Commercial Expectations and Cooperation in Symbiotic Contracts

Exploring the role played by cooperation in the law and management of modern, complex contracts, this book contrasts an in-depth review of case law with a large-scale empirical study of the views of commercial actors responsible for the outcomes of these contracts.

The possibility of aligning these expectations with the law is considered from the perspective that there is a general duty for parties to cooperate and ensure constructive engagement. The book examines how this might translate into constructive communication, professional governance, genuine attempts to settle issues, a right to fix defects and a duty to take decisions in a fair and rational manner. It argues that statutory adjudication should be extended to all commercial contracts and more ambitious use of available remedies, including those for prevention and cost penalties, would help provide incentives for parties to cooperate more fully.

The book will be of interest to academics in the fields of contract law and of contract management, as well as legal and commercial practitioners.

Dr C. Haward Soper (Haward) is an Honorary Associate Professor of Law at the University of Leicester. He retired in 2014 after a 35-year commercial/contracting career in industry.

Commercial Expectations and Cooperation in Symbiotic Contracts

A Legal and Empirical Analysis

C. Haward Soper

Routledge
Taylor & Francis Group

LONDON AND NEW YORK

First published 2020
by Routledge
2 Park Square, Milton Park, Abingdon, Oxon OX14 4RN

and by Routledge
52 Vanderbilt Avenue, New York, NY 10017

Routledge is an imprint of the Taylor & Francis Group, an informa business

British Library Cataloguing-in-Publication Data
A catalogue record for this book is available from the British Library

Library of Congress Cataloging-in-Publication Data
A catalog record has been requested for this book

ISBN: 978-0-367-27211-1 (hbk)
ISBN: 978-0-429-32810-7 (ebk)

Typeset in Galliard
by Swales & Willis, Exeter, Devon, UK

Contents

Figures

Tables

Foreword

When awarding the 2016 prize for Economics, the Nobel committee observed "Modern economies are held together by innumerable contracts". Given the prevalence and importance of contracts, it is remarkable how little research there has been about their practical use and impact. Many hours are spent in their negotiation, but does it matter? Extensive fees are paid to lawyers for their preparation, but is it worthwhile? Millions of contract managers are appointed to oversee their management, but is it effective?

This book sets out to provide insights and answers to some of these questions. It is based on extensive and wide-ranging conversations and surveys involving those from the front line – the lawyers, contract managers, commercial managers, engineers, project managers and other professionals who prepare, negotiate and manage thousands of these contracts. Business relationships are becoming more complex, yet underlying legal principles have not adapted. The book reveals the importance of the contracting ritual, but the reluctance of parties to then invoke their legal rights when things start to go wrong. It discovers that there are typically high levels of cooperation as the parties seek to build common ground and establish a firm footing for their relationship.

This book offers many thought-provoking insights into modern contracting and relationship management. It brings valuable knowledge and understanding to those who are charged with establishing agreements and making them work – so that the world is indeed "held together by contracts".

Tim Cummins
President, International Association of Contract
and Commercial Management
www.iaccm.com

Acknowledgments

I am lucky to be here. More than 90% of those diagnosed with oesophageal cancer on the 13 February 2013 are now with their maker. I will be making a contribution from earnings from this book to charities promoting awareness of this awful disease. Awareness and early diagnosis can materially improve outcomes from this, the sixth most common cancer and one of the deadliest. I am a survivor, but my cost is an unpredictable digestive system. Many of you reading this would benefit from wondering whether you are at risk.

Over the decades, in good times, great times and bad times, my small friend and tolerant companion Celia has been a constant source of everything; especially support and good cheer. Thank you dear.

I am incredibly grateful for the massive amount of work my 500+ respondents put into my survey.

Francois du Bois, the Head of the Law School at Leicester, pushed me very hard and forced me to justify things I thought obvious. It wasn't, I hope, a lesson too late for the learning. My two other supervisors Sebastian Peyer and Richard Craven were extremely helpful.

My colleagues at the University of Leicester have been sensational. Many non-academic staff provided answers to my survey. I must also mention those who trained me in the use of software, especially Hazel Guyler. I have spent decades with secretaries doing the word processing. Developing my own expertise, as well as taking months off my PhD, was a useful exercise in reminding me of how lucky I have been to operate in senior roles with great assistants.

Industrial colleagues, too many to name, made much of my work possible.

Lastly, I am alive because of the extraordinary expertise, kindness and decency of the medical fraternity, including my friend Colin Trask, my diagnosing physician, Ryan Ponnudurai, in Kuala Lumpur, my oncologist, Azrif Annuar, my surgeon, Mr William Allum and their teams.

Table of cases

All cases cited

Scotland

United States

Canada

Bermuda

Hong Kong

South Africa

Gold Coast (now Ghana)

East Africa Protectorate (now Kenya)

1 Introduction

> To cooperate [kəʊˈɒpəreɪt] is to Act or operate jointly with another,
> to concur in action, effort or effect Cooperation is the act of
> cooperating ...[1]

In this book I argue that, to make symbiotic contracts successful, to make
them "work" those managing them at the sharp end need and expect active
cooperation. This commercial expectation can be defined and distilled into
readily accessible legal duties to cooperate. My intent is to create improved
alignment between commercial contract law and the commercial world; finding a way to meld law with the expectations of those managing complex
modern contracts. I take a pragmatic, instrumental, approach, working on
the mechanics as opposed to the structure of contract law, the aim being to
determine what cooperation means in these contracts, and what incentives
the law can and should offer to commerce to help make them successful, all
under the general assumption that contracts are made to be performed.
I apply a three-pronged methodology, combining doctrinal analysis and theoretical reflection with a real-world empirical investigation; seeking
a pragmatic way to implement the views of commercial actors while preserving the commercial strengths of the Law. I engage in a critical analysis and
evaluation of the current law by examining whether and when a duty to
cooperate does and should exist and I identify consequent needs for legal
reform; mainly comprising more imaginative and flexible use of currently
available remedies, and more attention to context and contractual purpose
when considering party intention.

---

1 *Webster's New International Dictionary of the English Language* (G. Bell & Sons 1928). See
also *The Oxford English Dictionary* (OUP 1970); "co-operate" and "cooperate" have been
alternatives since the 17th century. I use cooperate. The *OED* adds a gloss "with another
person or thing, to an end or purpose or in a work". Christopher Clarke J said of a cooperation
clause that it required parties "to work together to achieve a common object" in *Lexington
Insurance Co. v Multinacional de Seguros SA* [2008] EWHC 1170 at [50].

The first appearance of "cooperation" in terms in an English contract case seems to be in 1843 in *Startup v MacDonald*, Rolfe J referring to delivery in shipping as "that common act which can only be effected by the cooperation of both".[2] In 1892, in *Harris v Best* Lord Esher refers to shiploading activity as "joint", meaning that "Each is to do his own part of the work, and to do whatever is reasonable to enable the other to do his part."[3] The word "cooperation" then vanishes from the judicial vocabulary until 1941 when Lord Simon remarks:

> where B is employed to do a piece of work which requires A's cooperation – eg to paint A's portrait, – it is implied that the necessary cooperation will be forthcoming – eg A will give sittings to the artist.[4]

In ground-breaking work, in 1963, Stewart Macaulay made the now uncontroversial observation that:

> businessmen often fail to plan exchange relationships completely, and seldom use legal sanctions to adjust these relationships or to settle disputes. Planning and legal sanctions are often unnecessary and may have undesirable consequences.[5]

Lord Devlin recognised a similar issue in 1951, saying that businessmen think of the contract as "merely a seal"[6] whereas the law is apt to "canonise"[7] judicial statements, and is insufficiently flexible to react to changes in commercial practice, ending with a plea "that the law might go further than it does towards meeting the business attitude".[8] Since Macaulay's work, many empirical studies[9] have supported

---

2   *Startup v Macdonald* (1843) 134 ER 1029; (1843) 6 Manning and Granger 593 at 611. I ran a word search on multiple databases. I am reasonably confident that this is correct.

3   *Harris v Best* (1892) 68 LT 76; [1891–94] All ER Rep 567 at 569.

4   *Luxor (Eastbourne) Ltd v Cooper* [1941] All ER 33 (HL) at 39. See also *Samuels v Davis* [1943] 2 All ER 3 (AC); patient/dentist cooperation. In an earlier Irish case – *Langham Steamship Co. v. Gallagher* [1911] 2nd Ir Rep 348 (KB) at 376 – Kenny J ruled: "The act of discharge … requires co-operation on the part of the ship and on the receiver" at 376.

5   Stewart Macaulay, 'Non-Contractual Relations in Business: A Preliminary Study' (1963) 28 *Am Sociol Rev* 55, perhaps the most-cited article in legal history – Fred R Shapiro, 'The Most-Cited Law Review Articles Revisited' (1996) 71 *Chi-Kent L Rev* 751.

6   Patrick Devlin, 'The Relation between Commercial Law and Commercial Practice' (1951) 14 *MLR* 249 at 265.

7   Ibid. at 263.

8   Ibid. at 266.

9   Hugh Beale and Tony Dugdale, 'Contracts between Businessmen: Planning and the Use of Contractual Remedies' (1975) 2 *Br J Law Soc* 45, Terence Daintith and Gunther Teubner (eds), *Contract and Organisation: Legal Analysis in the Light of Economic and Social Theory* (De Gruyter 2011), Simon Johnson, John MacMillan and Christopher Woodruff, 'Courts and Relational Contracts' (2002) 18 *J Law Eco Org* 221, a study in post-communist economies which found a mix of formal and informal preferences. See John Tillotson, *Contract Law in Perspective* (Butterworths 1985), 19, observing that the Macaulay article is "rather narrow in

the claim that much commercial activity is characterised by cooperation, problem-solving, relationship building and maintenance and ad-hoc deal-making, together with a reluctance to enter into black letter negotiation or initiate formal end-game mechanisms.[10] As Robson points out, surveys used to turn the world into data, create knowledge or tell a story, are not new, the Domesday Book and 17th-century efforts to assess the effects of the plague being notable landmarks.[11] I tested Macaulay's conclusions using a survey involving 500 experts. The results largely agreed with him, but with an undertone suggesting that the contract, qua contract, was somewhat more important than his analysis suggests.

Most major English Law texts deal descriptively, rather than analytically, with the duty to cooperate.[12] Much of the theoretical literature, legal and law and economics, is predicated on a binary dichotomy between discrete transactions and long-term iterative contracts. Neither model accurately describes modern business contracts which are often medium/long-term, fixed-term, complex and multi-layered/multi-disciplinary/multi-site, incorporating management provisions which deal with change through, for example, unilateral powers to vary and termination for convenience provisions which allow the parties to adjust their relationship without court intervention or renegotiation.

Cooperation debates are dominated by classical contract theory, probably best described by Patrick Atiyah,[13] and relational contract theory, the latter being spawned by Macaulay's work. Crudely, but typically, classical contract theorists are asserted to support a law red in tooth and claw, in which amoral and opportunistic self-interested commercial actors prey on the unwary, awaiting the chance to earn or save a quick buck.[14] This is not a plausible picture of contract law and the reality is more granular.[15] A comparable parody of relational theory is that it ends in support for a fluffy compromise which is subjective and cannot

---

its scope". See also Stewart Macaulay, 'The Real and the Paper Deal: Empirical Pictures of Relationships, Complexity and the Urge for Transparent Simple Rules' (2003) 66 *MLR* 44.

10 See the great Scots draughtsman, Sir Mackenzie Chalmers, *The Sale of Goods Act, 1893* (Clowes 1902), 129, that "Lawyers see only the pathology of commerce and not its healthy physiological action, and their views are apt to be warped and one-sided".

11 Colin Robson, *Real World Research* (3rd edn, Wiley 2011), 236.

12 See also David M Walker, *Principles of Scottish Private Law* (2nd edn, OUP 1975). A search in Harvey McGregor, *McGregor on Damages* (Sweet & Maxwell 2012) proved fruitless.

13 Patrick S Atiyah, *The Rise and Fall of Freedom of Contract* (Clarendon Press 1979), chapters 8 and 9 – 'Freedom of Contract in the Courts, 1770–1870'.

14 See Brownsword at 14 in David Campbell and Peter Vincent-Jones (eds), *Contract and Economic Organisation* (Dartmouth 1996) – "the classical model has it that contractors operate as ruthless utility maximisers, exploiting every opportunity to advance their own self-interest". But see Atiyah (n. 13) at chapter 9: "much of what has been said was somewhat theoretical, and at no time did this austere and amoral market law ever wholly represent the practice of the Courts".

15 See e.g. John Wightman, *Contract: A Critical Commentary* (Pluto Press 1996) especially at 86–91. Richard Lewis, 'Contracts between Businessmen: Reform of the Law of Firm Offers and an Empirical Study of Tendering Practices in the Building Industry' (1982) 9 *JLS* 153, suggests that his empirical findings need not imply a need for legal reform. Hugh Collins,

be expressed in default rules which allow parties a reasonable degree of certainty in analysing the end game.[16] This is also extreme and it is not impossible to envisage ways of effecting, at least in part, certain relational norms such as preservation of the relationship, conflict harmonisation and adjustment to new situations.

Some relational theorists and some law and economics scholars argue for cooperation as a general foundation or norm for contract law.[17] Jonathan Morgan, while accepting that cooperative relationships are important in business and agreeing that this proposition is well supported by empirical evidence, argues firmly against any reformulation of the law to bring cooperation into play:

> whether this means that the law of contract must be reformulated to promote co-operation rather than to resolve disputes in a clear-cut fashion is questionable. A "co-operative" law of contract may paradoxically fail to promote co-operation, or rather to curb opportunism ...[18]

This assumes that the debate lies between a contract law wholly based on cooperation and one in which there is no duty of cooperation or that cooperation simply means the opposite of opportunism.[19]

I argue that there is a "third way" in which an enlarged or deeper duty to cooperate can be envisaged for symbiotic contracts without creating uncertainty. I take a pragmatic, incremental approach, consistent with the general approach of the English and Commonwealth courts, arguing that these contracts should meet commercial expectations and that to help make symbiotic contracts successful courts must construe them, contextually, as including a deep duty to cooperate. I explore the possibility that the classical law is not quite so red in tooth and claw as sometimes claimed[20] and that an extensive duty to cooperate

---

Regulating Contracts (OUP 2005), 190–191, noted that "these business expectations provided the reason for leaving the law as it is".

16 Michael J Trebilcock, *The Limits of Freedom of Contract* (Harvard UP 1993), 141–142, argues that Macneil does not "yield determinate legal principles". Jonathan Morgan, *Contract Law Minimalism* (CUP 2013) agrees at 69.

17 See e.g. John Adams and Roger Brownsword, *Key Issues in Contract* (Butterworths 1995), 301–302.

18 Morgan, *Contract Law Minimalism*, 69. The article on which Dr Morgan bases this claim is less definite. The abstract notes that the right balance "requires establishing a monitoring/ bonding package that may well result in optimal output and a satisfactory risk-allocation". Charles J Goetz and Robert E Scott, 'Principles of Relational Contracts' (1981) 67 *VaLRev* 1089.

19 See also Catherine Mitchell, 'Publication Review – Contract Law Minimalism: A Formalist Restatement of Contract Law' (2014) 25 *ICCLR* 324 which she describes as an "excellent and comprehensive new contribution to the ongoing formalist-relationalist debate over the design and function of contract law", inferring, perhaps, that the debate is binary.

20 See Brownsword at 14 in Campbell and Vincent-Jones, *Contract and Economic Organisation*.

in symbiotic contracts is not likely either to cause major uncertainty or destroy the adversarial commercial spirit inherent in contracting. Indeed, it may increase certainty as it will be more in line with the expectations of those who manage and negotiate contracts. This "third way" differs from relationalism. It is less concerned with preserving a relationship in circumstances not planned for at the time the contract is made and more with the day to day, the pathways to success and performance, of an agreed deal.

I demonstrate that commercial expectations are that cooperation in the day-to-day work is vital in a commercial context. I argue that commercial expectation is based on party respect for the deal, on a perceived need for successful performance, hedged by realism and a pragmatic approach. Recognising that the pathways to success in performing these contracts lie in cooperation characterised by communication and problem-solving, those at the sharp end know that they must build relationships to discern what drives the other party, which, in turn, provides a foundation for solid communication and practical problem-solving activity, requiring some "give and take". As Robert Frank advises, failure "to recognize that we live in Darwin's world rather than Smith's" prevents us "seeing that competition alone will not solve our problems".[21]

The structure of the book is that I begin by discussing some of the "countless" cases which feature in law reports.[22] I draw out six threads from the basic duty not to prevent the other party from performing through to a duty of active cooperation in which constructive engagement and problem-solving are of the essence, and further consider decision-making powers where these impinge on enabling performance. This is a functional approach, differing from Samuel Stoljar's influential, seminal, 1953 work,[23] in which he created a breakdown of Building, Commission, Employment and Notice categories.[24] Finally I consider whether abandoning implying terms and employing commercial construction would provide coherence. In Chapter 3 I discuss my survey, which involved asking some 500 experienced contract managers, an elite group,[25] for their views on what success means in contract management, whether cooperation is required, what cooperation means and how to achieve it. I found no other empirical work on the source of reasonable or commercial expectations, and my work shows that these can be uncovered and defined at a level of abstraction

---

21 Robert H Frank, *The Darwin Economy: Liberty, Competition, and the Common Good* (Princeton UP 2012), meaning, unfairly, Adam Smith.

22 J W Carter, *Carter's Breach of Contract* (Hart 2012) at 2.027.

23 SJ Stoljar, 'Prevention and Cooperation in the Law of Contract' (1953) 31 *CanBar Rev* 231. Building cases cited are mainly prevention cases, subsequently the law has developed more towards positive duties.

24 Ibid.

25 Bill Gillham, *The Research Interview* (Continuum 2000) – those in positions of authority, with power or with special knowledge, at 81 onwards. On interviewing elites see Rosalind Edwards and Janet Holland, *What is Qualitative Interviewing?* (Bloomsbury Academic 2013).

that can underpin a duty to cooperate, despite the claim that "In fact, there is good reason to believe, both in theory and from empirical studies, that commercial contractors do prefer a formalist law of contract".[26] Respondents overwhelmingly consider cooperation to be important or even mission critical. The theme which runs through responses is management/problem-solving. Sometimes that is by problem avoidance: seizing on issues early. At other times respondents build a relationship, through communicating formally and informally, allowing the creation of an atmosphere in which give-and-take can work.[27] When matters become difficult, unravelling the problem, whether through escalation or fast track dispute resolution, and getting on with the business are leitmotifs. The least acceptable option is always abandonment of the contract: termination. Punitive action, deducting money or charging money, is also eschewed.

Tit-for-tat, reciprocity is not regarded as effective, and there is an interesting lack of variation between male and female responses. In Chapter 4 I discuss the basis on which a duty to cooperate could be incorporated into symbiotic contracts. I show that there has been significant change in the commercial reality and I explore theoretical writings, concentrating on those of Catherine Mitchell, Hugh Collins and Roger Brownsword, on commercial expectations, following this up by examining the tools available to judges and litigants to evince commercial expectations in trial conditions. I show, using case law, that commercial expectations are neither external to the contract nor subjective and can be uncovered by conventional evidentiary methods. I argue that current restrictions on contract interpretation such as those limiting the use of previous dealing practices, negotiation evidence or post-agreement conduct are illogical and could be relaxed without opening any floodgate. In Chapter 5 I examine various definitions of cooperation in contract, from academics and from the notion of good faith, and assess them against my review of existing law and the views of commercial actors. I suggest a Transcendent Duty to Cooperate creating a concrete, detailed, modern duty to cooperate, requiring solid communication, constructive engagement, problem-solving and active cooperation. The case law demonstrates that judges can lay down fairly clear definitions of cooperation in practice. It sometimes seems that theorists have trouble matching judicial levels of definition and creativity in describing cooperation. In Chapter 6 I examine remedies and legal process. Where a party fails to engage constructively, fails to communicate effectively or will not try to resolve problems can the courts provide incentives to make them more likely to do so? My proposition is that fast-track adjudication works well in the construction industry, was considered helpful by survey respondents and could be extended. I also examine what were once called Wrotham Park damages (now narrower hypothetical release fees), damages for failure to negotiate and cost penalties. I also consider remedies,

---

26 Morgan, *Contract Law Minimalism*, 42.
27 See Alison Coleman, 'Spot the Signs of a Failing Project' (2015) *Sunday Times* (2 August).

conventional but seldom used, which lean towards abuse of rights remedies or extend those available where prevention occurs, including judges taking matters into their own hands. In Chapter 7 I undertake a detailed, fact-driven analysis of various hard cases. I ask whether on the facts my third way full-blown duty, in part or in whole, could be incorporated. Had it been would this have changed the outcome, and, if so, would that be preferable? In part, this is to answer criticism that academics do not do enough "design", but it is also intended to demonstrate that the duty can work in concrete cases without reducing certainty. I review the emerging English Law notion of good faith, concluding that in each of the recent "relational" cases the notion is supernumerary and merely adds complexity. I also consider how the duty might be enforced in these cases, building on my Chapter 5 discussion of remedies. I conclude by summing up the performance-based analysis I have made, providing, in diagrammatic form, a conception of contract which shows formal, informal and cloudy elements, reflecting the "messy reality" (a phrase stolen from David Ibbetson) of contractual relations.

1.1 Justifying an expectations approach

My thesis is that parties to symbiotic contracts (indeed all contracts) have expectations which can and should be enforced by the State. Insofar as they are necessary to the success of these contracts such expectations should be respected as a necessary incident of a presumption that contracts are made to be performed. Being joined in a "common enterprise" parties "engaging in a contractual relation A and B become no longer strangers to each other".[28] Voluntarily creating expectations, an expression of individual liberty, carries with it an obligation not to dismantle those expectations without the consent of the affected party.[29] Contract law should, therefore, protect the reasonable expectations of autonomous parties who have voluntarily created contractual rights, whether commercial or non-commercial. Accordingly, I suggest that when symbiotic contracts threaten to break down, a mutual duty to cooperate may well reinforce the mutual or symbiotic nature of the contract and provide courts and parties with options to deter, manage or prevent breakdown.[30]

This rights-based claim is coupled with an instrumental purpose,[31] or social policy, that contract law can, should and does encourage exchange relations, in

---

28 Charles Fried, *Contract as Promise* (Harvard UP 1981) at 72.

29 See TM Scanlon discussing "unjustified manipulation" of expectation in Peter Benson, *The Theory of Contract Law: New Essays* (CUP 2001), chapter 3 Promises and Contracts at 88.91.

30 This may be seen as explicitly relational – see Ian Austen-Baker, 'Comprehensive Contract Theory – A Four Norm Model of Contract Relations' (2009) 25 *JCL* 216 at 222.

31 The Oxford Dictionary online defines instrumentalism as a "pragmatic philosophical approach which regards an activity (such as science, law, or education) chiefly as an instrument or tool for some practical purpose". See also *Webster's New International Dictionary*, 1928 "serving as a means". Morgan, *Contract Law Minimalism*, refers to the "central purpose" of the law of contract in the preface.

order to ensure that the bargains parties make can be fulfilled, in the light of prevailing circumstances and changing realities. Exchange relations tend to enhance individual and societal welfare and enrich individuals and society, notwithstanding that rights created should be (and are) enforced even if they do not have this effect. Emphasising that contract does not need trust Dori Kimel describes contract law as making arms length commerce possible by providing "a modicum of assurance or a safety-net of sorts in case of an unforeseen breakdown of the relationship".[32]

I make two observations on instrumental claims, intending to answer two of Stephen A Smith's criticisms of what he refers to as utilitarian theories.[33] Smith says that explicit consideration of the effects of judicial rulings on commercial activities is not "in the main" the way judges reason.[34] Jonathan Morgan says, correctly, that "Great Judges have consistently kept the needs of commerce before them"[35] and refuses to defend the opposite case "in detail" since "any English contract lawyer would recognise the truth in it".[36] By way of example, and one could fill a book with examples, as Lord Wright reminds us, there is an instrumental commercial thread in judicial thinking: "Businessmen often record the most important agreements in crude and summary fashion ... It is, accordingly, the duty of the court to construe such documents fairly and broadly."[37] In a famous phrase in the Antaios Lord Diplock observed that: "if detailed semantic and syntactical analysis of words in a commercial contract is going to lead to a conclusion that flouts business common sense, it must be made to yield to business common sense".[38] As Lord Tomlin advocated in *Hillas v Arcos*, the law should not be a "destroyer of bargains"; which also applies to the parties.[39] This is not new. In 1898 Lord Herschell observed that provisions should be "construed in a business fashion ... in the way businessmen would interpret them".[40]

The second of Smith's criticisms is stronger and that is that utilitarian theories inevitably mean that individual interests are subverted, wrongly, to "broader social goals".[41] When he makes this criticism of economic efficiency-based

---

32 Dori Kimel, 'The Choice of Paradigm for Theory of Contract: Reflections on the Relational Model' (2007) 27 *OJLS* 233 at 248.

33 Stephen A Smith, *Contract Theory* (OUP 2004), 132–136 where Smith concentrates on efficiency-based accounts of contract law.

34 Ibid. 133.

35 Morgan, *Contract Law Minimalism*, 6.

36 Ibid.

37 *Hillas & Co. Ltd v Arcos Ltd* (1932) 38 Com Cas 23, [1932] All ER Rep 494 at 503.

38 *The Antaios* [1984] 3 All ER 229 at 233. For numerous examples of judicial use of common sense see Neil Andrews, 'Interpretation of Contracts and "Commercial Common Sense": Do Not Overplay This Useful Criterion' (2017) 76 *CLJ* 36.

39 *Hillas v Arcos* (n. 37 above) at 499.

40 *Southland Frozen Meat and Produce Export Company v Nelson Brothers Ltd* [1898] AC 442 PC.

41 Smith, *Contract Theory*, 139.

approaches, he is correct, as these claims mean that "remedies are awarded not in order to do justice between the parties, but to induce others to enter contracts in the future".[42] This would be a desirable side effect but it should not be the purpose. The individual liberty in focus is the freedom to create contractual rights. If the law supports the creation of those rights, by analysing them properly, in accordance with party intention, and enforces them directly or indirectly that seems to me to be a tool of social policy directed immediately at the promotion of individual liberty. The argument can be extended by pointing out that enforcement is a public event. Courts are visible and their discussions are public and reported. In promoting the liberty of one party (or two), courts will demonstrate to others that these liberties exist and will be protected and fostered, creating confidence for putative exchangers to enter the arena. Individual rights are not sublimated to the broader social goal, rather they create the landscape which is represented by that broader social goal.

Catherine Mitchell, Jonathan Morgan and Hugh Collins take a similar line on contract law's purpose in their key works. Catherine Mitchell, in a subtle and nuanced work, which asks all the right questions, positing misalignment of expectation and law, says that a claim that there should be alignment "cannot be assessed without considering larger questions concerning how contract law best facilitates commerce", inferring, inevitably, that that is the purpose of contract law.[43] In a sweeping, holistic and masterful exposition of the world of contract, Hugh Collins asks us to consider "what kinds of laws and legal institutions are good for commercial transactions, and what sorts of legal regulation are efficient and effective in retail sales to consumers".[44] Jonathan Morgan opens his energetic and coruscating work, in which one is sometimes unsure whether the bludgeon or the rapier is being utilised, advocating a "minimalist" law of contract with one of three theses being that the law's purpose is "to provide a suitable framework for trade".[45]

Lord Steyn makes a similarly clear claim – that the "prime function of the law of contract, ... is to facilitate commercial dealings".[46] Richard Austen-Baker asserts that the law of contract is "about" doing business.[47] In a wide-ranging historical review, Stephen Waddams says that courts have "often taken account of social economic and political considerations".[48]

Although I agree that contract law is "a tool of social policy",[49] I am not convinced that judicial aims comprise the enabling of exchange relations. Much contract law is policy based, and much policy is obscure. Some is technical and

---

42 Ibid.
43 Catherine Mitchell, *Contract Law and Contract Practice: Bridging the Gap between Legal Reasoning and Commercial Expectation* (Hart Publishing 2013), 3.
44 Collins, *Regulating Contracts*, 6.
45 Morgan, *Contract Law Minimalism*, preface.
46 Johan Steyn, 'Contract Law: Fulfilling the Reasonable Expectations of Honest Men' (1997) 113 *LQR* 433 at 436.
47 Richard Austen-Baker, *Implied Terms in English Contract Law* (Edward Elgar 2011).
48 SM Waddams, *Principle and Policy in Contract Law* (CUP 2011), 217.
49 Morgan, *Contract Law Minimalism*, 3.

nebulous, some illogical. In other words, the instrumental account does not fit the legal rules, unless it can be shown that these policy-based or technocratic rules are truly underpinned by a desire to reinforce party intention. It is hard to think of a defence based on party intention for rules which, for example:

- Allow courts to analyse a document for the purposes of determining whether a contract has come into existence but debar the court from using the same document to interpret the contract.
- Debar courts from using pre-contract documents not incorporated into the contract even when those documents make the meaning of the contract "crystal clear".
- Claim that in-contract decision-makers suffer from a "clear conflict of interest".
- Morph open ended provisions such as to "co-operate with each other in good faith and ..." into specific, narrow provisions, stripping them of much contractual power.

Judges often speak of the need to make contracts effective or workable. They rationalise choices between competing, potentially equally meaningful outturns,[50] and emphasise business common sense and business efficacy. It would be improper and misleading to say that judges do not mean what they say.[51] But this is not all they say, and some rules appear to bespeak the primacy of legal policy or elevate judicial comfort over party intention As Aditi Bagchi argues, the internal point of view must also be defended by showing that judicial reasons could be accepted as valid by parties.[52] When senior figures such as Lady Arden, Lord Steyn and Lord Reed offer considered animadversion on some of the above rules it is worth exploring the issues.

In another example there is a Common Law thread which asserts that the primary requirement of the law of commercial contract is the achievement of certainty.[53] As I discuss in Chapter 3, there is more breadth than this implies and parties also want, in more or less equal measure, fairness and flexibility.

---

50 See e.g. Lord Hoffmann in *Investors Compensation Scheme v West Bromwich Building Society* [1998] 1 WLR 896.

51 Smith, *Contract Theory*, 24, suggests that transparency requires that the reasons Judges give must be the "real reasons".

52 Aditi Bagchi, 'The Perspective of Law on Contract' (2013) 88 *Washington LR* 1227 at 1233.

53 See e.g. JS Hobhouse, 'International Conventions and Commercial Law' (1990) 106 *LQR* 530 at 532 "The first and paramount requirement [of the commercial community] is the achievement of certainty ... The commercial man needs to be able to obtain prompt and accurate advice about the effect of contracts ..." See Chadwick LJ: "it is reasonable to assume that the parties desire commercial certainty" in *EA Grimstead and Son v McGarrigan* [1999] All ER (D) 1163. See also *Vallejo v Wheeler* (1774) 1 Cowp 143, 153; 98 ER 1012, 1017. See the qualification in *Golden Strait Corporation v Nippon Yusen Kubishika Kaisha* [2007] UKHL 12, (Transcript) Lord Scott at [38]: "Certainty is a desideratum and a very important one, particularly in commercial contracts. But it is not a principle and must give way to principle".

Adopting a neo-Realist approach, John Gava, while accepting a coincidental "commercial hue", argues that any market utility of contract law is accidental, the law being developed through legal reasoning, doling out rough and ready justice: "the best reading of its history is that a restricted corps of judges, trained in the common law, developed the law in relative isolation and with a heavy doctrinal influence".[54] The clarity of instrumental judicial expression cannot easily be confuted, and he produces no serious argument that judges operate as if in a silent order, closed off from the real world.[55]

1.2 What is a symbiotic contract?

A symbiotic contract is one in which active cooperation is required to make the contract work, to make it a success. It may, at one extreme, possess the incidents of "a mini society with a vast array of norms beyond those centered on the exchange and its immediate processes".[56] At the other end of the spectrum the quotidian includes the installation of a new kitchen in one's home. Symbiotic contracts include:

- Facilities management, back office support and other "continuing, highly interactive contracts"[57] where "internal" enterprise work is outsourced.
- Long/medium-term service and maintenance contracts.
- Infrastructure contracts, including many construction, petrochemical and engineering contracts.
- Domestic contracts such as the creation of an extension or a garage, and the installation of a kitchen.
- Joint land development deals.
- Research and development contracts where confidential information, know-how and intellectual property are shared in pursuit of a common goal.
- "Alliance" or Joint Venture type contracts.
- Information technology (IT) or management system implementation contracts.
- Contracts referred to as "relational" in *Yam Seng Pte Ltd v International Trade Corporation Ltd*: "some joint venture agreements, franchise agreements and long-term distributorship agreements".[58]
- Agency contracts; albeit some agency duties are fiduciary rather than contractual.

---

54 John Gava, 'What We Know about Contract Law and Transacting in the Marketplace – A Review Essay (2014)' (2014) 35 *U of Adelaide Law Review* 409 at 422.
55 John Gava, 'Taking Stewart Macaulay and Hugh Collins Seriously' (2016) 33 *JCL* 108 and Gava, 'What We Know about Contract Law' at 422.
56 Gillian K Hadfield, 'Problematic Relations: Franchising and the Law of Incomplete Contracts' (1990) 42 *StanLRev* 927 footnote 9.
57 As Goetz and Scott (n. 18) above describe relational contracts at 1090.
58 *Yam Seng Pte Ltd v International Trade Corporation Ltd* [2013] EWHC 111 (QB) Leggatt J at [142].

Illustrating complexity, Price Waterhouse Cooper describe the expectations of sophisticated clients, and the complexity of modern arrangements, in facilities management contracting as including flexibility, innovation (using technology), complex risk management, "Self delivery", "real time performance metrics and response", as "drivers of value".[59]

Symbiotic contracts may require details to be adjusted to make the contract work,[60] they may require reasonable solutions to be agreed,[61] they may require parties to work together constantly. Their distinctive characteristic is that parties must enable or facilitate the obligations undertaken by the other or work together to ensure that acts which are joint can be efficaciously performed.[62]

This is a significantly wider "specie" than that of relational contract described by Fraser J in the PO litigation[63] in that it does not have to be long-term, trust and confidence are not necessary incidents and no significant degree of investment is necessary.

1.3 Summary

In describing and defending my concept of a duty to cooperate I recognise that this is second-order question, a content question; which I answer instrumentally.[64] My argument is incremental and pragmatic, characteristic of the Common Law method, seeking greater emphasis on context and more imaginative use of current remedies; and, to that extent, it is not revolutionary. It is underpinned by an argument that there has been a material change in the commercial landscape from transactional contracts (one-off or iterative) to complex multi-layered contracts which require cooperation in the shape of constructive engagement for their success.

The hard-boiled contextualist proposition[65] at the heart of this book is that for symbiotic contracts (and some others) a deep, active, duty to cooperate, arising through recognition of mutual commercial party expectation and based on the need for successful performance, should be recognised and articulated more clearly and coherently by the courts. This is close to Charles Fried's analysis of

---

59 https://www.pwc.co.uk/services/transaction-services/insights/facilities-management-a-quiet-revolution.html.

60 *Hillas v Arcos* n. 37 above.

61 *Anglo Group plc v Winther Brown & Co. Ltd* [2000] EWHC Technology 127 (TCC).

62 *Compass Group UK and Ireland Ltd (t/a Medirest) v Mid Essex Hospital Services NHS Trust* [2012] EWHC 781 (QB).

63 *The Post Office Group Litigation* [2019] EWHC 606 (QB) at [725]; see a detailed account in Chapter 7 below.

64 Smith, *Contract Theory*, 269–270, describing rules for determining content.

65 "Committed" is another way of putting it. See Hugh Collins, 'Objectivity and Committed Contextualism in Interpretation' in Sarah Worthington (ed.), *Commercial Law and Commercial Practice* (Hart 2003), 189.

contractual relations – which is, in turn, described by Ian Macneil[66] as "excellent relational thinking":

> [parties] stand closer than those who are merely members of the same political community … [T]hey are joined in a common enterprise, and therefore they have some obligation to share unexpected benefits and losses in the case of an accident in the course of that enterprise.[67]

Fried goes too far in this passage – contracts are not all equal, and sharing goes too far in the commercial world, despite his limitation of the concept to situations in which "there are no rights to respect",[68] except in the sense that the parties must make efforts to engage, give and take, solve problems and make serious efforts to make the contract work. I do not assume that parties must wholly abandon their own interests, nor that they must entirely put opportunism aside.[69]

My broad thrust is that party intention is at the heart of contract; that "affected individuals are usually the best judges of their own welfare";[70] and that putting more effort into finding actual intention, expressed and unexpressed, would do no harm and much good.

I could consider a Critical Legal Studies approach, concentrating on criticising the law as a whole but, while I agree with Baroness Hale that "an important project of feminist jurisprudence has been to explode the myth of the disinterested, disengaged, and distant judge",[71] I take the law as fact; as a systematic, to which end, value-based analysis is unnecessary. I could place myself squarely in the Realist School insofar as I agree that law should include the study of other disciplines, that practising and researching law requires skills and knowledge which go beyond legal skills and knowledge; as Karl Llewellyn observed: "substantive rights and rules should be removed from their present position at the focal point of legal discussion, in favour of the area of contact between judicial behaviour and the behaviour of laymen".[72] The description of

---

66 Ian R Macneil, 'Relational Contract: What We Do and Do Not Know' (1985) *WisLRev* 483 at 520. Peter Rosher, 'Good Faith in Construction Contracts under French Law' (2015) *ICLR* 302 at 306 quotes Professor Demogue on French Law – "the obligation of cooperation means that parties 'must work together towards a common goal, which is the sum of their individual goals'".

67 Fried, *Contract as Promise*, at 72.

68 Ibid. 71.

69 See Guido Alpa and Mads Andenas (eds), *Private Law beyond the National Systems* (British Institute of International and Comparative Law London 2007) – Ewan McKendrick at 693 citing *National Grid Co. plc v Mayes* [2001] UKHL 20, [2001] 2 All ER 417 "a good faith obligation does not ordinarily require a party to neglect its own interests".

70 Benson, *Theory of Contract Law*, 10, citing Richard Craswell.

71 Baroness Hale, 'Maccabean Lecture in Jurisprudence – A Minority Opinion' (2008) 154 *Proceedings of the British Academy* 319–336. This seems a little unfair on John AG Griffith, *The Politics of the Judiciary* (Fontana 1997) who could be claimed to have "exploded" the myth.

72 William Twining, *Karl Llewellyn and the Realist Movement* (CUP 2012), 547–548.

the rest of us (especially my expert respondents) as laymen seems a bit old-fashioned nowadays. My work is, however, as he recommends, based on method, less on theory: "The only tenet involved is that the method is a good one. 'See it fresh', see it as it works".[73]

The overarching norms of relationist theory are too ambitious and remain amorphous. The approach of classical theory, minimalists or formalists is limited and incongruent with modern commercial practice and expectation. I identify a third way to import cooperation, at an abstract level, supported by worked examples at a detailed level asserting that cooperation is expected, core to the deal and can be exposed by evidence in proceedings. The third way, derived from the commercial expectation of commercial experts, requires for symbiotic contracts a construction demanding a high level of cooperation. Cooperation, active cooperation and constructive engagement, essential to successful performance, is characterized by good communication between the parties, problem-solving, timeous and accurate information flow, solid formal and informal governance, good management and leadership worked in formal and informal channels, creation of mutual understanding and fair decision-making. The unique and detailed empirical evidence, from contract practitioners, those in the field, with the hard-day-to-day experience of managing contracts, demonstrates that reciprocity and punishment are not regarded as effective; the goal is almost always performance. A properly defined and circumscribed duty to cooperate can and should be incorporated into (mainly) symbiotic but also some less complex contracts, such as those where, for example, parties must exchange information to make them work. There is no tension between a deep duty to cooperate and the commercial need for certainty.

73 Ibid. 574, citing Karl N Llewellyn, *The Common Law Tradition: Deciding Appeals* (Little, Brown 1966).

2 Duty to cooperate – case law and comment

Where action or abstention by one contracting party is required to enable or facilitate action or performance by the other party, Courts will infer a duty, or construe a contract, or find an obligation which will make the contract "work"[1] or "effective"[2] or "operative".[3] The Courts intervene in a variety of ways and will infer obligations requiring parties:

- not to prevent performance,
- to do what is "necessary",[4]
- to use "diligence",[5]
- to do what is necessary to make the contract "workable",[6]
- or to do what is "reasonable".[7]

In the first subchapter below I discuss the basic principles of English Law applying to contractual cooperation. In subsequent subchapters I break cases down functionally. I discuss prevention by one party, a generalised negative duty or obligation not to get in the way or create obstacles, followed by a discussion of basic facilitation/

---

1 See McNair J in *Pavia & Co. v Thurmann Nielsen* [1952] 1 Lloyds Rep 153 'Otherwise the contract simply will not work' and Longmore LJ in *Swallowfalls Ltd v Monaco Yachting & Technologies SAM* [2014] 2 All ER (Comm) 185 at [35]. In *Richard Pease v Henderson Administration Ltd* [2018] EWHC 661 (Ch) Spearman J observed that the contract would be "unworkable" without an obligation to cooperate – at [132].
2 Lord Tomlin in *Hillas & Co. Ltd v Arcos Ltd* (1932) 38 Com Cas 23, [1932] All ER Rep 494 at 499 and Lord Backburn in *Mackay v Dick* (1881) 6 App Cas 251 (HL) using "effectually". Lord Hobhouse, JS Hobhouse, 'International Conventions and Commercial Law' (1990) 106 *LQR* 530: contract law is a tool which enables commercial people to conduct "commercial activity effectively and efficiently" at 533.
3 *William Stirling the Younger v Maitland and Boyd* (1864) 122 ER 1043 (KB) – Cockburn CJ.
4 *Butt v MacDonald* (1896) 7 QLJ 68 at 70–71.
5 *Ford v Cotesworth* (1868) LR 4 QB 127 (QB) at 134, *Garcia v Page & Co. Ltd* (1936) 55 Ll L Rep 391 (KBD) at 392.
6 *Mona Oil Equipment & Supply Co. Ltd v Rhodesia Railways Ltd* [1949] 2 All ER 1014 at 1018.
7 *Harris v Best* (1892) 68 LT 76 at 569 in [1891–94] All ER Rep 567.

diligence duties which require positive action to ensure that a contract can be performed. I then review rights to cure defects, an emerging right. Then I review duties to communicate or provide suitable information. Finally, I review "active" cooperation, arguably a modern duty, which has older roots. At its apex this hierarchical breakdown delimits duties to cooperate in symbiotic contracts.

In addition to these positive and negative rules, regulatory rules come into play when Courts control contractual decision-making powers, ensuring that they are used purposively; to enable or facilitate performance requiring, for example, that decision-makers act fairly and impartially when making decisions in relation to valuation of work.[8]

I consider how judges go about the process of interpretation of contracts and argue that it may be better for Courts to make reasoning more explicit and differentiate more clearly between construction and gap-filling. I use construction to mean the extrication of meaning and description of obligations by reading the contract or by reading the contract and considering the background or matrix.[9] I use gap-filling to describe the process whereby judges, having read the contract and considered the background, conclude that there is something missing; and that they must fill that gap either to give the contract "efficacy" or for policy reasons.

The cases show that the duty to cooperate often emerges through construction, sometimes as gap-filling and sometimes, illogically, using both methods. Practitioners, accordingly, cannot predict results, nor resources or evidence required at trial, with anything approaching certainty and I argue that construction is possible, and more efficient.

2.1 Basic principle – duty to cooperate

The basic principle of English Law which can be fairly described as the duty to cooperate in contract requires consideration of three key cases.

In 1881, in *Mackay v Dick*, still cited today,[10] Lord Blackburn, lucidly and economically, adumbrated the basic positive duty to cooperate (the *MvD* duty or principle):

> where in a written contract it appears that both parties have agreed that something shall be done, which cannot effectually be done unless both concur in doing it, the construction of the contract is that each agrees to do all that is necessary to be done on his part for the carrying out of that thing, though there may be no express words to that effect.[11]

---

8 *Sutcliffe v Thackrah* [1974] 1 All ER 859.

9 See Chitty, *Chitty on Contracts* (ed. Hugh Beale, 33rd edn, Sweet & Maxwell 2018) at 13.041, construction is how "a court arrives at the meaning to be given to the language used by the parties in the express terms".

10 *Ukraine v Law Debenture Trust Corp plc* [2018] EWCA Civ 2026 *St Shipping & Transport Inc. v Kriti Filoxenia Shipping Co. Sa (The "Kriti Filoxenia")* [2015] EWHC 997 (Comm).

11 *Mackay v Dick* (n. 2 above) at 263–264.

The "prevention principle", the basic negative duty, articulated by Vaughan-Williams J in *Quilpué (Barque) Ltd v Brown* means that each party to a contract is obliged not do anything to "prevent the other party from performing a contract or to delay him in performing"[12] and, as Lord Alverstone CJ added the following year, in *Ogdens Ltd v Nelson,* to "abstain from doing anything which will prevent him from fulfilling [his] obligations".[13]

These "correlative and generalised" terms, as Ian Duncan-Wallace QC describes them,[14] should, as Professor Carter argues, "be seen as an inference – drawn from construction of the contract".[15] The *Mackay v Dick* principle, described as "austere" by JF Burrows,[16] encapsulates the generality in an elegant and economical way, while lucidly stressing that the interpretive technique is construction. It is notable that Lord Blackburn is clear that a correlative duty to permit testing was inferred from construction whereas Vaughan Williams J prefers to anchor the prevention principle in an "implied contract":

> in this contract, as in every other, there is an implied contract by each party that he will not do anything to prevent the other party from performing the contract ... such a term is by law imported into every contract[17]

One must be careful with the language when considering what this means. Vaughan Williams J is very clear that this is an immanent term; incorporated into "every contract" and not a term dependent on the tests to which implied-in-fact or implied in law terms are subjected. Lord Atkin said of the principle

---

12 *Quilpué (Barque) Ltd v Brown* [1904] 2 KB 264, 73 LJKB 596 (KB) at 271, saying that the principle was "implied in every contract". The delay in question, from August to October, was no breach of contract. In the "regular turn" of the colliery the ship had been unloaded in accordance with the "usual custom and manner" of the colliery. See similar phrasing in the US – *Patterson v Meyerhofer* 204 NY 96 (NY 1912) (Court of Appeals NY).

13 Lord Alverstone CJ at trial ([1903] 2 KB 287 at 295) – approved in the House of Lords in *Ogdens Ltd v Nelson* (HL): [1905] AC 109.

14 Alfred A Hudson, *Hudson's Building and Engineering Contracts* (ed. Nicolas Dennys and Robert Clay eds, 13th edn, Sweet & Maxwell 2015) at 3.127. Interestingly the 10th edn, Alfred A Hudson and IN Duncan Wallace, *Hudson's Building and Engineering Contracts* (Sweet & Maxwell 1970), neither cites Mackay v Dick (n. 2 above), nor mentions cooperation; my first professional textbook, bought for £52 and still with me. Scots law is similar to English Law see David M Walker, *Principles of Scottish Private Law* (2nd edn, OUP 1975) at 777–778.

15 JW Carter, *Carter's Breach of Contract* (Hart 2012) at 2.27.

16 JF Burrows, 'Contractual Co-operation and the Implied Term' (1968) 31 *MLR* 390 at 402.

17 *Quilpué (Barque) Ltd v Brown* (n. 12 above) at 271–272. *Carter's Breach of Contract* refers to Cockburn CJ's language in *Stirling v Maitland* (n. 3 above) at 1047 – an "implied engagement".

that "I should not so much base the law on an implied term, as on a positive rule of the law of contract"[18] and Lord Alverstone CJ said, in a passage approved by the House of Lords, that the principle was "clearly established as a general proposition".[19]

It is a general proposition; not "highly restrictive"[20] nor an "extraordinary power".[21] The right approach is for judges to ask whether, correlative to the parties' obligations, the conduct or inactivity in question illegitimately prevented or delayed the other party's performance, at which point, the answer being "yes", the principle becomes operative. Reflecting Lord Alverstone CJ and Hudson, Lewison notes, having already observed that the expression "implied term" is used by lawyers in "a wide variety of senses"[22]: "In general, a term is necessarily implied in a contract that neither party will prevent the other from performing it".[23]

He goes on to say that it is:

> "necessarily implied" as parties "must be taken to have agreed that neither will actively prevent performance". It is possible that the duty does not rest upon the implication of a term, but may be a positive rule of the law[24]

Although this is tolerably clear, some judges seem to have read implied as implied-in-fact. This may be because Lewison also makes this much-cited comment: "since ultimately the rule of law (if such it is) depends upon the intention of the parties, ... it may properly be categorised as an implied term".[25]

For example, citing this passage, in *Royal Bank of Scotland plc v McCarthy*, Picken J seemed to hedge his bets by using construction ("the natural conclusion here is ... that Holdings should be bound by an obligation not to take active steps to prevent that thing being done")[26] and on both the *MvD* rule

---

18 *Southern Foundries (1926) Ltd v Shirlaw* [1940] AC 701 (HL) at 717. The House of Lords implicitly approved Vaughan Williams J's ruling. Burrows (n. 16 above) at 391 refers to it as "an inarticulate premise which underlies legal reasoning".

19 Cf. *Ogden* (n. 13 above). Vinelott J 'Described it as a general duty in Merton London Borough Council v Stanley Hugh Leach Limited' (1985) 32 *BLR* 51 at 80.

20 See Lord Carnwath at [66] in *Marks and Spencer plc v BNP Paribas Securities Services Trust Company (Jersey) Limited* [2015] UKSC 72.

21 Ibid. Lord Neuberger at [29] "the law imposes strict constraints on the exercise of this extraordinary power", quoting Sir Thomas Bingham MR in *Philips Electronique Grand Public SA v British Sky Broadcasting Ltd* [1995] EMLR 472.

22 Sir Kim Lewison, *The Interpretation of Contracts* (6th edn, Sweet & Maxwell 2015) at 6.01. See also Lord Wright in *Luxor (Eastbourne) Ltd v Cooper* [1941] All ER 33 (HL) saying "The expression 'implied term' is used in different senses" at 52.

23 Lewison, *Interpretation*, at 6.11.

24 Ibid. 6.14 and at 6.11.

25 Ibid. 6.14.

26 *Royal Bank of Scotland plc v McCarthy* [2015] EWHC 3626 (QB) at [270] citing Sales J – see n. 32 below.

and implication-in-fact.[27] He accepted two possibilities, one being that "this is what the agreement, read as a whole against the relevant background, would reasonably be understood to mean" and the other "that this term is necessary to make the contract work".[28] Spearman J appeared to take this approach in *Richard Pease v Henderson Administration Ltd*, referring to "the guidelines ... above [implied-in-fact tests]" and to Chitty, in which the mechanism is described as construction but also says that the implied-in-fact "guidelines ... must be **taken into account**",[29] finally keeping it simple – "Clause 3.6.1 would be unworkable without co-operation ..."[30]

In a recent construction law case Coulson LJ, having reviewed the 19th- and 20th-century law on extension of time clauses, noting that their purpose is to overcome the prevention principle, by way of providing a Contractor with a remedy for Employers' acts or omissions, says that the principle "can only sensibly operate by way of implied terms" and notes that Lewison "deals with the prevention principle in the chapter concerned with implied terms".[31] He does not differentiate between Lewison's description of the term as "necessarily implied" and implied-in-fact terms, despite dealing with both in the Judgment. This is confusing; but not exceptional.[32]

In *Swallowfalls Ltd v Monaco Yachting & Technologies SAM*, however, in which the shipbuilder financed the build of a yacht by a loan repayable on demand from the buyer, Longmore LJ, also relying on the *MvD* rule and Cockburn CJ's Judgment, agreeing with Counsel that the test is one of necessity (reflecting Lewison's language that the term is "necessarily implied"), correctly refers to prevention as "an ordinary implication in any contract for the performance of which co-operation is required". He goes on to observe:

> A shipbuilding contract is such a contract since ... the builder only earns a stage payment when the buyer's representative signs a certificate that the relevant stage or milestone has been achieved. If the relevant milestone has

27 Ibid. at [269] and especially [271], "the term in question is properly to be implied ... on the basis of the principles governing implication of terms set out in" *A-G of Belize v Belize Telecom Ltd* [2009] UKPC 10 and [145].
28 *RBS v McCarthy* (n. 26 above) at [271]. See *Scottish Power plc v Kvaerner Construction (Regions) Ltd* 1999 SLT 721 (CSOH) – Lord MacFadyen seems to use both grounds at 725.
29 *Chitty on Contracts*, at 14.023. Spearman J cites the 32nd edn at 14.104.
30 *Richard Pease v Henderson Administration Limited* at [132].
31 *North Midland Building Ltd v Cyden Homes Ltd* [2018] EWCA Civ 1744 at [28]. The case [1] "concerns the validity of a clause ... which provided that, where there was a delay caused by an event for which the contractor was responsible, and that delay was concurrent with a delay for which the employer was responsible, such concurrent delay would not be taken into account when calculating any extension of time".
32 See Lewison, *Interpretation*. See also *F&C Alternative Investments v Barthelemy* [2011] EWHC 1731 (Ch) where Sales J, seems to assume that there is only one kind of implied term, also quoting Lewison, *Interpretation*, at [268] and Lord Blackburn at [269].

in fact been reached, the buyer must so certify as part of his implied obligation to co-operate in the performance of the contract ...[33]

If one takes Lewison at face value and the term is necessarily implied, parties
being "taken" to have agreed not to get in the way, then the implied-in-fact
hurdle merely duplicates matters. A natural corollary to agreement, as Carter
and Lewison indicate, must be that parties covenant not to prevent the
object of the agreement from being achieved. Explanations based on business
efficacy, or necessity, or reasonableness, merely serve to complicate the position, prolong argument and increase cost.

In these cases, the primary task of the judge is, as JF Burrows describes it, to
"apportion out the required acts according to who is better positioned to do
them".[34] *Chitty* says, correctly: "the degree of co-operation required is to be
determined, not by what is reasonable, but by the obligations imposed-whether
expressly or impliedly upon each party by the agreement itself, and the surrounding circumstances".[35] The clearest example is Lord Esher's illustration of
practical cooperation in *Harris v Best*, answering the question "What is the obligation created by the agreement 'to be loaded?'"

> Loading is a **joint act** ... Each is to do his own part of the work, and to **do
> whatever is reasonable to enable the other to do his part** ... the shipper
> has to bring the cargo alongside so as to enable the shipowner to load the
> ship within the time stipulated ... and to lift that cargo to the rail of the
> ship. It is then the duty of the shipowner to be ready to take such cargo on
> board and to stow it ... **What is a reasonable course of action for both
> parties?** The shipper ... **must act reasonably** and bring the cargo alongside
> in sufficient time to enable the shipowner to do his part ...[36]

Scrutton describes these as common law obligations.[37]

Lord Blackburn referred to "a very early case [of 1489] in England",[38] in
which the great bell of Mildenhall was to be delivered to the Defendant brazier

---

33 *Swallowfalls* (n. 1 above).

34 Burrows (n. 16 above) at 403.

35 *Chitty on Contracts*, at 14.023. But see n. 30 above. Chitty is less than certain on this, saying
that the implied in fact "guidelines ... must be **taken into account**". See Cooke J in *James
E McCabe Ltd v Scottish Courage Ltd* [2006] EWHC 538 (Comm) at [17] – "It is self-
evident that any implied term of co-operation or prevention from performance can only be
given shape in the light of the express terms ..."

36 *Harris v Best* (n. 7 above) at 78.

37 Henry Bernard Eder and Sir Thomas Edward Scrutton, *Scrutton on Charterparties and Bills
of Lading* (Sweet & Maxwell 2011), 9.064.

38 *Mackay v Dick* (n. 2 above); Lord Blackburn's Judgment "the Year Book of 9th Edward IV.,
Easter Term, 4 A" i.e. 1489. Lord Watson's Judgment reflects the fact that *Mackay v Dick* was
a Scottish case – "They have been thwarted in the attempt to fulfil that condition by the neglect
or refusal of the Appellant to furnish the means of applying the stipulated test ... they must be

in Norwich, weighed, put in the fire in the presence of the men of Mildenhall and tuned to "agree with" the other Mildenhall bells. Emphasising the result and the "obvious good sense and justice" of this case in which the Court had found against the Defendant brazier, and that it was his job to put the bell in the fire, Lord Blackburn ruled that outcomes in such cases depend on an analysis of "what is the part of each". In *Mackay v Dick* the parties had agreed that payment of £1115 for a new type of railway cutting machine, a "patent steam excavating machine", would follow testing at a cutting in Carfin, Lanarkshire. The Defendants would not allow it to be tested there and thence refused to pay. The corollary of the seller's obligation to test was the buyer's duty to facilitate testing.

One might reconstruct the *MvD* rule into a basic principle:

> where in a contract it is necessary that something must be done, which cannot be done unless both parties effectuate it, the construction of the contract is that each agrees to do all that is necessary to be done on his part for the carrying out of that thing, and that each party is bound not to do anything, and to abstain from doing anything, which would prevent or delay the performing of any part of the contract, though there may be no express words to that effect.

In the following subchapters I consider a variety of the "something"s which have to be done through cooperation.

2.2 Prevention of performance

As I have described in subchapter 2.1 the essence of prevention is that one party acts or fails to act, placing the counterparty in a position where it cannot perform one or more of its contractual obligations or take advantage of the bargain struck. Courts will neutralise such action or inaction. Accidents such as fire[39] or third-party prevention[40] are not prevention.[41] For the purposes of an extension of time clause in a construction contract the phrase "causes beyond the contractor's control" may include acts of prevention.[42]

---

taken to have fulfilled the condition. The passage cited by Lord Shand from Bell's Principles ... 'If the debtor bound under a certain condition have impeded or prevented the event, it is held as accomplished'".

39 *Appleby v Myers* (1865–66) LR 1 CP 615 (Court of Common Pleas).

40 *Porter v Tottenham UDC* [1915] 1 KB 776.

41 Even new bye laws, issued by the Employer, acting under its statutory powers, which increase the cost of performance, are not covered by the principle. *Cory Ltd v City of London Corp* [1951] 2 KB 476 (AC).

42 See Hudson at 6.027 and *Group Five Building v Minister of Community Developments* [1993] 3 SA 629.

Cases are legion; best developed in construction and engineering.[43] "Commonly cited"[44] as the earliest modern case is *Holme v Guppy*[45] in which late handover of the site prevented commencement of the building of the Mersey Porter Brewery. The Court found that this vitiated the liquidated damages clause. This can lead to apparent absurdity. The "Rapid Building Group" was delayed from entering site by a man, his wife and a dog squatting in an old Austin Cambridge. The Contractor finished ten months late. The twenty-four-day squatting delay, not covered by the extension of time clause, vitiated the liquidated damages clause, Lloyd LJ saying that he was "startled" by this outcome.[46] Clients who interfere with the activity of a certifier or otherwise prevent the proper operation of the contractual machinery, breach their duty to cooperate; Lord Thankerton observing that it was "almost unnecessary" to cite precedent and the House of Lords agreeing with this "construction".[47] If an employer becomes aware that a certifier is not acting fairly and impartially, she must intervene, else she will be in breach.[48]

Keating J referred to *Holme v Guppy* as "consistent with the most ancient authorities ... founded on the most invincible reason and good sense".[49] These ancient authorities include a 1586 case where access to site was denied (prevention),[50] and a 1599 case in which the betrothed, Bridget Andrews, was called a whore and threatened with being tied to a post (not prevention).[51]

More conventional cases include one where a writer was commissioned to produce content for the "Juvenile Magazine"; this periodical then being "put an end to" by the publisher, thereby preventing the author from publishing.[52] Similarly where a corporate reorganisation was used to justify the removal of a managing director the Court found that this breached his fixed-term

---

43 For a detailed treatment of the cases see Hudson, at 6.025–6.030.

44 Michael Sergeant, 'No EOT Provision for Variations: Why the Right to LADs Should Not Be Lost' (2016) *Const LJ* 352.

45 *Holme v Guppy* (1838) 150 ER 1195 – Guppy Rees & Co. were the Kent Street brewers. See *Macintosh v The Midland Counties Railway Company* (1845) 153 ER 592 (Court of Exchequer). The principle has applied in Scotland since the 19th century – *McElroy v Tharsis Sulphur Co.* (1877) 5 Rettie (Ct of Sess) 161.

46 *Rapid Building Group Ltd v Ealing Family Housing Association Ltd* (1984) BLR 5 CA.

47 See Michael Sergeant and Max Wieliczko, *Construction Contract Variations* (Informa Law 2014) at 10.058 and *Panamena Europea Navigacion (Compania Ltda) v Frederick Leyland & Co. Ltd* (J Russell & Co.) [1947] AC 428 at 435.

48 *Cantrell v Wright and Fuller Ltd* [2003] EWCA Civ 1565.

49 *Russell v Viscount Sa da Bandeira* (1862) 143 ER 59 (Common Pleas) – Byles J at 83.

50 *Barker v Fletwel* (1586) Godb 69.

51 *Blandford v Andrews* (1599) Cro Eliz 694. See Samuel J. Stoljar, 'Prevention and Cooperation in the Law of Contract' (1953) 31 *CanBar Rev* 231, for an "extraordinary" case, *Foreman S T and S Bank v Tauber* (1932) 348 Ill 280, in which Max Tauber and Frances Bleier agreed an ante-nuptial contract that Tauber would pay Frances $20,000 in the event of his predecease. Tauber shot and killed Frances, then shot himself; dying of the wound the following day. Shooting his wife operated to "waive the condition of survivorship".

52 *Planche v Colburn* (1831) 131 ER 305 (Court of Common Pleas).

contract.[53] A company contracted to clear waste rock, which was to be crushed by the Defendant's machinery. An inadequate crusher prevented the Contractor from clearing the waste rock – relieving him of liability.[54] In another case a dental practice was sold, the vendor then wilfully incapacitating himself and thereby damaging the business.[55] In another case, cited by Pollock,[56] a master gave up the corn-factor trade, subsequent to which an indentured apprentice left his service. Pollock CB observed that the master "cannot be heard to complain that the other party has not done that which he has wilfully made it impossible that he should do".[57] In a diametrically opposed situation he found that "the apprentice would not be taught, and by his own wilful acts prevented the master from teaching him.".[58]

More recently a haulier was found to have breached an exclusive road haulage contract by ceasing to trade and merging with another company.[59] Lady Hale found that "On the true construction of the contract, the defendant had agreed that the claimant should exclusively provide its haulage and transport requirements" and implied a term in-fact that "a term that NLL would do nothing of their own motion to bring to an end their own requirements".[60] Once the true meaning has been divined by the Court it is hard to see the point of going on to imply a term when it is clear that cessation of the business is a breach, which is how Pollock CB and Willes J dealt with matters.

Hobhouse J found that a defendant oil trader had prevented performance of a contract by allowing its employee, a Miss Taber, to fail to answer a late afternoon telephone call, in a falling market, preventing the shipper from declaring the cargo, essentially closing the office early and landing itself with a liability of over $1,000,000.[61]

In *Sparks v Biden* Mr Sparks had sold a parcel of land to Mr Biden with a proviso that, once developed, a share of the "overage", calculated by reference to sale prices, would be paid to Sparks. Biden let the properties out to tenants, thereby preventing the overage proviso crystallising. The Court implied a term obliging Mr Biden to sell the properties in a reasonable period of time.[62]

---

53 *Shirlaw v Southern Foundries (1926), Limited.* [1939] 2 KB 206 (n. 18 above). See also *Shindler v Northern Raincoat Co Ltd* – [1960] 2 All ER 239.

54 *Kleinert v Abosso Gold Mining Co. Ltd* (1913) 58 Sol Jo 45 (Privy Council).

55 *Patrick M'Intyre the Elder v Belcher* (1863) 143 ER 602 in which Willes J said "(I)f I grant a man all the apples growing on a certain tree, and I cut down the tree, I am guilty of a breach" at 606.

56 Frederick Pollock, *Principles of Contract* (5th edn, Stevens 1889) at 409.

57 *Ellen v Topp* (1851) 155 ER 609.

58 *Raymond v Minton* (1866) LR 1 Exch. 244.

59 *CEL Group Ltd and others v Nedlloyd Ltd* [2003] All ER (D) 323 (Feb).

60 Ibid. [2003] EWCA Civ 1716 at [18].

61 *Nissho Iwai Petroleum Co. Inc. v Cargill International SA* [1993] 1 Lloyd's Rep 80. The call was made at 4:59:40 pm and should have been answered within ten seconds.

62 *Sparks v Biden* [2017] EWHC 1994 (Ch). In a similar case, *Renewal Leeds Ltd v Lowry Property Ltd* [2010] EWHC 2902 (Ch), Mr Elleray QC, using implied-in-fact principles, came to the same conclusion.

In *Marten v Whale* Scrutton LJ found an "implied provision" that the plaintiff was obliged to appoint a solicitor, to make the contract effective; and failure to appoint was a breach.[63] In *Cream Holdings Ltd v Stuart Davenport*, Mr Davenport, on leaving the company, was obliged to offer his shares to the remaining Directors. The value of the shares was to be determined by an accountant. Davenport refused to sign the letter of appointment. This persuaded the Court to imply an "obvious and necessary" term requiring cooperation in the appointment.[64] A more robust approach was taken where a party had, per Lord Diplock "flouted" "sensible [valuer appointment] machinery" by Lord Fraser resting his decision on the Court's general power to substitute its own machinery.[65]

2.3 Reasonable endeavours, diligence/facilitation

When action by one party is necessary to facilitate or enable performance by the other Courts infer duties to take such action and promote the duties through requirements which ensure that such actions are carried out timeously or otherwise reasonably. In *Hick v Raymond and Reid*, Lord Watson ruled that where there was no time specified for cargo discharge by the consignee, the law implies a rule of "general application" that unloading "shall be performed within a reasonable time".[66] In *Sparks v Biden*, above, HHJ Davis-White QC decided that a term requiring the Defendant to market and sell the houses within a reasonable period of time should be implied.[67] The best developed law in these cases is to be found in engineering and construction contracting.[68] Vinelott J, citing the *MvD* rule, implied a term into the 1963 JCT form, which requires significant interaction (see the partial list in 2.7 below), and ruled: "the building owner would do all things necessary to enable the contractor to carry out the work … the Courts have not gone beyond the implication of a duty to co-operate whenever it is reasonably necessary". The term was implied on the basis of a "fourth" category, which seems to mix implied-in-law and "implicit in the contract".[69]

---

63 *Marten v Whale* [1917] 2 KB 480.
64 *Cream Holdings Ltd v Stuart Davenport* (2011) [2011] EWCA Civ 1287 at [37]. See also *Al-Waddan Hotel Ltd v Man Enterprise SAL (Offshore)* [2014] EWHC 4796 (TCC) where an engineer's decision was a condition precedent to commencement of arbitration proceedings. The hotel owner failed to appoint an engineer and was unable to rely on the condition.
65 See generally *Sudbrook Trading Estate Ltd v Eggleton* [1983] 1 AC 444 (HL), and *Alstom Signalling Ltd v Jarvis Facilities Ltd* [2004] EWHC 1232 (TCC). See also *Richardson v Smith* (1870) LR 5 ChApp 648 – an order for specific performance was made and *Hooper v Herts* [1906] 1 Ch 549, where, given that there was a refusal to register a share transfer, such an order might have been appropriate.
66 *Hick v Raymond & Reid* [1893] AC 22 at 32.
67 *Sparks v Biden* (n. 62 above).
68 See for detailed treatment – Hudson at 3.127 and Sergeant and Wieliczko.
69 *Merton London Borough Council v Stanley Hugh Leach Limited* (n. 19 above) at 200 in (1986) 2 Const. LJ 189. At 123 Elisabeth Peden, *Good Faith in the Performance of Contracts*

Keating, paraphrasing Lord Simon in *Luxor (Eastbourne) v Cooper*,[70] says: "the employer impliedly agrees to do everything that is necessary on his part to bring about completion of the contract".[71] Construction contracts will be interpreted to include obligations that site must be handed over in a reasonable time,[72] possibly immediately,[73] and drawings and instructions provided in a reasonable time.[74]

Where cash is to be paid, money must be given at a time to allow it to be counted.[75] John Stannard lists cases in which a receiver of goods must be given enough time and the right facilities to inspect them; otherwise there will be neither tender nor delivery.[76] In *Croninger v Crocker* the New York Court found "little doubt that time should be given the tenderee for such examination before sunset and by daylight".[77] The principle is ancient; in 1597, in *Withers v Drew*, a distinction was drawn between matters requiring personal attendance (such as payment of rent) and those not; "things done in the night, where personal attendance of another is not necessary, are good".[78] What is reasonable changes over time; in *Proudfoot v Montefiore* an agent was held obliged to use the novel "electric telegraph" to communicate efficaciously with his principal.[79]

In the US there are some contracting contexts where Courts will infer obligations on employers to use best endeavours in coordination of contractors.[80]

In shipping cases obligations to act reasonably to facilitate the other's performance have been long inferred. In *Ford v Cotesworth* Blackburn J ruled that in the joint act of cargo "each party shall use reasonable diligence in performing his part", saying

---

(LexisNexis Butterworths 2003) says that construction of the architect's obligations would procure the same result.

70 *Luxor (Eastbourne) Ltd v Cooper* (n. 22 above) at 39.

71 Stephen Furst and others (eds), *Keating on Construction Contracts* (Sweet & Maxwell 2006) at 3.052.

72 *Arterial Drainage Co. v Rathangan Drainage Board (1880) 6 LR Ir 513*, Alfred A Hudson and IN Duncan Wallace, *Hudson's Building and Engineering Contracts* (11th edn, Sweet & Maxwell 1995) at 4.133–4.146 citing *Roberts* – "there must be an implied term that the site will be handed over to the contractor within a reasonable time". John E Stannard, *Delay in the Performance of Contractual Obligations* (OUP 2007) at 5.90–91.

73 *Freeman v Hensler* (1900) JP 260.

74 *Roberts v The Bury Improvement Commissioners* (1870) LR 5 CP 310 (Exchequer). This includes nomination of specialist contractors – Hudson at 3.148.

75 *Wade's Case* (1601) 5 Co Rep 114A.

76 Stannard, *Delay,* at 4.07–4.13.

77 *Croninger v Crocker* 62 NY 158.

78 *Withers v Drew* (1597) 78 ER 913. In *Oakdown Ltd v Bernstein & Co.* (1984) 49 P & CR 282; the Court dismissed as "ridiculous" an argument that posting cash through a letter box at midnight on Good Friday was tender.

79 *Proudfoot v Montefiore* (1867) LR 2 QB 511, 8 B & S 510 (QB) Cockburn CJ at 519.

80 *H. E. Crook Co., Inc. v United States* 270 US 4 (1926) (Supreme Court) cited in Hudson and Wallace, Hudson 1970 (n. 14 above) at 1.189.

that this obligation was implied by law.[81] Lord Esher mentions reasonable/reasonably three times in the passage from *Harris v Best* quoted above.

In numerous cases the Courts have determined which party should obtain an import or export licence where these are required for performance[82] and have inferred obligations which ensure that each party has the necessary information to make the applications.[83] Best endeavours obligations, or a duty to take "all reasonable steps", have been inferred where an export licence is required.[84] Where a party is entitled to a bill of lading the bill must be delivered "forthwith" or as soon as it can conveniently be delivered.[85] In an Australian case, a purchase "subject to finance" was read as requiring reasonable efforts to obtain finance.[86] That obligation was construed rather than implied.[87]

In international trade payment may be secured through documentary credits which guarantee payment by a bank on production of "conforming" documents such as bills of lading and/or invoices. In *Garcia v Page & Co. Ltd*, Porter J held as a matter of construction (Morris LJ referring to "true construction") that: "the buyer must have such time as is needed by a person of reasonable diligence to get that credit established".[88] This goes beyond strict necessity. The seller could ship without the credit and sue for the price (not always a practical proposition where the buyer is based overseas) but the absence of the credit relieves a seller of its obligations.[89] As Todd observes, the "advantages ... are mutual. The seller [obtains] sure knowledge he will be paid ... The buyer can use a credit to raise funds."[90] Denning LJ ruled in *Pavia & Co. v Thurmann-Neilson*, without using implied-in-fact language: "the seller

---

81 *Ford v Cotesworth* (n. 5 above) Blackburn J at 134. See also *Sunbeam Shipping Co. Ltd v President of India (The "Atlantic Sunbeam")* [1973] Vol. 1 Lloyd's Rep 482.

82 *Kyprianou v Cyprus Textiles Ltd* [1958] 2 Lloyds Rep 60.

83 *Chitty on Contracts*, at 14.025, citing *AV Pound* (n. 118 below) and *Kyprianou* (n. 82 above).

84 *Société d'Avances Commerciales (London) Ltd v A Besse & Co. (London) Ltd* [1952] 1 Lloyd's Rep 242, [1952] 1 TLR 644 (QBD) Sellers J at 249. See *Re Anglo Russian Merchant Traders & John Batt* [1917] 2 KB 679 (AC) and *Taylor & Co. v Landauer & Co.* [1940] 4 All ER 335, 85 Sol Jo 119 (KBD) "steps necessary" at 341. Clive M Schmitthoff and others, *Schmitthoff's Export Trade* (12th edn, Sweet & Maxwell 2011) at 32 says that sellers are more likely to be "sufficiently acquainted" with relevant rules and practices.

85 *Barber v Taylor* (1839) 5 Meeson Welsby 527 (Exchequer) – Parke B the bill should be delivered "forthwith".

86 *Meehan v Jones* (1982) 149 CLR 571.

87 AF Mason, 'Contract, Good Faith and Equitable Standards in Fair Dealing' (2000) 116 *LQR* 66 at 74–75 says "I considered that there was an obligation on the purchaser to make reasonable efforts".

88 *Garcia v Page & Co. Ltd* (n. 5 above) at 392 approved in MG Bridge and JP Benjamin, *Benjamin's Sale of Goods* (Sweet & Maxwell 2014) at 12.084.

89 *Trans Trust S.P.R.L. v Danubian Trading Co.* [1951 T 507], [1952] 2 QB 297 (AC) Denning LJ at 306. See AJ Bateson, 'The Duty to Cooperate' (1960) *JBL* 187 at 189. See also *Nichimen Corporation v Gatoil Overseas Inc.* 1987 2 Lloyd's Rep 46.

90 Paul Todd, *Bills of Lading and Bankers' Documentary Credits* (Lloyds of London Press 1998) at 22. See Ali Malek and David Quest, *Jack: Documentary Credits: The Law and Practice Including Standby Credits and Demand Guarantees* (4th edn, Tottel 2009) at 1.2.

is entitled, before he ships the goods, to be assured that, on shipment, he will get paid".[91] He subsequently modified this to "the buyer must provide the letter of credit within a reasonable time before the first date for shipment".[92]

In 1973 Manchester United bought the Scots striker Ted MacDougall from Bournemouth with a proviso that on his scoring 20 goals the final £25,000 instalment of the £200,000 fee (a Third Division record) became payable. They appointed a new manager, Tommy Docherty, whose plans did not include McDougall, who seldom played and who was sold at the end of the season. The 20-goal target was not reached and the £25,000 not paid. On appeal the £25,000 was determined to be due: "Manchester United were bound to afford Mr. MacDougall a reasonable opportunity of scoring 20 goals."[93] In this case the "something" was that reasonable opportunity. Other impresarios have received the same treatment; Romilly MR found, construing an agreement reviewing its purpose and background, that an actor must "have an opportunity of shewing what his abilities were before a London audience".[94] As we can see the Courts use a mixture of mechanisms for inferring the duty or its content. In some, the matter is resolved by construction; in others by gap-filling.

To achieve high-level coherence and reflect actual outcomes, one could draft a supplement or explanation of the *MvD* principle when reasonable diligence or reasonable action is required to make a contract work:

> Among the somethings which have to be done is the use of reasonable diligence in, and the undertaking of those things that are reasonably necessary to ensure that each party might properly perform its part of the contract.

2.4 Defects and rights to cure

In general, there is no right to cure a breach in English Law.[95] A seller may be able to cure a defect before expiry of the time for performance, Benjamin referring to "a certain amount of authority … most of it concerned with tender of documents", such as in *Borrowman, Phillips & Co. v Free and Hollis*, in which tender of a cargo of maize had been refused due to the failure to produce shipping documents,

---

91 *Pavia & Co. v Thurmann Nielsen* (n. 1 above) at 157.

92 *Sinason-Teicher Inter-American Grain Corpn v Oilcakes & Oilseeds Trading Co. Ltd* [1954] 3 All ER 468 at 472.

93 *Bournemouth & Boscombe Football Club Ltd v Manchester United Football Club Ltd* 1974 B No 1531 (AC). At 66 Edwin Peel and Sir GH Treitel, *Treitel on the Law of Contract*, vol. 13 (Sweet & Maxwell 2011), refers to the case as one of prevention but it seems to require positive cooperation.

94 *Fechter v Montgomery* (1863) 23 Beav 22; (1863) 55 ER 274 at 276. See *Kelly v Battershell* [1949] 2 All ER 830.

95 *Clegg v Andersson* [2003] All ER (D) and *Buckland v Bournemouth University Higher Education Corporation* [2010] All ER (D) 299. AS Burrows, *A Restatement of the English Law of Contract* (OUP 2016) – there is "some uncertainty on this" at 116.

a second, conforming, tender being held valid on appeal.[96] but that right might be lost where confidence has evaporated.[97] The law is complex; for example, a right to cure defects will probably be implied, either as an incident of the type of contract[98] or, possibly, construed; based on market practice, in bespoke software contracts.[99] Roy Goode expresses regret that Sale of Goods legislation does not provide such rights.[100]

Staughton J recognised that, in bespoke software contracts, as an incident of the type of contract, there will likely be some defects and that the supplier should be given time to cure those defects because the inevitable modifications and tests required in such contracts were something that a supplier should have both the right and the duty to carry out.[101]

Although the Court did not deal directly with a right to cure, in a case involving two squabbling joint managers of an oil-and-gas investment fund, the fund owner ordered them to sort out their differences so that they could work together. Five weeks later they had failed to do so, and their contracts were terminated.[102] Their failure to try to work matters out, instead trying to obtain individual advantage from the situation, appears to have weighed with Popplewell J.

In another case the purchaser withheld money from the supplier, Rubicon, claiming that there were defects in its system.[103] Rubicon then time-locked the system rather than fixing the defects. Euan Cameron says "it was the spectacular disabling of the system ... that gave the clue that the supplier was no longer going to co-operate in seeking to remedy the problems".[104] Where defects are

---

96 *Benjamin's Sale of Goods,* at 12.032. See e.g. *Borrowman, Phillips, & Co. v Free & Hollis* (1878) 4 QBD 500 and see Vanessa Mak, 'The Seller's Right to Cure Defective Performance – a Reappraisal' (2007) *LMCLQ* 409 .

97 *Benjamin's Sale of Goods,* at 12.032–12.033. See also *Maple Flock Co. Ltd v Universal Furniture Products (Wembley) Ltd* [1934] 1 KB 148.

98 *Saphena Computing Limited v Allied Collection Agencies Ltd* [1995] FSR 616, *Anglo Group plc v Winther Brown & Co. Ltd* [2000] EWHC Technology 127 (TCC).

99 *Eurodynamic Systems Plc v General Automation Ltd* unreported; Steyn J ruling that "The expert evidence convincingly showed that it is regarded as acceptable practice to supply computer programmes that contain errors and bugs. The basis of the practice is that, pursuant to his support obligation the supplier will correct errors and bugs ..."

100 Royston Miles Goode and Ewan McKendrick, *Commercial Law* (4th edn, LexisNexis 2009) at 364. At 413–414 Mak (n. 96 above) notes that this is the direction in which EU consumer law is headed, doubting that its application in the UK matches this ambition.

101 *Saphena Computing Ltd v Allied Collection Agencies Ltd* n. 98 above. See also *Eurodynamics* n. 99 above. The principle may not apply to tried and tested systems; *SAM Business Systems Ltd v Hedley & Co.* [2002] EWHC 2733.

102 *Qogt Inc. v International Oil and Gas Technology Ltd* [2014] EWHC 1628 (comm).

103 *Rubicon Computer Systems Ltd v United Paints Ltd* (Unreported Court of Appeal 12 November 1999).

104 Euan Cameron, 'Major Cases' (2000) 14 *IRLCT* 259. I dealt with a supplier who remotely locked a ship unloader bought for a Qatari contract; a call on the on-demand bond in our possession brought him to the negotiating table.

relatively minor there will be no right to terminate.[105] Defects before completion, which become apparent during performance, if "genuinely temporary"
defects, may be classified as "temporary disconformities" but where these cannot
be easily remedied, they may be regarded as breaches. Termination might be
premature especially if it remained possible to remedy the defect, or where
remedy would be inexpensive.[106] Burrows considers that the duty to mitigate
may "override an intention to cure",[107] meaning that clients are virtually forced
to organise rectification by the contractor. Cairns J ruled that defects which
would cost £174 to rectify were not minor in the context of a £560 contract.[108]
Such technicalities serve only to promote uncertainty. Vanessa Mak may go too
far saying that: "The balance is generally struck in favour of the buyer, who, by
exercising his right to reject the goods and terminate for breach, can put an
early stop to any attempts at cure ..."[109] Where an employer has an express
right to require a contractor to return to cure defects, should the employer
instead appoint an alternate, recovery will be limited to consequential loss plus
the cost which the defaulting contractor would have incurred.[110] Almost all
modern standard forms (including GC/Works1 and CiOB forms), contain such
a provision and most contractors would resist any general right for the employer
to use a substitute. This also virtually forces an employer to organise rectification
by the contractor. Beale and Dugdale noted that if a buyer attempted to repair
the defect himself without authorisation his labour costs would not be paid and
frequently such interference was treated as invalidating the warranty.[111]

The position is clearer in Scotland; Lady Cosgrove ruled: "it is a basic principle of the law of contract that if one party is in breach, the innocent party is
not entitled to treat the contract as rescinded without giving the other party an
opportunity to remedy the breach".[112] Where such a right exists, it is ineluct-
able that one party must enable the other to carry out repairs; by providing
access to an IT system or a building or a defective part. A right to cure, along
the lines of Lady Cosgrove's Judgment, is arguably market practice and what

---

105 Sergeant and Wieliczko at 4.17.
106 Hudson at 4.074–4.075.
107 AS Burrows, *Remedies for Torts and Breach of Contract* (3rd edn, OUP 2004), at 223.
108 *Bolton v Mahadeva* [1972] 1 WLR 1009, and see *Hoenig v Isaacs* [1952] 2 All ER 176 (the
      full price should not be withheld for minor defects).
109 Mak n. 96 above.
110 See e.g. *Pearce and High Ltd v Baxter and Baxter* [1999] EWCA Civ 789 and *Woodlands
      Oak Ltd v Conwell & Anor* [2011] EWCA Civ 254.
111 Hugh Beale and Tony Dugdale, 'Contracts between Businessmen: Planning and the Use of
      Contractual Remedies' (1975) 2 *Br J Law Soc* 45 at 56 and see also 57.
112 *Strathclyde Regional Council v Border Engineering Contractors Ltd* 1997 SCLR 100; at 104.
      This idea may only apply where the breach is capable of remedy – a logical position – see
      Neil Morrison, 'Once Bitten, Twice Shy' *Journal of the Law Society of Scotland*. See the Scot-
      tish Law Commission paper rejecting this – www.scotlawcom.gov.uk/files/1115/2222/
      5222/Report_on_Review_of_Contract_Law_Formation_Interpretation_Remedies_for_
      Breach_and_Penalty_Clauses_Report_No_252.pdf at 150–151.

parties reasonably expect. My experience is that most industrial contractors' policies require a right to cure defects and a warranty conditional on being provided that opportunity.[113]

In the next subchapter I deal with a number of cases where a right to terminate was denied by Courts, one because the "ordinary reaction" of a shipowner tendered too little money is "point out the deficiency ... in no uncertain terms".[114] It really does not feel sensible for the law to draw elusive distinctions between temporary disconformities or bugs on the one hand and defects on the other, nor on defects which would entitle one to terminate and defects which would not. The common-sense position, I suggest, almost certainly market practice, is that a contractor should have a right to be notified of defects and a right to attempt to cure.[115]

Consider your own experience. If you have had work carried out in your house, such as a kitchen installation or an extension built, it is likely that there were defects. I suggest that you didn't read the contract or consider terminating but picked up the phone and spoke to the builder – your "ordinary reaction" or, as Jenkins LJ put it, "the simple and reasonable step, which [anyone] would take".[116]

In the event that cure is impossible or refused then normal service should resume, with termination possible where the defect makes the contractual objective unattainable and damages available otherwise.

To achieve high-level coherence and reflect actual outcomes, one could draft a supplement or explanation of the *MvD* principle as it applies when defects emerge or are detected, and cure is required to make a contract work:

> The something which has to be done is the cure of defects and to achieve that end the supplier's part is to make him/herself available to make or attempt the cure and the employer's part is to make available to the supplier reasonable opportunity or opportunities to enable the supplier to make or attempt the cure.

2.5 Communication or constructive engagement

Communication is critical to the successful performance of symbiotic contracts which require sedulous attention to detail and seamless performance. Parties must engage constructively and effectively to communicate, clarify details of the

---

113 The following provision is typical (my drafting) "The Contractor's obligation hereunder is limited to making good by repair, replacement or modification at the Contractor's option any defect in the goods appearing ... [time limits]".

114 *Tradax Export SA v Dorada Compania Naviera SA (The "Lutetian")* [1982] 2 Lloyd's Rep 140 – Bingham J at 157.

115 See e.g. *Yeoman Credit Ltd v Apps* [1962] 2 QB 508, [1961] 2 All ER 281 – the buyer terminated a hire purchase contract after several requests to the seller to put the car into roadworthy condition had been ignored.

116 *Peter Dumenil & Co. Ltd. v James Ruddin Ltd* [1953] 1 WLR 815 (AC) at 824.

contract (such as time and place of delivery), organise access, provide information, tackle problems and correct actual and potential misunderstandings. Courts infer express duties to communicate on parties who hold or must create information required by a counterparty and provide incentives to communicate by refusing remedies where communication might have perfected a contract. In a simple example, a shipowner must give notice of readiness to load.[117]

In *AV Pound Ltd v MW Hardy Inc.* (*AV Pound*), the House of Lords considered a contract for the sale of 300 tons of turpentine to be bought from a Portuguese supplier. Under Portuguese law an export licence was required. The sellers possessed the information required. Viscount Simmonds ruled that the seller had a duty to obtain the licence and to cooperate with the buyer: "by telling him the destination of the contract goods and otherwise as may be reasonable".[118] Goddard CJ dealt with a similar issue, also by construction, where Syrian authorities required evidence that seed was not destined for Israel, in a case of a Cypriot trader buying cotton seed, saying:

> it clearly was the duty of the buyers to co-operate with the seller … : it was their duty to supply the information … It was quite obvious that the only people who could supply that information were the buyers.[119]

A letter of credit is "opened" once the contract between the bank and the buyer has been made and the letter communicated to the buyer to enable the buyer to make appropriate shipping and insurance arrangements.[120] It is not enough simply to open a credit.

A fraternity club leased a Hong Kong property for the playing of mah-jong. The landlord attempted to forfeit the lease alleging a failure to obtain a gaming licence but was ordered to provide the lessee with the information it needed to obtain the licence.[121] Centuries old agency law obligations require an agent to keep the principal informed of matters which are his or her concern.[122] Judge Heppel QC described the obligations of an estate agent: "if … he becomes aware of any significant event in the market that might influence his principal's instructions, to inform the principal thereof and to advise him accordingly".[123]

---

117 *Stanton v Austin* (1872) LR 7 CP 651 (Common Pleas).
118 *AV Pound Ltd v MW Hardy Inc.* [1956] 1 All ER 639 (HL) at 648. See Peden, *Good Faith*, at 33–34.
119 *Kyprianou* (n. 82 above) at 64–65.
120 *Bunge Corpn v Vegetable Vitamin Foods (Pte) Ltd* [1985] 1 Lloyd's Rep 613.
121 *Quick Switch Ltd v Shining Star Super Seafood Ltd* [2011] HKEC 232.
122 Peter Watts, FMB Reynolds and William Bowstead (eds), *Bowstead and Reynolds on Agency* (20th edn, Sweet & Maxwell 2014) at 6.021 at 196. See *York Buildings Co. v Mackenzie* (1795) 8 Bro Parl Cas 42, 3 ER 432 (HL).
123 *John D. Wood & Co. (Residential & Agricultural) Ltd v Knatchbull* – [2002] EWHC 2822 (QB) which sits comfortably with RICS, *Professional Standards and Guidance, UK – UK Residential Real Estate Agency* (2017): "The agent should report to the client … no less than once a month with a summary of the data … The report should also include an opinion

A manufacturer seeking a new distributor has no duty to advise the incumbent.[124] This may not be true where the parties are engaged in a "relational" contract, Leggatt J finding, in a case arising from a joint venture between a Greek businessman and a member of the Abu Dhabi Royal Family, that it was inconsistent with the duty of good faith implied in this relationship for one party to enter into negotiations to sell his interest without informing the other.[125]

In a case arising from delayed construction of a new sewage works, Diplock J said that the time for providing instructions, information or drawings is that "which is reasonable having regard to the point of view of [the engineer] and his staff and the point of view of the [employer], as well as the point of view of the contractors".[126] The law is of long standing – see *Holme v Guppy* (1838)[127] and *Roberts v The Bury Improvement Commissioners* (1870).[128] Hudson notes that failure to provide drawings and information in time is "probably the commonest cause of claims by contractors".[129]

In *JH Ritchie v Lloyd Limited (Ritchie)*, an agricultural harrow broke down, being replaced with a loaned second-hand item and repaired. Lord Hope described Mr Ritchie's enquiries, concluding that no one

> would reveal what the nature of the problem was or what had been done to the harrow to repair it. All he was told was that it had been repaired to what was described as "factory gate specification". Mr Ritchie then asked for an engineer's report on the harrow. This too was refused. … the Respondents were under an implied obligation to provide … the information that Mr Ritchie asked for.[130]

In *Ritchie* the harrow was "conform" in Scots terms, but the farmer needed the information for reassurance; to allow him to make an informed judgement as to whether to accept it.

There are cases in which a misunderstanding or an error has resulted in the destruction of a contract and in which it can be inferred or argued that the Court

as to any change in the market conditions, with advice as to whether the market price should be adjusted …"

124 *Ilkerler Otomotive Sanayai v Perkins Engines Co. Ltd* [2015] EWHC 2006 (Comm).
125 *Sheikh Tahnoon Bin Saeed Bin Shakhboot Al Nehayan v Ioannis Kent (AKA John Kent)* [2018] EWHC 333 (Comm).
126 *Neodox Ltd v Swinton and Pendlebury Borough Council* (1958) 5 BLR 34 QBD at 42; cited in *City Inn Ltd v Shepherd Construction Ltd* [2007] CSOH 190 (OH) and *Wells v Army & Navy Co-operative Society* (1902) Hudson BC Vol. 2. In *Consarc Design Ltd v Hutch Investments Ltd* (2003) 19 Const LJ 91 (QBD (T&CC)) HHJ Bowsher referred to "full and coordinated" information.
127 *Holme v Guppy* (n. 45 above).
128 *Roberts v The Bury Improvement Commissioners* (n. 74 above) – see Kelly CB at 329.
129 Hudson at 2.130.
130 *J & H Ritchie Ltd v Lloyd Ltd* [2007] UKHL 9; [2007] 1 WLR 670 at [19].

has subsequently settled liability on the basis of a failure to communicate. Owing to a misunderstanding of the position by the seller in *Mona Oil v Rhodesian Railways (Mona Oil)*,[131] which could have been resolved easily through either party making sensible enquiries, a seller did not deliver 75 oil tanks. Payment was conditioned on receipt of signed confirmation by T&Co, the buyer's agent, that the goods were at the buyer's disposal. Once that had been effectuated Mona Oil approached T&Co, who demurred, requiring written instructions, subsequently received but not communicated to Mona Oil. Devlin J's Judgment, saying that the buyer's desire to do business "evaporated" after a meeting, suggests that there may have been some dispute. Devlin J's much quoted, almost regretful, peroration says:

> every business contract depends for its smooth working on co-operation, but ... the law can enforce co-operation only in a limited degree – to the extent that is necessary to make the contract workable. For any higher degree of co-operation, the parties must rely on the desire ... that the business should get done.[132]

Mona Oil remains a difficult case. It would have been easy for T&Co to communicate with the seller to remove the misunderstanding, which would have made the contract work. Devlin J added that: "the removal of misunderstanding is quite beyond the reach of implied contractual obligation".[133] In *Peter Dumenil & Co. v James Ruddin Ltd (Dumenil)*, Jenkins LJ put paid to that notion. A warehouseman, asked for 25 cases of skinned rabbits, advised that he had "GPL" rabbits but no "Gaythorn"; notwithstanding that they are the same. Jenkins LJ said, using marvellous Old English language:

> it behoved them, before they jumped to the conclusion of repudiation, to take the simple and reasonable step, which any businessman would take, of going to the defendants and saying:
> What has happened about our rabbits? We are told by the Crown Wharf Cold Stores that none of them are there.
> As soon as they said that the whole matter would have been explained at once.[134]

Bateson says that the buyer's failure to make enquiries "led to the failure of his claim for repudiation".[135]

---

131 *Mona Oil* n. 6 above.
132 Ibid. at 1018.
133 Ibid.
134 *Dumenil* (n. 116 above) at 824.
135 Bateson (n. 89 above) at 187.

In *AE Lindsay & Co. Ltd v Cook* the seller repudiated on the buyer's error in calculating a credit. Reflecting that it would have been easy to communicate the error Pilcher J, wryly, said:

> Businessmen ... do stand on their rights. It would have been quite competent for Colimpex to have cabled the plaintiffs and said: "You must open credit for a larger sum ..." There was no real reason why [the buyer] should not have been able to estimate with considerable exactitude the sum for which he ought to have opened credit; he might, moreover, have inquired, but he did not.[136]

In this case, the party making the error was left with the consequences because he could have double-checked. It seems unlikely that *AE Lindsay* would be followed today. In a rising market case, *Tradax Export SA v Dorada Compania Naviera SA (Tradax)* a charter was determined on the charterer's mistakenly paying too little. Bingham J said:

> None of the relevant witnesses in this case had any hesitation in agreeing that the ordinary reaction of an owner who is tendered too little hire is to point out the deficiency to the charterer in no uncertain terms ... I have no doubt that the owners knew that the charterers believed they had paid the right amount. It was their duty, acting honestly and responsibly, to disclose their own view to the charterers.[137]

In a similar case, Proudman J said that it was:

> obvious that Mr Tunnicliffe knew that a mistake had been made and that it would be unfair and unconscionable to ignore the terms ... in circumstances where Mr Tunnicliffe was surprised by the terms ... but said nothing about them.[138]

These are estoppel by convention cases but seem not quite to fit the normal requirements for estoppel which are complex[139] and, for this work, I rely on the

---

136 *A. E. Lindsay & Co. Ltd v Cook* [1953] 1 Lloyd's Rep 328 (QBD) at 333.

137 *The Lutetian* (n. 114 above) at 157. In *Starbev GP Ltd v Interbrew Central European Holdings BV* [2014] EWHC 1311 (Comm) – a failure to disclose the existence of a dispute might create an estoppel and *Raffeisen Zentralbank Osterreich AG v Royal Bank of Scotland* [2011] 1 Lloyd's Rep 123. The question may not arise again after the decision that timeous payment is not a condition in *Spar Shipping AS v Grand China Logistics Holding (Group) Co. Ltd* [2016] EWCA Civ 982.

138 *Process Components Ltd v Kason Kek-Gardner Ltd* [2016] EWHC 2198 (Ch) at 132.

139 Catherine Mitchell, *Contract Law and Contract Practice: Bridging the Gap between Legal Reasoning and Commercial Expectation* (Hart 2013) describes estoppel as "nebulous" at 100 and "useful" at 264–265.

brief description in Wilken: "Silence will probably only give rise to ... estoppel where there is a duty to disclose ... [the representation must be] clear and unequivocal."[140] Silence in response to a request to provide assurance as to performance might allow a party to terminate after the *Pro Victor* case. A concerned shipowner made several requests to a charterer for assurance that the charter would be performed. Receiving no reply, the owner terminated, Flaux J ruling:

> The court has to look at the totality of the relevant words and conduct relied upon ... including the history of the contractual relationship, to determine whether ... the defendant has evinced an intention not to perform[141]

Ritchie is another case in which silence in response to commercially sensible[142] queries led to a rejection being upheld.

Hugh Collins, unimpressed by *Mona Oil*, says that it has "stifled the development of a duty to disclose information during ... performance" .[143] In later work, he asserts that the case reflects the view that to do differently would "conflict with a more basic right of every individual to go about his business as he pleases, even where the exercise of that right obstructs successful performance of existing contracts".[144] *Mona Oil* is not cited in *Schmitthoff's Export Trade,*[145] is never cited in trade documentation cases and some near contemporaneous cases such as *Kyprianou v Cyprus Textiles Ltd*[146] suggest that it would not be followed today.

---

140 Sean Wilken, *The Law of Waiver, Variation and Estoppel* (OUP 2012) at 7.40. In the US a silent response to a notice to cure a lack of progress may justify a termination. See *Composite Laminates, Inc. v United States* 27 Fed Cl 310, 323–324 (1992) and *International Verbatim Reporters, Inc. v United States* 9 Cl Ct 710, 715 (1986).

141 *SK Shipping (S) Pte Ltd v Petroexport Ltd (The Pro Victor)* [2009] EWHC 2974 (Comm); [2010] 2 Lloyd's Rep 158 at [88]. See Reza Beheshti, 'Anticipatory Breach of Contract and the Necessity of Adequate Assurance under English Law and the Uniform Commercial Code' (2018) *LMCLQ* 276 for a review of the US doctrine of adequate assurance. See for a review of Louisiana Law Jumoke Dara and Olivier Moreteau, 'The Interaction of Good Faith with Contract Performance, Dissolution, and Damages in the Louisiana Supreme Court' (2018) 10 *J Civ L Stud* 261.

142 Counsel in *Ritchie* (n. 130 above), Mr Tyre, accepted that Lloyd's silence had not been commercially sensible practice – see Lord Brown at [41]. A pre-contract letter which attempts to interpret the contract will be inadmissible, even if ignored – see, in Canada, *Phoenix Commercial Enterprises Pty Ltd v City of Canada Bay Council* [2010] NSWCA 64.

143 Hugh Collins, 'Implied Duty to Give Information during Performance of Contracts' (1992) 55 *MLR* 556.

144 Hugh Collins, *The Law of Contract* (CUP 2008) at 337.

145 *Schmitthoff's Export Trade*.

146 *Kyprianou* n. 82 above.

Jonathan Morgan approves of *Mona Oil* (without explaining what the "higher degree" might have meant) seemingly because Lord Devlin has limited the scope of cooperation in contract:

> Some great commercial judges have displayed a more convincing grasp of the role of extra-legal sanctions in curbing opportunism. ... The fact that that co-operative spirit had 'evaporated' was 'unfortunate' ..., but the law ... would not imply a term to assist their plight. Devlin J clearly saw that, despite its vital importance, co-operation is ... properly a matter for ... extra-legal relations.[147]

The Judgment refers to misunderstanding, not to opportunism. It appears from Devlin J that the behaviour of Mr Chamberlain, of T&Co, whose willingness to cooperate had "evaporated", caused the problem but Devlin J would not accept that Mr Chamberlain was under any duty to inform Mona Oil that he had received instructions. He ruled that the law will only enforce cooperation if that is necessary to make the contract "workable".[148]

It's an odd comment because the result was that the oil tanks remained undelivered and a duty on T&Co to communicate their instructions to Mona Oil does not seem oppressive. However, Mona Oil could have made enquiries, and it might be better that the risk lies with the party failing to double check. Hugh Collins makes a similar point, his logic being economic, that avoidance of wasted cost, and the desire for performance, is a good argument for imposing some disclosure obligations:

> if costs could be avoided at the price of a telephone call, the criterion of wealth maximization suggests that an implied duty of disclosure ... should be imposed ... would assist the successful completion of contracts by requiring a minimal and inexpensive mutual duty to safeguard the other contracting party's interests[149]

A duty to safeguard the other party's interests may go too far. A simple obligation to make that telephone call (or send a text or an email) would be sufficient.

In a case which is interesting because the supplier did not know of the duty of the supplied GRP pipe until sometime after the contract had been made, Coulson J, citing several duties to warn authorities, said:

> It would be absurd if, say, JP knew or ought reasonably to have known that foam concrete was an inappropriate environment for their GRP pipe, but

147 Jonathan Morgan, *Contract Law Minimalism* (CUP 2013) at 144.
148 *Mona Oil* (n. 6 above) at 1018.
149 Collins, 'Implied Duty to Give Information', at 556–557.

had no obligation to pass such information on to Murphy, simply because the contract had been made before JP found out about the use of foam concrete.[150]

In this case the duty to warn was implied as "as a consequence of JP's role as a specialist supplier of GRP pipe".[151] Where a contractor's actual knowledge is that designs are dangerous or inadequate, a single warning may be insufficient, May J saying that "they could have protested more vigorously"; a somewhat subjective and unhelpful formulation.[152] In an insurance claim case, Clarke LJ, finding an estoppel by acquiescence resulting from the conduct of negotiations, said:

> In the light of what had passed between the parties, TB was, in my view, entitled to expect that if the insurers regarded [material] as outstanding, due, and unparked, then, acting honestly and responsibly, they should have told her.[153]

It is hard to understand why a more general duty that information is outstanding would be cumbersome. The principle underlying the decision follows Blair J's Judgment in which he held that a "duty to speak ... may arise ... where one party is proceeding on the assumption that something is agreed, whereas the other party knows that it is in dispute".[154]

Where the US Government withheld vital information, the Court held that the Government "could not properly let [suppliers] flounder".[155] The position in the US originates in good faith principles, Judge Posner holding in one well-known case that "To be able to correct your contract partner's mistake at zero cost to yourself, and decide not to do so, is a species of opportunistic behavior that the parties would have expressly forbidden."[156]

In *Mannai Investment Co. Ltd v Eagle Star Assurance Co. Ltd (Mannai)* the Court would not allow one party to take advantage of a minor and obvious error. A tenant purported to determine a lease on the 12 January 1994 under a lease providing for determination on notice on the "third anniversary of the

---

150 *J Murphy & Sons Ltd v Johnston Precast Ltd [2008] EWHC 3024 (TCC)* at [129]. See also *Lindenberg v Canning*, 29 ConLR 71 – the builder should have queried the plans he was given.

151 Ibid. (*Murphy*) at [130].

152 *Plant Construction PLC v Clive Adams and Associates* [2000] BLR 137. The Judgment reviews a number of earlier cases.

153 *Ted Baker PLC and another v Axa Insurance UK PLC and others* [2017] EWCA Civ 4097 at [87].

154 Ibid. at [74] paraphrasing Blair J in *Starbev GP Ltd v Interbrew Central European Holdings BV* (n. 137 above).

155 *Helene Curtis Industries, Inc. v The United States* 312 F2d 774 (United States Court of Claims).

156 *Market Street Associates Ltd Partnership v Frey* 941 F2d 588 (7th Cir 1991) at 597. See Melvin A. Eisenberg, 'The Duty to Rescue in Contract Law' (2002) 71 *Fordham LRev* 647.

term commencement date" – 13 January 1994.[157] The House of Lords refused to allow the landlord to take advantage of a "latent ambiguity".[158] There are echoes of the above "mistake" cases in that the "reasonable recipient" of the notice could easily have double-checked the intention of the departing lessee.[159] It would have been better, and coherent, for the House of Lords to use the same language as that deployed by Jenkins LJ in *Dumenil* – that it "behoved" the recipient to make enquiries. In a similar case Christopher Clarke J said: "[A] helpful test is whether a reasonable representee would naturally assume that the true state of facts did not exist and that had it existed, he would have been informed of it."[160] This might be better expressed as requiring a party terminating a contract, or receiving a possibly ambiguous notice, to make enquiries as to whether the latent ambiguity, the insufficient credit or the lack of instructions were deliberate or accidental, perhaps allowing them to warn that if there is an error it must be corrected within a defined timeframe.

There are other situations in which Courts will insist that communication is a necessary pre-condition to the finding that a contract has been breached. In a principle of general application, a tenant cannot sue a landlord for failure to repair demised premises unless she has given the landlord notice. Bramwell B described the "introduction and interpolation" of words requiring such notice as necessary to prevent a "monstrous absurdity" risking a result "preposterous and unreasonable".[161]

Where notice requirements are clear, and the contract requires precise adherence, Courts will not usually relieve parties of their obligations.[162] In recent

---

157 *Mannai Investment Co. Ltd v Eagle Star Life Assurance Co Ltd* [1997] AC 749, [1997] 3 All ER 352 (House of Lords). See also *Doe d. Cox v Roe* (1803) 4 Esp 185 – a tenant leasing the Bricklayer's Arms was given notice to quit "the premises ... commonly ... known by ... The Waterman's Arms". There was no "The Waterman's Arms" in Limehouse. The error was treated as a latent ambiguity. *Mannai* was followed in Scotland in *Tyco Fire & Integrated Solutions (UK) Ltd v Regent Quay Development Co. Ltd* [2016] CSOH 97 – Lord Tyre at [16] – "I am satisfied that the reasonable recipient would not have been perplexed in any way by the error ..."

158 See also *General Nutrition Investment Co. v Holland and Barrett International Ltd* [2017] EWHC 746 (Ch) at [97] – Warren J paraphrased the principle "if a notice unambiguously conveys a decision to determine a court may nowadays ignore immaterial errors which would not have misled a reasonable recipient". Lord Steyn in 'The Intractable Problem of the Interpretation of Legal Texts' at 148 in Sarah Worthington (ed) *Commercial Law and Commercial Practice* (Hart 2003) says that *Mannai* caused Chancery practitioners to "hoist a black flag over Lincoln's Inn".

159 In *Sackville UK Property Select II (GP) No. 1 Ltd v Robertson Taylor Insurance Brokers Ltd* [2018] EGLR 13 the error would not have been understood as an error by a reasonable recipient.

160 *Raiffeisen Zentralbank Osterreich AG v RBS* (n. 137 above) at [85].

161 *Makin v Watkinson* (1870) LR 6 Ex 25 (Exchequer) at 28, *Torrens v Walker* [1906] 2 Ch 166. See Burrows, *Remedies*, at 404.

162 *Hoe International Ltd v Martha Andersen and Sir James Aykroyd* [2016] CSOH 33. See also *Multiplex v Honeywell* [2007] BLR 195 and the review in *Sackville UK Property Select II (GP) No. 1 Ltd v Robertson Taylor Insurance Brokers Ltd* (n. 159 above).

construction cases "draconian" requirements operating as time-bars have been construed strictly; potentially devastating consequences notwithstanding.[163] These express duties to communicate clearly and unequivocally are intended to prevent ambush tactics by enforcing a clear process of communication.[164]

The limits of a duty to communicate depend on the obligations under the contract and in a case where professionals carried no site supervision responsibility the duty to warn was severely curtailed in a "sad case" with terrible consequences for a house-owner.[165]

In a high-profile City case, the parties were syndicated lenders to Yorkshire Food Group which encountered financial difficulties, and its lending was placed by the banks into "work-out". On the evidence, it was considered good practice for co-work-out banks to disclose only information those concerned with the work-out personally considered material, and no further disclosure was required.[166] This brutal dog-eat-dog ethos of the City prevailed – being the relevant market practice.

Citing *AV Pound*, Hugh Collins asserts:

> At most, the courts have been prepared to imply a duty to disclose information where that information is exclusively in the possession of one party and, without it, the other party cannot perform a central obligation ...[167]

As we have seen this goes too far. The Courts take a more flexible approach than Professor Collins claims. To achieve high-level coherence and reflect actual outcome, one could draft a supplement or explanation of the *MvD* principle as it applies when good communication is required to make a contract work:

> Among the somethings which have to be done is the provision of information or the making of enquiries and to that end the part of each party is to provide such information, in reasonable time, as the other party might need to perform their part of the contract and to make such enquiries as are reasonably necessary to ensure that misunderstandings do not arise, or have not arisen, or can be corrected in good time.

2.6 Active cooperation/accepting reasonable solutions

By active cooperation I mean that parties are required to engage constructively inter se, take positive and/or proactive steps, find ways around problems, fill

---

163 See Coulson J's summary of case law in *Severfield (UK) Ltd v Duro Felguera UK Ltd* [2015] EWHC 3352 (TCC) *Van Oord UK Ltd v Allseas UK Ltd* [2015] EWHC 3074 (TCC).
164 For a detailed review see Hudson at 6.031–6.033.
165 *Goldswain v Beltec* [2015] EWHC 556 (TCC).
166 *National Westminster Bank plc v Rabobank Nederland* [2007] EWHC 1056 (Comm).
167 Collins, 'Implied Duty to Give Information' at 561.

gaps, clarify details – all to make the contract work. Lord Blackburn's conception merely requires parties to take steps to effectuate the other's performance but does not envisage the need for concessions or agreement.

Where a music hall artist, Victoria Vesta, and a promoter were in dispute about performance dates, the performer having a right to "transfer" dates, Eady LJ ruled that the parties should act reasonably in making efforts to agree dates.[168] In *Hillas v Arcos* the contract included an option expressed as:

> of entering into a contract ... for the purchase of 100,000 standards for delivery during 1931 ... to stipulate that ... buyers shall obtain the goods on conditions and prices which show to them a reduction of 5 per cent on the fob value of the official price list at any time ruling during 1931.

Construing this clause Lord Wright ruled that: "in contracts for future performance over a period, the parties may not be able nor may they desire to specify many matters of detail, but leave them to be adjusted in the working out of the contract".[169] The question is one of degree and context and dependent on how much of the contract the Court might have to write and whether the wording or the context indicates an "agreement to agree" (no contract ensues) or have left "matters to be adjusted" (the Courts will help them do that).[170] Interestingly, Hugh Collins claims that the result "flies in the face of formal legal rationality" because the contract lacked an object and a price, saying that the House of Lords balanced documentation against expectation.[171] Zoe Ollerensaw, saying that English Law currently "demonstrates a conflicting and ambivalent approach to good faith", describes *Hillas v Arcos* as "recognising a more co-operative approach to contracting".[172] It is hard to determine just where the line is drawn between judges declining to write a contract and determining that there are objective criteria, as in *Hillas v Arcos*, by which they can perfect a deal. Where disagreements arose over crude oil handling fees between an incumbent contractor and a new refinery owner, Rix LJ said: "There is no evidence that the resolution of a reasonable fee would cause any difficulty at all ... these parties .... had managed to agree a handling fee throughout the best part of 20 years ..."[173] In *Hillas v Arcos* delivery dates

---

168 *Terry v Moss's Empires* (1915) 32 TLR 92. See *Wood v Lucy, Lady Duff-Gordon* 118 NE 214 (NY 1917).

169 *Hillas v Arcos* (n. 2 above) at 504. He referred to other cases including *Dominion Coal Co. Ltd v Dominion Iron and Steel Co. Ltd and National Trust Co. Ltd* [1909] AC 293, 78 LJPC 115 in which the obligation, upheld as workable, was to supply to the latter "all the coal that the steel company may require for use in its works as hereinafter described".

170 *Teekay Tankers Ltd v STX Offshore & Shipbuilding Co. Ltd* [2017] EWHC 253 (Comm).

171 Hugh Collins, *Regulating Contracts* (OUP 2005) at 190.

172 Zoe Ollerenshaw, 'Managing Change in Uncertain Times' in Larry A DiMatteo and others (eds), *Commercial Contract Law: Transatlantic Perspectives* (CUP 2013).

173 *Mamidoil-Jetoil Greek Petroleum Co. SA v Okta Crude Oil Refinery AD* [2001] EWCA Civ 406 at [14]. See also *Teekay* (n. 170 above).

and quantities per delivery are plainly left to be agreed. In contrast, in *Teekay* Walker J found that a provision that delivery dates for optional tankers would be "mutually agreed" left an essential term incomplete – the contract therefore being void for uncertainty.[174]

In *iSoft v Misys* the contract provided for the sale of a business on its "fair market value". Carnwath LJ agreed with the trial judge that the Court could not "construct a complete contract from scratch".[175]

In *Jet2.com Ltd v Blackpool Airport Ltd* the parties agreed to "co-operate together and use their best endeavours to promote Jet2.com's low cost services from BA and BAL will use all reasonable endeavours to provide a cost base that will facilitate Jet2.com's low cost pricing". Moore-Bick LJ found the first leg enforceable: "the promotion of Jet2's business did extend to keeping the airport open to accommodate flights outside normal hours". But not the second: "an obligation to ... facilitate some essential element of another person's business seems to me to pose greater problems, because it is much more difficult to identify its content".[176] An obligation to establish a two-aircraft operation at Durham Tees Valley Airportt and to operate the aircraft by flying them commercially was upheld despite no detail of the number of flights required or other detail being expressed.[177] In a distributorship dispute the Court would not imply a term of active cooperation that minimum purchase requirements would be fulfilled as too vague.[178] In another case Rose J found that an arbitrator should be able to decide how a contract should be amended to reflect a "major physical or financial change in circumstances".[179]

There is little doubt that a contractual requirement to undertake "friendly discussions" or negotiate in good faith is enforceable; Lord Ackner's notorious repugnance notwithstanding.[180] Longmore LJ ruled that to declare unenforceable a clause requiring parties to negotiate "legal content", would "defeat the reasonable expectations of honest men" and be a "strong thing".[181] Sir George Leggatt has suggested that refusing to meet to discuss the effects of a price review clause might breach a good faith obligation; I would treat this as a refusal to cooperate. He also suggests that, in negotiation, knowingly to

---

174 *Teekay* n. 170 above.

175 *iSoft Group plc v Misys Holdings Ltd* [2002] All ER (D) 217 (Oct) at [27].

176 *Jet2.com Ltd v Blackpool Airport Ltd* [2012] EWCA Civ 417 [2012] 1 CLC 605 at [31].

177 *Durham Tees Valley Airport Ltd v BMI Baby Ltd* [2010] EWCA Civ 485, [2011] 1 All ER (Comm) 731. Mitchell, *Bridging the Gap,* refers to the result as enforcing, "in an oblique way, an obligation to be co-operative" at 257.

178 *James E McCabe Ltd v Scottish Courage Ltd* (n. 35 above).

179 *Associated British Ports v Tata Steel UK Ltd* [2017] EWHC 694 (Ch); [2017] 2 Lloyd's Rep 11 at [22].

180 *Walford v Miles* [1992] 2 AC 128.

181 *Petromec Inc v Petroleo Brasileiro SA Petrobras* [2005] EWCA Civ 891 at [121]. Colin Reese QC refused to allow parties to "thwart" an obligation to make reasonable endeavours to agree a pain/gain sharing provision in *Alstom Signalling Ltd v Jarvis Facilities Ltd* (n. 65 above) at [61].

mislead must fall foul of a good faith obligation, adding that "it is arguable that the obligation would also include a duty to disclose relevant information, at least on request".[182]

Where a contract required negotiation in good faith and engagement in mediation before arbitrating Allsop J, drawing an analogy with modern civil procedure, construed this to oblige parties to "exercise a degree of co-operation to isolate issues for trial that are genuinely in dispute and to resolve them as speedily and efficiently as possible".[183] Teare J ruled that an obligation to seek to resolve a dispute using "friendly discussions" meant that parties must undertake honest and genuine discussions: "Where a party clearly fails to honour such standards of conduct judges and commercial arbitrators will have no particular difficulty in recognising and identifying such failures."[184] In a case where a landlord failed to consult tenants affected by redevelopment works Alan Steinfeld QC found that the landlord should have taken the tenants' interests into account and agreed a pattern of quiet and noisy times for the works. In addition, despite there being no evidence that the tenant had lost profit, the Court awarded a 20% discount on the rent, indicating that this should have been considered by the landlord.[185] The case shows that a duty to negotiate can bite.

The limits of Court tolerance of negotiating tactics can be found when deals are revoked for economic duress.[186] However, "no single factor is determinative".[187] In one case the defendant refused to make further deliveries unless Carillion agreed to the terms of a settlement agreement. The Court struck the agreement down for duress.[188] This adds some limited weight to Teare J's assertion that the Courts can spot improper conduct.

Leggatt J's decision in *Sheikh Tahnoon Bin Saeed Bin Shakhboot Al Nehayan v Ioannis Kent* appears to mean that, where the contract is relational, it may be

---

182 Sir George Leggatt, 'Negotiation in Good Faith: Adapting to Changing Circumstances in Contracts and English Contract Law' (Jill Poole Memorial Lecture, 2018) at [56]–[60]. See *Sanderson Ltd v Simtom Food Products Ltd* [2019] 442 (TCC) where Halliwell J found a refusal to attend a kick-off meeting breached the duty to cooperate.

183 *United Group Rail Services Ltd v Rail Corporation* NSW [2009] NSWCA 1707 at [70]–[71].

184 *Emirates Trading Agency LLC v Prime Mineral Exports Private Ltd* [2014] EWHC 2104 (Comm) at [53]. See also *Willmott Dixon Housing Ltd v Newlon Housing Trust* [2013] EWHC 798 (TCC); Vivian Ramsey QC ruling that provisions requiring cooperation extended to solicitors managing disputes between the parties and communicating effectively.

185 *Timothy Taylor Ltd v Mayfair House Corporation* [2016] EWHC 1075 (Ch).

186 Nelson Enonchong, *Duress, Undue Influence and Unconscionable Dealing* (2nd edn, Sweet & Maxwell 2012); the elements are illegitimate pressure or a threat; that the innocent party had no practical choice but to enter into the agreement; and that the pressure or threat had been a significant inducement.

187 Ibid. at 79. Lord Mance at 638 in *Pao On v Lau Yiu Long* [1980] AC 614, [1979] 3 All ER 65 (PC).

188 *Atlas Express Ltd v Kafco (Importers and Distributors) Ltd* [1989] QB 833, [1989] 1 All ER 641.

a breach of an implied duty of good faith to make plans to exit the business through negotiations with third parties, without informing one's current partner.[189] This inherently involves forcing a negotiation between the existing parties.

Courts can force parties into deal-making in quasi-contractual situations. In somewhat specialised situations parties may agree that one will buy land intending that they will split it later; the calculation being that they will be worse off if both bid. If the successful bidder then rats Courts will impose a *Pallant v Morgan* equity and order the parties to try to reach a deal, failing which the Court will do so for them.[190] The exact juridical basis of this "equity" is unclear but Bowstead treats it as an agency concept.[191]

Discussing modern forms of contract, recognising that change is "heavily planned for"[192] and that parties must be free to disagree,[193] Zoe Ollerenshaw proposes content for express duties to negotiate in good faith which include that parties:

- commence negotiation
- enter negotiation with an open mind not intending to not agree
- do not ignore the other side's suggestions
- consider suggestions in the spirit of cooperation and mutuality
- disclose required information
- if withdrawing to tell the other party why, allow a response
- not to withdraw if that would be reasonably unacceptable to the other party

In one case, which gives similar guidance, showing that elements of this proposal are practical, the ADR Handbook was referred to by Briggs J, who said that it advised parties faced with ADR requests but who were reluctant to use ADR that "constructive engagement" was the right response. Parties should not ignore an ADR offer, respond promptly, giving clear and full reasons why ADR is not appropriate, raising with the opposing party any shortage of information or evidence, together with consideration of how to overcome the shortage and not closing off ADR.[194] In Australia Einstein J ruled that a commitment to

---

189 *Sheikh Tahnoon Bin Saeed Bin Shakhboot Al Nehayan v Ioannis Kent (AKA John Kent)* (n. 125 above).

190 *Pallant v Morgan* [1953] Ch 43. See also *Banner Homes Plc v Luff Developments Ltd* [2000] Ch 372, CA.

191 Watts and others, *Bowstead and Reynolds*, 6.110. See Tiffany Scott, 'Failed Joint Ventures: The Search for the "Pallant v Morgan equity"'.

192 Zoe Ollerenshaw, 'Managing Change in Uncertain Times' in DiMatteo and others, *Commercial Contract Law*, at 217–218.

193 Victor Goldberg, *Readings in the Economics of Contract Law* (CUP 1989) at 18–19 indicates that economic incentives will take care of matters, whereas sophisticated parties appear to consider solid terms necessary.

194 *PGF II SA v OMFS Co. 1 Ltd* [2013] EWCA Civ 1288 at [30].

ADR meant entering it with an open mind, a willingness to consider options put forward by the mediator or the other party and a willingness to put forward one's own proposals.[195]

In *Yam Seng*, a case concerning a short, eight-paragraph, distribution agreement in which Yam Seng was granted the exclusive rights to distribute fragrances bearing the brand name "Manchester United" in specified territories; Leggatt J said that the distributor "was arguably entitled to expect that it would be kept informed of ITC's best estimates of when products would be available to sell and would be told of any material change in this information without having to ask".[196]

In the context of an IT system contract in which special needs, or detailed requirements, tend to emerge during contract execution, Judge Toulmin QC said:

> It is well understood that the design and installation of a computer system requires the active co-operation of both parties ... There would be aspects of the system which did not immediately fulfil the customer's needs and there would have to be a period of discussion between customer and supplier to see how the problems could be resolved. The duty of co-operation in my view extends to the customer accepting where possible reasonable solutions to problems that have arisen. In the case of unimportant or relatively unimportant items that have been promised and cannot be supplied each party must act reasonably, consistent, of course, with its rights.[197]

In this case a standard IT package called Charisma had been sold to Winther-Brown, a distributor of mouldings and the like to DIY stores. One commentator says that this seems "to be a code of reasonable behaviour ... rather than a statement of unexpressed intentions".[198] In *Eurodynamics* Steyn J observed that "It is of some significance, however, that in the intervening period of more than two months GA made no attempt to render support or assistance in respect of any of the technical problems."[199]

In *Medirest*[200] the relationship between an NHS Trust and its facilities management contractor fell apart over deductions for service failures by the Trust. The Court of Appeal appeared to reverse modern interpretation trends by

---

195 *Aiton v Transfield* (2000) 16 BCL 70.
196 *Yam Seng Pte Ltd v International Trade Corporation Ltd* [2013] EWHC 111 (QB) at [143]. Yam Seng is a Cantonese toast meaning "drink to success".
197 *Anglo Group* (n. 98 above) at [125]–[127]. Approved in *Yam Seng*. Cited by Steyn J in *Micron Computers v Wang (UK) Ltd* (1990) unreported, 9 May.
198 Cameron (n. 104 above) at 264.
199 *Eurodynamics* n. 99 above.
200 *Compass Group UK and Ireland Ltd (t/a Medirest) v Mid Essex Hospital Services NHS Trust* [2012] EWHC 781 (QB).

making a very narrow interpretation of a cooperation clause and inventing new canons of construction. Clause 3.5 of the contract provided that the parties will:

> co-operate with each other in good faith and will take all reasonable action as is necessary for the efficient transmission of information and instructions and to enable the Trust ... to derive the full benefit of the Contract.

The Court of Appeal described this, in an unnecessary discourtesy to the draughtsman, as a "jumble of different statements, set out in an incoherent order",[201] deciding that:

> the obligation to co-operate in good faith is not a general one which quali-fies or reinforces all of the obligations on the parties in all situations where they interact. [it] is specifically focused upon the two purposes stated in the second half of that sentence.[202]

The reasoning appears to be founded on two startling, acontextual, canons of construction.[203] One is that, had the parties intended the clause to apply gener-ally, "they would have stated this in a stand-alone sentence with a full stop at the end".[204] The other is that a general and potentially open-ended obligation to "co-operate" or "act in good faith" should not be taken to cover the "same ground as other, more specific, provisions, lest it cut across those more specific provisions". Catherine Mitchell comments that that the result is that "the good faith obligation is emptied of any substantive content".[205] One could say the same of the cooperation obligation. Cranston J had described the context:

> the duty to cooperate necessarily required the parties to work together con-stantly, at all levels of the relationship, otherwise performance of the con-tract would inevitably be impaired. The duty ... necessarily encompassed the duty to work together to resolve the problems which would almost cer-tainly occur from time to time in a long-term contract of this nature[206]

201 Johan Steyn, 'Contract Law: Fulfilling the Reasonable Expectations of Honest Men' (1997) 113 *LQR* 433 at 439 describes such commentary as "tiresome".
202 *Mid Essex Hospital Services NHS Trust v Compass Group UK and Ireland Ltd (t/a Medirest)* [2013] EWCA Civ 200 at [106].
203 Jan van Dunné, 'On a Clear Day, You Can See the Continent' (2015) 31 *ConstLJ* 3 at 14; context is "lost out of sight" by the Appeal Court.
204 The Trust's submission in *Medirest Court of Appeal* (n. 202 above) at para [103]. See Morgan, *Contract Law Minimalism*, 62, quoting Oliver Williamson that "it is easy to draft a cooperation clause ... showing the danger of prediction" ("especially about the future" – Niels Bohr).
205 Mitchell, *Bridging the Gap*, 133.
206 *Medirest High Court* (n. 200 above) at [27]. A similar duty to *Anglo Group* n. 98 above.

It is a very similar comment to that of Judge Toulmin. A realistic view of cooperation clauses was taken by HHJ Humphrey Lloyd when he said that: "people who have agreed to proceed on the basis of mutual co-operation and trust are hardly likely at the same time to adopt a rigid attitude to contract formation".[207] Morgan J dealt with an express good faith obligation that parties, in all matters, would "act with the utmost good faith towards one another and will act reasonably … at all times" as imposing: "a contractual obligation to observe reasonable commercial standards of fair dealing".[208] This is a good answer to Lewison LJ's inability to understand "in what sense the unilateral decision by the Trust to award SFPs or to assert a right to levy Deductions … is something that requires co-operation at all".[209]

The wording of GC/Works 1, the most common contract standard used for Government works, which provides that parties "shall deal fairly, in good faith and in mutual co-operation with one another", seems to be designed to cut across "specific" provisions.[210] Would it be construed purposively or in a very narrow, technical manner as in the Court of Appeal in *Medirest*? It may be that the Court of Appeal is changing its attitude; Jackson LJ observing, in a "comment", in a case involving an enormous and complex maintenance contract (over 5,000 pages long, with 200 pages of definitions) between Amey and Birmingham City Council:

> Any relational contract of this character is likely to be of massive length, containing many infelicities and oddities. Both parties should adopt a reasonable approach in accordance with what is obviously the long-term purpose of the contract. They should not be latching onto the infelicities and oddities, in order to disrupt the project and maximise their own gain.[211]

The similarity to Toulmin J's comment is obvious but *Anglo Group* is not cited.

To achieve high-level coherence and reflect actual outcome, and hoping for a relaxation of the *Medirest* principles, one could draft a supplement or

---

207 *Birse Construction Ltd v St David Ltd* [1999] BLR 194.
208 *Berkeley Community Villages Ltd v Pullen* [2007] 3 EGLR 101 at 113.
209 *Medirest High Court* (n. 200 above) at 146.
210 For this and many other examples of similar drafting see Richard Cockram, *Manual of Construction Agreements* (Jordan Publishing 2016) at A3; "all three [I Chem E] forms include mutual obligations to co-operate and to deal with each other fairly, openly and in good faith". See Edwards-Stuart J, construing a stand-alone clause, 44.4.1, requiring the parties to "deal fairly, in good faith and in mutual co-operation with one another", applying this only to the rest of clause 44 in *Portsmouth City Council v Ensign Highways Ltd* [2015] EWHC 1969 (TCC) at [91]–[101].
211 *Amey Birmingham Highways Ltd v Birmingham City Council* [2018] EWCA Civ 264 at [93].

explanation of the *MvD* principle as it applies when active cooperation is required to make a contract work:

> Among the somethings which have to be done is constructive engagement, the adoption of a reasonable approach in accordance with what is obviously the purpose of the contract, through working together constantly, at all levels, proposing, discussing and considering reasonable solutions to such problems as inevitably arise, and to that end the part of each party is to work together to agree on schedule or resourcing matters, resolve the problems which would almost certainly occur from time to time, to provide information which allows the other party to make informed judgements, and to accept where possible reasonable solutions to problems that have arisen.

2.7 Control of contractual decision-making

In the course of execution of complex, symbiotic contracts, it usually comes to pass that a decision, varying the obligations of one or both parties under the contract, is made or required to be made by one party under "extremely common" provisions.[212] Many such decisions are made under powers granted to one party to ensure that there is a mechanism in place to facilitate decisions which can be envisaged as a matter of prediction but not with particularity. Richard Hooley suggests that their incorporation makes the contract "unbalanced" and they might be incorporated to "get the deal done".[213] Hugh Collins indicates that discretion might be a price worth paying for a deal and that it helps to manage future uncertainty.[214] Most such provisions appear to be boilerplate or semi-boilerplate. The reason for their inclusion is practical necessity. David Foxton says that powers to vary interest rates in a mortgage "reflects the difficulty in fixing this feature of the contract for all time at the outset".[215] Hudson says that if the employer had no unilateral variation rights this would require reliance "on the willingness of the Contractor to agree [enabling] the Contractor to place unacceptable pricing or other pressures on the Employer".[216] Variation clauses are wholly uncontroversial

---

212 Lady Hale at [18] in *Braganza v BP Shipping Ltd (The "British Unity")* [2015] UKSC 17. "Commonplace particularly in relational contracts" – Paul Finn in 'Fiduciary and Good Faith Obligations under Long Term Contracts' in Kanaga Dharmananda (ed) *Long Term Contracts* (Federation Press 2013) at 149.

213 Richard Hooley, 'Controlling Contractual Discretion' (2013) 72 *CLJ* 65 at 67.

214 Hugh Collins, 'Discretionary Powers in Contracts' in David Campbell and others (eds), *Implicit Dimensions of Contract: Discrete, Relational, and Network Contracts* (Bloomsbury 2003), 219 at 226–231.

215 David Foxton, 'A Good Faith Goodbye? Good Faith Obligations and Contractual Termination Rights' (2017) *LMCLQ* 361 at 364.

216 Hudson at 5.019. See also Sergeant and Wieliczko:-without such clauses the Employer would be in a "weak commercial position" at 5.1.

in modern, symbiotic contracts, particularly in construction, facilities management and outsourcing. They are the norm, capable of abuse by both parties. I doubt that any industry player finds them unacceptable.

One finds such decision-making powers examined by the Courts in multifarious situations (see Appendix A, subchapter 2.7.8). Unless "performance according to the terms of the contract" constitutes cooperation,[217] it can be said that not all decisions described come into the category of decisions which enable or effectuate performance. Some decisions are required to allow a contractor to plan towards a completion date and/or allocate appropriate resources.[218] Enabling/facilitating decisions include:

- Decisions regarding the effects of events affecting progress. In *Sutcliffe v - Thakrah*,[219] Lord Reid described decisions made under the RIBA standard contract:

  whether the contractor should be reimbursed for loss under clause 11 (variation), clause 24 (disturbance) or clause 34 (antiquities), whether he should be allowed extra time (clause 23); or when work ought reasonably to have been completed (clause 22). … whether work is defective.[220]

- Valuation of work carried out; allowing a contractor to submit invoices.[221]
- Decisions relating to quality of work.[222]
- Approval of documents such as Quality Plans, or weld set-up procedures. Network Rail requires Contractors to submit:

  information pertaining to the methods of construction …. which the Contractor proposes to adopt or use and, if requested … such calculations of stresses, strains and deflections …[223]

- Approval of management teams or senior personnel.
- Decisions to vary the contract. The CiOB form allows changes to numbers of personnel (Article 6), additions to or omissions from services or changes to working hours (Article 8).[224]

---

217 Collins, *Law of Contract*, 329.
218 See *Balfour Beatty Civil Engineering Ltd v Docklands Light Railway Ltd* 49 Con LR 1. The generality is described by The Hon Justice Carmel McClure: in 'Long Term Contracts: Principles for Determining Content' in Dharmananda, *Long Term Contracts*, 117.
219 *Sutcliffe v Thackrah* (n. 8 above) at 737 (AC).
220 See also *Neodox Ltd v Swinton and Pendlebury Borough Council* (n. 126 above).
221 See Hudson generally at Chapter 4.
222 *Bluewater Energy Services BV v Mercon Steel Structures BV* [2014] EWHC 2132 (TCC).
223 Network Rail, standard suite of contracts (2016) http://www.networkrail.co.uk/browse%20documents/standardsuiteofcontracts/documents/nr11%20mf1%20(rev%205)%20v3%204(tp).pdf.
224 Chartered Institute of Building, *CIoB's Facilities Management Contract* (John Wiley 2015).

When Courts examine such decisions, there are four common outcomes:

- Courts may decide that no control is necessary.
- A Court may decide that discretion must not be exercised in an arbitrary, capricious or irrational manner.
- Certifiers may be required to take decisions fairly and impartially.
- The interests of the other party must be considered.

In this subchapter I review the general principles associated with decision-making in contracts, then I review the approach of the Courts to so-called binary decisions and decisions involving absolute rights, commercial contracts, construction contracts and instances where the interests of the other party should be taken into account.

I make an argument for clearer advice from the Courts to those who are entrusted with decision-making, setting this out as a process with guidance notes.

2.7.1 *General principles*

The Supreme Court has concluded that Lord Greene's two-limb test from *Associated Provincial Picture Houses Ltd v Wednesbury Corporation*[225] "usually" applies to contractual decision-making; Lady Hale SCJ recapitulating that test:

> The first limb focusses on the decision-making process – whether the right matters have been taken into account … The second focusses upon its outcome – whether even though the right things have been taken into account, the result is so outrageous that no reasonable decision-maker could have reached it.[226]

Neither limb, the first sometimes called the relevancy review and the second the rationality review,[227] creates onerous controls[228] and the circumstances in which a Court will interfere are "extremely limited".[229] Richard Hooley says that the

---

225 *Associated Provincial Picture Houses Ltd v Wednesbury Corporation* [1948] 1 KB 223, [1947] 2 All ER 680.
226 *Braganza* (n. 212 above) at [24].
227 See e.g. Ernest Lim and Cora Chan, 'Problems with Wednesbury Unreasonableness in Contract Law: Lessons from Public Law' (2019) 135 *LQR* at 93.
228 Sergeant and Wieliczko say it is a "relatively low standard" at 315. Ewan McKendrick in 'Good Faith in the Performance of a Contract in English Law' in Larry DiMatteo and Martin Hogg (eds), *Comparative Contract Law: British and American Perspectives* (OUP 2016) at 200 describes it as "not an onerous standard". Jonathan Morgan, in 'Resisting Judicial Review of Discretionary Contractual Powers' (2015) *LMCLQ* 484 describes them as "ill-defined standards of review" at 486.
229 Brooke J at [62] in *Ludgate Insurance Co. Ltd v Citibank NA* [1998] EWCA Civ 66, [1998] Lloyds Reports IR 221.

limitations are "at the lower end of the [good faith] scale".[230] Michael Bridge says that the "standard is not particularly demanding".[231] Showing how limited the controls are, Dyson LJ, in *Nash v Paragon Finance plc* (*Nash*), reached for a breathtakingly unlikely scenario: "where the lender decided to raise the rate of interest because its manager did not like the colour of the borrower's hair".[232] Arden LJ was more realistic in *Lymington Marina Ltd v Macnamara* (*Lymington*): "it would not be enough that the proposed sub-licensee, say, has in the past lived outside the United Kingdom".[233] Explaining the policy of the Courts on the exercise of such powers Lady Hale said, in a passage "redolent" of implication-in-law:[234]

> the party who is charged with making decisions which affect the rights of both parties to the contract has a clear conflict of interest. ... The courts have therefore sought to ensure that such contractual powers are not abused. They have done so by implying a term as to the manner in which such powers may be exercised, a term which may vary according to the terms of the contract and the context in which the decision-making power is given.[235]

The contention that the decision-maker has a clear conflict of interest goes much too far. The owner of a marina, asked to approve a sub-licencee, has no conflict of interest, nor does a client who needs extra work to be performed. This is not new law; despite Dr Morgan's claim that its vitality springs from "youthful exuberance".[236] In 1837 a Court ruled against a lessor who "capriciously" withheld approval of repairs to be performed to his approval.[237] In 1861 Wightman J rejected an insurance company's pleading that a term permitting the request of such evidence as they "think necessary" allowed capricious requests, saying that this contravened "the proper and reasonable construction to be given to this clause".[238]

---

230 Hooley, 'Controlling Contractual Discretion', Conclusion.

231 Michael Bridge, 'The Exercise of Contractual Discretion' (2019) 135 *QR* 227 at 247.

232 *Nash v Paragon Finance Plc* [2001] EWCA Civ 1466 at [31].

233 *Lymington Marina Ltd v Macnamara* [2007] All ER (D) 38 (Mar) at [28].

234 Wayne Courtney, 'Reasonableness in Contractual Decision-Making' (2015) 131 *LQR* 552 at 555.

235 *Braganza* (n. 212 above) at [18]. Rix LJ said in *Socimer International Bank Ltd (in liquidation) v Standard Bank London Ltd* [2008] EWCA Civ 116 at [61] that "the concern is that the power should not be abused".

236 Jonathan Morgan, 'Resisting Judicial Review of Discretionary Contractual Powers' (2015) *LMCLQ* 484 at 484.

237 *Dallman v King* (1837) 132 ER 729. PS Atiyah, *The Rise and Fall of Freedom of Contract* (Clarendon Press 1979) at 418 considers that the case was "almost distinguished away" in *Stadhard v Lee* (1863) 122 All ER 138 (Queen's Bench) but this case appears to revolve around a clear express term which in context reflected a particularly stringent main contract – see at 141.

238 *Braunstein v The Accidental Death Insurance Co.* (1861) 121 ER 904 at 909.

2.7.2 *Decisions to exercise absolute contractual rights*

In this subchapter, I explore how the Courts deal with so-called binary decisions or decisions to exercise absolute contractual rights. The treatment of binary decisions, making a choice between two positions, is variable and illogical.[239]

In a contract for the provision of catering and ancillary services, an NHS Trust was empowered to award "service failure points" and adjust payments accordingly. The Court of Appeal declined to apply any limitation to the making of such adjustments, Jackson LJ saying that this "discretion"

> is very different from the discretion which existed in the authorities discussed above ... [it] ... simply permits the Trust to decide whether or not to exercise an absolute contractual right. There is no justification for implying ... a term that the Trust will not act in an arbitrary, irrational or capricious manner. If the Trust awards more than the correct number of service failure points ... that is a breach of the express provisions ...[240]

This logic was followed in a case involving a yes/no decision to subordinate loan notes; potentially making them worth less to their holders.[241] The approach has become known as "binary" and has been criticised on that basis.[242] Under another loan agreement a "shall we make further advances; yes or no?" decision was to be made at the lender's "sole discretion", Aikens J ruling that this decision must be exercised in good faith and not irrationally, capriciously or arbitrarily.[243] His ruling, arrived at by construction, was that the decision not to make further advances was legitimate because "[Centurion] was not satisfied with the ATE insurance that was being offered".[244]

Mary Arden provides an overview of *Lymington*,[245] an "unusual"[246] case. The holder of a 98-year license for a marina berth, inherited from his father, Commodore MacNamara, wished to sub-license to his brothers. Permission to sub-license was in the owner's (LML) "absolute discretion"; another yes/no decision. She has "some difficulty" with the decision in *Medirest*.[247] In *Lymington* she noted LML's "fears":

---

239 Bridge, 'Exercise', 229, says the line is difficult to draw. Chitty says that this is not "straightforward" – at 1.061.

240 *Medirest High Court* (n. 200 above) at [91]–[92].

241 *Myers and another v Kestrel Acquisitions Ltd and others* [2015] All ER (D) 11 (Apr). See also *Greenclose Ltd v National Westminster Bank* [2014] EWHC 1156 (Ch).

242 Emmanuel Sheppard, 'Good Faith in the Aftermath of Yam Seng' (2015) 7 *JIBFL* 407 says "it is not clear how coherent or useful this dichotomy ... is" at 409.

243 *McKay v Centurion Credit Resources* [2012] EWCA Civ 1941 at [17]. See *CTN Cash and Carry Ltd v Gallaher Ltd* [1994] 4 All ER 714 – a similar discretion being held to be absolute.

244 *McKay v Centurion Credit Resources* (n. 243 above) at [21].

245 *Lymington* n. 233 above.

246 Mary Arden, 'Coming to Terms with Good Faith' (2013) 30 *JCL* 199 at 205–206.

247 *Medirest Court of Appeal* n. 202 above.

that sub-licensees would be casual users of berths in the marina ... much less likely to make use of the repair facilities than long-term users. ... a concern that the sub-licensees may not fit into the ethos of the marina, [which] would discourage annual licence holders, who are attracted by the social atmosphere of the marina.[248]

The second of LML's concerns may be a tolerably polite expression of a "No riff-raff" proviso[249] but it provides a fair encapsulation of the purpose of the approval requirement. Arden LJ said that the grounds of refusal must "arise out of his proposed use of the marina. ... if [he] were known to have avoided payment of mooring fees in other marinas, this ... might ... afford a good ground for refusing approval".[250] It seems entirely legitimate that LML would want a busy marina, both for social and business reasons. Had the parties wished to impose limits on LML's absolute discretion, there are, however, established means of doing so.[251] In *International Drilling Fluids Ltd v Louisville Investments (Uxbridge) Ltd* Balcombe LJ provided a solid résumé of the law when a lease expressly provides that consent to assignment will not be "unreasonably withheld". The first proposition that he "deduces" from the extensive authorities is: "The purpose .... is to protect the lessor from having his premises used or occupied in an undesirable way, or by an undesirable tenant or assignee."[252]

At first instance, in *Medirest*, Cranston J reviewed the deduction provision: "the purpose of the Trust's power ... was to curb performance failure not ... to generate discounts".[253] In other words, this is a power to manage the contract, providing a remedy in circumstances where damage would be almost impossible to prove and, correlatively, an incentive for Medirest to perform. It would be difficult, even impossible, to recover over £43,000 in damages for the bare fact of finding a spoon wedging open a fire door.

Where service point deduction was on a sliding scale Mr Justice Edward-Stuart ruled that PCC, the Employer, must act on proper grounds and not in an arbitrary, irrational or capricious manner.[254] It is hard to see the difference

---

248 *Lymington* (n. 233 above) at [7].
249 From Basil's advertisement for the Gourmet Night in *Fawlty Towers.*
250 *Lymington* (n. 233 above) at [28].
251 As Jonathan Morgan, 'Against Judicial Review of Discretionary Contractual Powers' (2008) *LMCLQ* 230 at 239 argues – "It should be for the parties to state so expressly if such judicial control is desired."
252 *International Drilling Fluids Ltd v Louisville Investments (Uxbridge) Ltd* [1986] 1 Ch 513. See *Cudmore v Petro-Canada Inc.* 1986 Carswell BC 93 – a landlord must not "refuse his consent arbitrarily or unreasonably" and *Rotrust Nominees Ltd v Hautford Ltd* [2018] EWCA Civ 765. See *Rickman and another v Brudenell-Bruce* [2005] EWHC 3400 (Ch) – such a term would be in line with the "reasonable expectations" of the parties. See *Addison v Brown [1954] 1 W.L.R. 779* – a term that approval would not be withheld unreasonably was implied into a father's contract to pay those of his son's school bills he approved.
253 *Medirest High Court* (n. 200 above) at [43].
254 *Ensign* (n. 210 above) at [112].

between a decision to deduct or not deduct points and a decision to deduct three points or four.[255]

Medirest has become somewhat notorious,[256] due to the "absurd" nature of the "cavalier" calculations which included:

- Box of out of date ketchup sachets found in cupboard – £46,320;
- Failure to sign off a cleaning schedule – £71,055;
- No temperature on refrigeration display – £ 94,830;
- Butter sachets with no use-by date – £94,830.

For each deduction, a decision must have been made whether Medirest was in breach. The next decision is whether the breach was Minor, Medium or Major; attracting deductions of £5, £15 or £30 respectively. Having decided that the box of ketchup sachets in a fridge was a Major failure, a further decision was made that each individual sachet was a breach, and then a decision was made that each day that the box was in the fridge was an independent breach attracting a separate deduction. In another example the contract required "areas" to be cleaned and Mid-Essex contended/decided that each dirty cooker, toaster or so on was an "area". Cranston J said that this was "artificial", and an "area" would typically be a kitchen.[257]

These decisions precede and inform the exercise of a binary right. Lewison LJ recognised this, referring to the "control mechanism" under which the Trust calculated deductions.[258] No limit on the misuse of the control mechanism was imported. David Foxton observes: "the suggestion that the existence of a control mechanism renders a contractual right 'absolute', such that the more extensive the control mechanism the more absolute the right, is a curious one".[259] The Court of Appeal simply failed to consider examining the failure of the control mechanism, the underlying rationale for the deductions, despite Cranston J's finding of absurdity.[260] Curiously, Jackson LJ asserted that the Trust "rightly demands high standards from all those with whom it contracts", in the face of Cranston J's findings that the Trust's behaviour had not exactly been of a high standard.[261] Michael Bridge notes that this seems to allow the state to demand high standards from Contractors while misusing its own powers; appearing "to turn upside down the notion that the state should be held to a higher standard of conduct".[262] It is not clear

---

255 See Sheppard (n. 244 above) at 409 citing other binary cases.
256 Dunné (n. 203 above) describes it as a "running gag" at 11.
257 *Medirest High Court* (n. 200 above) at [118].
258 *Medirest Court of Appeal* (n. 202 above) at [139].
259 Foxton, 'A Good Faith Goodbye?', 373.
260 *Medirest High Court* n. 200 above.
261 *Medirest Court of Appeal* (n. 202 above) at [91]. Cranston J ruled that the Trust "as a public body must be devoted to high standards of behaviour" *Medirest High Court* (n. 200 above) at [26].
262 Bridge, 'Exercise', 244.

whether the Supreme Court in *Braganza* intended that binary decisions should be subject to control, although *Socimer* was specifically approved.[263]

Courts will not imply limitations into termination clauses, even termination at will clauses,[264] although they may consider the reasonable expectations of parties in assessment of compensation in the latter case, which might come to the same thing.[265] The Court of Appeal has said that the "right to terminate was no more an act of discretion … than the right to accept a repudiation".[266] Briggs J held that the right "was plainly to be exercised in such a way as the Non-defaulting party considered best served its own interests".[267] The Privy Council has explained the rationale in employment contracts; saying that its very nature "is that its exercise does not have to be justified".[268] Aikenhead J described a mutual right to terminate as "an unqualified right available to either party".[269]

Richard Hooley argues that differentiating between termination decisions and others risks "doctrinal incoherence".[270] He argues, rightly, that in making a choice to terminate a party exercises "judgement in making a choice" which is, clearly, "an exercise of discretion".[271] Michael Bridge's answers that where damages are an adequate remedy a judicial control on the discretion may not be necessary, but this is not a full response because it is the breach of the contractual control that should create liability in some cases.[272] The reasoning may be satisfactory where there is fault, a defined event or mutuality.[273] In deciding whether to renew or extend an existing contract a party will not be subjected to controls, because the parties are not engaged in the endeavour but "considering whether that joint endeavour should continue".[274]

Arguing that termination is fundamentally different, involving a "choice" as opposed to a judgement,[275] David Foxton says, making the dubious claim that it can be "priced in":

---

263 *Braganza* (n. 212 above) at [22] and [102]. Neil Andrews, *Contract Rules* (1st edn, Intersentia 2016) says, at Rule 104, that *Medirest* "goes against the grain".

264 *TSG Building Services PLC v South Anglia Housing Ltd* [2013] 1151 (TCC) the contract provided that they "shall work together and individually in the spirit of trust, fairness and mutual co-operation". See also *Petroleo Brasileiro SA v Ene Kos 1 Ltd* [2012] UKSC 17 and *Monk v Largo Foods Ltd* [2016] EWHC 1837 (Comm). See Foxton, 'A Good Faith Goodbye?', 382–384.

265 *Willmott Dixon Partnership Ltd v London Borough of Hammersmith and Fulham* [2014] EWHC 3191 (TCC).

266 *Lomas v JFB Firth Rixson Inc* [2012] EWCA Civ 419 at [36] – the argument was "hopeless". See *Monde Petroleum SA v Westernzagros Ltd* [2016] EWHC 1472 (Comm).

267 *Lomas v JFB Firth Rixson Inc.* (n. 266 above) at [93].

268 *Reda v Flag Ltd* [2002] UKPC 38 at [42].

269 *TSG Building Services PLC v South Anglia Housing Ltd* (n. 264 above) at [152].

270 Hooley, 'Controlling Contractual Discretion', 83 and 89.

271 Ibid. at 86.

272 Bridge, 'Exercise', 231–232.

273 As in *TSG Building Services PLC v South Anglia Housing Ltd* (n. 264 above).

274 *Monk v Largo Foods Ltd*. See *Ilkerler* n. 124 above. The Canadian Courts impose good faith based limits on these powers: *Data & Scientific Inc. v Oracle Corp* 2015 ONSC 4178.

275 Foxton, 'A Good Faith Goodbye?', 384.

the very purpose of a termination clause ... is fundamentally different from discretions which arise in the course of ... contractual performance. Termination clauses fall to be exercised in a context in which considerations of self-interest have displaced the implementation of a joint endeavour ...[276]

Interestingly, Fraser J held in the Post Office litigation that, as an incident of the contract being relational, the Post Office could not "terminate [or suspend] Claimants' contracts ... arbitrarily, irrationally or capriciously".[277] It is possible to provide express limitations on rights to terminate. Under the MF/1 form, termination (clause 49.3) is only possible where under-performance continues "despite previous warnings" and in my own standards I incorporated easy to follow words:

> A party proposing to terminate this Contract shall first give the other party written details of any alleged breach and a reasonable time to cure such breach.

David Foxton's reasoning appears correct. There is a difference in class between clauses regulating a relationship and clauses allowing a party to end a relationship. The primary consideration for any decision-maker must be to consider the purpose behind the power that they are about to use. In other words, this is not a doctrinal issue; it is a matter best examined by reference to the presumed intention of the parties. In termination matters the (rebuttable) presumption should be the same as it is in matters of formation; that the party terminating has the absolute right whether to form a contract or to decide to unform it. In matters of powers to make decisions which regulate in-contract behaviour the (rebuttable) presumption should be that there are context-based limitations on the use of such powers.

As a general principle a contractor must be permitted to carry out the whole of the work. Variation clauses, which allow omissions, cannot be used to transfer work to a lower priced contractor, which will be a repudiatory breach[278] unless there are clear words in the provision which allow "redistribution"[279] of the work by omission.[280] HHJ Humphrey Lloyd said, construing one provision "carefully", that the purpose of the provision was to allow the omission of work "no longer required".[281] Why then should a termination for convenience clause not, at the very least, be subject to a control that it should not be used to

---

276 Ibid. at 383.

277 *The Post Office Group Litigation* [2019] EWHC 606 (QB) at [746].

278 Sergeant and Wieliczko at 5.144.

279 Hudson at 3.151. See *Carr v J. A. Berriman Proprietary Ltd* [1953] 89 CLR 327; *Commissioner for Main Roads v Reed and Stuart Proprietary Limited* (1974) 12 Build LR 55.

280 *Abbey Developments v PP Brickwork Ltd* [2003] EWHC 1987 (TCC) "carefully" at [46].

281 Ibid. at [69]. See Jackson J approving this in *Trustees of The Stratfield Saye Estate v AHL Construction Ltd* [2004] EWHC 3286 (TCC), where an omission provision was used to try to escape from a bad bargain.

transfer the work to a lower priced contractor?[282] Using variation terms to reduce volume requirements may breach EU Commercial Agency Law; possibly based on a breach of the good faith duty in EU Law.[283]

Other absolute decisions may include the right to issue a valid variation under an express power, if the variation is "for a purpose for which the power to vary was intended".[284] Another is in Conclusive Evidence Clauses where a lender may certify that certain monies are due and insist on payment of those monies on certification, overpayments being recoverable.[285]

2.7.3 *Commercial contracts*

In *Nash* Dyson LJ implied a term to "give effect to the reasonable expectation of the parties" that rates of interest would not be set dishonestly, for an improper purpose, capriciously or arbitrarily:

> If asked at the time … whether it accepted that the discretion … could be exercised dishonestly, for an improper purpose, capriciously or arbitrarily, I have no doubt that the claimant would have said "of course not".[286]

In *Socimer* Rix J provided detail on limb two saying that decision-making powers were limited, by "necessary implication" (which sounds like construction): "by concepts of honesty, good faith, and genuineness, and … the absence of arbitrariness, capriciousness, perversity and irrationality".[287] In *Gan Insurance v Tai Ping Insurance,* the scope of an inelegantly expressed power to approve settlements was disputed – "No settlement and/or compromise shall be made and liability admitted without the prior approval of Reinsurers".[288] In the Court of Appeal Mance LJ, observing that the purpose of the sub-clause was to protect the reinsurer which was "directly exposed to loss",[289] held that the limit was: "along the lines that the reinsurer will not withhold approval arbitrarily, or …. will not do so in circumstances so extreme that no reasonable company in

---

282 See Anthony Gray, 'Termination for Convenience Clauses and Good Faith' (2012) 7 *J Int Commer Law and Technol* 260 at 89 such a manoeuvre involves breaching the duty of good faith. In the US see *Sigal Constr Corp v General Services Admn* (13 May 2010) CBCA 508.

283 The Commercial Agents (Council Directive) Regulations, 1993. See Andrea Tosato, 'Commercial Agency and the Duty to Act in Good Faith' (2016) 36 *OJLS*.

284 *Abbey Developments v PP Brickwork Ltd* (n. 280 above) at [50]. See also *Blue Circle Industries plc v Holland Dredging Company (UK) Ltd* [1987] 37 BLR 40.

285 Sandra Booysen, '"Pay Now – Argue Later": Conclusive Evidence Clauses in Commercial Loan Contracts' (2014) *JBL* 31.

286 *Nash v Paragon* (n. 232 above) at [36].

287 *Socimer* (n. 235 above) at [66]. Bridge, 'Exercise', 277, describes this as "the baseline position".

288 *Gan Insurance v Tai Ping Insurance* [2001] EWCA Civ 1047 [2001] 2 All ER (Com) 299.

289 Ibid. at [64].

its position could possibly withhold approval".[290] Other terms which have been used to limit decision-making include a requirement of "genuineness",[291] or that it should not be "so outrageous in its defiance of reason".[292]

2.7.4 Construction contracts

In construction and engineering settings manifold powers are usually delegated to an independent professional acting on behalf of the client as an agent.[293] These powers allow clients to manage the contract, sometimes in circumstances where, without such provisions, contractors can walk away, such as powers to award an extension of time following acts of prevention.

Such decisions are subject to re-examination by judges or arbitrators.[294] The role of certifiers or approvers is to act in a fair and impartial manner.[295] In a leading case, *Sutcliffe v Thackrah*, Lord Reid said that the contract is made:

> on the understanding that … the architect will act in a fair and unbiased manner and it must therefore be implicit in the owner's contract with the architect that he shall … reach such decisions fairly, holding the balance between his client and the contractor.[296]

In *Balfour Beatty Civil Engineering Ltd v Docklands Light Railway Ltd,* where the certifier was an employee, Sir Thomas Bingham MR agreed with Vivian Ramsey QC that the employer must: "act fairly and reasonably, even where no such obligation was expressed in the contract".[297] Jackson J ruled that an employee might only be appointed as a certifier if expressly permitted by the contract, as the purpose of appointing a certifier was to provide protection to the contractor against under-certification.[298]

---

290 Ibid. at [73] and [76].

291 *Bluewater Energy Services BV v Mercon Steel Structures BV* (n. 222 above).

292 *Ludgate Insurance Company Ltd v Citibank NA* (n. 229 above) at [35].

293 Hudson at 2.076 "a Certifier [decides] matters such as value, quality of work or extension of time as part of an administrative function … the Certifier is … acting as agent".

294 *Modern Engineering v Gilbert-Ash Northern* [1974] AC 689.

295 See generally Hudson, chapter 4.

296 *Sutcliffe v Thackrah* (n. 8 above), at 737. Lord Morris – the architect must be "fair and honest", "he is not employed … to be unfair" at 740–741. Lord Salmon – the architect "must act fairly and impartially" at 759.

297 *Balfour Beatty Civil Engineering Ltd v Docklands Light Railway Ltd* (n. 220 above) at 10–11. At 10.85 Sergeant and Wieliczko note that this does not mean that the level of valuations must be reasonable. Ramsey J held in *Bluewater Energy Services BV v Mercon Steel Structures BV* (n. 222 above) that a clause requiring that Mercon "continuously proceed with action satisfactory to BLUEWATER to remedy such default" is "not … construed by reference to an objective standard. … there is a limitation on … to concepts of honesty, good faith, and genuineness, and the need for the absence of arbitrariness, capriciousness, perversity and irrationality".

298 *Scheldebouw v St. James Homes (Grosvenor Dock) Ltd* [2006] BLR 113.

Commenting that valuation is not an exact exercise Hobhouse J said in *Secretary of State for Transport v Birse-Farr Joint Venture* that the its purpose is to provide a fair progress payment system.[299] This is also not new law. In 1901 Sir AL Smith MR, commenting that final payment is "not a mere matter of arithmetic", said that the architect: "owed a duty to the builder ... to hold the scales fairly and to decide impartially ... the amount which the builder was entitled".[300] Mr Recorder Toulson QC referred to the position of the architect as "quasi-arbitral", ruling that when taking termination decisions the architect should act fairly; noting that the Courts are used to applying such a standard.[301] Even in a notoriously difficult environment, such as construction contracting,[302] neither Courts nor contracting parties appear to have difficulty with such standards.

2.7.5 Taking the interests of the other party into account

There are rarer cases where it has been held that the exercise of discretion must be balanced with the interests of the other party. This is more usual in employment contracts but in *The Product Star* Leggatt J ruled that an owner's discretion to allow or disallow a vessel to proceed to a particular port had to be used "honestly and fairly in the interests of all the parties".[303] In *IBM UK Holdings Ltd v Dalgleish* Warren J held, assessing an employer's discretion, that the reasonable expectations of employees are of central importance.[304] Acting contrary to those expectations, in the absence of a "compelling business justification", is a strong indication that an employer has breached the Imperial duty.[305]

Where a bank was obliged to act in a commercially reasonable manner the Court found the bank might still elevate its own interests over those of the other party.[306]

---

299 *Secretary of State for Transport v Birse-Farr Joint Venture* [1993] 62 BLR 36 at 53.

300 *Chambers v Goldthorpe* [1901] 1 KB 624 at 973. See also *Sutcliffe v Thackrah* (n. 8 above). See Hudson and Wallace, Hudson's 11th edn (n. 72 above) at 6.022–6.035 and Sergeant and Wieliczko at 10.88 – Wednesbury principles should be applied by certifiers together with Sutcliffe duties.

301 *John Barker Construction Ltd v London Portman Hotel Ltd* 83 Build LR 35 at 45E.

302 Stella Rimington, former Director General of MI5, in her autobiography, *Open Secret* (2002): "the Thames House Refurbishment was fraught with difficulties. It was clear that dealing with the building industry was just as tricky as dealing with the KGB."

303 *Abu Dhabi National Tanker Co. v Product Star Shipping Ltd, The Product Star (No. 2)* [1993] 1 Lloyd's Rep 397, (1992) *Times*, 29 December. See also *Reardon Smith Line Ltd v Ministry of Agriculture, Fisheries and Food* [1962] 1 QB 42 – Wilmer J ruled that nomination of a port was unconstrained save for the nomination of an "impossible port" at 110.

304 *IBM UK Holdings Ltd v Dalgleish* [2014] EWHC 980. See also *White v Reflecting Road Studs Ltd* [1991] IRLR 331, [1991] ICR 733.

305 *Imperial Group Pension Trust Ltd v Imperial Tobacco Ltd* [1991] 1 WLR 589 – at 597: "an employer would not, ... exercise a power vested in it in a manner calculated or likely to destroy or seriously damage the relationship of trust and confidence".

306 *Barclays Bank Plc v Unicredit Bank AG* [2014] EWCA civ 302.

2.7.6 How to make a decision

The right starting point is a consideration of generic decision-making processes. If a decision-maker wishes to raise interest rates, to refuse to approve an insurance settlement, to deduct monies for performance failure or to terminate, the first activity of the decision-maker must surely be to consider the power available.

Lady Hale emphasises in *Braganza* that consistency with "contractual purpose" is essential.[307] Decision-makers must, therefore, give serious consideration to the underlying purpose of the power, which one might think of in terms of the expectations of the parties;[308] parties plural.[309] Perhaps the clearest exposition of this was by Balcombe LJ explaining that the reason for the control in that case was to "protect the lessor from having his premises used or occupied in an undesirable way". Explained in simple English, any decision-maker can proceed with confidence.

The purpose of the clause may be the protection of the commercial interests of the decision-maker. Mance LJ observed, in *Gan*, that the purpose of the power was the protection of the reinsurer's interests because they were "directly exposed to loss" and Gan could plainly ensure their exposure should not be increased.[310] In a case arising out of the implosion of Lehman Brothers, Blair J said that the decision-maker was entitled to have regard to its commercial interests.[311] Longmore LJ found that a power conferred was for the protection of Barclays Bank's interest, noting that the term "commercially reasonable manner" "must be intended to be a control exercise of some kind", went on to say that Barclays could not, therefore, demand "a price which is way above what he can reasonably anticipate would have been a reasonable return".[312]

Ineluctably, a serious, professional, rational consideration of the purpose of the power will have the effect that only relevant matters and genuine considerations are taken into account.

---

307 *Braganza* (n. 212 above) at [30].
308 As in *Nash v Paragon* n. 232 above.
309 Collins, *Law of Contract* – A "limitation … inferred to protect the reasonable expectation of the subject" at 340. See Males LJ's reference to "justified expectations" in *Equitas Insurance Ltd v Municipal Mutual Insurance Ltd* [2019] All ER (D) 112 (Apr) saying at [143] – "The doctrine of good faith in this context requires a contractual power to be exercised in a way which is consistent with the justified expectations of the parties arising from their agreement, *construed* [my emphasis] in its relevant context".
310 *Gan Insurance v Tai Ping Insurance* (n. 288 above) at 64. See *Equitas Insurance Ltd v Municipal Mutual Insurance Ltd* (n. 309 above) at [143] and [152]–[155]. Males LJ reviewed indemnities allowing the lead insurer to decide on future contribution levels from reinsurers from long-term, asbestos liabilities, concluding that they were aimed at annual risk allocation.
311 *Lehman Brothers International (Europe) (In Administration) v Exxonmobil Financial Services BV* [2016] EWHC 2699 (Comm) at [331].
312 *Barclays Bank Plc v Unicredit Bank AG* (n. 306 above) at [18]–[19].

For verification, decision-makers should analyse the decision they propose to make, asking themselves whether it is aligned with the purpose of the power, rational or, in some contexts, fair. Where a party has power to levy an administrative charge, simply operating a "standard" scale of charges may not be a proper exercise of discretion. One must consider in each case what level of charge is appropriate.[313] Rix LJ, reviewing a complex financial transaction, concluding that its structure was designed to keep the lender free from risk, meant that the lender was "entitled to have an entirely proper regard for any danger to itself".[314]

In the US franchisors are obliged to "exercise … discretion reasonably and with proper motive … [consistent] with the reasonable expectations of the parties".[315] There may be some difficulty in identifying the "reasonable expectations" of the parties but these should become tolerably clear once the purpose has been identified.

To ask one's typical commercial actor to avoid being capricious feels ridiculous – I can imagine that the reaction of at least one former colleague would be a Frankie Howerdism: "ooh Missus". In fair comment Dr Morgan says that "it is quite impossible to define a 'capricious' or 'thoroughly unreasonable' decision in the abstract".[316] In *Esso v Addison* in which Esso held the right to adjust the amounts payable/receivable by its licensees, Tuckey LJ said, referring to the "construction" of the contract at first instance and following that on appeal:

> The question is whether the adjustments … were based on a genuine examination by Esso of the commercial factors affecting its retailing business in general and a rational response to the conclusions it reached.[317]

Next, decision-makers should consider what evidence is required. In *Braganza* the Supreme Court concluded that BP failed to give sufficient weight to the possibility of accidental death; and did not collect "cogent" evidence of suicide.[318] For example, Tuckey LJ approvingly recounts the evidence, "the product of a thorough

---

313 *BHL v Leumi ABL Ltd* [2017] All ER (D) 04 (Aug) a collector of receivables with discretion to charge up to 15% always charged 15%, the Court replacing this with its own calculation.

314 *WestLB AG v Nomura Bank International Plc* [2012] EWCA Civ 495 at [60].

315 *Interim Health Care of N. Illinois, Inc. v Interim Health Care, Inc.*, 225 F3d 876, 884 (7th Cir 2000).

316 Morgan, 'Against Judicial Review', 236.

317 *Esso v Addison* [2004] EWCA Civ 1470 at [36] quoting the trial Judge, Moore-Bick J. See also See Bridge LJ in *Shell UK Ltd v Lostock Garage Ltd* [1977] 1 All ER 481, [1976] 1 WLR 1187 – at 495 (All ER) "I … take as the test of the degree of discrimination prohibited … whether it is such as to render Lostock's commercial operation of their petrol sales business impracticable."

318 *Braganza* (n. 212 above): "Mr Sullivan's task was … [to] consider whether he was in a position to make a positive finding that Mr Braganza had committed suicide. He should have asked himself whether the evidence was sufficiently cogent to overcome the inherent

review" of Esso's retail operations, to support Moore-Bick J's conclusion that Esso had behaved properly.[319] In one case Board approval was required for a valuable share option and, as the Board had dealt with the matter "very casually" and with "no clear evidence", Judge Waksman QC ordered specific performance of the option agreement.[320]

Where the purpose of the power is the protection of one's own commercial interests a more lenient view may be taken, allowing a party to "have regard to such pricing sources and methods ... as it considers appropriate".[321]

In *Medirest* the Trust should have realised that the purpose of the power to make deductions was to create incentives to perform. Cranston J said that a reasonable person would consider the Trust to be required to "act consistently with that purpose of the mechanism".[322] Having performed a proper analysis, which should not have taken long, it should have considered whether the deductions being considered were made after a genuine examination, legitimate, and directed to encouraging performance. If not, then organising a long serious contract review to determine what a realistic approach to service point deduction might be would have been a sensible next step.

This guidance is easy to follow and collapses relevance and rationality reviews into a relatively easy to understand, linear process. It will be hard to take a capricious decision, having considered the purpose of the power available, taken only relevant matters into account, and collected and considered proper evidence.[323] Such guidance would allow decision-makers to reach decisions using, as Lord Hodge suggests: "literal and purposive elements [to achieve] results which ... are in accordance with the reasonable expectations of honest business people".[324]

2.7.7 Conclusion

Power is normally conferred on the party best placed to make decisions. Regarding interest rates a bank is clearly the better party to hold the power; a lessor better placed to determine whether work undertaken to her property is satisfactory. This intrinsically indicates that power is not conferred on an absolute basis but to ensure that a mechanism exists to manage affairs in a changing world.

---

improbability ...." – Lady Hale at [39]. And at [49] Lord Hodge says that he is struck by the "paucity and the insubstantial nature of the evidence".

319 *Esso v Addison* n. 317 above.

320 *Watson v Watchfinder.co.uk Ltd* [2017] All ER (D) 101 (Jun) at [116]–[120].

321 *Lehman Brothers International (Europe) (In Administration) v Exxonmobil Financial Services BV* (n. 311 above) at [331].

322 *Medirest High Court* (n. 200 above) at [43].

323 See e.g. Charles Wynn-Evans, 'Contractual Powers: How to Reach a Reasonable Opinion' (2015) EmpLJ – Employers' decisions will be all the less susceptible to challenge the more carefully they are structured by reference to the issues and the relevant evidence.

324 In 'Can Judges Use Business Common Sense in Interpreting Contracts?' in DiMatteo and Hogg, *Comparative Contract Law*, at 279.

Decision-making powers are sometimes circumscribed by analysing the purpose, sometimes by reference to fairness and impartiality, occasionally by requiring the decision-maker to take the interests of the other into account. Sometimes the limitation is implied-in-fact, sometimes construed ("necessary implication" in *Socimer*[325]), sometimes (perhaps post-*Braganza*, the norm) by implication-in-law.[326] As Sir George Leggatt says, Lord Sumption's language in *Braganza* – "it is well established that, in the absence of very clear language to the contrary, a contractual discretion must be exercised in good faith" – is the language of implication-in-law.[327]

Richard Hooley describes it as a two-stage process, saying that first the Court identifies the scope and purpose of the power by construction and then imposes controls through the implication of a term.[328] Dyson LJ's description of the "necessity" involved in incorporating these terms as "somewhat protean", adding that they are based on: "reasonableness, fairness and the balancing of competing policy considerations",[329] infers that the terms cannot be implied-in-fact. As Leggatt J said in *Product Star* that "The essential question is always whether the relevant power has been abused".[330] In many cases control of discretion is linked to the purpose of the clause. This infers that the context is the purpose.[331] Paul Finn quotes Sir Anthony Mason's justification for judicial interference: "the court will interpret the power as not extending to … action [which] exceeds what is necessary for the protection of the party's legitimate interests".[332]

In *Equitable Life*, Steyn LJ ruled that discretion could not be used to defeat the main purpose of the contract,[333] Dyson J held in *Nash* that interest rates could not be revised for an "improper purpose"[334] and Aikens LJ decided that

---

325 *Socimer* at [66], in *Product Star* (n. 303 above) and *Lymington* n. 233 above.
326 See Courtney, 'Reasonableness'. Bridge, 'Exercise', 228, characterises the control as a term implied in fact, as does Hooley, 'Controlling Contractual Discretion'.
327 Leggatt, 'Negotiation in Good Faith', saying this is "a general default rule" at [50].
328 Hooley, 'Controlling Contractual Discretion', 72.
329 *Crossley v Faithful and Gould* [2004] EWCA Civ 293, per Dyson LJ at [36], approved in *Société Générale v Geys* [2012] UKSC 63 (n. 301) by Lady Hale at [56]. See also *Chitty on Contracts*, at 14.005 – the courts do not confine themselves to a narrow test of necessity but instead can draw upon a broader range of factors, such as the reasonableness of the term, its fairness and a range of competing policy considerations.
330 *Product Star* (n. 303 above) at 404.
331 Hugh Collins, 'Objectivity and Committed Contextualism in Interpretation' in Worthington, *Commercial Law*, 205 – "purpose is a technique for constructing the understanding of a reasonable promisee". See for a good example of construction from purpose Lord Sumption in *Rock Advertising Ltd (Respondent) v MWB Business Centres Ltd (Appellant)* [2018] UKSC 24.
332 'Fiduciary and Good Faith Obligations under Long Term Contracts' in Dharmananda, *Long Term Contracts*, 150.
333 *Equitable Life Assurance Society v Hyman* [2000] 3 All ER 961 at 971, [2002] 1 AC 408.
334 *Nash v Paragon* (n. 232 above) at [36] "a contract where one party truly found himself subject to the whim of the other would be a commercial and practical absurdity".

one clause could "not be used so as to subvert the basis of the contract".[335] In *Hayes v Willoughby* Lord Sumption said that the object was: "to limit the decision-maker to some relevant contractual purpose".[336] Andrew Phang describes implied-in-law terms as "far more problematic" than terms implied-in-fact, due to the uncertainty that their existence generates.[337] He argues that it might be better to abolish them altogether, forcing parties to argue for implied-in-fact terms. I argue that in commercial contracts control should emerge through construction, by examination of background, purpose and expectation.

In *Nash* and *Socimer*, for example, an analogue of Tuckey LJ's construction of the obligation in *Esso v Addison* makes perfect sense and obviates the need to impose terms through policy; the italics show the replaced wording:

> The question is whether the adjustments to the *interest rates* which the *mortgag*ees criticise were based on a genuine examination by *Paragon* of the commercial factors affecting its *lending* business in general and a rational response to the conclusions it reached.

And in *Socimer*:

> The question is whether the *sale, and pricing of* the *Designated Assets* which the *liquidators* criticise were based on a genuine examination by *Standard* of the commercial factors affecting its *investment* in general and a rational response to the conclusions it reached.

In neither case would that formulation have changed the result. The evidence and the background would have shown that the right questions were asked, the decision taken for the right reasons and that sufficient evidence underpinned the decision-making process. It would certainly have changed the result in *Medirest*, the Trust, far from making a genuine examination of performance, indulging in "absurd calculations".

Determining whether power has been abused requires an analysis into the purpose behind the power; surely a construction question and not a policy matter. I have more than considerable sympathy with Lord Reed's confession:

> I am not sure that I understand …. the statement that there should be "an absence of arbitrariness, of capriciousness or of reasoning so outrageous in its defiance of logic as to be perverse", but that the court is not referring to "a decision lying beyond the furthest reaches of objective reasonableness"; or how that test is related to the causal connection between the purpose and the conduct.[338]

---

335 *McKay v Centurion Credit Resources* (n. 243 above) at [18].
336 *Hayes v Willoughby* [2013] UKSC 17 (n. 212) at [14].
337 Andrew Phang, 'The Challenge of Principled Gap-Filling' (2014) *JBL* 261 (n. 321) at 295.
338 *Hayes v Willoughby* (n. 176) at [28].

If these esoteric concepts cause Lord Reed some pause for thought it seems highly likely that an experienced commercial player will find them incomprehensible. It is possible to rebalance the interpretation of such provisions, looking more to purpose and context based considerations.

Commercial people might find a positive duty to act fairly, even (perhaps, taking the interests of the other party into account) respecting the purpose of the decision-making provision and the reasonable expectations of each party, easy to understand. Applying this to, for example, *Nash*, Paragon was logically correct to argue that Mrs Nash was free to hunt down another lender. She wasn't trapped. She could redeem the mortgage and remortgage elsewhere. In that sense, the reining in of Paragon's discretion was not necessary but must derive from appreciation of the purpose of the clause. Dyson LJ argued that the parties would have answered "of course not" if asked whether interest rates could be altered "dishonestly, for an improper purpose".[339] He found that the rates were set at the level they were because Paragon considered it "commercially necessary", given that Paragon itself was in financial difficulty, because many of its borrowers had defaulted and the price of its own borrowing had, accordingly, risen and its "aim is to make a profit by lending money".[340]

Although Lady Hale provides a plausible explanation for the imposition of controls and Karl Llewellyn defends controls as enforcing "minimum decencies",[341] they are founded on policy considerations with insufficient attention paid to the intentions of the parties.

One could write an *MvD* influenced principle, anchored in construction and obviating policy making:

> Where in a written contract one party is charged with making decisions which affect the rights of one or both parties, the construction of the contract is that the decision-maker will act honestly, fairly, and impartially, and that such decisions will be made in accordance with the contractual purpose for which the power to make decisions has been conferred [or agreed], taking into account relevant matters and genuine commercial factors, after [collecting and] considering appropriate evidence; though there be no express words to that effect.

2.7.8 Appendix A to Chapter 2.7 – typical contract decision-making powers

- Settlement approval by a reinsurer.[342]
- The ability of a mortgage lender to alter mortgage rates.[343]

---

339 *Nash v Paragon* (n. 232 above) at [36].
340 Ibid. at [41] and [47].
341 AS Burrows and Edwin Peel (eds) *Contract Terms* (OUP 2007) (n. 289); Gerard McMeel at 33, a phrase he returns to in Gerard McMeel, 'Foucault's Pendulum: Text, Context and Good Faith in Contract Law' (2017) *CLP*.
342 *Gan Insurance v Tai Ping Insurance* n. 288 above.
343 *Nash v Paragon* n. 232 above.

- The right of a marina owner to control sub-licensing[344] or of a landlord to approve sub-letting.[345]
- Whether to provide further interim loans.[346]
- A master's determination whether a port to which he was ordered to sail was dangerous.[347]
- Withdrawal of credit facilities.[348]
- Operation of provisions allowing deduction of monies for performance failures.[349]
- Who might accompany an academic at a disciplinary hearing (the University's literal stance being described as "unattractive").[350]
- Operating termination machinery, whether "for convenience" or otherwise.[351]
- Installation of sales monitoring equipment in pubs.[352]
- Employers' decisions to award or not award bonuses or discretionary payments.[353]

2.8 The apparatus of contract interpretation

In this subchapter I continue the argument that many judges are unclear in their language and their reasoning for incorporating duties to cooperate, sometimes using implied-in-fact terms, often creating legal policy as implied-in-law terms, and/or from a relatively straightforward process of interpretation and construction. I suggest that construction is the best, most efficient and the right method, for incorporating duties to cooperate.

The basic principle of cooperation in English contract law requires a consideration of what has to be done when "it appears to be necessary that something must be done" which requires the cooperation of both parties. This requires that judges first find what Elisabeth Peden calls the "fundamental"

---

344 *Lymington* n. 233 above.
345 *International Drilling Fluids Ltd v Louisville Investments (Uxbridge) Ltd* n. 252 above.
346 *McKay v Centurion Credit Resources* (n. 243 above). See also *Greenclose Ltd v National Westminster Bank* (n. 241 above) and *Barclays Bank Plc v Unicredit Bank AG* (n. 306 above).
347 *Product Star* n. 303 above.
348 *CTN Cash and Carry Ltd v Gallaher Ltd* n. 243 above.
349 *Medirest High Court* (n. 200 above). *Ensign* (n. 210 above).
350 *Stevens v University of Birmingham* [2015] EWHC 2300 (QB).
351 *Petroleo Brasileiro SA v Ene Kos 1 Ltd* (n. 264 above), *TSG Building Services PLC v South Anglia Housing Ltd* (n. 264 above) and *Ilkerler* (n. 124 above). In Canada there may be limitations (based on good faith) – see *Burquitlam Care Society v Fraser Health Authority*, 2015 BCSC 1343.
352 *Ludgate Insurance Co. Ltd v Citibank NA* n. 229 above.
353 *Horkulak v Cantor Fitzgerald International* [2004] EWCA Civ 1287.

obligation; the next task being to determine the meaning of the obligation.[354] Few judges seem to be willing to keep it this simple. There is a gallimaufry of judicial descriptions of the origin of the duty to cooperate; Peden describing a failure to apply the tests for implication while using "an implied term approach" as "judicial sloppiness".[355]

The language used includes "implied engagement",[356] "implied contract",[357] "implied provision",[358] a "positive rule",[359] the "construction of the contract",[360] "implication of a duty to cooperate",[361] "implied obligation",[362] "obligation to cooperate",[363] "do whatever is reasonable",[364] "natural implication",[365] "the duty of co-operation",[366] "implied contractual obligation",[367] "duty ... to disclose",[368] "implied understanding",[369] "ordinary and well-known principles",[370] "law implies an agreement",[371] "it must mean",[372] "by implication of law, an obligation to co-operate",[373] "implicit in the parties understanding",[374] "necessary implication upon a proper construction",[375] "inevitable inference",[376] "a general rule applicable to every contract",[377] rule of construction,[378] "an obvious implication",[379] "implicit in the contract",[380] "a general principle of construction",[381] "implicit in the contract".[382] In one case Mason J uses "implied obligation" citing *Mackay*

354 Peden, *Good Faith*, 129. See also *Carter's Breach of Contract* at 2.27.
355 Peden, *Good Faith*, 125.
356 *Stirling v Maitland* (n. 3 above) at 1047.
357 *Quilpué (Barque) Ltd v Brown* n. 12 above.
358 *Marten v Whale* (n. 63 above) Scrutton J at 486.
359 *Southern Foundries (1926) Ltd v Shirlaw* (n. 18 above) Lord Atkin at 717, cited with approval by Lewison, *Interpretation*, at 6.14.
360 *Mackay v Dick* n. 2 above.
361 *Merton London Borough Council v Stanley Hugh Leach Limited* n. 19 above.
362 *Swallowfalls* (n. 1 above), *Ritchie* (n. 130 above).
363 *Brookfield Construction Ltd v Foster & Partners Ltd* [2009] EWHC 307 (TCC).
364 *Harris v Best* n. 7 above.
365 *Ritchie* n. 130 above.
366 *Anglo Group* n. 98 above.
367 *Mona Oil* n. 6 above.
368 *The Lutetian* n. 114 above.
369 *Lister v Romford Ice & Cold Storage Co.* [1957] 1 All ER 125.
370 *Hick v Raymond & Reid* n. 66 above.
371 *Postlethwaite v Freeland* 5 App Cas 599.
372 *Hargreaves Transport v Lynch* [1969] 1 All ER 455.
373 *Martin Grant & Co. Ltd v Sir Lindsay Parkinson & Co. Ltd* 3 Con LR 12.
374 *Bristol Groundschool Ltd v Intelligent Data Capture* [2014] EWHC 2145 (Ch).
375 *Hart v McDonald* (1910) CLR 417.
376 *Nissho Iwai Petroleum Co. Inc. v Cargill International SA* n. 61 above.
377 *Butt v MacDonald* n. 4 above.
378 *Commonwealth Bank of Australia v Barker* [2014] HCA 32.
379 *Cream Holdings Ltd v Stuart Davenport* (2011) n. 64 above.
380 *Wmc Resources Limited v Leighton Contractors Pty Ltd* [1999] WASCA 10 *Hargreaves Transport v Lynch* n. 372 above.
381 *Park v Brothers* (2005) 222 ALR 421.
382 *Sutcliffe v Thackrah* n. 8 above.

v Dick, a "rule of construction", going on to observe that it is "easy to imply a duty to cooperate".[383]

Perhaps this apparently heterogenous language should not surprise us. Sir Kim Lewison rightly says that the phrase "implied term" is used "in a wide variety of senses".[384] The *OED* defines implicit, implied and imply as:

- implied though not plainly expressed,
- naturally or necessarily involved in,
- capable of being inferred from something else;
- necessarily intended though not expressed;
- or to involve or comprise as a necessary logical consequence.

This covers construction, implication-in-fact and implication-in-law (which might be inferred from the nature of a class of contracts). Arguably, then, judges use imply and variants in disparate ways; adding words (implied-in-fact), ascribing meaning inferentially (where there is an inevitable inference), incorporating custom, or practice, and attributing incidents to types of contract (implied-in-law).[385] Although Hugh Collins says that bases for implication can operate simultaneously and cumulatively, this is not a coherent, or defensible approach.[386] Sir Kim Lewison argues that there is no conflict between what Lord Blackburn says and the language of implication, which might be right in a technical, linguistic sense, but the more pressing issue is certainty and coherence.[387] There are differing tests for each base and where there is uncertainty as to which might be used this will add cost and complexity to litigation.

Lord Neuberger, quoting Lady Hale, says:

> there are two types of contractual implied term. The first ... is implied ... in the light of the express terms, commercial common sense, and the facts known to both parties ... The second ... arises because ... the law ... effectively imposes certain terms into certain classes of relationship.[388]

Even this is not quite correct. Judges use the language of implication relatively indiscriminately. If there is uncertainty as to the base for the term litigators will, must, cover both bases, meaning that cost and complexity increase. The "second", implication-in-fact, described by Lord Clarke as a "more ambitious undertaking", involves the "interpolation" of terms to fill gaps and make the

---

383 *Secured Income Real Estate (Australia) Ltd v St Martins Investments Pty* [1979] HCA 51.

384 Lewison, *Interpretation*, at 6.01.

385 Richard Austen-Baker, *Implied Terms in English Contract Law* (Edward Elgar 2011) at 1.12.

386 See Collins, *Law of Contract*, at 244.

387 Lewison, *Interpretation*, at 6.15.

388 *Marks and Spencer v Paribas* (n. 20 above) at [15] quoting Lady Hale in *Société Générale v Geys* (n. 329 above) at [55].

contract work.[389] As Lord Neuberger has ruled,[390] a term will only be implied in a "very clear case",[391] once a gap has been identified, if it is fair and the parties would have agreed it,[392] one of the tests of business necessity or obviousness are satisfied[393] and the business efficacy test satisfied; meaning that the contract would lack commercial or practical coherence in its absence.[394] Lord Carnwath remarks that it is a "useful discipline" that judges remember "that the object remains to discover what the parties have agreed or (in Lady Hale's words) 'must have intended' to agree".[395] To assist the "lazy reader" Sir Kim Lewison[396] suggests turning to Mance LJ's summary of the judicial task in interpreting commercial contracts:

> to construe the documents in a manner which effects the mutual intention of these commercial parties, against the background of the transaction as a whole, looking for the meaning which the language used … would convey to a reasonable person, having all the background knowledge which would reasonably have been available to the parties to the relevant documents, but excluding previous negotiations and evidence of subjective intent.[397]

He goes on – "the lazy reader may stop here". I didn't take this sage advice. In an illuminating article on how Courts approach this task, Lord Grabiner suggests that the natural starting point is the reading of the texts[398] after which "in many cases" Courts should then examine the factual background (or matrix),[399] noting that there is limited room for this when the words are clear.[400] As Lewison says, the primary material is the document, Burrows emphasising that there

---

389 *Mediterranean Salvage & Towage Ltd v Seamar Trading & Commerce Inc* [2009] EWCA Civ 531 at 18.
390 See, for a critical assessment – Joanna McCunn, 'Belize It or Not: Implied Contract Terms in Marks and Spencer v BNP Paribas' (2016) 79 *MLR*; Edwin Peel, 'Terms Implied in Fact' (2016) 132 *LQR* 531.
391 *Marks and Spencer v Paribas* (n. 20 above) at [50].
392 Necessary but not sufficient conditions – Lord Neuberger ibid. at [21].
393 Ibid.
394 Ibid.
395 Ibid. at [69].
396 Lewison, *Interpretation*, p. 3.
397 *Rank Enterprises Ltd v Gerard* [2000] 1 All ER (Comm) 449.
398 Lord Grabiner, 'The Iterative Process of Contractual Interpretation' (2012) 128 *LQR* 41 at 45 citing *Re Sigma Finance Corp* [2008] EWCA Civ 1303, and *Multi-Link Leisure Developments Ltd v North Lanarkshire Council* [2010] UKSC 47; [2011] 1 All ER 175 SC where Lord Hope said at [11]: "the court's task is to ascertain the intention of the parties by examining the words they used and giving them their ordinary meaning in their contractual context. It must start with what it is given by the parties". "iterative" is described as "modish" by McMeel, 'Foucault's Pendulum', 6.
399 Grabiner, 'Iterative Process', 46, where he also uses the term "factual matrix". Lewison, *Interpretation*, says "background" is more "fashionable" at 3.17, p. 162.
400 Grabiner, 'Iterative Process', 47, quoting Neuberger LJ in *Skanska Rashleigh Weatherfoil Ltd v Somerfield Stores Ltd* [2006] EWCA Civ 1732 at [21]–[22].

is a "rebuttable presumption" that the written terms are the only terms.[401] Lord Hoffmann describes the matrix as material "reasonably available to the parties … including" "absolutely anything which would have affected the way in which the language of the document would have been understood by a reasonable man".[402] Lord Hoffmann's examination of the background included analysing and comparing consequences of each of the argued-for interpretations.[403] Lord Steyn not empanelled; Lord Lloyd felt able to refer to "slovenly" drafting in his "construction"; also bringing in the background.[404] Proceeding with caution Courts may then consider whether a term should be added to the contract to make it work or for policy reasons.

This process is not serial, but an iterative process involving checking back and forward between rival meanings and, Lord Neuberger indicates, judges may use different starting points.[405] The process should be a four-fold, sequential, process. judges should first read the words and may reach conclusions on that basis. They may go on to consider background and reach conclusions based on the words and background. I use "construction" to describe these activities, which includes the first step of finding the fundamental obligation and the second step of ascribing meaning. As Sir Thomas Bingham MR described it, construction is a "a composite exercise, neither uncompromisingly literal nor unswervingly purposive".[406]

Once they reach the end of this process, they may consider whether the contract has gaps to be filled. If so, they then consider first whether the gap *must* be filled to provide business efficacy or *should* be filled, for policy-based reasons. I refer to this activity as gap-filling because in construction activity a Court may have to add words to the express words where custom or trade practice, for example, explain or supplement the express terms.

Lord Carnwath says that sequence has "little practical significance", but this is plainly not correct.[407] It is quite difficult to work out how one might determine that there is a gap in a contract without first getting around to reading it.

Elimination or limitation of the final steps of gap-filling creates significant benefit for litigants. Modish or no, should Courts interpret iteratively and find a way to persuade litigants that the norm in cooperation cases is construction, then step three, expensive gap-filling, can be eliminated from much litigation.

401 Burrows, *Restatement*, 80.
402 *Investors Compensation Scheme v West Bromwich Building Society* [1998] 1 WLR 896 at 912–913. See Brian Langille and Arthur Ripstein, 'Strictly Speaking – it Went Without Saying' (1996) 2 *Legal Theory* 63 (n. 257) at 81 "what another party means really is fixed by what others reasonably take him or her to mean".
403 *Investors* (n. 402 above) at 912.
404 Ibid. at [899].
405 Lord Neuberger, '"Judge Not, That Ye Be Not Judged": Judging Judicial Decision-Making' at [10].
406 *Arbuthnott v Fagan* [1996] LRLR 143.
407 *Marks and Spencer v Paribas* (n. 20 above) at [68].

Carter considers that the duty to cooperate is not an implied term but an incident of commercial construction;[408] describing the language of implication as "redundant".[409] Sir Kim Lewison says that parties are under a general duty to co-operate in the performance of a contract, citing *Mackay v Dick,* inferring that it is a general rule of construction.[410] The High Court of Australia has called the prevention principle a "general principle of construction".[411]

Gerard McMeel, however, says that: "the duty to cooperate ... which might be an aspect of good faith in civil law systems finds its expression through the familiar vehicle of the implied term".[412] Richard Austen-Baker thinks that McMeel goes too far, saying: "this is not a term implied by law at all. In each and every case it is necessary to demonstrate that the term is necessary ... The rule is too general to be formulated into an implied term in the English tradition."[413] This is also too wide. The test is not necessity but whether or not the contract includes obligations which require some measure of joint activity for their performance. It is not uncommon for a Court to conclude, from the words, that certain activities are joint or require concurrence.[414] Hobhouse J concluded in one case that an "inevitable inference" arose that a telephone call be answered in a reasonable time, finding that that an eight-second failure to answer a call, resulting in the delayed declaration of a cargo in a falling market, was a breach of the implied term of prevention.[415] The fundamental obligation was that Cargill must be ready to receive calls and the construction of the contract was that Cargill must answer calls without delay. Elisabeth Peden says that none of the implied-in-fact tests were used,[416] but this is unfair as Hobhouse J used the words "inevitable inference" as a direct, literal response to the Plaintiff's pleading and he said of the prevention principle this was an implied term of "a contract", meaning, I infer, a general term.[417]

In *Startup v MacDonald*, where bulk goods had been tendered during the hours of darkness, Rolfe B describes the corollary of that fundamental obligation of delivery; "as the attendance of the other is necessary ... to complete the act ... what is the true meaning of the contract?"; concluding that a "reasonable opportunity"[418] of inspection must be given to the receiving party. Denman CJ said in the case that it was obvious "that the lateness of the hour may make

---

408 *Carter's Breach of Contract,* 2.027.
409 Wayne Courtney and JW Carter, 'Implied Terms; What Is the Role of Construction?' (2014) 31 *JCL* 151 at 160.
410 Lewison, *Interpretation,* at 16.06.
411 *Park v Brothers* (n. 381 above) at [38].
412 Gerard McMeel, *The Construction of Contracts Interpretation, Implication, and Rectification* (2011), 10.29.
413 Austen-Baker, *Implied Terms,* 77–78.
414 *Mackay v Dick* (n. 2 above), *Harris v Best* (n. 7 above).
415 *Nissho Iwai Petroleum Co. Inc v Cargill International SA* n. 61 above.
416 Peden, *Good Faith,* 126.
417 Ibid. 122, however Peden accepts that imply may mean "infer or construe".
418 *Startup v Macdonald* (1843) 134 ER 1029 at 1042.

a tender unreasonable".[419] In *Hargreaves Transport v Lynch* the Court of Appeal described an obligation to "take all reasonable steps by way of attempting to get not only the outline planning permission" as "implicit" and Lord Denning said that it was required "to make [the condition] work sensibly"; language which indicates construction.[420] Peden describes this as "implication by construction", but implicit can mean inherent or obvious, and it seems to me to be straightforward construction (with confusing language thrown in).[421]

The background in *Anglo Group plc v Winther Brown & Co. Ltd* was a complex IT design and install contract. Toulmin J "implied" an active cooperation term as a standard for such contracts, without using implied-in-fact tests; saying that "It is important to understand the nature of the contracts ... It is well understood that the design and installation of a computer system requires the active co-operation of both parties". This is the language of construction.[422]

Saying that the "modern approach" is generally "permissive" in admissibility of evidence within the matrix and balances "loyalty to the text" against "purposive reasoning, which gives effect to business common sense", Gerard McMeel[423] refers us to Patrick Atiyah's reflections on construction, at a time when the "technique", he said, had become popular. Atiyah approved of its flexibility but warned that its "extreme flexibility" might lead to uncertainty:

> The familiar formula that the construction of a contract "depends on all the circumstances of the case" appears to be little more than a device by which ... the court is able to achieve what it regards as the most just result ... Similarly, the construction technique enables the court to avoid, where necessary, the suffocating grip of the doctrine of precedent.[424]

It can be argued that the same risks inhere in implication. David Ibbetson, analysing the history of implied-in-fact terms, describes the claim that they effect party intention as a "façade" which "did not necessarily affect the answer".[425] Waspishly, Austen-Baker describes implication as a judicial technique allowing the Court to discover interpretations "more aligned to its view ... of what is common sense or fair without ever having to admit to such a heinous thing".[426]

---

419 Ibid. at 1043.

420 *Hargreaves Transport v Lynch* (n. 372 above) – Russell LJ at 459.

421 Peden, *Good Faith,* 32–33. Andrew Robertson says that such terms "necessitated by language and logic" are still implied; which begs the question as to which of the meanings of imply he uses – see Andrew Robertson, 'The Limits of Interpretation in the Law of Contract' (2016) 47 *Victoria Univ Wellington Law Rev* 191 at 196.

422 *Anglo Group* (n. 98 above) at 125 and 128.

423 McMeel, 'Foucault's Pendulum', 3 and 10.

424 PS Atiyah, 'Judicial Techniques in the Law of Contract' (1968) 2 *Ottawa LR* 244 at 269 and 274.

425 DJ Ibbetson, *A Historical Introduction to the Law of Obligations* (OUP 1999) at 224–225.

426 Austen-Baker, *Implied Terms,* preface p. vi.

In summary, and grossly over-simplifying, Courts should first read the documents and, where necessary, examine the matrix. From that the Court will derive the "nature" or purpose of the contract and the fundamental obligations should then have become tolerably clear. The Court can then ask itself a straight question:

> In those obligations is there anything (the "something") which requires the concurrence of both parties in order for it to be effectuated? If so, pace Lord Esher, what is the part of each party?

Going back to my quotidian example of a kitchen installation these seem to me to be the right questions to ask:

- Is there a contract?
- Does it appear from that contract that there is something to which the parties have agreed which requires the concurrence of each?
- What part in that something does each have to do?

In this example I can think of the following possibilities:

- The trader must carry out work in the house; accordingly, access is required. The trader must turn up and the householder must admit the trader.
- The trader needs water and power to carry out the work. The householder must ensure a reasonable supply of both.
- The trader will require exclusive access to some areas of the house and non-exclusive access to others. The householder must facilitate this, agreeing on times and areas with the trader.
- In all likelihood, as work progresses, there will be changes of mind as to the location of electrical sockets, shelves and so on. The parties should make reasonable efforts to agree to effect these.

Although it is likely that these are set out in the trader's terms it is possible that they are not. But they would be in the natural understanding of the parties.

In *Cream Holdings Ltd v Stuart Davenport*, the fundamental obligation was that Mr Davenport's shareholding would be valued by a third-party accountant. The appointment required Mr Davenport's agreement. The construction of the contract (the Articles) should have been that Mr Davenport must sign up to reasonable terms of engagement for the third party.

In *CEL Group Ltd v Nedlloyd Lines UK Ltd*, the contract provided a haulier with exclusive rights to its client's transport requirements for a period of three years. This was the fundamental obligation. The client merged its business with that of a third party who decided to send much of the freight by rail. In this case the Court concluded that the construction of the contract included the continuation of the defendant's practice of significant use of road haulage. There was no need for an implied term.

In *Medirest* the fundamental obligation, in Cranston J's Judgment was that the parties "work together constantly, at all levels of the relationship … and … work together to resolve … problems". The corollary was that when problems arose the parties should engage constructively to resolve them. That is the problem-solving obligation. The Trust's absurd calculations produced problems and the fundamental obligation in operating the service point deduction provision was to use the deductions strictly in accordance with their purpose, to create an incentive for good performance and to compensate the Trust for shortfalls in performance and the correlative duty is that the Trust should make deductions acting fairly and impartially and not irrationally.

There are, then, several reasons for arguing that construction is preferable to gap-filling as a method of determining the obligations of the parties.

Adopting the theoretical perspective that words have public meanings and only public meanings, as Langille and Ripstein put it, "any intended departure from the ordinary requires some signal";[427] the first is that it can be argued to reflect the "public meaning" of their words. It sets out the real agreement between the parties, covering meaning of express terms and meaning exposed through examining background.

The second is that it requires less evidence, less argument and does not require subjective assessment of what is fair, or necessary or efficacious or reasonable or coherent. Less argument of what might happen if the term is not incorporated is necessary; as, arguably, is less witness evidence. Implying terms is controversial, as well as "intrusive". Jonathan Morgan, while accepting that the rules ensure that adding words is rare in commercial contracting, argues that the Courts should institute an "austere regime of non-intervention", resisting the temptation to make contracts fair, efficient or complete.[428]

The third is that it limits the ability of the judiciary to impose "protean" policy-based meanings to contracts; the Court should not rescue parties from a bad bargain; which may happen if a Court can be tempted to fill arguable gaps.[429]

Finally, it provides coherence and principle, together with a measure of certainty to the matter. The cases reviewed show that it is currently well-nigh impossible for a party to predict with certainty the principle on which a duty to cooperate should be pleaded.

---

427   Langille and Ripstein, 'Strictly Speaking', 79. See Stephen A Smith, *Contract Theory* (OUP 1993) at 273 "a purely private language is an impossibility".

428   Morgan, *Contract Law Minimalism*, 237–242.

429   Peel (n. 93 above) at 534. And see Rose J in *Libyan Investment Authority v Goldman Sachs International* [2016] EWHC 2530 (Ch) – the law will not intervene to save people from making improvident bargains – quoting Lord Hoffmann in *Union Eagle v Golden Achievement Ltd* [1997] 2 All ER 215; the notion that the Court has unlimited, unfettered, jurisdiction to grant relief from bad consequences of contracts is merely a "beguiling heresy".

2.9 Conclusion

JF Burrows believed that the law will go a little beyond "absolute necessity" but that "it stops short of demanding co-operation because that would be reasonable ... By and large the motto seems to be 'each man for himself'".[430] I am not sure why this is problematic. Why one would ask for much more than necessity is unclear to me. The case law, however, shows that the Courts, case by case, incrementally, incorporate duties to cooperate into commercial contracts because such cooperation is fundamental to the bargain under examination. Those contracts range from the day-to-day, relatively simple, to the highly complex and interactive. The duty incorporated varies with that context, growing from a mechanical duty not to get in the way to active managerial duties to find ways to resolve problems and allow defects to be cured.

I also show that the techniques used by judges to expose a duty are, if not incoherent, less than wholly coherent. Construction provides the best basis, and a coherent basis, for uncovering a duty to cooperate.

The "third way", in which an extensive, permeating, duty to cooperate can be envisaged for symbiotic contracts is possible using existing contract law principle. I do not think that the *Medirest* approach can survive long; *Braganza*, and possibly *Amey,* may have already limited its application. I have shown that the case law (perhaps melding the dicta of Cranston J, Lord Blackburn, Toulmin J, Sir Thomas Bingham MR, Allsop J and Vaughan Williams J) and some reconsideration of judicial language, including more emphasis on construction, demonstrate that this can be achieved and that lays the foundations for a more detailed consideration of the duty in later chapters. Optimism might be found in the fact that the requirement for a third-party certifier to act fairly and impartially has survived for more than 100 years, that the law applying to contractual decision-making has been clarified, and that a broader need for communication and problem solving in complex contracts has been identified and has survived. Pessimism derived from the unhelpful, and hopefully apotropaic, *Medirest* Judgment must be tempered by the fact that it appears to be case-specific, and it seems possible that Jackson LJ, at least, may be reconsidering his approach to such contracts.

---

430 Burrows (n. 16 above) at 390 and 404.

3 Empirical research
Survey and results

In this chapter I describe the results of a wide-ranging, complex and detailed survey of commercial experts on how one makes symbiotic contracts work and the role that cooperation plays in this. The original features of the survey are that it provides significantly more detail, at working level, of how these contracts are made to work, how cooperation is achieved in practice and that respondents are experienced professionals drawn from a wide variety of backgrounds. Over 500 participated, by online survey, interview or workshop.[1]

I want to tell a "convincing story ... in realist terms"[2] on the role played by cooperation in the management and success of symbiotic contracts. I investigate the dual contexts of the legal and business worlds, in an effort to illuminate the effect of challenging commercial conditions, changes, bad behaviour or disputes on the expectations of commercial actors and provide a basis for consequent desirable development of legal principle. I elicited expert opinion from experienced contract management professionals; through a real-world survey of people engaged in the management of symbiotic and other contracts. Contracts professionals are accustomed to expressing opinions in writing on diverse subjects. My survey is largely qualitative work and the story emerges through contextual analysis rather than number crunching. Variation in opinion is not easy to set out numerically; but it can be reduced to major themes. Contracts are messy and subjective, and meaning emerges from both the words and the performance. The survey provides a reliable guide to the objectively reasonable expectations of commercial players in symbiotic contract environments.

Respondents overwhelmingly consider cooperation to be important or mission critical. They are also able and willing to define cooperation and to advise us how to achieve it. They define cooperation as high-level active cooperation and constructive engagement. This is tested against four real-world case studies (using open and closed questions), based on adjudicated

---

1 Survey results take up 241 pages. Respondents answered a minimum of 18 survey questions and five demographic questions and a maximum of 52 survey questions and ten demographic questions. 27 hand-written pages of interview notes were taken.
2 Colin Robson, *Real World Research* (3rd edn, Wiley 2011) at 242–243.

situations, in which cooperation was arguably the better modus operandi.[3] Open questions ask, for example, how one achieves cooperation in symbiotic contracts and closed, scaled, questions ask for preferences in formal/legal reaction and commercial/managerial reaction to a situation in which the supplier of business-critical defective equipment refuses to provide an explanation for the defect; and, because these are experts, for other ideas in an open question at the end of each vignette.

Empirical survey work is a social science rather than a legal discipline and I found it easier to write it up in Grand Narrative[4]– a contextual social science style, typical for a normative researcher with a desire for regularity and a wish to make the world a better place, suitable for the investigation of natural or quasi-natural settings and in particular, for this work, for considering "inner connections" between contract law, legal theory, and contract management.[5]

The importance of creating a better understanding of how symbiotic contracts work successfully is underscored by the recent collapse of Carillion, one of the UK's largest providers of outsourced work to the Government (Figure 3.1).

A Parliamentary report concluded:

> Carillion was a hugely complex company … in the highly volatile construction and outsourcing services markets, and it entered into long contracts with uncertain returns. … A deeper engagement with the business at all levels is required, to gain an understanding of the company's culture … to enable any concerns affecting Government contracts to be detected and escalated early. While this may be a costlier system … *We recommend that the Government immediately reviews the role and responsibilities of its Crown Representatives … This review should consider whether devoting more resources to liaison with strategic suppliers would offer better value for the taxpayer.*[6]

---

3 These include *J & H Ritchie Ltd v Lloyd Ltd* [2007] UKHL 9; [2007] 1 WLR 670, *Compass Group UK and Ireland Ltd (t/a Medirest) v Mid Essex Hospital Services NHS Trust* [2012] EWHC 781 (QB) and *Williams v Roffey Bros and Nicholls (Contractors) Ltd* [1991] 1 QB 1 (AC).

4 A grand narrative or meta-narrative is a description coined by Jean-François Lyotard, Geoffrey Bennington and Brian Massumi, *The Postmodern Condition: A Report on Knowledge* (Manchester University Press 1984) of commentary which sees events as interconnected, and attempts to make sense of the interconnections.

5 Mats Alvesson and Stanley Deetz, *Doing Critical Management Research* (Sage 2000) at 32.

6 UK Parliament, *Work and Pensions and BEIS Committees Publish Report on Carillion* (2018). See also Rob Davies, 'Key Findings from the MPs' Report into Carillion's Collapse', *The Guardian* (www.theguardian.com/business/2018/may/16/mps-dole-out-the-blame-over-carillions-collapse) – "'Recklessness, hubris and greed' – Carillion slammed by MPs".

What did Carillion do?

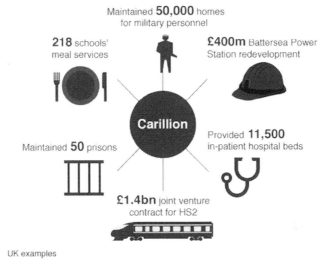

Figure 3.1 Carillion's Portfolio

In response to this crisis the Government has now issued a "Playbook".[7] This seems to recognise the need for better management of risk, and the need for contracts to be profitable, but there is no mention of cooperation, "deeper engagement" or improved contract management. There is vague reference to setting reasonable supplier expectations but, overall, it is a missed opportunity. Presciently, in 2003, David Parker and Keith Hartley counselled (not properly addressed in the Playbook) that the "long-term nature of PFP contracts requires a clear procurement policy with provision for changes, resolving disputes, risk management, contract pricing, performance incentives and exit strategies".[8]

My basic method was to "really dig into things ... [using] any technique [I] can ... [to] Find out how people organise their worlds".[9] I take the

---

7 UK Government, *The Outsourcing Playbook – Central Government Guidance on Outsourcing Decisions and Contracting* (https://assets.publishing.service.gov.uk/government/uploads/system/uploads/attachment_data/file/780361/20190220_OutsourcingPlaybook_6.5212.pdf 2019). As I write this, in mid-March 2019, in Shanghai, it is reported that another major supplier has entered administration. The effect of these collapses can be significant. The BBC reported that the NHS's costs had doubled after one. www.bbc.co.uk/news/uk-scotland-48169029.

8 David Parker and Keith Hartley, *Transaction Costs, Relational Contracting and Public Private Partnerships: A Case Study of UK Defence*, vol. 9 (2003) at 7.

9 Bruce L Berg, *Qualitative Research Methods for the Social Sciences* (7th edn, Ally & Bacon 2009). Herbert Blumer said this to Norman Wiley on fieldwork: "it's like being a good,

line that a critical management researcher with an interpretive slant would take, which is to place the social paradigm of organisation "in a wider cultural, economic and political context",[10] unearthing content and context for real-world cooperation-in-action, looking for connections and attempting to explain contradictions or illogicalities, or seeking a way through them. It is not easy to pigeon-hole the survey into a mainstream social science paradigm. My paradigm is fundamentally Denzin-Lincoln constructivist,[11] with lived experience, critical-realist, normative and cultural investigatory elements, meaning that the narration is an interpretive case study, using the lived experience of subjects (more typical in cultural studies).

I seek to establish whether there is sufficient congruence between respondents' views and the legal principles described in Chapter 2 to assist in drafting a duty to cooperate at a level of abstraction similar to that in *Hadley v Baxendale* or *Donoghue v Stevenson*.[12] I will consider whether players are likely to lean more towards Cranston J, who thought that cooperation meant "the parties work together constantly at all levels of the relationship ... to resolve the problems",[13] or Lewison LJ, who was so baffled by the concept of cooperation where one party was empowered to make deductions he said that he could not see "in what sense the unilateral decision [to deduct monies for under-performance] ... is something that requires co-operation at all".[14]

I obtained 481 survey responses which included 27 interviews. From a mini workshop in Rome in May 2016, I obtained 22 responses. I received a further 13 responses, using vignette 4 below, in an executive education workshop at the University of Leicester in June 2018.[15] As expected, I received substantial comment in answers to open questions (Table 3.1).

investigative reporter, ... Really digging into things ... no fixed field-work techniques. Use any technique you can ... Find out how people organize their worlds and how they fit actions together." Blumer's fundamental view was that contextual understanding of human action is intrinsic to valid social research (Wikipedia). See also Norman K Denzin and Yvonna S Lincoln, *Collecting and Interpreting Qualitative Materials* (Sage 1998) that "attempting to make sense ... of phenomena in terms of the meaning people bring to them ... product is a complex, dense, reflective, collagelike creation" (3–4) and "qualitative work is multimethod", there is "no single interpretive truth", it is not "value-free", that it involves an "interpretive, naturalistic approach" (30).

10 Alvesson and Deetz, *Doing Critical Management Research*, 32.
11 Denzin and Lincoln, *Collecting*, see Table 1.2.
12 *Hadley v Baxendale* (1854) 23 LJ Ex 179, 9 Exch 341, *Donoghue v Stevenson* [1932] UKHL 100.
13 at [27].
14 *Mid Essex Hospital Services NHS Trust v Compass Group UK and Ireland Ltd (t/a Medirest)* [2013] EWCA Civ 200 [2013] EWCA Civ 200 at [146].
15 The results are recorded in subchapter 3.3.4.

Table 3.1 Survey Responses in Numbers

Question	No. of respondents	No. of comments	No. of words (approx.)
Tell me what you enjoy about managing contracts	475	475	16000
What does success mean in the outcome of a contract? How does contract management contribute to success?	472	472	21600
Vignette 1 – the machine that didn't work	418	225	13800
Vignette 3 – a supplier refuses to perform without additional payment	454	134	8700
Vignette 4 – the ketchup vignette, in which a client makes unfair deductions from the price	360	109	6200
How do you achieve cooperation?	404	404	15500
What other contract provisions drive cooperation?	104	104	3600
Other definitions of cooperation	23	23	860
Rome workshop	22	21	650
		1946	82810

Around 5000 words were written down in interviews.

I tested survey results against other empirical studies, and in combination with analysis of the data for coherence, I can be confident that the data are robust and credible.

3.1 Methods and results

I selected experienced contract managers (whom I refer to as "real people" to differentiate them from avatars such as students) who can be expected to understand in broad terms the relevant background[16] to symbiotic contracts, in possession of some underlying commercial common sense[17] and who could also be described as reasonable parties, reasonable readers or the notional reasonable people referred to by Lord Neuberger.[18] I elicit from the "lived experience"[19]

---

16 Lord Hoffmann's phrase in *A-G of Belize v Belize Telecom Ltd* [2009] UKPC 10 at [16].

17 See Neil Andrews, 'Interpretation of Contracts and "Commercial Common Sense": Do Not Overplay This Useful Criterion' (2017) 76 *CLJ* 36 reviewing the use of "common sense" by judges.

18 In *Marks and Spencer plc v BNP Paribas Securities Services Trust Company (Jersey) Ltd* [2015] UKSC 72 at [21].

19 Svend Brinkmann, *Understanding Qualitative Research: Qualitative Interviewing* (OUP 2013) at 47 quotes Marshall and Rossman: "qualitative interviews … lend themselves most naturally to the study of individual lived experience".

of this powerful, creative elite a sense of what business necessity and commercial coherence[20] means, in the management of symbiotic contracts.

As between qualitative and quantitative methods, says Martin Davies, the "ethos of a particular course" may be the deciding factor, qualitative (non-numeric) methods being arguably "more human" and quantitative (numeric/statistical), more geared toward contemporary "scientific principles and techniques".[21] I am not a "quantophreniac",[22] nor am I a softy or a ninny.[23] One must use appropriate techniques to unearth social phenomena and I used a combination of qualitative and quantitative methods.[24]

Miles and Huberman advise that qualitative researchers should be familiar with the setting, utilise a multidisciplinary approach, be able to draw people out and possess good investigative skills.[25]

It can be tempting for researchers and theorists to take numbers at face value. Eisenberg and Miller reviewed choice of law clauses in public merger filings and, analysing the data statistically, concluded that it showed a marked tendency to choose the laws of Delaware and New York, drawing the conclusion that a desire for formalism underlay that "flight".[26] Juliet Kostritsky, using qualitative methods, including interviews, asked practising lawyers to explain their choice of law clauses in 343 agreements and found that formalistic law was not the motivating factor; the reasons for their choices being "so variegated that they cannot support the argument that formalism is driving".[27] Another study in which corporate counsel explained their rationale

20 Lord Neuberger in *Marks and Spencer v Paribas* (n. 18 above) at [21] refers to practical or commercial coherence being a requirement of an implied term.

21 Martin Davies, *Doing a Successful Research Project: Using Qualitative or Quantitative Methods* (Palgrave Macmillan 2007).

22 Robert Dingwall, 'Quantophrenia is Back in Town' www.socialsciencespace.com/2014/05/quantophrenia-is-back-in-town/- "the term coined by Pitrim Sorokin for the 'cult founded on the belief that quantification is the most, or indeed the only, valid form of knowledge'".

23 S Gherardi and BA Turner, 'Real Men Don't Collect Soft Data' (1987) 13 *Quaderno*. A parody: "soft data are weak unstable impressible squashy and sensual … softies and ninnies who carry it out have too much of a soft spot for counter-argument".

24 See Stacey M Carter and Miles Little, 'Justifying Knowledge, Justifying Method, Taking Action: Epistemologies, Methodologies, and Methods in Qualitative Research' (2007) 17 *Qual Health Res* 1316.

25 Matthew B Miles and AM Huberman, *Qualitative Data Analysis: An Expanded Sourcebook*, vol. 2 (Sage 1994) at 38.

26 Theodore Eisenberg and Geoffrey P Miller, 'The Flight to New York' (2009) 30 *Cardozo LRev* 1475. Of 89,000 contracts reviewed 49,000 contained a choice of law clause, 67% choosing New York or Delaware. That means that around 33,000 of 89,000, around 37% of the contracts chose New York or Delaware; rather a saunter than a flight? Jonathan Morgan, *Contract Law Minimalism* (CUP 2013), 185–186, agrees with their analysis. Lisa Bernstein cites it in 'The Myth of Trade Usage: A Talk for KCON', 11, as do Alan Schwartz and Robert E Scott, 'Contract Interpretation Redux' (2010) 119 *Yale LJ* 926. I used to advise against New York Law due to the impossibility of contracting out of gross negligence liability – see *Red Sea Tankers Ltd v Papachristidis (The Hellespont Ardent)* [1997] 2 Lloyd's Rep 547 (QBD).

27 Juliet P Kostritsky, 'Context Matters – What Lawyers Say about Choice of Law Decisions in Merger Agreements' (2014) 13 *DePaul Bus Com Law J* 211, 248. Reviewing over 1,000,000

for choice of law clauses concluded that the "most important factor is the perceived neutrality and impartiality of the legal system, (66%), followed by the appropriateness of the law, (60%) and familiarity with and experience of the particular law (58%)". The authors conducted 136 surveys and 67 interviews.[28]

Numbers are not mere numbers, not vacuum packed; they exist in a context and empirical researchers must avoid crude equation of correlation with causation.[29]

3.1.1 Respondent sample and demographics

I took a realist and judgemental approach to finding the right people.[30] In such a sample, the researcher's judgement is the leading selection criterion.[31] Berg recommends finding an "appropriate" population, describing the use of special expertise or knowledge in finding it as "judgemental" or "purposive".[32] I spent more than 30 years working in global commercial contracting environments, in shipbuilding, oil industry fabrication, power, defence and marine contracting, nuclear fuel reprocessing, industrial energy and compression, airport baggage handling, automated warehousing, oil and gas, and compressor and gas and steam turbine manufacture. I have been a Principal Contracts Consultant, a Company Secretary, a Commercial Manager, Vice President, General Counsel in blue chip organisations including Shell, ALSTOM, GEC, Siemens, NEI and British Shipbuilders. I deploy "special knowledge or expertise" and I am qualified to use my own judgement.[33]

Non-random samples are typical in such studies.[34] A random sample, using a defined population, selecting a representative sample, is not practically possible

---

contracts, Sarath Sanga, 'Choice of Law: An Empirical Analysis' (2014) 11 *JELS* 894, explains the "flight" by possible network or lock-in effects; see the abstract.

28 London School of International Arbitration, *2010 International Arbitration Survey* (2010)

29 See Etienne Joly, 'Baseball and Jet Lag: Correlation Does Not Imply Causation' (2017) 114 *Pro Nat Acad Sci US Am* E3168. Consider a read of Tyler Vigen, 'Spurious Correlations': www.tylervigen.com/spurious-correlations.

30 See Denzin and Lincoln, *Collecting*, 204 – they "recommend that the qualitative researcher thinks purposively and conceptually about sampling". Mandy Burton, 'Doing Empirical Research' in Mandy Burton and Dawn Watkins (eds) *Doing Empirical Research* (Routledge 2012) – "opportunistic approaches and the use of personal contacts can be valuable" (59) and there "may be a large element of luck involved" (60). I found one contact after complaining about a botched fire drill in a major hotel.

31 Robson, *Real World Research*, 275.

32 Berg, *Qualitative Research Methods*, 49–51. See also Earl R. Babbie, *Survey Research Methods* (2nd edn, Wadsworth Publishing 1990), 97–98 and 99.

33 Berg, *Qualitative Research Methods*, 50–51.

34 Richard N. Landers and Tara S. Behrend, 'An Inconvenient Truth: Arbitrary Distinctions between Organizational, Mechanical Turk, and Other Convenience Samples' (2015) 8 *Ind Organ Psychol* 142 – "virtually all samples used in I-O psychology are convenience". Alan Bryman, *Social Research Methods*, vol. 4 (OUP 2012), 191 – "may be typical in management and business studies".

for contract managers.[35] Commercial enterprises are generally unable or unwilling to provide population data to researchers.[36] And, as Robson notes: "The exigencies of carrying out real world studies can mean that the requirements for representative sampling are very difficult, if not impossible, to fulfil."[37] Evocatively, Miles and Huberman observe: "social processes have a logic and a coherence that random sampling can reduce to uninterpretable sawdust".[38]

I located potential respondents from my LinkedIn and Facebook contacts (weeded to avoid contacts with no contract experience), and LinkedIn groups (20-odd responses). Twelve of 25 members of the Academy of Experts who profess contract management expertise completed the survey. I asked for listeners to an Ask the Expert[39] seminar (I was the expert) to respond (six did), and a request to original respondents resulted in a "snowball" response from 56 people.[40]

My 481 respondents constitute a variegated, heterogeneous sample; having in common experience of contracting, more specifically, of complex contracting. This is a cross-business, variegated, diverse, global sample with profound, wide-ranging experience and background, including a former CEO of a FTSE company, a former Executive Vice President and a Vice President of an oil supermajor, partners in City Law firms, an internet gambling company's IT manager, the University of Leicester's estates department managers, a psychedelic music festival organiser, a commercial executive in warship building, facilities managers, gas turbine salespeople, outsourcing specialists, IT consultants, project managers, credit card managers, housing managers, industrial electrical contractors, geologists, engineers, lawyers, finance executives, procurement professionals and architects.[41] They make the world go around. They build and maintain LNG plants, aircraft carriers, highways, track and trains, power stations (big and small), student housing, baggage handling facilities and nuclear fuelling machinery; they run petrol stations, hotels and the cafes in

35 Bryman, *Social Research Methods*, 166–170. In double checking my sample, I discovered that one institution, which tried to identify as many of its contract managers as possible, had missed out a large number. This is not surprising – the same phenomenon is common in industrial settings.

36 Robson, *Real World Research,* 276.

37 Ibid. 276. Alvesson and Deetz, *Doing Critical Management Research,* 192.

38 Miles and Huberman, *Qualitative Data Analysis,* 27. See Berg, *Qualitative Research Methods,* 8: "If humans are studied in a symbolically reduced, aggregated fashion" conclusions may "fail to fit reality".

39 Run by the International Association for Contract and Commercial Management.

40 I didn't have the sampling problems experienced by Richard T Wright and Scott H Decker, *Burglars on the Job: Streetlife and Residential Break-ins* (Northeastern UP 1996) (worth reading as a read) – they needed active burglars and hired one "Street Daddy", a wheelchair-bound former thief with a solid street reputation who provided 105 burglars – 75% without convictions. Offering an Italian dinner improved results. They paid for interviews, resulting in "pimping" – informants taking a cut of the fee.

41 There is a suggestion in Matthew T Jones, 'Strategic Complexity and Cooperation: An Experimental Study' (2014) 106 *J Econ Behav Organ* 352 that those with higher ACT scores may be more cooperative. I think that my respondents are in this cohort.

many offices; they decommission nuclear plants. One has been in the Panama Canal widening project. Another cut her teeth on site at Hinckley B nuclear power station. The type of contracts they manage can mostly be described as symbiotic or complex, requiring planning and communication, and close cooperation.

I interviewed a selected 27 people. The selection was, generally, of very senior, very experienced people. Among them were a former FTSE 250 CEO, a former FTSE Finance Director, a partner in a big six consultancy firm, a Director of a listed outsourcing company, two partners in a City law firm, one project manager, a defrocked British Ambassador (now in the electricity business) and a former Executive Vice President of an oil supermajor. Without specific intent, although this seems to have support, my interviews were generally conducted on neutral territory, nine being carried out at home, nine in their office, three in the pub, one at a party, one by Skype and one in a coffee-shop.[42]

Responses came from far and wide (Figure 3.2) – with around 150 companies providing at least one response.

To tell a convincing story Robson stresses that explanation and interpretation depend on the incorporation of variables and subsequent analysis of correlation.[43] To provide a framework for analysis, I collected demographic data

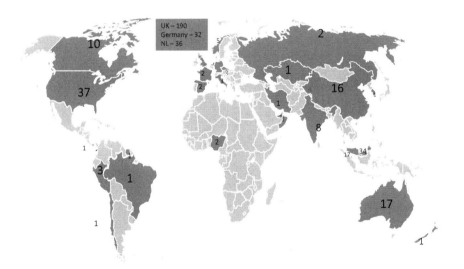

Figure 3.2 Respondent Location

42 Alvesson and Deetz, *Doing Critical Management Research*, 195 – "managers are more open and free when interviewed outside their offices".
43 Robson, *Real World Research*, 242–243.

(variables) to enable comparison/triangulation between subsamples to determine robustness and consistency of the data.[44]

Of those responding 80% are male, 18.9% female, with one other and four who preferred not to say. Professionally, (rounded numbers) 19% are project managers, 17% technical/engineers, 25% contracting/procurement specialists, 13% lawyers and 8% others. I "coded" my relationship with participants to allay concern that the sample might be biased due to my extensive use of contacts: finding that I don't know 35%, slightly know 23%, know 24% well and consider 18% as close friends or close colleagues. 60% emanate from an English common law legal culture, 10% from US common law, 21% civil law, 2% China, 3% mixed (Scotland, Philippines or South Africa), 3% other and 1.5% emerging jurisdictions such as Former Soviet Union. Because they might show that as people move up the greasy pole they become more, or less, cooperative in their outlook, I collected data on seniority, finding that 31% were executive managers or directors, 12% general managers, 25% contract or project managers, 20% managers and 11% other. I also wondered whether attitudes would change with portfolio value; 7% had portfolios of up to $1m, 17% between $1 and $10m, 30% $10–$100m, 26% between $100m and $1bn and 17% more than $1bn (in my final roles I held portfolio values of $7–$18bn). As less experienced respondents might be more inclined to manage in "tell" mode and use formal contractual mechanisms more than those with significant experience; as people gain experience they may become more, or less, cooperative in their outlook; I collected longevity data, finding that 10% have one to five years of experience, 17% six to ten, 32% have eleven to twenty, and 43% over twenty years. By industry they are shown in Figure 3.3.[45]

I also asked them to tell me what types of contract they manage; this was justified by the result recorded in 3.1.12 below, showing that those managing simpler supply contracts rate cooperation as less important.

3.1.2 Survey and interview design

I collected data by interviews and using an online survey, asking the same questions in each setting.[46] Survey design took into account multiple requirements:

---

44 Miles and Huberman, *Qualitative Data Analysis,* 267, Robson, *Real World Research,* 158, Denzin and Lincoln, *Collecting,* 199–200. Denzin coined the term "triangulation" for carrying out studies in different locations, using multiple theories, multiple researchers, multiple data technologies, different sources, collection methods, quota samples, age and gender, and datatypes to ascertain how far one might generalise from a non-random sample. See also Berg, *Qualitative Research Methods,* 7, who says that "research literature continues to support Denzin's recommendation to triangulate".

45 Robson, *Real World Research,* 277, suggests considering comparing early and late respondents. I took his steer – which is that this is a "counsel of perfection".

46 Brinkmann, *Understanding Qualitative Research,* 83, saying "the most general rule across paradigmatic differences is; describe what you have done and why".

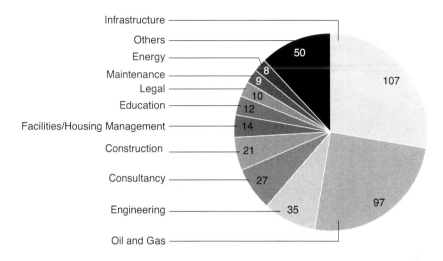

Figure 3.3 Respondents by Industry

- I sought lived experience. Questions were realistic, based on real-life cases.
- The conversation was with an elite. The survey reflected this is in complexity and the use of open questions.
- Demographic questions provided quantitative data, which in turn allow analysis of consistency between answers and facilitate some generalisation.
- In early discussions, trials and pilots it became clear that I should ensure that initial questions were open, with case studies and demographic questions following.[47]
- The availability of online survey tools, easy to distribute by email or social media, made an online survey an easy option despite the risk that vast amounts of data would be returned for analysis.
- Some questions bore similarity to questions asked by other empirical researchers. This also allowed comparison and strengthened generalising claims.[48]

Context matters. It is vital to place people into contexts they may understand. After conducting an experiment using military officers asked to make a counter-terrorism decision, Mintz replicated it using student avatars. Whereas over one-third of

---

47 This advice was of a severely practical nature; respondents would complete demographic questions to avoid wasting the work already performed on open and closed questions; which might not be true vice versa. For solid advice on constructing questions and sense-checking them see e.g. Valerie M Sue and Lois A Ritter, *Conducting Online Surveys* (Sage 2007) (especially to consider whether interviews will add anything), Robson, *Real World Research*, 255–256, G Nigel Gilbert, *Researching Social Life* (Sage 2008), 188, and Brinkmann, *Understanding Qualitative Research*, 49.

48 The Bristol Online Survey tool (www.onlinesurveys.ac.uk/) made realising my design easy.

students recommended doing nothing, over 90% of military officers recommended doing something.[49] Mintz concludes:

> It is unrealistic to expect students to play the role of elites in political science and international relations experiment … as the groups are very different in their sociodemographic characteristics, expertise, level of professional responsibility, and other significant factors.[50]

I avoid the use of "x-phi" games or experiments – Ultimatum Games, Prisoner's Dilemma games, variant trolleyology (a British invention I call tramification) – which all suffer from the disadvantage that real-world application or generalisation to the real world is not possible. In one Prisoner's Dilemma experiment the game was called the Cooperation Game for half the participants and the Wall Street Game for the others. Those playing the Wall Street Game were "dramatically" less likely to cooperate. Commenting, Jesse Prinz concludes that strategies adjust in "dramatic ways based on culturally meaningful contexts".[51] Other studies show, for example, that placing posters with eyes on them on the wall during x-phi experiments varies participant behaviour (Figure 3.4).[52]

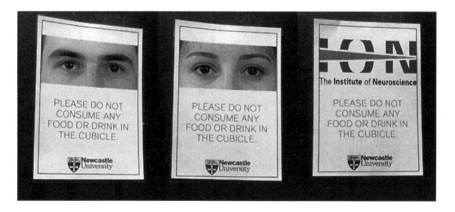

Figure 3.4 The Watching Eyes Experiment – The Posters

49 Alex Mintz and others, 'Can We Generalize from Student Experiments to the Real World in Political Science, Military Affairs, and International Relations?' (2006) 50 *J Conflict Resolut* 757 in abstract.
50 Ibid. 771.
51 Jesse J Prinz, *Beyond Human Nature* (1st edn, Allen Lane 2012), 313–314. For a note on possible cultural issues in such studies see Natalie Gold, Andrew M Colman and Briony D Pulford, 'Cultural Differences in Responses to Real-Life and Hypothetical Trolley Problems' (2014) 9 *Judgm Decis Mak* 65.
52 Daniel Nettle, 'The Watching Eyes Effect in the Dictator Game' (2013) 34 *Evol Hum Behav* – abstract. In this game researchers placed a questionnaire and instructions,

This strengthens the case for asking questions designed from real-life case studies and seeking the reaction of experienced managers to them.[53] Experiments should be transferable and should test real-world hypotheses.[54] Edmonds observes:

> In the real world we are not constrained by having just two options, X and Y: we have a multitude of options, and our choices are entangled in complex duties and obligations and motives. In the real world, crucially, there would be no certainty.[55]

Engel makes the point in an extended way, emphasising that

> The [iterated PD] model makes a lot of assumptions. Interaction is anonymous. There is no communication. It is not possible to solve the conflict by agreement. There is no room for third-party intervention. Interaction is one-shot. It is an interaction between only two individuals. Each individual has to make a yes or no decision and cannot make intermediate choices. There are no dynamics.
>
> All these assumptions matter for the dissolution of cooperation problems.
>
> Individuals are less selfish if they are identified. Communication increases the willingness to take others' legitimate interests into account. If people are able to choose their partners ... similar partners, they cooperate more. A credible threat with third-party intervention almost perfectly removes the dilemma.[56]

Analysing responses to a questionnaire designed "to explore the circumstances when financial incentives can overcome the moral scruples of contractual parties about breaching the contract", Tess Wilkinson-Ryan asserts that it

> is intended to be closely analogous to a real-world contracts context, but there are limits to that analogy. The stakes were real but very low; there

---

a cardboard box and two envelopes, one marked "For you to take away", the other "For a random student", in the cubicle. Also on the desk was £5 comprising four £1 coins and two £0.5 coins. Participants were instructed to put whatever money they wanted to keep into the "take away" envelope, which they could then pocket, and whatever money they wished to donate to a random student in the "random student" envelope.

53 As I observe above, it is difficult to persuade commercial actors to take part in such surveys. Nevertheless, we should be cautious about drawing conclusions from experiments in which the participants are avatars.

54 See Russell Korobkin, 'Empirical Scholarship in Contract Law: Possibilities and Pitfalls' (2002) *U IllLRev* 1033 especially at 1052 and Dennis Patterson, 'The Limits of Empiricism' (2000) 98 *MichLRev* 2738.

55 David Edmonds, *Would You Kill the Fat Man?* (Princeton UP 2013) at 100.

56 Christoph Engel, 'The Proper Scope of Behavioral Law and Economics', Discussion Papers of the Max Planck Institute for Research on Collective Goods (2018) at 8 with references. See also Samir Okasha, reviewing *The Origins of Human Cooperation: Samuel Bowles and Herbert Gintis: A Cooperative Species* (Princeton UP, 2011) at 28 *Biology and Philosophy* 873: "The [folk] theorem only demonstrates the existence of cooperative Nash equilibria; but this says nothing about how or why agents will arrive at them. ... if players have private rather than public information about each other's past moves, as seems quite likely, then the folk theorem does not go through."

was no legal framework in which parties were negotiating and operating; there were no reputation costs, transactions costs, or even social costs to breach.[57]

It might have been easier to list the respects in which a real-world analogy existed; and it is unlikely that the subjects had a meaningful understanding of the context.

It is also important to ensure that there are no credible alternative explanations for phenomena experienced; (the error made by Eisenberg and Miller). In another example, Jonathan Morgan, relying on an experiment carried out on 94 Midwestern University students presented with iterated "Prisoner's Dilemmas", apparently showing trust increasing with repeated interaction, says: "attempting to enforce vague obligations of trust and cooperation will not only be difficult and expensive, but may be counterproductive".[58]

In laboratory conditions, the 94 were offered "non-binding" (whatever that means) contracts, then, in a later transaction, offered a "contract". On acceptance, they were informed, electronically, that "the computer would automatically enforce it".[59] At that point trust apparently decreased. The chief problem with this and similar experiments is the assumption that one can transcribe experimental results from trials involving students to the real world. As Robson notes, this is dangerous.[60] My survey shows that experience may change perspective, so the use of inexperienced avatars arguably reveals little except the reaction of inexperienced avatars.

The second problem is that the researchers appear not to have appreciated the nature of the enforcement advice. I double-checked by asking some of my contacts to consider the short case study in Table 3.2. I received 105 responses and 170 comments.

My respondents are hard-bitten contract professionals; not ingénues. My short survey shows that the "enforce" language may provoke a reduction in trust or other reaction that casts serious doubt on the claim that entering into a formal contract reduces trust. The blatant reference to enforcement arouses suspicion and creates a negative reaction. I cannot pretend that the sample is random. For my purpose, that does not matter. I demonstrate an alternative, plausible, explanation for the so-called reduction in trust.

Interviews work best as conversations, in which the interviewer listens carefully, rather than as question and answer sessions.[61] Allowing online respondents

---

57 Tess Wilkinson-Ryan, 'Incentives to Breach' (2015) *ALER* 290.
58 Morgan, *Contract Law Minimalism*, 69, the claim deriving from Deepak Malhotra and J. Keith Murnighan, 'The Effects of Contracts on Interpersonal Trust' (2002) 47 *Administrative Sci Q* 534. Deakin and others, 'Contract Law, Trust Relations, and Incentives for Co-operation: A Comparative Study', in Jonathan Michie and SF Deakin (eds) *Contracts, Co-operation, and Competition: Studies in Economics, Management, and Law* (OUP 1997), chapter 5, show using an empirical survey that these results may be hard to replicate in the real world.
59 Malhotra and Murnighan. 'Effects'.
60 Robson, *Real World Research*, 4. And see Mintz and others, 'Can We Generalize'.
61 See Robson, *Real World Research*, 281.

Table 3.2 Do Contracts Reduce Trust?

You are negotiating a contract and the negotiations are proceeding normally. Things seem to be reaching the point at which you can both sign. At a late stage in the negotiations your counterparty says to you – "we will enforce this contract".
What do you make of this? How do you react?

Reaction	No.	Comment
I feel threatened I am suspicious Trust is damaged Have I missed something?	26 34	I would show and express my astonishment The word "enforce" implies a battle ahead, it's very "them and us" I would consider that to be slightly hostile and to a certain degree combative behavior. On a positive note – this is a good thing because the counterparty intends to honour the terms; On a negative note – there will be a lot of contract management required if the intention is to adhere strictly to the contract
I would ask what they meant	35	Depends on the tone That would freak me out a bit I would definitely ask the other party what they meant. Definitely would not just ignore.
I wouldn't sign until I have clarification	14	Just raises that sense of chronic unease that we Contracts folks have about our counterparts It is a very odd thing to say (maybe they are French, and their English is not that good?) I would take this as a warning to tread carefully when seeking any further concessions or compromises Why? budget or pressure constraint, dirty trick to get some more advantage, other?
I'm relaxed; this is normal	45	Clients say all kinds of stern and ominous things during a negotiation. Serious businesspeople know that what counts is building a solid relationship and delivering as promised Good, so will we He is testing our resolve
It's aggressive or irritating	15	Slightly aggressive ... I'd probably just let them know that we will too. Aggressive gets an aggressive response This is huffing to inhabit a dominant position. I would make sure that my side was very diligent during the contract to ensure that our actions were well documented

to offer up their opinions in open questions, and to provide written opinion, was intended, as far as possible, to replicate the interviews.

The strength of interviewing is flexibility and the ability to steer conversations. Good interviews allow the interviewee to do most of the talking. Extracting rich, refined, considered data from very senior participants would be difficult using an online survey. As Dr Jennifer Fleetwood observed, in the qualitative training I undertook, an interview is "easy to do badly and hard to do well".[62] Managing an elite elite, a super group, required patience and expertise on my part together with a degree of flexibility. Control was not possible with this group but my background, as a peer, enabled me to identify with them, understand their responses and steer them in the desired direction.[63]

In interviews and online I asked two open questions at the start, asking respondents what they enjoyed about managing contracts and what success meant. I expected this to provide a guide to expert commercial opinion on commercial coherence or business efficacy in generating advice on how these complex contracts work, and are managed, in practice. This definition would be at a relatively high level of abstraction, necessarily so because the question is very wide.

It was important to ask at least some questions that were not too general. For example, in 2005 Vogenauer and Weatherill surveyed 175 enterprises in eight countries.[64] They found that respondents wanted law that enabled trade (87%), is predictable (79%), fair (78%), flexible (61%) or prescriptive 39%. This is useful, but is clearly an example of survey data which worried Adams and Brownsword; showing expectations shared only at a "very high level of generality".[65] I followed open questions with four vignettes, case studies, developed from difficult and controversial cases covered in my thesis.[66] The thread that runs through the vignettes is uncooperative behaviour.

In vignettes, I asked respondents to assess "standard" current options and for advice on how the law and the contract could support them. I expected that a majority would identify communication and governance to create cooperation as important but that legal remedies such as fast-track dispute resolution would be considered extremely useful. I expected enforcement and threat-based

---

62 I like her advice on methodology (in an email): "I'd say that most academics ... learn on the job ... trialling with students, and then with ex-colleagues will be sufficient. Have confidence – there is no such thing as a perfect interview. ... interviews are all different, so even if your guide is fantastic, it will not do the magic in all circumstances and with all respondents. All you can do is your best, and see what happens!"

63 Rebecca E Klatch, 'The Methodological Problems of Studying a Politically Resistant Community' (1988) 1 *Studies in Qualitative Sociology* 73 suggests that young female interviewers may have more success with elites. As a 62-year-old male; I disagree. A peer, an expert, is more likely to be successful. Alvesson and Deetz, *Doing Critical Management Research,* 195, suggest that I am correct.

64 Chapter 7 'The European Community's Competence to Pursue the Harmonisation of Contract Law – An Empirical Contribution to the Debate' in Stefan Vogenauer and Stephen Weatherill (eds) *The Harmonisation of European Contract Law: Implications for European Private Laws, Business and Legal Practice*, vol. 1 (Hart 2006) at 137.

65 John Adams and Roger Brownsword, *Key Issues in Contract* (Butterworths 1995) at 326.

66 On vignettes see Christiane Atzmüller and Peter M Steiner, 'Experimental Vignette Studies in Survey Research' (2010) 6 *Methodology* 128.

remedies to be considered helpful but insufficient. In my vignettes fast-track binding adjudication would almost certainly deter some of the behaviour if a duty to cooperate formed part of the contract.

I considered other vignettes; for example, the Coombes case where a manager had referred to his Secretary as a "bitch". In informal trials, I detected very strong emotional recoil from this and decided against including it.[67] I also considered *Horkulak v Cantor Fitzgerald International* but decided that the use of very strong language would deter respondents.[68] Case studies were part quantitative, with scaled responses, usually using discrete variables, and part qualitative, allowing respondents to offer alternative solutions or other comment.

After that I asked respondents to rate the importance of cooperation and to tell me what cooperation means and entails and how one achieves it. The purpose of these questions was to determine whether cooperation is considered necessary by my respondents, to allow me to assert that cooperation is necessary to business efficacy or commercial coherence in these complex contracts and, in defining cooperation, whether I can find analogies or authority which would allow me to put forward a transcendent concept of cooperation.

3.1.3 Survey – general results

In analysing results variables were reduced to graphs and tabulated to uncover outliers and major variance. I have included a visual map of the results in Table 3.3, which was produced by visual inspection of the graphical data. From this snapshot one can see that the data are robust. Around 70% of cells show little or no variance, 8% show variance in one answer. Approximately 16% of cells show some variance.

3.2 Open questions – enjoyment and success

To provide a framework for the survey and to persuade participants to consider issues in the round I presented respondents with open questions asking what they enjoy about managing contracts and what success means in contract management.[69] Allowing them space and time to expatiate was intended to provide insight into their general thinking about contracts and contract management. That should provide, I hoped, a good introduction to the survey which would allow them to consider fully the difficult questions in the vignettes. I hoped to find many volunteering that cooperation of some kind leads to enjoyment or spells success – saying "win–win", referring to both parties, talking about sharing, common goals,

---

67 *Isle of White Tourist Board v Coombes* [1976] IRLR 413, EAT.
68 *Horkulak v Cantor Fitzgerald International* [2004] EWCA Civ 1287. The Judgment records one incident in which a manager, Mr Amaitis, after a presentation, shouted: "get this shit out of here", "it will never fucking work". Stronger language is also recorded.
69 Robson, *Real World Research*, 256 – the desire to use open-ended questions tends to diminish with experience. This was my first major survey and responses have not diminished my appetite.

Table 3.3 Variance Overview/Snapshot

	Minimal variance		Some variance		Variance – too few responses to draw conclusions		Variance in one answer			Outlier [o/I]	
Subgroup / Question	Co Code	Industry	Seniority	Portfolio	Experience	Gender M/F	Legal Culture	Relational	Familiarity	Profession
4.1											
4.2											Legal [o/I]
4.3											Legal
4.4		o/sour finance [o/I]									
4.5											
5.1											
5.2	17										
5.3	4+14			1–10M							
5.4								US			Legal / Commercial
5.5			Others								
7				<1M							
8.1											
8.2											P.Man / Legal
8.3											
8.4	3							Civil			
8.5	3 [o/I]										Comm [o/I]
8.6			GM								
8.7				<1M							

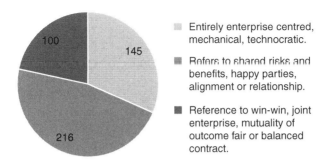

Entirely enterprise centred, mechanical, technocratic.

Refers to shared risks and benefits, happy parties, alignment or relationship.

Reference to win-win, joint enterprise, mutuality of outcome fair or balanced contract.

Figure 3.5 Respondent's Relational Attitude

teamwork, relationships or partnership. I am trying to establish what it is that makes contracts work – in legal terms, what coherence or efficacy means. An explanation of what makes contracts work will play into the development of legal theory and principle. I also wanted to determine whether the opinions of respondents were consistent with those uncovered in other empirical work. The first exercise I undertook when reviewing the 16,000 words and 947 comments made by respondents was to create a rough breakdown to see how many volunteered cooperation or win–win or partnership or joint enterprise or similar terms in open answers (Figure 3.5).

On opening the survey respondents were confronted with a direct open question "what do you enjoy about managing contracts?" Their responses could be broken out into four themes and several sub-themes; the four themes being

• management,
• intellectual challenge,
• meeting people or variety and
• outcomes/performance.

One, a former direct report, taking advantage of a new relationship, said: "Much like you, I enjoyed a good fight in the early part of my career. More recently, I have learned the value of collaboration and am always now seeking to have the other party working for/with me."

I read the data (opinions and comments) several times before tabulating[70] themes and sub-themes and these tables appear below in this subchapter. Scheurich counsels that coding may mask "intractable uncertainties", and that "data reduction techniques" can overlay indeterminacy with our own determinacy, replacing ambiguity with "findings or constructions".[71] I tried to avoid this by keeping coding at

---

70 Created "ordered displays" – Miles and Huberman, *Qualitative Data Analysis,* 90.
71 James Joseph Scheurich, *Research Method in the Postmodern* (Falmer 1997), 61–75.

quite a high, relatively abstract level, quoting directly from respondents to support the coding, and taking the words contextually, rather than basing it on keywords or threads (which is how much coding software works). The quotations I provide are intended to assist in understanding my method.

Management, mentioned by 266, involves the creation and management of relationships, negotiation, collaboration and teambuilding, problem solving and conflict resolution (Table 3.4). Respondents refer to working to the spirit rather than the letter of the contract, using the contract to "drive a strong relationship", being "collegiate" and "achieving common aims".

Intellectual challenge, mentioned 159 times, is described by one respondent: "The enjoyment is orchestrating all these elements to work coherently and achieve the individual and overarching goals. A bit like getting the pieces of a jigsaw to fit together. Two analogies for the price of one!" Turning conceptual business needs into hard and soft obligations, dealing with complexity,

Table 3.4 Management Theme – Enjoying Contract Management

Themes		*Sub-themes*		*Respondent Comment*
Management 266	Creating/ managing relationships 48	Stakeholder management 28		Ensuring you are more aligned to the spirit of the contract, rather than the "letter" I would also want to complete a Project leaving the customer with a positive view of the Business I represent
	Negotiation 70			Reach mutually acceptable outcomes
	Collaboration 35	Joint enterprise 14 Coordination of activities 9	Teambuilding 12 Create happy work environ- ment 2	Working with a partner to achieve common aims Success is when you have been able to develop and create a win-win situation, and the client/supplier would be more than happy to engage in future business collaborations.
	Problem solving or conflict reso- lution 36	Managing chan- ging environ- ment 7	Avoiding escalation 2	If put together and executed properly, it really drives a strong relationship between the parties

Table 3.5 Intellectual Challenge Theme – Enjoying Contract Management

Themes	Sub-themes			Respondent Comment
Intellectual challenge 159	Turning business needs into a contract 64	Dealing with complexity 24	Learning about contracts or contract law 21	I enjoy when I see a Contract stimulates the right behaviour from Contractor.
	Creativity Innovation 33	Wordsmithing 9	Anticipating the future 6	No two contracts are alike

innovation, wordsmithing, recognising that "no two contracts are alike", are part of what respondents enjoy about managing contracts (Table 3.5).

I found 109 mentions of meeting people, variety, interaction or cultural learning (Table 3.6). They said that contracts are each unique, one that"Contracts come to life when people get involved."

Outcome or performance was indicated by 285 comments as an enjoyable aspect (Table 3.7). It is grouped into sub-themes of managing risk, finding "clarity", minimising disputes, making the business smoother, creating value and even "making a difference". Creation of value, delivery to time and budget featured in many responses. One mentioned "the sense of order" and others:

> I enjoy building something that will be providing power after I'm dead.
> Make the world a better place – progress.

Around 20 said that they don't enjoy it – "It's a job".

At first blush this may not seem to educate us as to what a duty to cooperate entails. It does, however, help in assessing what commercial actors expect of contracts and how they manage them, how they make them work. The few who admitted to not enjoying it much still referred to contracts as a necessary evil. Nobody said that they provided a mechanism for punishing the other party or behaving

Table 3.6 Meeting People/Variety Theme – Enjoying Contract Management

Themes	Sub-themes		Respondent Comment
Meeting people Variety 109	Variety 36		Not every day is the same, not every contract is the same, nor every customer etc.

	Interaction with people 57	Cultural learning 16	What I enjoyed was the sheer variety of the work, the opportunity to meet other contract professionals whether they be customers, suppliers, advisers or colleagues.
			    one has to be creative, open minded and culturally interested.
			    Creating a business-to-business relationship is always a person-to-person matter.

Table 3.7 Outcome/Performance Theme – Enjoying Contract Management

Themes		Sub-themes		Respondent Comment

Outcomes, performance 285	Management of risk 29	Achieving clarity 39	Minimise disputes 3	I like the sense of order they bring
				  Everyone stays safe
				  Execution is "fairly painful".

	Make the business possible or smoother 35			Beneficial for both parties
				  The enjoyment comes from finding the sweet spot whereby both (all) parties meet their objectives to a large extent.
				  Business on the basis of a contract that one party is nervous about from day one is not a good way to start a project.

	I don't enjoy it! Not a lot. It's a job. 20	Pragmatic – has to be done 6		A necessary evil to get the job done [contracts] are just a necessary evil

	Win/win create value 54 Make the world a better place – progress 11	Achieve best value for my company 41	Deliver to time and budget 47	Delivering good outcomes
				  Make a difference
				  When I see smiles from recipients, I feel motivated

opportunistically; although a few may have disguised this in making comments about creating value for their company (perhaps the dog that didn't bark).

My next question was directed at what success means in contract management. The main themes which emerged involved contract formation and negotiation, contract execution and contract delivery.

Respondents explained contract formation (Table 3.8) as providing structure ("rules of the game"), aligning objectives, identifying risks, creating clarity, balancing risk and reward, and providing a forum for discussing expectations to be discussed openly to allow each organisation to succeed ("establishing a contractual relationship where each party fully understands the asks, needs and even the future beyond the paper"). Fairness was mentioned 24 times and "win-win" 21 times. Fairness meant different things. In around half the cases it meant a fair contract, followed closely by meaning it was fairly managed. A few thought it meant a fair price (which might be the same as generally fair).

Contract execution (Table 3.9) contained sub-themes of conflict minimisation, consideration and management of risks, managing the relationship and maintaining a safe working environment. Communication was mentioned as one way to ensure good execution ("even when things have gone wrong") and the

Table 3.8 Negotiation and Contract Formation – Success Themes

Themes	Sub-themes		Respondent's Comment
	What is success?		
Contract formation Negotiation	Providing structure 35 Business needs landed 53	Aligned objectives 27	The rules of the game Contract should be a checklist which helps the parties decide on their actions
	Create relative certainty or clarity 81	Identifying the risks 41	Sets the scene for expectations, the framework for delivery and the rules for engagement Ensures no unnecessary scope drift or gold plating
	A fair contract 24	Mutual benefit. Win-win 21	Allowing service expectations, delivery, management information and costs to be discussed openly and for an understanding between to develop so that both organisations can succeed. This ability of [Contract Management] to see things in a holistic way ensures their effectiveness and overall success for all
	Focus on outcomes 5	Acceptable compromises 32	Balance of risk and reward in the contracting experience was properly and fairly reflected

contract described as the "ultimate fallback when nothing works anymore". Minimising conflict and maintaining a good working relationship were mentioned 113 times; one respondent saying that this involves "leading and managing what is not written in the contract" and another that "management is more important than the contract itself".

Unsurprisingly, perhaps, under contract delivery (Table 3.10) the main output was (187 comments) safe and on-time delivery, to price; "key success factors achieved or bettered". Win-win or each party being happy was mentioned by 120 respondents; one saying, "with all heart-valves and relationships intact". Future business ("evokes a common focus to achievement and ultimately … longer term/future working alignment") was mentioned 49 times, which might be fewer than relationalists would anticipate. Obtaining "best value" was mentioned by 34 respondents and, although this might mask some opportunism, some made it clear that this is a mutual concept ("best value outcome for both parties"). One respondent said: "Success to me means when both … work mutually together to maximise their business needs in a harmonise relationship and have mutual respect and trust for each other."

Figure 3.6 gives a selection of interviewees comments; in themes.

The answers reflect the fact that contract in the real world is multidimensional with delivery and relationships at its heart. Interviewees made 19 comments on what they enjoy and 13 on the meaning of success. They referred

Table 3.9 Contract Execution – Success Themes

What is success?			Respondent's Comment
Themes	*Sub-themes*		
Contract execution	Minimum conflict 57 Fair dealing 15	Vigilance to opportunities and risks 14	If done fairly should be the route to success but invariably biased towards one party Handle the contract issues in accordance with the contract fairly
	Safety not compromised; nobody hurt; we all go home. 24	Risks are managed 23 No surprises 4	On balance, contract management is more important than the contract itself, i.e. you can manage a bad contract to a good outcome, and you can mismanage a great contract to a poor outcome.

	Relationship management 21	Good working relationship 45	When you communicate correctly, timely and effectively this ensures a smooth execution of the project, even in cases where things have gone wrong.
			    like to rely on my own ingenuity and ideas and problem-solving skills to avoid escalations or use of contract levers
			    the parties have stated their respective motivations and aspirations, and work together to reach that and actually achieving it
			    Reputation confirmation

Table 3.10 Contract Delivery – Success Themes

What is success?		Respondent's Comment
Themes	*Sub-themes*	
Contract delivery	Project delivered in time, safely and to price 187	All parties' key success factors achieved or bettered within a safety-first driven culture.
	Win-win, each party happy 83	Satisfied customer 37	That all parties involved are content or even better, excited about the outcome. with all heart valves and relationships intact
	Obtain best value 34	Reputation enhanced 5 Trust enhanced 5	Shepherding the deliverers to improve their understanding of the contract,

(*Continued*)

Table 3.10 (Cont.)

	What is success?	Respondent's Comment
Themes	Sub-themes	
	Future business 49	Another key to success is to implement the contract in the way it is meant to be, not in a word-by-word approach
	Lessons learned 5 Continuous improvement 9	Success to me means when both the Operator and the contractor work mutually together to maximise their business needs in a harmonise relationship and have mutual respect and trust for each other.

to the contract as – "For planning"; "A governance mechanism"; "A roadmap for successful business"; and "A management tool". Other comment included – "Get it right up front"; "Working together is success"; "Outcome is more important".

There is a strong focus on management, getting the contract performed and, even in the "intellectual" cadre, a strong focus on converting abstract business

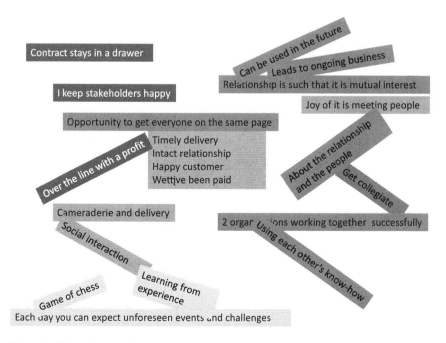

Figure 3.6 Interviewee Comment – Contract Management

needs into a contract. The focus is highly practical, desirous of a relationship, clarity, delivery; all in a complex, diverse world.

I expected to be told that outcome/delivery was success. What I also found was clear emphasis on the joint nature of the contract, and a desire for successful perform-ance which meant delivery/completion. The contract was not seen as a tool for opportunistic behaviour; rather as a framework with hard written elements and softer behavioural elements. The hard elements are a construct within which the parties can fulfil agreed goals and the softer elements are the how. Each is required for success.

3.3 The vignettes/case studies

These case studies were developed from experience and from real-life, adjudi-cated cases. They provide a platform from which one can draw comparison between judicial pronouncement and the needs of the contract manager in the firing-line. I asked respondents to consider both their reactions to the vignettes and the support they need from the contract and the law when things go wrong.

- Vignette 1 considers a situation in which a supplier, having fixed a defective machine, refuses to provide an explanation of the cause.
- Vignette 2 considers how a manager under pressure allocates site accommo-dation where he/she has complete discretion.
- Vignette 3 considers how to manage a situation where time is tight, and a critical subcontractor refuses to perform unless more money is offered.
- Vignette 4 considers next steps when an employer is making thoroughly unreasonable monetary deductions against alleged defective performance.

Against some questions in the following subchapters, I have copied graphs showing variance in some cases and no variance in others. A fuller graphical pic-ture can be found in my PhD thesis.[72]

3.3.1 Vignette 1 – the power and the story – the machine that didn't work and the reluctant supplier

You are George Reynolds, the owner of a business which makes and sells MDF, a material used in many different applications, but most widely known for kitchen worktops and you are the market leader for these. As the business expands you need new premises and you find a suitable location in the North of England but there is no connection to the electricity grid. The Grid's price for a connection is very high

72 C Haward Soper, 'Contract, Conflict and Cooperation: A Critical Analysis of the Common Law Approach to the Breakdown of Modern, Complex, Symbiotic Contracts' (PhD, Leicester University 2018).

and you elect to buy a gas engine, as there is a high-pressure gas supply to the site, and you also install a back-up diesel generator for emergencies.

At first all goes well. The gas engine produces a stable supply and you are able to run at full capacity. However, it develops a vibration and, after consultation with the supplier, you continue to run it. The vibration gets worse and the engine shuts down. The supplier returns, carries out some work on the gas engine, assures you that all is well and leaves. It works again but the vibration returns after a short period, the supplier comes back to the factory, fixes the gas engine again, assures you, again, that all is well and leaves.

This pattern repeats until the supplier advises you that the engine will have to be returned to their factory for repair and you agree to it being uninstalled and returned. During the absence of the engine your line is running at 60% of capacity and other options such as arranging a Grid connection, or a further diesel generator are extremely expensive and very difficult.

After a short period, the machine is returned, reinstalled and appears to work well. You ask the supplier for a report on what had caused the problem, how it had been fixed and reassurance. The supplier refuses to provide a report. The supplier takes the view that you have a working gas engine and that this is the extent of his responsibility. You are pretty surprised and pressurise the supplier for a report, escalating matters because you need the reassurance and the gas engine is critical to you; another interruption in power supply would cause you major problems. You explain this to the supplier. The supplier continues to refuse to supply a report.

This vignette was developed from *J & H Ritchie Ltd v Lloyd Ltd*, involving a used harrow, purchased for around £14,000, which reached the House of Lords.[73] I used the case in training seminars in industry and I was struck by how many commercial/contract/legal players would react with a lawsuit rather than picking up the phone. Four interviewees were presented with this vignette – they wondered just what was going on:

– How much trust do I have? I'm not comfortable.
– Escalation and assurance that the problem won't recur would be enough for me.
– I need an absolute guarantee – I think "the things work by magic anyway".
– Why won't they tell you? They're hiding something!
– First indicate that there may be commercial consequences. In the end escalate.
– Keep Boy Scout badges polished – don't give them any bricks to throw back.
– A great question – I would get an independent assessor in and ask the supplier to work with me.
– Don't reciprocate; don't terminate.

Two hundred and twenty-five other respondents provided comment. The most common option was to talk to the supplier or to try to obtain a better understanding

---

73 *Ritchie* n. 3 above.

of the relationship and what was driving the supplier's behaviour. Some wondered what the supplier had to hide, others whether aggressive price negotiation had contributed. Finding an incentive, a managed solution, such as long-term service agreements, removing "fear of claims", online monitoring services (typical in high-speed rotating machinery contracts[74]), was suggested to help cut through the problems:

- Firstly sit down with the customer to try and negotiate a suitable outcome.
- If the understanding of the report is the goal rather than using the report as evidence to claim compensation, there ought to be some compromise.
- Ultimately you have to find a working relationship to get through these type of issues. Life is too short to continue along this stand-off vein!
- A discussion can be fruitful for both sides, if this will result in a win-win. GR needs warranty and the supplier expects comprehension. Both have to cooperate with each other … to understand the whole picture.
- Is there scope for improving communication to find out WHY supplier is behaving as they are? There may be other reasons why this information is not shared.
- Holding back payment is a one-off trump card and if Client is reliant on the supplier in the longer term this may make matters worse.

One respondent aged "at least ten years" in a similar situation. In general, reaction is analytical. Respondents want to understand why the supplier is behaving like this and want to find a way of getting the report; mainly by discussion and negotiation. A few respondents thought that threats, like blacklisting, or taking service business elsewhere might help. Escalation or leveraging the relationship was mentioned by several. Termination is not regarded as sensible, or practical. Answers are characterised by a desire to play it straight, get to the heart of the problem and find a commercial solution. In discussing fast-track dispute resolution one interviewee said that a judge "should force him to act reasonably".

I asked detailed questions to determine what respondents would do next and for their rankings of normal commercial, contractual and legal remedies (Figure 3.7).

Question 4.1 – Sigh. Reluctantly accept the situation

This is the result I expected; with an overwhelming majority, almost 90%, loath to accept the supplier's brush-off. Some respondents maintained that a report would not solve the problem. It might, however, begin to restore any confidence that had been lost in the machine.

---

74 See e.g. S Inabuaye-Omim, 'Industrial Gas Turbine Condition Monitoring System: An Overview' (39th Engine Systems Symposium, Cranfield University).

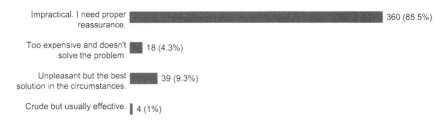

Figure 3.7 Overall Answers to Question 4.1 – Sigh, Accept the Situation?

Question 4.2 – Make sure the user group for this model hears of the problem

Around 73% of participants rate this possibility (Figure 3.8). User groups, usually "by invitation" fora, hosted by manufacturers, allow users to exchange experiences and opinions.[75] They can be a threat or an opportunity in that one might find that the defect is uncommon and minor or that it is serious and the cause unknown. Lawyers are outliers in these answers; apparently much less willing to accept that the user group might be the best solution.

Question 4.3 – Refuse to pay outstanding bills

Over 75% of my respondents thought this the best or an effective solution (Figure 3.9). Of course, it only works if there are outstanding bills. In the case of a sophisticated machine like a gas turbine a manufacturer may make serious money, possibly 90% of their income, in the aftermarket[76] so that a threat

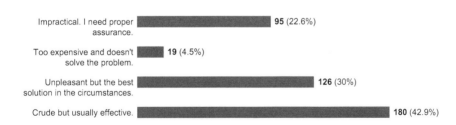

Figure 3.8 Overall Answers to Question 4.2 – Tell the User Group?

75 Stewart Macaulay, 'Non-Contractual Relations in Business: A Preliminary Study' (1963) 28 *Am Sociol Rev* 55 at 64 refers to "gossip exchanged by purchasing agents and salesmen at meetings … of associations".
76 See Aditya Ambadipudi and others, 'Industrial Aftermarket Services: Growing the Core'.

targeted at future revenue may be effective; one respondent pointed out that this remedy may only be effective if there is future business. Another notes that this damages the relationship, and another that it causes hurt in the long term. The reaction of respondents is fairly consistent across subgroups. Interestingly, many lawyers see it as impractical.

Question 4.4 – Terminate; reject the machine; you have wholly lost confidence in the machine and the supplier

Overwhelmingly, 83% considering this too expensive or impractical, consistent across sub-groups, commercial players eschew termination (Figure 3.10). They want to make the contract work. There is a willingness to use self-help remedies as we can see from Figures 3.8 and 3.9 but those remedies fall short of termination. Around 40% of outsourcing respondents thought termination effective whereas 100% of finance people thought it too expensive.

Question 4.5 – Find a reputable third party to inspect the machine, review the problem and report; tell the supplier that you expect them to pay for the report

This third self-help remedy was also thought to be workable, only 24% considering it impractical or too expensive, with 59% considering it the best solution or effective. Female respondents were slightly more positive about it than males.

   The next questions ask respondents to choose between various options designed to produce a cooperative result by forcing the supplier to act reasonably through sanctions or mandatory orders.

Question 5.1 and 5.2 – Provide for fast-track binding procedure allowing you access to the supplier's internal reports or a fast-track process which could force the supplier to provide you a report

Of the respondents, 76% and 89% respectively choose options which say that these would be helpful; 42% and 38% saying they'd be insufficient (if helpful). Insufficient indicated that respondents would not consider this the end of the matter. I had hoped that these remedies, which each provide a report, would be popular as they preserve the contract and provide the reassurance of a report. These results appear to support wider access to fast-track adjudication, now available in the construction industry. There's little apparent difference between them bar the possibility that the supplier may not always produce a full report or that internal reports may be indigestible to the commercial user. Respondents support a remedy furnishing a report which might create the confidence they need in this essential piece of machinery. Oil and Gas majors' respondents are less enthusiastic about fast-track processes.

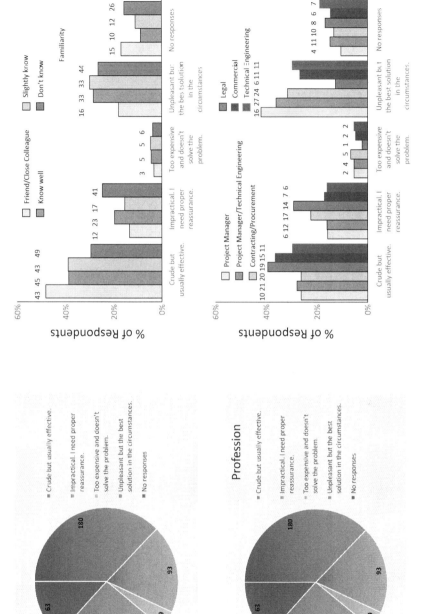

Figure 3.9 Bar Chart and Pie Chart Showing Breakdown of Answers to Question 4.2 by Familiarity/Relationship of Respondent to Author and Professional Discipline

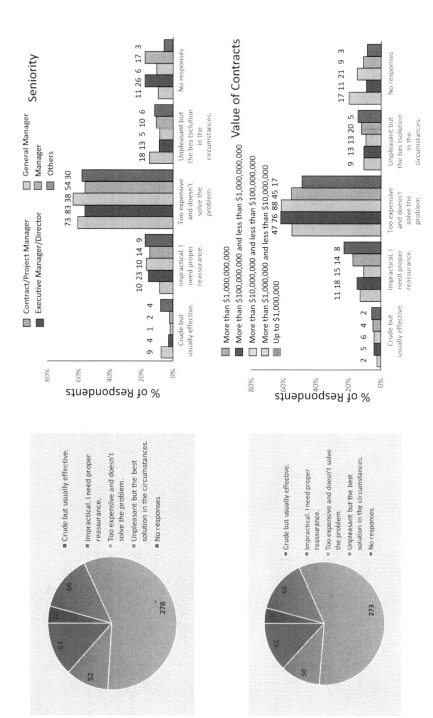

Figure 3.10 Bar Charts and Pie Charts Showing Breakdown of Respondent Answers to Question 4.4, Terminate?, by Seniority of Respondent and by Portfolio Value of Respondent

Question 5.3 – Use the machine and delay commencement of warranty and acceptance until the supplier gives you a report

Of the interviewees 52.8% considered this helpful and sufficient and 40.3% helpful but insufficient. This self-help remedy, described as "powerful" by one respondent, depends on the terms of the contract. Clients often insist on express terms which extend the warranty by the length of time that a machine is out of action. In this case, one is faced with a machine that does work but in which the client's confidence is low or non-existent.

Question 5.4 – Allow termination and rejection for non-cooperation or unreasonable behaviour

Of the interviewees 26.6% thought that this might put an end to the matter; 73.5% considered it helpful but insufficient or insufficient. In *Ritchie* Lord Brown described Lloyd's behaviour as unreasonable.[77] Notwithstanding the egregious nature of the refusal (Lord Hamilton referred to a "lack of candour" and Lord Brown noted that Lloyd's "adamantly refused to reveal the nature of the problem"[78]) respondents show a significant preference for information over termination.

Those with a US common law background were more likely to find termination to be helpful (Figure 3.11). Those with lower value portfolios are also more amenable to termination.

Question 5.5 – Provide that the supplier pays you for the time you have spent in trying to resolve this

Only 29.4% of respondents thought this helpful and sufficient. Like other punitive measures this is not generally viewed as sufficient. It may be helpful, but it will not solve the problem.

3.3.2 Vignette 2 – decide or concur? You have a decision to make: on a multi-contractor site how do you allocate accommodation space?

You are the project manager for Fracking Heaven, a well-known and popular player in the shale oil industry. You are running FH's latest major project in a sensitive location in Europe where you have been allowed to build a significant gas gathering and storage facility. The site is not as large as you would like, one of the concessions made during negotiations with local authorities. Part of the site is reserved for the accommodation of the temporary workforce you need. This space will be divided between

---

77 *Ritchie* (n. 3 above) at [41].
78 Ibid. See Lord Brown at [41] and [43] quoting Lord Hamilton.

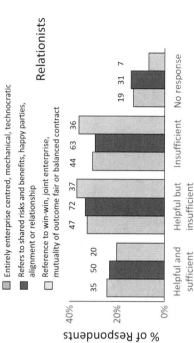

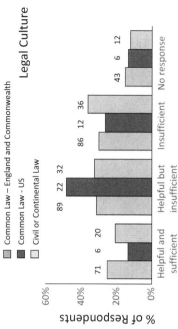

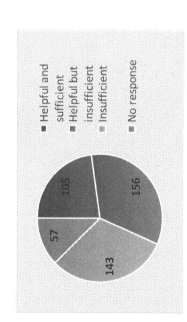

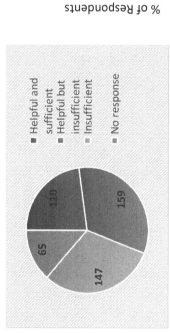

Figure 3.11 Bar Charts and Graphs Showing Breakdown of Answers to Question 5.4 ('Termination for Non-Cooperation?') by Legal Culture and Relational Attitude

multiple contractors. The contract provides that allocation of space is to be determined by you, in your absolute discretion.

As contractors begin to apply for space on site serious differences arise as to how much space each should be allocated for accommodation. Typically, a balance is struck between "Jack and Jill" units where a shower room and toilet is shared, and Executive Units for more senior people. The differences, and these are, as you know, difficult and sensitive issues in such camps, tend to revolve around the question of who is senior and who isn't, and the definition of senior is not the same for each contractor.

You are extremely busy, very pressed for time, and this doesn't appear to be a priority. But a decision is needed urgently as contractors are preparing to set up their sites.

You ask your Commercial Manager to look out Fracking Heaven's manual and policy. You allocate space on the basis of that policy. You have the discretion and you have no time.	*16.5%*
You have found the FH manual and policy. You circulate this to all affected contractors and ask for comment. Once you have received comment you allocate space on the basis of the FH manual and policy. At least you have given out the appearance of consultation.	*9.2%*
Bring everyone together quickly. Take a round table discussion on the issue. Try to gain agreement. Make policy based on the best possible option for all.	*58%*
As the second option but this time you have read all the submissions and you really do think that FH's policy is best for all.	*16.3%*

This vignette is designed to test decision-making when the decision-maker seems to have unlimited discretion. It does not directly deal with an enabling decision. Instead I address a fairly typical management decision in which a busy manager has to decide how to accommodate members of his wider team in a tight location under time pressure. There were 410 responses (Figure 3.12).

There is a danger in this vignette of social acceptability bias; that respondents will give the "correct" answer. It is present in all vignettes but more so in this one which involves a manager and her/his relationship with people in a more direct way than the others which are more corporate matters.

In interviews, many respondents asserted that this is the sort of decision they would take very seriously, chiefly because fairness ("fair and equitable", "establish commonality", "treat each group fairly") was important. The vulnerable, such as disabled personnel or females working late, must, for example, be given appropriate consideration.

The creation of team spirit by joint decision-making and consultation was vital. Of the 14 interviewees who addressed this topic one said; "get on with it". Others insisted that one "make time", "find time", "walk the site", don't "apply rules dogmatically"; that it is "critical" that people are happy, in one case

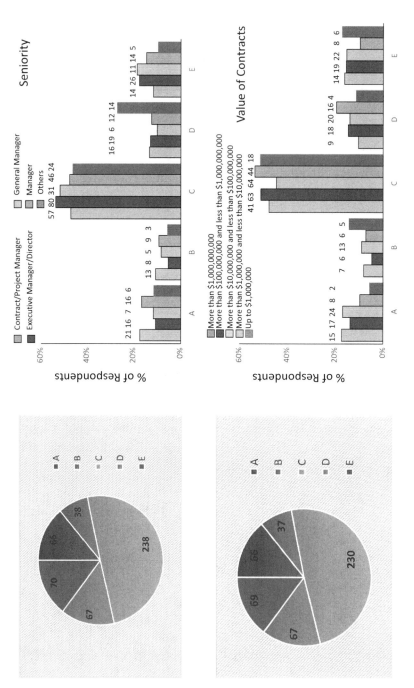

Figure 3.12 Bar Charts and Pie Charts Showing Answers to How to Use Discretion, by Respondent Seniority and Portfolio Value

asserting "it's their home!" and another that "it's worth the effort". The words felt real. They didn't appear to be for effect or approval (I detected no social acceptability bias). Those with less experience were marginally more likely to allocate based on company policy. Overwhelmingly even that group prefers consultation to instruction. Although this does not demonstrate directly that respondents believe that discretion should be controlled it shows a tendency to self-discipline, elevating the managerial imperative of the contract over the levers of power.

I advised respondents that I was not directing them to the best way to make a decision but was asking them to be honest and say how they would really react in a difficult situation. I predicted "an overwhelming number to choose the third answer below in the hypothetical context but in a real situation where there is little time to think I wonder whether that really reflects what would happen". The widest claim I can make is that it seems unlikely that commercial actors would object to being required by contract to take these decisions in a fair and impartial manner.

The only reference I can find to empirical work in contractual discretion is Jonathan Morgan's assertion of a "documented preference" for leaving control of "abuse" to extra-legal mechanisms.[79] Dr Morgan describes objections by "merchants" to Karl Llewellyn's proposed reform of the perfect tender rule in the US,[80] that they could find extra-legal methods of dealing with opportunism,[81] and extends this to a claim that merchants disapprove Court imposed rules on the use of contractual discretion, saying in other work that: -"it is in the highest degree doubtful that sophisticated commercial parties would want anything to do with it".[82]

I reviewed various modern forms of construction and engineering contract to determine whether merchants feel the need to limit judicial control of discretion. I reviewed the Joint Contracts Tribunal Standard Form of Building Contract 2005, the LOGIC Construction Conditions (for North Sea Oil work), the Institution of Civil Engineers Form of Contract 7th edn 1999, their New Engineering Contract and their Design and Construct contract form. None contained provisions which tried to water down judicial control.[83] The MF/1 form,

79 Jonathan Morgan, 'Resisting Judicial Review of Discretionary Contractual Powers' (2015) *LMCLQ* 484 at 488.

80 Zipporah Batshaw Wiseman, 'The Limits of Vision: Karl Llewellyn and the Merchant Rules' (1987) 100 *HarvLRev* 465 at 494.

81 Jonathan Morgan, 'Against Judicial Review of Discretionary Contractual Powers' (2008) *LMCLQ* 230 at 238–239.

82 Morgan, 'Resisting Judicial Review', 484.

83 Stephen Furst and others (eds) *Keating on Construction Contracts* (Sweet & Maxwell 2006) at 801–2 – the architect under the JCT form must act in a fair and unbiased manner in every function. Noting that clause 2(8) of the ICE form provides that the engineer shall act impartially and that this does not appear in the design and construct form, Brian Eggleston, *The ICE Design and Construct Contract: A Commentary* (Blackwell Scientific Publications 1994)

published by the Institution of Mechanical Engineers, provides that: "Wherever ... the Engineer is required to exercise his discretion: he shall exercise such discretion fairly within the terms of the Contract and having regard to all the circumstances." There is no evidence that merchants feel the need to respond to more than 100 years of judicial control over the activities of certifiers and decision-makers.

3.3.3 Vignette 3 – an offer he can't refuse? The blackmailing subcontractor – that's you!

You are the owner of Downhole Giftig, and you are a subcontractor to Fracking Heaven, a major and popular player in the shale oil industry. You supply drilling and analytics and you are absolutely critical to the success of their latest project which is very expensive and has been allowed a limited window in which to carry out a drilling programme.

As the project progresses and as you are in the final stages of setting up on site it becomes apparent to you that you have badly under-priced the work. The under-pricing is so serious that it may result in the business going broke; and closing down. Next week you have to commence an activity which is critical, that is – any delay to it will delay the entire project. Once started this activity cannot be stopped except in the event of a very serious accident or major emergency. You know how critical this activity is to the client.

You decide that the best way to deal with this is to speak to the client, advising Fracking Heaven that they must pay you more. If not, you explain, you will have to stop work and leave the site. You know that it is impossible for Fracking Heaven to replace you in time.

This vignette was developed from *Williams v Roffey Bros and Nicholls (Contractors) Ltd,*[84] with extreme elements of duress added – and is not an uncommon situation for businesspeople (as indicated by survey respondents).

Interviewees were interested, as usual, in why the problem had arisen; some taking a pragmatic approach:

– This is business.
– Sub can only do this once.
– Done deal – live with it!
– Once you've paid the money wave goodbye to it.

---

asserts at 148 that this makes no difference. I also reviewed a standard form used by an oil super-major – with the same result.

84 *Williams v Roffey Bros and Nicholls (Contractors) Ltd* n. 3 above. I have twice experienced existential threats in my career.

Others were less relaxed:

- It's an outrage. Try "weasel" words in deal. Contractor has you over a barrel – live with it!
- Like the Greek Government.

Others had ethical and procedural concerns, saying, "Corporate governance is an issue" and there should be "Ethical consideration of other bidders".

Others advised negotiating, "Should be a sensible conversation", and cIf they really have a major problem".

There were 134 comments made by respondents; over forty commenting that the best solution was renegotiation.

Over 30 questioned the contracting process saying that the client may have created the mess by poor bid management and market analysis. In that case they had little sympathy. Others differentiated between major and minor players ("I wouldn't negotiate if it was Schlumberger"):

- A professionally capable client would have recognised at the outset that the offered price was less than the necessary price. It is a poor business entity which – led by its lowest-cost focussed procurement function – must accept responsibility for the failure here ... Business realists now need to take control.
- Here's where we really appreciate the need for a proper RFP due diligence activity.
- In real world terms, Fracking Heaven would have tendered this part of the project and had several quotes. It follows that Downhole was significantly lower in cost than the others and Fracking Heaven should have questioned the costs before awarding a contract that was much lower than the others. Fracking Heaven owns a part of the problem.
- Accepting a lo-ball bid from a "weak" contractor is at the Client's risk. As they say: you get what you pay for.

Others suggested helping with cash flow or procurement to alleviate the financial burden. Many were familiar with such practices and differentiated between deliberate underbidding and errors in bidding.

Other comments included:

- Depends on who it is. If it's a major, they should live with the problem. If we knew about the under-pricing I may renegotiate. Costs me a fraction of the cost if the sub goes bust. I might tell them they'd be blacklisted. It's also an ethical issue. We may have got our subcontractor selection wrong.
- Never been a blackmailer therefore unable to comment further.
- Have frequently paid all or a significant part of the sum demanded as it was in our interests to do so.
- A lot depends on the relation between DG and my business.
- Prop him up for your project and when that is delivered, cease to support.
- I would negotiate if there has been a genuine error.
- The client should know whether the price is fair but in the end this is business.
- Pay up. The sub has abused the position but there is no time to deal with it.

Although one can detect fatalism or realism in responses most consider the best approach to be discussion or negotiation. Context remains one key; it depends on the cause and it depends on who is making the threat. The project remains worth protecting, and that means keeping the contract alive, even in the face of an existential threat.

Question 8.1 – Fracking Heaven tells you to get on with it; they will not discuss price or progress on these terms

Respondents seem to consider it essential to do something, over 95% recognise that stonewalling won't work, with almost no variance between subgroups (Figure 3.13 and Figure 3.14).

Question 8.2 – Fracking Heaven pays up angrily, reserving its rights and makes it clear that this is not an acceptable way to do business

Few, 25.7%, regard this as practical; most, 59.9% considering it likely to lead to delay or cause major problems. Those with higher portfolios and more experience were less likely to agree that it is practical. Project managers were most likely to agree that it is practical and lawyers least likely.

Question 8.3 – Fracking Heaven makes an offer to pay roughly enough to cover a major part of your loss

This is regarded, by over 78%, as a constructive approach and one that will work (Figure 3.15). Russell Weintraub finds, in a survey of corporate General Counsel, that, overwhelmingly, a request for price modification would be considered.[85] My respondents observed:

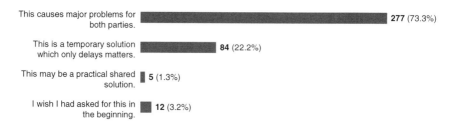

Figure 3.13 Bar Chart Showing Overall Answers to Question 8.1 – The Client Tells You to Get on with it and Refuses to Discuss Terms

---

85 Russell J Weintraub, 'A Survey of Contract Practice and Policy' (1992) *WisLRev* 1 at 19.

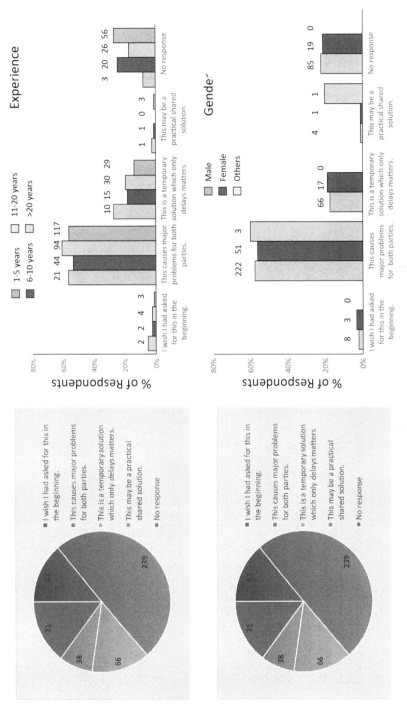

Figure 3.14 Bar Charts and Pie Charts Showing Answers to Question 8.1 by Gender and Length of Experience

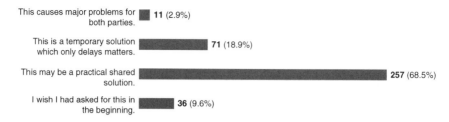

Figure 3.15 Bar Chart Showing Overall Answers to Question 8.3 – Does an Offer to Cover a Major Part of the Loss Solve the Problem?

– If there has been an inadvertent under-pricing, sometimes it is best to accept that a re-negotiated price is needed. … But if the under-pricing appears to have been tactical or reckless, that is another matter …
– Vital to try to deal with the problem through a negotiated settlement.

A later vignette in Weintraub's article poses a similar question to mine except that there is no real fault by the seller who has offered to sell oil at a price which would now ruin him. Around 35% of Counsel took a "too bad" approach while 60% thought that performance should be excused, or the price adjusted to give something like a fair outcome for both.[86] One of my respondents said, "keep away from the lawyers" and one or two others made similarly depressing comments. Likewise, one of Macaulay's interviewees claimed that one "can settle any dispute if you keep the lawyers and accountants out of it".[87]

Question 8.4 – Fracking Heaven terminates the contract forthwith and orders you to leave site, and to deliver all technical data immediately

Over 90% considered this to cause major problems or create delay. One respondent said "I have rarely, if ever, heard of a client terminating when faced with a dilemma such as this – it's suicide". In the scenario described termination might be impractical. I followed up 111 respondents of the 310 who said that termination would cause major problems and asked whether, were time available, their answer would be different. Of 66 replies six indicated that they would now terminate (another said: "as a last resort"). Even in this extreme example respondents baulk at termination. Many explained their thinking in commercially pragmatic terms (which law and economics scholars might recognise as transaction cost analysis); that replacing DG might end up costing more

---

86 Ibid. at 41.
87 Macaulay, 'Non-Contractual Relations', 61.

than a negotiated solution.[88] One said he'd still negotiate "but only after first ascertaining the actual reasons for DG's initial failure".

Another said:

– This scenario may not be plausible unless the Customer already has another vendor on standby ... If the sub made an honest error and there is no competitive vendor that can be engaged in time, I would renegotiate the contract and ensure that the there is an appropriate sharing of the financial risk. My experience suggests that bringing a vendor at such a late time period would drive higher risk in terms of technical and safety performance ...

One of the six said: "It´s a thin line. The assumption was that getting another supplier as a 'serious option' includes confidence on cost and timing. If that´s not there, the answer would be to further negotiate."

Question 8.5 – Fracking Heaven talks to your bank, in an effort to determine whether it can buy you out

Just over half, 54.2% considered that this would cause major problems or create delays, with 39.6% thinking it a practical shared solution. Ambivalence best describes the responses to this complex option.[89]

Question 8.6 – Fracking Heaven asks you to attend urgent meetings, saying that it should be possible to find a shared, fair solution

This option commands serious support, only 14.7% considering it to cause major problems or create delays. It reflects respondents' expressed preference for communication, negotiation and give and take.

Question 8.7 – Fracking Heaven offers third-party expert facilitation or mediation to resolve the problem without any preconditions

The proportion considering this to be a practical solution is 66.4%, slightly higher than that which said the same to 8.3 (paying a major part of the loss). A high number (33.3%) thought it would cause major problems or create delays. But it doesn't command the support that urgent meetings does.

Respondents were able to select more than one answer when asked to consider whether certain remedies or next steps would help.

Question 9.1 – Force you to repay any extra monies the client has paid in order to keep you working

This question asks respondents to rate possible solutions for deterring such behaviour, although, if the subcontractor is truly on the verge of

---

88 Some respondents quoted in Lisa Bernstein, 'Beyond Relational Contracts: Social Capital and Network Governance in Procurement Contracts' (2015) 7 *J Legal Anal* 561 at 570–571 say much the same.

89 Suggested by a fellow student – Dr Robert Coles.

bankruptcy, little can be done to deter. 271 respondents feel that forcing disgorgement is impractical, with 184 feeling that it might be practical.

Question 9.2 – Force you to repay any money over and above a reasonable price for the work

246 think that forcing repayment of some or all of the money might act as a deterrent, with 188 disagreeing. Roger Halson suggested this possible outcome.[90]

Question 9.3 – Make parties enter into open and constructive negotiation overseen by neutral Court appointed expert

225 respondents thought that this might work, with 250 less enthusiastic. I wonder whether using the prefix "fast-track" might have made this option more attractive. Time may be the factor that makes the option less attractive, especially when compared to the next option.

Question 9.4 – Provide fast-track dispute resolution with the power to make you perform

This solution is felt to be practical. 319 thought that it would act as a deterrent and/ or "might work". 132 thought that there was unlikely to be enough time or that it was impractical. From a legal perspective any solution involving specific performance involving complex activities is likely to be difficult to manage. I expected those from continental legal cultures to be more attracted to this specific implement but that is not borne out by the results (Figure 3.16).

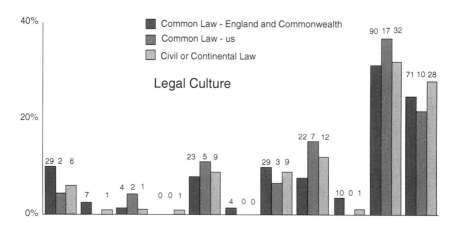

Figure 3.16 Responses by Legal Culture to Would Fast Track Dispute Resolution Help?

---

90 Roger Halson, 'Opportunism, Economic Duress and Contractual Modifications' (1991) 107 *LQR* 649 – at 677 suggesting that the law recognise contract "modification" if it is "reasonably related to the impact of unanticipated circumstances upon the performing party".

Question 9.5 – Enable the client to take control of your equipment and manpower and perform in your place

276 thought this impractical, with 165 thinking it might work. Many contracts make such provisions, but it is extremely unusual for them to be used.

Question 9.6 – Support solutions reached by negotiation if the parties have been open and cooperative and outcome has been "fair"

370 thought this right, with 79 considering that passing of time or other factors might make it impractical. This reflects the basic thrust of much of the comment on this and other vignettes that negotiation, communication and problem solving are at the heart of good management of contracts.

Macaulay found in a survey of ten purchasing people that "They expected to be able to cancel orders freely subject only to an obligation to pay for the seller's major expenses."[91] It is not clear what the contract(s) said about this, which is, in effect, recovery of the reliance value. In my experience, this is a typical express provision in purchasing contracts in a manufacturing environment. Andrew Robertson therefore misinterprets the data when he says that this reflects a disjunction between law and practice.[92] Beale and Dugdale did not replicate Macaulay's finding, but found that "the practice appeared to be quite close to the legal position", especially that lost profits would be recovered where the cancellation was non-consensual.[93]

The general view expressed by this group reflects the views of those who took part in vignette 3; even where the "adjustment" (Macaulay's term) is created by egregious behaviour, businesspeople want to talk it through and avoid invoking the law or terminating. This is consistent with Daintith's work on long-term iron ore contracts (LTCs): "Despite their rigidity and lack of sophistication, iron ore LTCs are, with rare exceptions, still in place after a very violent shake-up in the industry."[94] Daintith posits a reason for his findings as: "The LTC creates a privileged trading relationship … of great importance in times of difficult markets, of glut or scarcity, … by rendering unambiguous each party's claim to remain in business relations with the other."[95] That is similar to those respondents who talked to me of the risks of and costs of change. In the LTC

---

91 Macaulay, 'Non-Contractual Relations', 61, and Hugh Beale and Tony Dugdale, 'Contracts between Businessmen: Planning and the Use of Contractual Remedies' (1975) 2 *Br J Law Soc* 45 at 53.
92 Andrew Robertson, 'The Limits of Voluntariness in Contract' (2005) 29 *MULR 179* at 209. See Beale and Dugdale, 'Contracts between Businessmen', 52.
93 See also Beale and Dugdale, 'Contracts between Businessmen', 52–53.
94 Terence Daintith and Gunther Teubner, *Contract and Organisation: Legal Analysis in the Light of Economic and Social Theory* (De Gruyter 1986), 186.
95 Ibid. 187–188.

example this would be exacerbated by the fact that in that market there were relatively few players.

Deakin and Michie find "hardship" clauses, providing for adjustment in the event of an unforeseen contingency, prevalent in German contracts; in contrast to a common British view that they "could be confusing".[96] Oliver Williamson makes a hollow claim that when purchasing customised material buyers can feel safer since sellers will not withhold supply.[97] I would rather expect the opposite; customised stuff will require a longer lead time and the transaction is more complex than widgetting so the supplier has considerably more leverage. One can see from the survey that more cooperation is required or expected in non-supply type contracts. No participant expressed surprise that a provider of a customised solution would behave like this.

Williamson also claims, with no data given, that, in the case of plant construction, a "presumption of joint profit maximisation is warranted" through the emergence, "ordinarily", of vertical integration under single ownership.[98] Not one participant mentioned the idea of vertically integrating the business to attain better governance; and, indeed, the answers to questions 8.5 and 9.5 militate against vertical integration.

3.3.4 Vignette 4 – is it about the ketchup? – the opportunistic and unreasonable client who poisons the relationship

You are the Vice President of Terrible Grub Inc, a major facilities management contractor, and one of your many contracts is with a large hospital, the Titchborne Trust. The contract is complex and includes maintenance of non-medical equipment, catering, cleaning, retail facilities, car parking and other ancillary work.

After a messy bedding down period the work begins to go well but relationships between your personnel and those of your client begin to break down.

The Trust is allowed to deduct money if a performance failure occurs – £5 (Minor), £15 (Medium) and £30 (Major). The Trust makes many very large deductions, for example £46,000 because a small box of out-of-date tomato ketchup sachets is discovered in a store (the ketchup wasn't a type used by you and you don't know how the sachets got there and the £46,000 is calculated by multiplying the number of sachets by £30 by the number of days the Trust claims they were in the store), £71,055 because a supervisor has not signed off a cleaning schedule (the Trust claimed that a multiple Major deduction would be made every day until the fault was remedied but this fault can't be remedied), £25,000 because the temperature readings of refrigerators were not taken on one ward in the afternoons even though that ward isn't used in the evenings. A similar approach is taken by the Trust on so many issues that around 35% of your annual fee was to be deducted.

96 Michie and Deakin, *Contracts, Co-operation, and Competition*, 124.
97 Oliver E Williamson, *The Economic Institutions of Capitalism* (Free Press 1985), 77.
98 Ibid. 78–79.

Patient satisfaction with your performance is very high and, in your opinion, and on the basis of your monthly reports, you are performing very well. There has been a lot of correspondence between your managers and the Trust, but this has failed to resolve matters and it is clear that the atmosphere is very bad, and people are very frustrated.

You write to your opposite number questioning the calculations, showing that they are far out of line with the contract, saying that the Trust's attitude and behaviour was demoralising and suggesting a meeting so that the parties could work together in a more positive manner. Unhelpfully, the Trust's Manager tells you something along the lines that the Trust's stance is: "how much do you want to pay to retain the contract?"

Squalid behaviour like this is notoriously part of life in the construction industry.[99] One author records that "Commercial intimidation was rife, ... thousands of firms were forced out of business".[100] The vignette is based on the facts in *Medirest*, a case in which the commercial decision-making in an NHS Trust was described as "absurd" by Cranston J in the High Court.[101] Even with the Trust retaining large sums of money and refusing to negotiate or explain, the attitude of commercial players is that one plays a long game, talks, manages. Even when furious with bad behaviour ("They don't give a shit about the contract") termination is not considered a sensible way to assuage wrath.

The nine interviewees who addressed this vignette enjoyed it. Many felt that management had failed and indicated a need to find a way to restart dialogue:

– I am pretty pissed off with my account manager – annoyed it wasn't picked up earlier.
– Regain relationship. Recoup losses later.
– Have a conversation that recognises I have stepped in late.

Trust and confidence came up several times:

– Why has trust and confidence evaporated?
– Fundamental trust problem.

Others wanted to understand why things had happened

– Is there another agenda?
– Is it about the ketchup? [rhetorical]
– It is probably a budget issue.

---

99 See Stella Rimington, quoted in Ch. 2 n. 302.
100 James Pickavance, *A Practical Guide to Construction Adjudication* (John Wiley & Sons 2015), 1.2.
101 *Medirest High Court* n. 3 above.

And in reviewing their options opinions varied although most still believed that talking things out would be best:

– Tiered relationship needed. Carry on and hope.
– Fighting fire with fire will make matters worse/digs deeper trenches.
– No value in keeping this contract. There is no alignment.
– Draw line in sand. I'm not prepared to pay a penny.
– Can be straightened out but not through threats.

In Rome, I asked 22 participants to write down their reactions. Four would prepare an exit strategy, one would use it immediately. Five mentioned root cause analysis or understanding the context. One thought that mediation might be the next step and eight that negotiation was the right approach. Eight wondered whether they could find a way to resolve the problem through increasing scope and finding a way to help the Trust with what they assumed to be a budget problem. Seven went into transaction cost analysis, pointing out that both parties would be hurt in any permanent breakdown. Seven mentioned governance. Here is a selection of their observations:

– Express shock/concern/anger.
– Meet in person with opposite number and talk like a human not a contract.
– Bring the box of ketchup to the meeting and get a discussion going on the reality … do they want to be in the press … Ridicule.

In Leicester responses were similar. They included:

– Repair the relationship … prefer to have discussions.
– Trust will carry on until they get a lawyer's letter. Flush it out.
– Softer issues … Speak to CEO …
– Escalate … pick up the phone … at VP level.
– Go to Trust Board … legal letter in back pocket … Infer it's not easy to replace us.

One hundred and nine respondents commented on the vignette. A few wondered whether there was an ethical issue:

– [B]ehaviour of Trust management may be a hint for bribery.
– Is [this] an attempt to discredit in order to appoint a more favoured contractor?
– Their behaviour seems to be directed at getting us out without telling us why. Maybe they can get the services cheaper or someone in the Trust does not like us. It can be anything, even corruption.
– I see a compliance aspect in the comment from Trust's manager.

Others felt that it might be possible to rescue things through good management and communication:

– [A]lignment, team building, and other ways of building a collaborative relationship right from the beginning, with sponsor level support is needed …
– [D]ifficult to get a feel for whether the trust are operating an informal policy of using the fines as a type of discount scheme or there is somebody in the organization that has some personal issue with your business … necessary to find the decision-maker behind this trust policy and work on them. After that I would want to review if the contract is worthwhile.
– [F]ind the single person in the Trust responsible for this behaviour and attempt to address personally.
– Adversarial relationships very hard to break and will poison the contract.
– [F]ile a claim in court or request arbitration. This action will elevate the issue to the executives of the Trust.
– [B]end over backwards to support the customer and work through the areas of dispute, but when your head touches the floor it's time to reconsider the approach. Ultimately I would escalate to CEO, even shareholders and ask them if this is how they expect their company to operate (with a lack of moral fibre) and driven by a lack of values. If they come back and say Yes – get out as quickly and as prudently as you can and then sue them!

A few had direct NHS experience; the differences are striking:

– Misguided target-driven NHS contracts along with badly motivated or incapable managers, are a particular target for my own ire.
– I am a NED in a NHS Foundation Trust! Given the values in the UK NHS I doubt if this situation is UK based.
– Experienced this behaviour on a PFI contract … Negotiation and dialogue worked in the end.

Other comment included:

– [D]etermine what is the knot of the problem, is it an individual unreasonable behaviour, in this case, you negotiate the termination of the bad apple. If it is a bullying corporate behaviour, then run away.
– The value of the business is key here – this may only be a contract for one hospital but a reputation for being difficult can have a ripple effect on other contracts …
– [U]nlikely that the Trust's management will back down on a systematic decision to "kill the contractor".

Reciprocating:

• was not a viable choice because it included "inflating" invoices;
• (in accordance with tit for tat, game theory) may be a temporary solution if carried out in a controlled manner;
• Fighting fire with fire not very attractive, stooping to their level.

– Both parties are failures. "Everyone end with a black eye" … when we first hear of anything like this we walk away. The trust can afford to waste money, the supplier cannot.
– I would also suggest to install a CCTV system to find out who is smuggling stale ketchup into my stores.
– [T]ake action immediately when the client acts unreasonably thereby clearly demonstrating that you will not tolerate this behavior.

Almost all would try to find a way to resolve the issue short of walking away; preferring to manage the issue.

I asked respondents what they would do next, ranking answers 1–5 in preference.

Question 11.1 – Rely on the contract. It may take time, but things will work out in the end

Respondents split roughly 2–1 in their answers with two-thirds prepared to rely on the contract.

Question 11.2 – Keep trying. Keep asking for the removal of unreasonable managers. Tell the trust your patience isn't unlimited

This more active solution attracts more support with over 80% selecting options 1–3, meaning that they keep asking the Trust to deal with the manager making the deductions.

Question 11.3 – Terminate. Walk away. Take them to court. You've tried everything else

Only 19% selected options 1–2, with over 80% selecting 3–5. Very few wish to terminate and start legal action.

From these responses, it is tolerably clear that respondents overwhelmingly wish to make the contract work. Optimism abounds. Termination is slightly more attractive to those of a continental legal culture than others; it may be that they are less familiar with such behaviour (Figure 3.17). Those in contracting/procurement are more likely to terminate.

Question 11.4 – Reciprocate. Fight fire with fire. Inflate invoices. Make claims. Record every minor and major problem. Notify the Trust in detail often

Only 18.3% of respondents selected options 1–2, with 81.7% being neutral or less and selecting 3–5.

Question 11.5 – Work to rule. Read the contract very carefully. Do the minimum necessary. Query instructions insisting on clarity and detail

This tactic gained more traction, with over 82% selecting options 1–3, and just 17.5% 4–5. I suspect that the difference in the attractiveness of 11.5 when

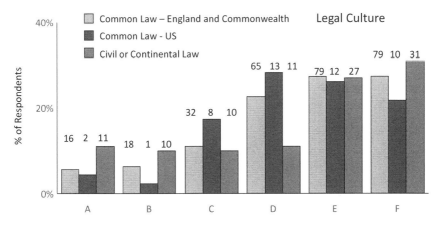

Figure 3.17 Bar Chart Showing Responses by Legal Culture to Question 11.3 (Terminate?)

compared to 11.4 is that it keeps players onside, working to contract, respecting the contract, whereas fighting fire with fire is seen as behaving just as deplorably as the Trust. One respondent described inflating invoices as "unethical and illegal". One thought reciprocating might work if carried out in a "controlled manner". Work to rule is a sulking approach but it might well be effective especially if the source of the trouble is one manager. Those with less experience and those in one major engineering/infrastructure enterprise appeared to be more favourable to a work to rule approach (Figure 3.18).

I asked respondents to rank remedies on a 1–5 scale for their effectiveness in deterring the Trust.

Question 12.1 – Fast, effective governance allowing senior level intervention

84.6% selected 1 or 2 and 13% selected 3. Only 2.2% thought this not very or ineffective. Facilities managers, those in outsourcing and IT were more likely to agree that this would be very effective, as were project manager and commercial respondents (Figure 3.19). One respondent said "Contractually oblige the parties to participate in regular meetings and include disputes on the agenda: Minutes ... distributed to senior management/board level."

Another said that only senior level intervention would resolve the conflicts – in *Medirest*, it didn't.

Question 12.2 – Dispute Resolution Board by a third party capable of making fast, binding decisions

71.5% chose answers 1 or 2, with 21.9% selecting 3 and only 6.4% saying this would either be ineffective or not very effective. This shows a clear preference

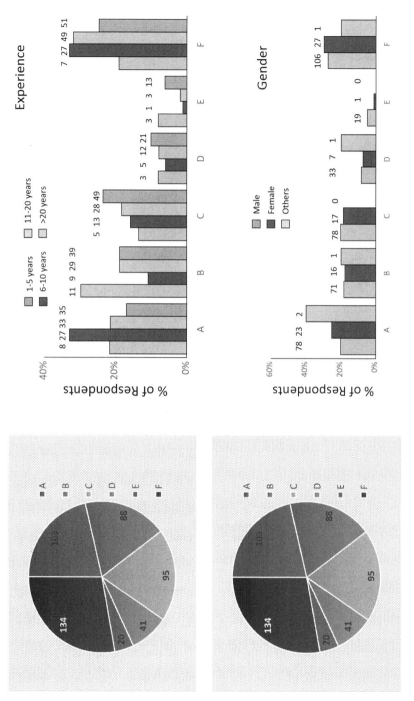

Figure 3.18 Bar Charts and Pie Charts Showing Responses by Experience and Gender on Whether Working to Rule Would Be Effective

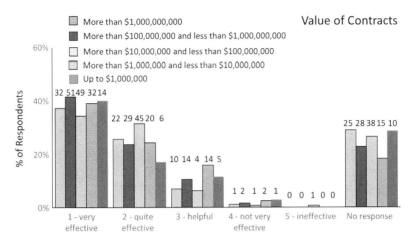

Figure 3.19 Bar Charts Showing Responses on whether Fast Effective Senior Management Intervention Would Be Effective by Respondent's Portfolio Value
and Seniority

for fast solutions, whether created by management intervention or a third
party.

Question 12.3 – Provisions which allow either party to demand the removal of uncooperative or aggressive managers

Most respondents, 67.3%, with only 8.6% thinking it very effective, thought that
this might be helpful or effective. I have seen contracts which translate this into
contract terminology. On the only occasion that I have experienced it in practice
a senior engineer was removed from the team, which caused major progress problems, poisoned the atmosphere (who's next?) and resulted in commercial confron-
tation. One respondent in the process of removing a manager said that this was
"very difficult". Another said that removal should be confined to serious failures
such as those that endangered life. Those with a US common law background were
more likely to think that this might work; the opposite being true for those with
less experience. One respondent offered another possibility: "often the only way to
gain their attention is to pull people off site when it comes to a critical event … combined with a demand for outstanding monies".

Question 12.4 – High interest rates to be charged for underpayment of invoices or overcharging

Over 60% of respondents considered this ineffective or not very effective, with nearly
25% thinking it merely helpful. My experience is that, unless delay or default is negli-
gent or deliberate, these terms are rarely used other than as negotiating positions.
There are exceptions in the construction industry and in the automotive industry.

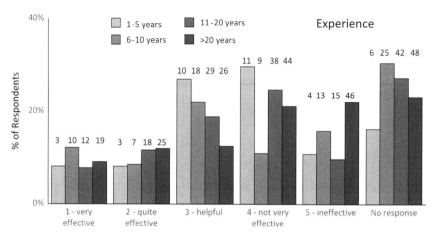

Figure 3.20 Bar Chart Showing Responses to Question 12.5 (Termination) by Length of Experience

Question 12.5 – Termination for long-term and repeated failure to operate in a cooperative manner

26.9% thought this effective, with 49.3% taking the opposite line and 23.3% selecting merely helpful. As with 11.3 commercial actors prefer to talk, manage, play the long game. Those of a US common law background are more likely to find this idea unhelpful; as are those with more experience (Figure 3.20).

Question 12.6 – Payment for management time wasted on sorting these issues out

Even fewer, 18.8% thought this effective, with 20.8% selecting helpful and 60.4% considering it ineffective or not very effective. As with 12.5 I suspect that this remedy is seen as a sideshow. Performance will not be helped by commercial recovery mechanisms. There is a similar result in question 5.5 which asks whether the supplier should pay for time wasted in managing the matter. This is no surprise – Beale and Dugdale uncovered a reluctance to enforce liquidated damages clauses in their famous paper.[102]

3.4 Themes from the vignettes

Vignettes contained common themed questions which allowed some internal triangulation; determining whether answers to would attract similar responses. In

---

102 Beale and Dugdale, 'Contracts between Businessmen', 55 – late delivery is primarily regarded as a commercial problem solved commercially through negotiation.

general responses were consistent across vignettes and align with much other empirical work, sometimes even with work carried out at a different level of abstraction.

3.4.1 Governance questions

These governance questions focus on managerial solutions.

- 11.2 and 12.3 ask whether it is worth asking for the removal of unreasonable managers. 12.3 has a more imperative character, providing for a right for either party to demand removal, and, perhaps for that reason, is less attractive to respondents – 67% taking one of the three top options, to 80% in 11.2. One respondent said: "Governance, if it's possible to go "higher" in the organisation seems to work well."
- 8.6 asks whether a request to attend urgent meetings would be worthwhile and over 80% of respondents respond positively to this.
- 12.1 asks whether fast and effective governance allowing senior management intervention would work. Only 2% rate this negatively.
- Over 96% rated as helpful or likely to promote cooperation, clauses which provide "Open and constructive governance provisions with regular, multi-level, reviews of what is going well and is not going well inbuilt and fast-acting escalation possibilities."

Give and take, honesty, balance, reciprocity and trust are mentioned by respondents together with dealing with issues early, not allowing them to "fester": "Regular communication on every topic is likely to result in successful outcome."

The most popular solution is early senior level intervention. In the ketchup vignette respondents observed:

- [Q]uick and effective senior dispute resolution/relationship panel is in my experience very helpful.
- The conflict can only get resolved by senior level interventions, … the replacement of most exposed squabblers is necessary.

The shadow of the contract "sets the scene" – as a framework. One of my respondents says – "Following the contract mechanically doesn't work". In Beale and Dugdale's work one sales manager described the contract, as did one respondent, as an "umbrella under which we operate".[103] Larson says that "the day-to-day operating relationship is not managed by the verbiage contained in a contract".[104]

---

103 Ibid. 48.
104 Debbie Harrison, 'Is a Long-term Business Relationship an Implied Contract? Two Views of Relationship Disengagement' (2004) 41 *J Manage Stud* 107.

3.4.2 Negotiation questions

Questions 8.3, 8.6, 8.7 and 9.6 elicit a very high level of support (over 75%) for negotiation in the first instance, and for Court support for negotiated solutions. Question 9.3, which suggests open and constructive negotiation supervised by a Court appointed expert, does not find majority support; perhaps because it is not fast-track.

Arrighetti says that give and take is typical in Britain – "less stress was placed on strict contract performance: the attitude could be described as one of flexible pragmatism".[105] Christine Jolls asserts that: "commitment to stick with an original contract, even if both parties later want to modify that contract, may improve contractors' welfare".[106] Nothing any of my respondents said supports that view. My respondents asserted that "give and take is what makes the process enjoyable" and that one should "Give and take". In the Fracking Heaven vignette many respondents suggested negotiated solutions in which FH would cover the cost of the job, ensuring that Downhole made no profit. "But I would want to be reasonable. I want them to recover their costs if it is a pricing issue."

One respondent to the ketchup vignette said "Need to keep negotiating to improve the situation. Termination is really a last resort." Another observed: "Outsourcing relationships are often described as marriages where give and take is required. If one side is obstinate it is only going to end in tears." See also Steven McCann observing that the hard elements of the contract are balanced by the need to work together:

> Only a small percentage of PPP projects in the UK have been subject to penalties applied for under-performance … penalties may be deferred to improve working relationships … (or to prevent them from deteriorating further) or to off-set under-performing services with other services rendered …[107]

I will argue later that the law should support this desire for negotiated outcomes, not by taking the decisions but by creating legal incentives for parties to cooperate actively and engage in the process of problem solving.

3.4.3 Punitive measures

I include as "punitive" measures, involving some financial disadvantage to the defaulter, those in 5.5 and 12.6 where the supplier pays employer for management

---

105 Alessandro Arrighetti, 'Contract Law, Social Norms and Inter-firm Cooperation' (1997) 21 *Cambridge J Econ* 171 at 191.
106 Christine Jolls, 'Contracts as Bilateral Commitments: A New Perspective on Contract Modification' (1997) 26 *JLS* 203.
107 Steven McCann, 'Managing Partnership Relations and Contractual Performance in the Operating Phase of Public Private Partnership' (2014) 15 *Int Public Manage Rev* 111 at 115.

costs, in 9.1 repaying costs paid to keep a supplier working, and in 12.4 the payment of high interest charges. None found significant support. As I note above the
reluctance to use punitive provisions is in line with Beale and Dugdale's
findings.[108] It was interesting that a slim majority considered forcing the contractor
to repay any monies over and above a reasonable cost was acceptable. It may be
that this is regarded as fair and not punitive. This is very much in line with my
experience, except in the construction industry. One respondent (a former direct
report with huge experience), said that: "Although 'High interest rates to be
charged for underpayment of invoices or overcharging' might seem appealing, my
experience is that such charges are never invoked."

Macaulay quotes a survey of Polish managers who advise that penalties work
well as a threat and should be used "intelligently".[109] Steven McCann and one
respondent also indicate that the value of punitive measures lies less in use than
as a threat in the background, which squares with question 5.5, in which the
possibility of termination was viewed more favourably than terminating.[110]

In the ketchup vignette one respondent said: "I would not actually use [punitive
measures] but indicate that I could do. Then say, that would do harm to both
sides, so let's rather focus on establishing an effective dispute resolution mechanism." Steven McCann quotes a senior PPP manager saying something similar:

> why would you abate, even if you're entitled to ...? It doesn't serve any
> purpose. ... the state has a very big stick, but you want to use it wisely. If
> you abate them, it hurts them financially, but the relationship is important
> and it's about give and take.[111]

In another study based on experiments using avatars, in a "controlled laboratory
experiment", Hoeppner, Freund and Depoorter suggest that "express damage
stipulations trigger negative reciprocity and moral hazard, reducing
performance".[112] They do not cite any real-life studies such as Beale and Dugdale's or Macaulay's showing that such stipulations are rarely used. It may have
been worth linking their finding to those studies and considering the

---

108 Beale and Dugdale, 'Contracts between Businessmen', 55. See also Bernstein, 'Beyond
Relational Contracts', 571–572.

109 Jacek Kurczewski and Kazimierz Frieske, 'Some Problems in the Legal Regulation of the
Activities of Economic Institutions' (1977) 11 *Law Soc Rev* 489 at 497 – and Stewart Mac-
aulay, 'Elegant Models, Empirical Pictures, and the Complexities of Contract' (1977) 11
Law Soc Rev 507 at 519–520.

110 Bernstein, 'Beyond Relational Contracts', 571, cites an example where punitive measures
were used when the relationship was deteriorating or when the VP interviewed wanted to
get the attention of more senior managers

111 McCann 'Managing Partnership Relations' 125.

112 Ben Depoorter and others, 'The Moral-Hazard Effect of Liquidated Damages: An Experiment on Contract Remedies' (2016) 173 *JITE* 1 – abstract.

implications. Certainly, my respondents refuse to consider reciprocity as a response to the misuse of damage stipulations.

3.4.4 Termination

Actual termination, represented in 4.4, 11.3 and 12.5, carries very little support. Potential termination, see 5.4, carrying threat, is found to be helpful but insufficient or unhelpful by a large majority. This underlines respondents' general desire to solve problems and keep the contract alive. It may derive from the fear of the cost of change; mentioned by a number of my respondents.[113] It may arise from recognition that a replacement, especially in a commodities transaction, or in a tight market, may not be much different to the current supplier. One vignette 3 respondent observed:

– I'd still negotiate. Termination is still disruptive for both parties and it's possible after negotiation with Downhole that they're still cheaper, especially taking into account the cost to change. If after negotiation they're more expensive, then I'd go for the next cheapest, time allowing.

Other vignette 3 respondents said:

– Termination is dirty business … nothing sweet about divorce.
– [B]etter the devil you know.

Simon Deakin, Christel Lane and Frank Wilkinson wonder whether trust can flourish without institutional support, having observed that: "Interpersonal trust and cultural norms are essential elements in long-term trading relationships."[114] They found that Macaulay's work did not apply in that the "vast majority" of the 61 firms surveyed wanted definite binding legal contracts[115] and that 50% of their sample would deal with a lack of trust by immediate termination of the relationship.[116] That shows a major difference to my sample, although one German interviewee said: "If you trust someone you do not need a contract but if you don't trust them no contract will help you!"

3.4.5 Fast-track dispute resolution measures

Fast-track proceedings with the aim of producing a decision, as in 5.1 and 5.2, is attractive to many respondents – only 10% and 13% rating it insufficient. Third-

---

113 See also Bernstein, 'Beyond Relational Contracts', 571.
114 Michie and Deakin, *Contracts, Co-operation, and Competition,* 134. Andrew Cox, *Strategic Procurement in Construction* (Thomas Telford 1998) criticises "simplistic" assumptions that trust alone, "without effective hierarchy of control", will achieve better outcomes.
115 Michie and Deakin, *Contracts, Co-operation, and Competition,* 123.
116 Ibid. 128.

party expert facilitation, 8.7, is attractive to 66% of respondents and this may be because of the involvement of an expert. Enforced/supervised negotiation, 9.3, is rated positively by 57% whereas fast-track dispute resolution with specific performance powers, 9.4, is a popular option, with 70% rating it positively. This seems to reflect the interest respondents show in performance of the contract. Some respondents were aware of the statutory adjudication process available in construction contracting and this group was positive about the benefits:

– [B]inding procedure, fast track process will help.
– Third party overseen fast track solution with executive power seems the best and most practical solution.

However, the attitude of small businesses to mediation, expressed in the responses to a consultation on creation of a Small Business Commissioner (I imagine it's the business that is small) is mixed with almost half saying that they would not use mediation, a fear being recorded that mediation could be expensive, time consuming and slow.[117]

3.4.6 *Question 16 – Self-help remedies*

Accepting that withholding payment is crude (see question 4.3), there is a slim majority (52%) which considers it effective and a smaller number (26%) who consider it unpleasant but the best option. Exploring matters with other users, in user group fora, as suggested in question 4.2, is rated positively by over 70% of respondents as is bringing in a third party to inspect and report (see question 4.5). Extending the warranty period and allowing use of the machine pending resolution of the problem seems to be another practical method of dealing with the problem, with only 7% finding this insufficient (see 5.3). Working to rule, sulking, making life difficult (82% choosing the top three options in 11.5), is more popular than reciprocating (36% choosing the top three options in 11.4), which is seen as behaving as badly as the client.

3.5 Cooperation themes

3.5.1 *Question 14 – How important is cooperation in managing your contracts?*

I asked respondents to rate cooperation from mission critical (meaning that the contract will fail without it) to unnecessary. I hoped to find a strong correlation between mission critical/important answers and those who manage symbiotic contracts. 283 respondents or 58.6% of the total selected "mission critical" and 195 or 40.6% selected "important".

---

117 'A Small Business Commissioner: Summary of Responses' (www.gov.uk/government/uploads/system/uploads/attachment_data/file/468368/BIS-15-248-summary_of_responses-a-small-business-commissioner.pdf, 2015).

This is an unexpectedly definite result which is consistent across sub-groups. I had thought that around 70–5% of respondents would select the top two options. Taken in conjunction with the result below showing a preference for high-level cooperation, not mechanical cooperation but real working together for a common objective, this is a very striking finding. Lawyers are outliers, more likely to be in the "important" group than "mission-critical" (Figure 3.21).

A small number, around 20, describe their experience as being long-term supply contracts or other, more transactional contracts. Of that group 60% say that cooperation is important, and 30% say that it is mission critical, differing, expectedly, from the 30.5% and 58.5% respectively in the whole sample.

3.5.2 *Question 16 – What does cooperation mean in contract management?*

The first possibility, "working together, sharing responsibility for outcomes, putting aside party interests, working towards a joint or mutual goal in a relationship underpinned by mutual trust", was ticked by 277 respondents, 57.3% of the total. The second, "each party acting reasonably, and objectively, not opportunistically, when problems occur, being flexible with solutions where the problem is not fundamental", an edited version of Toulmin J's definition of active cooperation, was ticked by 340 respondents or 70.4% of the total. "Flexible decision making and change management, especially in administering changes and variations" received 144 votes or 29.8% of the total, while "use of the same programme management tools and management systems, good day to day coordination of activities" was ticked by 91 respondents or 18.8% of the total. I received 23 suggestions for other definitions of cooperation. Most could be fitted into the definitions above.

Interviewees talked of flexibility, give-and-take (11), communication and mutual understanding (7), the need to "talk things out", resolve issues (15), communication (10) and escalation, keeping "friction to one side" or other management points (14). One counselled that cooperation can "descend to a nice chat" and that some formality is required. The theme throughout is that soft and hard issues are in play. One observed that it isn't a question of "fairness". Another that "woolly stuff" was insufficient. One said that it is "implicit that people act in a rational manner". Another raised the importance of "face time" and one said that "blackmail is old school"; a "little more upfront", "recognise issues" and "behave reasonably" were mentioned. No one used good faith, in terms, although trust, respect and honesty were mentioned. Others said:

– The sum is greater than the parts.
– About problem solving, sorting out the issues, not being too formal …

3.5.3 *Question 15 – Which contract terms promote cooperation?*

I identified a number of provisions which help achieve cooperation. I asked respondents to identify others.

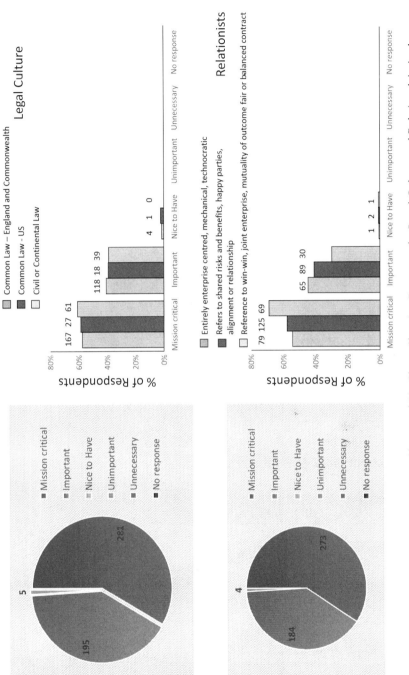

Figure 3.21 How Important is Cooperation – Bar Charts and Pie Charts Showing Responses by Legal Culture and Relational Attitude

Question 15.1 − Open and constructive governance provisions with regular, multi-level, reviews of what is going well and is not going well inbuilt and fast-acting escalation possibilities

360 respondents, 74.8%, thought this very likely to promote cooperation, with 108 or 22.5% thinking it helpful; 2.7% of the total (10) thought it not very useful and 3 thought it unlikely (Figure 3.22). This governance question, covering issues of communication, review and management, showed strong support, consistent across sub-groups, for strong contract governance provisions.

The Common Law can, as we have seen in Chapter 2, provide such particularity and, I argue in Chapters 2 and 6, provide support for deterrence of bad practice, characterised for this purpose as poor communication, lack of openness or candour, failure of management to intervene and solve problems.

Question 15.2 − Clear, fair and fast change management and decision-making provisions allowing, where necessary, fast track, binding, dispute resolution

357 respondents, 95.3% of the total thought this very likely to promote cooperation or helpful. Poor change management, or opportunistic behaviour when changes and delays occur, has provided fertile soil for disputes especially in the construction industry.[118] The balance between very likely and helpful is different between 15.2 and 15.1, perhaps showing a preference for management over mechanics.

Question 15.3 − Late notification of problems is heavily discouraged. Disincentives are applied. Open and constructive communication is regarded as essential

184 or 38.6% thought this very likely to promote cooperation with 218 or 45.7% thinking it helpful. The responses are similar to 15.2 above, with a slight change in the balance between very likely and helpful. One respondent suggests "Celebrate interventions and early warnings. Reward good behaviour". The difference between this question and 15.1 is in the mention of disincentives.

Question 15.4 Risk and reward sharing mechanisms which ensure that there is a mutual or joint interest in the outcome of the contract whether the outcome is success or failure or something in between

418 or 86.7% thought such provisions likely to promote cooperation or be helpful.

Question 15.5 A pricing mechanism which means that the weaker party can't lose their shirt; possibly even a cost-plus type of mechanism

This was less attractive to respondents with 60 or 12.5% agreeing that such provisions are likely to promote cooperation, 215 or 44.9% thinking them helpful and 42.6% or 204 thinking them unhelpful or unlikely to promote cooperation.

118 See generally Sir Michael Latham, *Constructing the Team* (1994) and Pickavance, *Practical Guide*, 1.07.

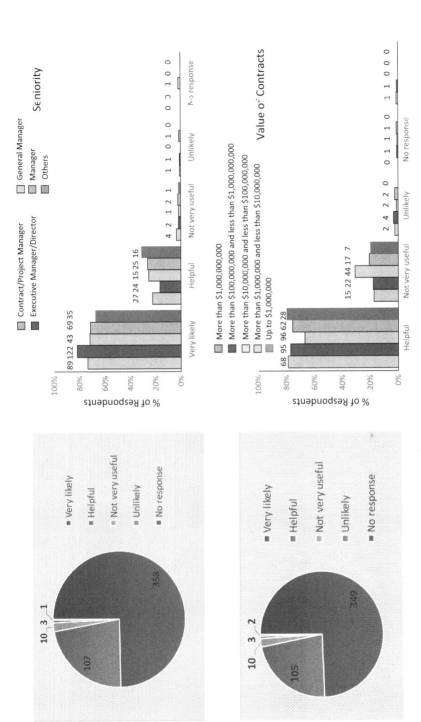

Figure 3.22 Bar Charts and Pie Charts Showing Respondent's Answers to Question 15.1 – Do Governance Contract Provisions Encourage Cooperation, by Seniority and Portfolio

Question 15.6 Flexible, proportionate remedies for problems and defects, which mean that remedies are proportionate to harm. That means, for example, that termination is only possible for reasons that go to the heart of the contract

146 or 30.4% thought this very likely to promote cooperation, and 231 or 48.1% thought it helpful.

Overall the answers to these questions are consistent with those to open questions. Respondents look to good governance and communication to drive cooperation.[119]

I then asked whether respondents considered other provisions to drive cooperation. Interviewees suggested escalation provisions (7), fast-track dispute resolution provisions (6), pain/gain provisions, communication (4) and "softer" provisions. I received 105 other responses (around 3,700 words). Many repeated, in different forms, the ideas floated in the questions. Other suggestions included:

– De minimis provisions in contracts help to avoid a lot of little claims removing focus from bigger issues – but these need to be applied correctly …
– Joint innovation or customer excellence forums.
– Value engineering … sharing cost benefits as a result.
– I cannot imagine that a contract provision with the obligation of good cooperation is really practicable. To promote cooperation it is helpful that the rights and obligations of each party are specified in the contract.

3.5.4 How is cooperation achieved?

Interviewees spoke passionately about how one achieves cooperation (Figure 3.23). The snapshot below reflects the basic themes of management, mutual understanding, reasonable behaviour, relationship management, governance and problem solving. My sample saw the building of personal relationships as essential to success and the creation of cooperation through mutual understanding, role clarity, good communication and the creation of formal and informal problem-solving mechanisms.

I received 404 comments. I broke them down into five basic categories/themes, or, in process terms, inputs (Table 3.11). I considered working on a Six Sigma SIPOC (Supplier, Input, Process, Output, Client). A SIPOC summarises or tabulates process inputs and outputs, providing a high-level process overview. It is used as a Six Sigma device or a LEAN guide, but it has a client at one end of the chain and the supplier at the other end.[120]

In this case we need both parties to appear each end of the chain, so I created an IVAR which provides me with a method of analysing the results into a properly configured "how".

---

119 My evidence is on all fours with the conclusion in Oliver Schilke and Fabrice Lumineau, 'The Double-Edged Effect of Contracts on Alliance Performance' (2018) 44 *J Manage* 2827 "the effects of contracts depend on the types of provisions included and differentiate between the consequences of control and coordination provisions".
120 See e.g. www.projectmanager.com/training/what-is-sipoc. See also Table 3.16 in Appendix B to this Chapter providing a very simple SIPOC for a new kitchen installation.

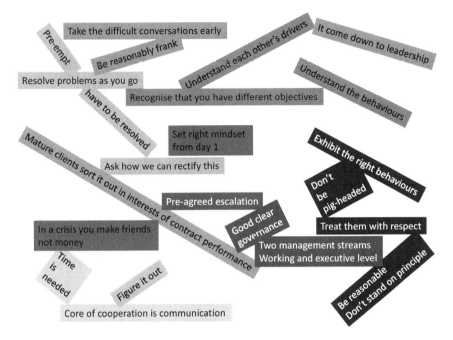

Take the difficult conversations early

Pre-empt

Be reasonably frank

Understand each other's drivers

It come down to leadership

Resolve problems as you go

Understand the behaviours

have to be resolved

Recognise that you have different objectives

Mature clients sort it out in interests of contract performance

Set right mindset from day 1

Ask how we can rectify this

Exhibit the right behaviours

Don't be pig-headed

Pre-agreed escalation

Good clear governance

Treat them with respect

In a crisis you make friends not money

Two management streams
Working and executive level

Time is needed

Figure it out

Be reasonable
Don't stand on principle

Core of cooperation is communication

Figure 3.23 How to Achieve Cooperation

Input (or theme) – **A**greement **C**ommunication **M**anagement **A**ttitude **V**alues
Vector – Direction of Travel for each Input, which creates or informs Activity
Activity
Result

The first theme or Input, mentioned 171 times, was Agreement/Contract, which creates "the ground rules", and through the Vector of contract content (clarity, scope, incentives, obligations, escalation formalities), one creates Activity (in this case kick off meetings) which should Result in alignment.

The second Input is Communication, mentioned 290 times, and through openness, clarity, active communication and pre-empting problems (Table 3.12). Sharing information and expectations creates mutual understanding and alignment. Some respondents were emphatic about communication (communication, communication, communication) and others mentioned "constructive challenge" or a no-fault culture.

The third Input is Management, mentioned 345 times, and through the Vectors of problem solving, dealing with change, team-building and role clarity (rigorous, tiered governance), Activities such as performance reviews, relationship building, escalation or involvement of senior management, one achieves clear responsibilities ("establish boundaries" so everyone knows who does what), open

Table 3.11 Achieving Cooperation in Complex Contracts – Agreement/Contract Theme

How to achieve cooperation in the management of complex contracts 404 comments received – number made against each dimension shown

Inputs	Vectors	Activity	Results	Comments
Agreement/ Contract 171	Clarity 30 Scope, obligations and management 19 Objectives 17	Kick off meetings 19	Alignment 13 Contract/ Project Management Plan 11	Agree the ground rules
	Balance (fairness?) 17			Balance trust and control
	Escalation formalities 11			Accessible and graduated escalation process
	Incentives 19	Reward good behaviour, penalise bad behaviour 9	Skin in the game 1	

Table 3.12 Achieving Cooperation in Complex Contracts – Communication Theme

How to achieve cooperation in the management of complex contracts 404 comments received – number made against each dimension shown

Inputs	Vectors	Activity	Results	Comments
Communication 290	Openness 47 Firmness/ clarity 19		Mutual understanding 46 Understanding each other's drivers 30	Communication Communication Communication
	Active communication 19	Share expectations 7 Share information 1	Alignment 1	Constructive challenge
	Early – don't let it fester 36			No fault culture Pre-empt problems
	Listening 14			

lines of communication, and allows effective dispute resolution (Table 3.13). Respondents commented that important dimensions included "no personal ego", "quality of leadership is the thing". In relationship management, they said, "you can't fall out with the guy next door very day" and that achieving it isn't easy – "one team building piss-up at the start of the job isn't enough!". Other advice included "don't deal with idiots".

Attitude, mentioned 125 times, is characterised by reasonableness, working together and taking responsibility ("be bold and brave"), and to achieve Results of active cooperation and win-win, managers utilise flexibility, give and take (Table 3.14). It is necessary to be objective and unemotional, to be "unconditionally constructive", to be "firm but fair" and to be guided by a "genuine desire to do the right thing".

Values/behaviour, mentioned 112 times, is characterised by honesty (don't be afraid to say something that isn't popular), respect and reliability ("keep to your word") (Table 3.15). Being transparent will create trust (although one used the Reaganism "trust but verify") and common goals. One respondent said: "Everyone knows that things can go wrong ... most people will be gentle if you explain what happened."

Respondent opinion inspirits Charles Handy's definition of management, providing the missing "x" which makes resource = output.[121] Communication[122] was often mentioned. Respondents spoke of "less finger pointing", recognition that issues need to be resolved, the need for "soft skills training"[123] ("how can I help?"), poor management of "information flow" causes "99%" of problems,[124] the need to "know the contract in the broadest sense", formal and informal dialogue, the need to "lead" or to "take responsibility", do the "right thing"/exhibit the "right behaviours", work out socially/informally how to work together, treat each other with respect, formal meetings (use "set pieces"), proper reporting, clear lines of communication "at the right level", openness (no "Chinese whispers"). The essence of comment was that the role of the Contract Manager is to manage, find ways through problems, keep one's eye on the ball, to accept that there will be problems (even conflict) and to behave professionally, honestly and openly.

---

121 Charles B Handy, *Understanding Organizations* (4th edn, Penguin 1993).

122 Communication and reporting is among the "top ten" important contract terms according to IACCM surveys – *2013/2014 Top Terms* (IACCM, 2014).

123 From a Senior Counsel who once worked for me, who reminded me that I could have benefited from this.

124 Lord Brown's references to "adamant" refusal to provide information and others in *Ritchie* (n. 3 above) come to mind.

Table 3.13 Achieving Cooperation in Complex Contracts – Management Theme

How to achieve cooperation in the management of complex contracts 404 comments received – number made against each dimension shown

Inputs	Vectors	Activity	Results	Comments
Management 345	Problem solving 5 Deal with change 2	Regular performance reviews – mutual 81	Clear responsibilities for actions and issue resolution 6	No personal ego. Quality of leadership is the thing. Share the highs and lows
	Plan 2		Management Plan and activity plan 2	
	Team building 29	Build relationship – formal and informal 85	Open lines of communication 8	You can't fall out with guy next door every day. Build a shared vision. One team building piss-up at the start of the job isn't enough! Joint extra-curricular activities. Bowling and barbeques in North America. Suckling pig roasts and dancing in East Europe. Petanque tournaments in France. Banquets in China
	Role clarity	Clear roles 43 Tiered roles 17 Senior/executive management involved 17	Someone owns the actions 6 Everyone understands roles/responsibilities 4	Establish boundaries – who does what and what happens if this does not work. Don't deal with idiots. Keep away from the lawyers
	Escalation 27	Clear tiers of management 15	Quick and effective dispute resolution	Understand the downside of conflict a two-way "service management" clause defining how each party will act and the different people within the business who'll be part of any "escalation" seems to work. Rigorous, tiered governance. Pay on time!
	Empowerment 3			

Table 3.14 Achieving Cooperation in Complex Contracts – Attitude Theme

How to achieve cooperation in the management of complex contracts 404 comments received – number made against each dimension shown

Inputs	Vectors	Activity	Results	Comments
Attitude 125	Reasonableness 19	Flexibility 16	Active cooperation 1	Firm but fair approach Find solutions instead of allocating blame Not sweating the small stuff
	Working together 20	Give and take 15		Unconditionally constructive
	Assist each other 13	Reciprocity 7	Win-win 21	Treat suppliers and customers as you would expect to be treated.
	Be brave and bold. Take responsibility 6	Compromise 9		Don't fudge Genuine desire to do the right thing.
		Objective/ unemotional 6		Do not make it personal

Table 3.15 Achieving Cooperation in Complex Contracts – Values/Behaviour Theme

How to achieve cooperation in the management of complex contracts 404 comments received – number made against each dimension shown

Inputs	Vectors	Activity	Results	Comments
Values/ Behaviour	Honesty 28	Transparency 9	Trust 32	Don't be afraid to say something that isn't popular. Open, honest, honourable. Everyone knows that things can go wrong and most people will be gentle if you explain what happened.
	Respect 11		Common goals 22	Focus as team on contract delivery success, not finger pointing.
	Reliability 10			Keeping to your word, be it a threat or a promise Trust but verify

3.6 Conclusions from this empirical evidence

The purpose of my survey was to "generate data on what cooperation means to commercial players and to determine the needs of those commercial players in the management of complex contracts". I wanted to determine whether cooperation is important, what it means and how it can be, and is, achieved.

3.6.1 Cooperation is important

99% of respondents said that cooperation is mission critical or important. Interviewees described cooperation variously as mission critical (5), "everything", "key", "absolutely critical", critical or extremely important (3), "key to success", or "don't get the job done without it". One said symbiotic, another important and another very important. Of the 22 answers in Rome, two said important, eight very important, others essential, fundamental, key, crucial, top-max, vital.

3.6.2 What cooperation means

There were 481 responses to the request for a definition of cooperation. Respondents could select more than one answer; 46% did so. 275 respondents selected the "high-level" mutual answer: "Working together, sharing responsibility for outcomes, putting aside party interests, working towards a joint or mutual goal in a relationship underpinned by mutual trust". And 340 selected this edited version of Judge Toulmin's deathless definition:[125] "Each party acting reasonably, and objectively, not opportunistically, when problems occur, being flexible with solutions where the problem is not fundamental." More than 99% selected one or other of these options, either on its own or in combination with others. Around 23% chose the top option alone and 30% option 2 alone. A further 11% chose options 1 and 2. Conversely, around 1% chose only one of the two bottom options. I have not seen any such clear definition of cooperation in other empirical legal research.

3.6.3 Cooperation is achievable

The social and business nature of the management of complex contracts is apparent from responses.[126] Relationship building, communication, meeting people, cultural experience, teambuilding, minimising or solving conflicts, are mentioned by large numbers of respondents. However, it is business-like, unemotional, clearly focused on outcomes with an underlying tenor of performance; getting the business done.

---

125 *Anglo Group plc v Winther Brown & Co. Ltd* [2000] EWHC Technology 127 (TCC) at [125] "The duty of co-operation ... extends to the customer accepting where possible reasonable solutions to problems that have arisen. In the case of unimportant or relatively unimportant items that have been promised and cannot be supplied each party must act reasonably."

126 Jane M. Wiggins, *Facilities Manager's Desk Reference* (Wiley 2010), 476, says that facilities managers need "highly developed communications skills" which will enable them to build "excellent customer relationships".

Consistent with other answers 96% of respondents identified governance provisions promoting formal communication, review and dispute resolution as likely to assist in creating cooperation and 95% thought the same of provisions ensuring clear fair and fast decision-making together with fast-track dispute resolution. 84% agreed that discouraging late notification of problems assists in promoting cooperation. 78% thought that proportionality, ensuring that termination is only possible where matters go to the heart of the contract, would assist. Risk/reward sharing mechanisms were viewed as helpful or more by 86%. Pricing conditions providing protection, preventing a party from "losing its shirt", were less attractive than risk/reward sharing mechanisms. Few other suggestions were made, allowing me to infer, given that I had received 90,000 words of advice from this erudite group, that my list was about right.

3.6.4 Summary

There are major differences between my study and previous studies. My study asks experienced commercial players to answer open questions about the wider frame of reference, their day-to-day actuality. I wanted to draw out coalface meaning for business necessity and commercial coherence.

My survey used real-life vignettes, drawn from real cases, which allow me to determine respondents' attitude to situations already adjudicated; and to compare those answers to those given to open questions. The coherence of the data, seen in the "variance snapshot" (above at 3.1.3), together with the triangulation work, shows that they are broadly comparable with other empirical studies when questions and context can be directly compared, allowing me to claim that they unearth certain commercial expectations.

It is worth considering Macaulay's conclusion: "Contract, then, often plays an important role in business, but other factors are significant."[127] Macaulay appears to mean by "contract" the "legal", hard, black-letter element of the deal. To respondents, the hard part of the contract is part of a framework, the "rules of the game", which comprises hard and soft elements; each of which must work.[128] The contract comprises a hard core of legal terms and, for example, scope definitions and processes, and a softer penumbra of communication, give and take, and relationship building.

The hard elements are of two types. One is the "contract" which few want to use and that, I infer, means the "terms and conditions", the "legal" elements, which many, in line with Macaulay's findings, don't want to wave at the other

---

127 Macaulay, 'Non-Contractual Relations', 67.
128 See Schilke and Lumineau, 'Double-Edged Effect', 2853 – "if coordination provisions help align activities and goals ..., goal-direction through control provisions will bring about comparatively less conflict than if no coordination provisions are present".

party, although they recognise their necessity. As Deakin, Lane and Wilkinson concluded:

> the vast majority of firms saw both the use of writing and attachment of legal force as an important means of clarifying the agreement ... it would be "complacent" to assume that a "voluntaristic attitude" to the legal system is "conducive to cooperation".[129]

The other hard element includes scope, objectives, risks and governance and there is a clear desire for clarity in these elements. As one respondent says, it allows "service expectations, delivery, management information and costs to be discussed openly". Macaulay quotes businessmen on how you solve problems:

– You get the other man on the telephone ... you don't read legalistic clauses at each other if you ever want to do business again ...
– Customers had better not rely on legal rights ... [I will] not be treated as a criminal.[130]

One of my respondents says, "I might get the contract out but that's a failure for everyone". Others made similar points, one (a finance director) saying "Non-enforcement is the key. Success means getting to the objectives without looking at the terms and conditions." This means talking, picking the telephone up, trying to resolve problems in a business-like manner. The contract, the hard contract, is a key part of the background to this work.

The soft elements also comprise two types. One is the informal element of governance and deal-making. The other is informal relationship-building. Relationship-building underpins success by helping each party to understand others' drivers and opinions and ensures that formal and informal channels of communication are kept open and used appropriately. Informal channels, which work both in having "boots on the ground" and in social events, are equally valuable in management terms; if not easy to describe in legal principles. Lyons and Mehta describe building personal relationships as assisting in the development of socially oriented trust (SOT), meaning that a "history of social relations creates shared values, moral positions, affection and friendship".[131] And that investment in personal relationships turns on "perceived inadequacies in the law of contract".[132] In my sample, not one respondent mentioned affection or friendship. One mentioned a team building "piss-up" as being insufficient; perhaps

---

129 Michie and Deakin, *Contracts, Co-operation, and Competition,* 123 and 134, as quoted at n 114 above.
130 Stewart Macaulay, 'Freedom from Contract: Solutions in Search of a Problem?' (2004) 2004 *WisLRev* 777 at 793.
131 Michie and Deakin, *Contracts, Co-operation, and Competition,* chapter 2, 'Private Sector Business Contracts: The Text between the Lines', 53.
132 Ibid. at 59.

consistent with Lyons and Mehta's references to investments in SOT, even by firms which had covered "every feasible aspect" of the deal in writing, such investments including visits to the opera and ballet.[133]

The purpose of formal and informal relationship-building is to ensure that communication channels are open and clear; that everyone knows who does what, or, when things go awry, who to talk to and how to talk to them and what fixes are possible within reasonable boundaries. It also recognises that contracts are neither perfect nor complete and that there is room for legitimate debate as to what they mean, notwithstanding that such debate should be conducted openly and constructively. There is no emotional content; it is business driven, allowing the contract work to proceed in a recognisable form. Steven McCann says that: "there is a link between the public partner's contract management style ... and satisfactory delivery of VfM [value for money]".[134] This is another reason why parties cooperate, communicate, try to make it work. It is cheaper!

Cooperation in contract management involves complex human and corporate interaction. It is a social and a business process, intellectual and managerial in nature, structured and unstructured. It requires business-like interaction, efficacious, formal and informal, between people and within businesses/enterprises working towards a successful contract outturn.

My survey respondents were offered the option of reciprocation in vignette 4 and few found the idea attractive; just 6% rating as their first choice and 12% as their second choice. It was said that it involved "stooping to their level", would dig "deeper trenches" or "relationships would sour". I was surprised at this finding, but it is consistent with the relationship-building, communicate and make-it-work philosophy of those engaged in management of these contracts. Tit-for-tat, the bedrock of PD games, simply does not figure in the management of these modern complex contracts. It is ditched in favour of pragmatism; a realistic, problem-solving approach to the contract and its difficulties. Those differences reflect the real-world nature of my study and the closeness of respondents to the actuality of managing contracts. It is at once too simplistic, binary in nature and does not provide the basis for a solution to the problem. Parties recognise that they will have to talk at some stage and that to reciprocate will only put that day off.

The themes from the vignettes disclose a marked reluctance to use punitive measures or to terminate but see value in fast-track dispute resolution, negotiation, communication and professional governance. These require constructive engagement, that the parties talk, communicate and work together to find the cause of the problem and agree solutions. It is interesting that respondents

---

133 Ibid. 59.
134 McCann, 'Managing Partnership Relations', 126, also quoting other sources; "Developing good working relationships ... can decrease the amount of corrective action ... that might otherwise be needed", from Ernst & Young, 'The Journey Continues: PPPs in Social Infrastructure' (2008) http://infrastructureaustralia.gov.au/policy-publications/publications/Ernst-Young-.

seemed to pick up the fact that management had become involved late in *Medirest;* which was one of Cranston J's findings – that the delay in setting up meetings was "partly due to inadequate drive on Medirest's part". This requires time and effort, as parties must make proper endeavours to find space and time to consider and unravel issues and to put the lid back on the can of worms. This underlines the conclusion that respondents are more interested in performance than in revenge, the task is about making the contract work.

There is some, limited, evidence that lawyers are more often outliers than other groups. They are, for example, least likely to agree that paying up and preserving your rights is a practical solution, and more likely to see cooperation as important than as mission-critical.[135] Another interesting point is that there is considerably less gender-based divergence than some authors might think likely.[136]

In broad terms, what I have gleaned from my respondents is consistent with other studies. However, there are significant differences in that what I have heard is that the contract creates the relationship; not vice versa. The relationship may pave the way for future business, but its raison d'être is that of making the contract at hand work. It follows the contract or contracting process; it does not lead it.

Parties do not cooperate in a vacuum. They cooperate to make the contract work, in part because people are generally cooperative, and partly because making the contract work is part of the deal that they have done; they feel somewhat obliged to cooperate. Cooperation is also necessary to make these symbiotic contracts work – another reason why they cooperate. The question is what parts of the cooperation/relation can be regulated and what part of that should be regulated. Most of the time aeroplanes don't crash. Most of the time people don't get cancer. Most of the time contracts don't go wrong. The argument is the same in each case. When these things happen, the job of the engineer, the doctor or the lawyer is to find out what happened and try to prevent it from happening in future.

The survey provides a definition of cooperation, a clear opinion that cooperation is necessary and many hints and tips on how to achieve it. The requirements of good communication between the parties, timeous and accurate information flow, solid formal and informal governance, and reasonable attempts to solve problems and disputes (constructive engagement) are essential to successful performance.

---

135 See also Schilke and Lumineau, 'Double-Edged Effect', 37: "legal experts tend to be more risk-averse than their clients". In my opinion this is a good thing. Management is a team enterprise and different attitudes and viewpoints help rational decision-making.

136 Rosemary C Hunter and others (eds) *Feminist Judgments: From Theory to Practice* (Hart 2010) – Linda Mulcahy in Commentary on *Baird Textile Holdings v Marks Spencer Plc* at 188, discussed below in subchapter 5.2.1.

Appendix A

Sample SIPOC for a new kitchen

A SIPOC summarises or tabulates process inputs and outputs, providing a high-level process overview. It is used as a Six Sigma device or a LEAN guide. This is a highly simplified SIPOC for one of you who wants a new kitchen installed.

Table A3.1 Sample SIPOC for a New Kitchen

Supplier	*Input*	*Process*	*Output*	*Customer*
Kitchen designer	Kitchen location, dimensions, equipment and facilities requirements	Create overall design and drawings. Buy large items. Supervise installation.	Agreed specification for kitchen. Who buys (e.g.) the fridge? Instructions to tradesmen. Price. Complete kitchen. Happy customer.	You
Electrician	Number and location of sockets, lighting, extractor units etc.	Price work, buy components, install; liaising with other trades and customer.	Agreed price. Complete electrical system.	You
Plumber	Location of sink, dishwasher, washing machine, taps, boiler etc.	Price work, buy components, install; liaising with other trades and customer.	Agreed price. Complete plumbing system. All machines installed and tested.	You
Carpenter	Cupboard, worktop and shelving requirements	Price work, buy components, instal; liaising with other trades and customer	Agreed price. Complete kitchen infrastructure.	You

4 The source, justification and application of the duty to cooperate

Legal recognition of expectations must be argued for.[1] My claim is essentially a hard-boiled contextualist position claiming that the expectations uncovered by the survey are shared, normative, core to the contract and necessary incidents of successful performance; evidenced by the practices, assumptions or understandings of the morally reasonable and commercially experienced. The commercial experts who manage modern, symbiotic contracts say that contract success depends on expectations which include constructive engagement, give and take, problem solving, hard-legal and hard-scope/governance and soft-formal and soft-informal relationship building.

I explore theoretical writings on commercial expectations in subchapter 4.1, considering definition and sources, and follow up in subchapter 4.2 by examining the tools available to judges and litigants to evince commercial expectations in trial conditions.

4.1 Theoretical perspectives on commercial expectations

The best-known claim for expectations is Johan Steyn's: "A thread runs through our contract law that effect must be given to the reasonable expectations of honest men … that are, in an objective sense, common to both parties … which satisfy an objective criterion of reasonableness."[2] Sarah Worthington rightly says that this "touchstone" is "too vague to provide a useful normative yardstick".[3] Robert Bradgate describes Steyn's touchstone as a "litmus test" which "identifies the principle which underlies the detailed doctrinal rules".[4] Sebastien

---

1 Francois du Bois, *Good Faith, Good Law?* http://www.archive.legalscholars.ac.uk/edinburgh/restricted/download.cfm?id=312 at 7.
2 Johan Steyn, 'Contract Law: Fulfilling the Reasonable Expectations of Honest Men' (1997) 113 *LQR* 433.
3 Sarah Worthington (ed.) *Commercial Law and Commercial Practice* (Hart 2003), Introduction, p. xiii.
4 Bradgate, 'Contracts, Contract Law and Reasonable Expectations', in Worthington, *Commercial Law*, 667.

Grammond suggests that reasonable expectations at "the operational level" are "too imprecise.[5] Steyn, however, counsels that: "usages and practices of dealings ... will be prime evidence of what is reasonable".[6] Steyn is clear that expectations are objective and shared; therefore, typically contractual. Paul Finn describes them as constructed from the "raw materials" of: "The character and terms of the contractual relationship ... its context and on how the parties have conducted themselves".[7]

To justify my claim that the law should be repositioned to give effect to some of the norms described in Chapter 3, I describe the significant increases in contracting complexity, changes in commercial needs and commercial reality which have occurred over the last 30 or so years. I consider various theoretical works on the definition and source of commercial expectation, arguing that my, Steynite, normative approach to commercial expectation works in theory. I argue that what parties have agreed "subjectively" or "objectively" in negotiation, by practice or usage, or by conduct should be enforced. This is a rights-based claim which can supplement and justify instrumental claims.

Using Stephen Smith's taxonomy, I argue that justification for enforcing or taking into account commercial expectation is normative. He refers to expectations of the morally reasonable party;[8] and I equate morally reasonable with commercially experienced players who know what it takes to make performance possible and successful in a symbiotic contract.

4.1.1 The change in commercial reality and commercial practice

The commercial world has changed since Stewart Macaulay first investigated the phenomenon of non-contractual relations in business.[9] Macaulay's contacts, and Beale and Dugdale's,[10] came from manufacturing entities involved in transactional buying and selling (long-term and iterative). Many contracts managed by survey participants, including IT services, design and/or management, outsourcing and facilities management, were unknown in the 1960s and 1970s. Catherine Mitchell says that changes in contracting practice include

---

5 Sebastien Grammond, 'Reasonable Expectations and the Interpretation of Contracts across Legal Traditions' (2009) 48 *Can Bus LJ* 345 at 364

6 Steyn, 'Contract Law', 434.

7 In 'Fiduciary and Good Faith Obligations under Long Term Contracts' in Kanaga Dharmananda (ed.) *Long Term Contracts* (Federation Press 2013) at 137.

8 Stephen A Smith, 'Reasonable Expectations of the Parties: An Unhelpful Concept' (2009) *CBLJ* 366 at 369.

9 Stewart Macaulay, 'Non-Contractual Relations in Business: A Preliminary Study' (1963) 28 *Am Sociol Rev* 55.

10 Hugh Beale and Tony Dugdale, 'Contracts between Businessmen: Planning and the Use of Contractual Remedies' (1975) 2 *Br J Law Soc* 45.

umbrella agreements,[11] which are usually non-binding frameworks allowing call-off ordering by reference to a master contract.[12]

Ian Macneil discussed relational contracts involving an automobile manufacturer ordering "from another manufacturer with which it regularly deals, thousands of piston rings".[13] Even these widgetty contracts may now be highly complex. The Mini's crankshaft, an example used to illustrate integration of EU markets, a Brexit leitmotif, crosses the Channel several times before final installation (Figure 4.1). The crankshaft is cast in France, machined in the UK, installed in the engine in Germany, returning to Oxford for final installation.

These significant changes have not penetrated law and economics literature which still assumes that there are basically two types of transaction, being one-off, arms-length, or long-term, relationship based, transactional or iteratively transactional.[14] In the game theoretical examples discussed in Chapter 3, none involves much more than a single transaction or a series of iterative transactions. In a still typical example Baird claims that "the principal measure of the success of our contract law is whether it in fact induces cooperation", using a dichotomy between the one-off transaction (a book sale) and the long-term contract.[15]

The "essence" of Oliver Williamson's work on contractual governance is that "particular mechanisms or structures will emerge as responses to the characteristics of transactions" (Figure 4.2).[16] The contracting world he describes comprises

11 Catherine Mitchell, *Contract Law and Contract Practice: Bridging the Gap between Legal Reasoning and Commercial Expectation* (Hart 2013) at 61.

12 See Lisa Bernstein, 'Beyond Relational Contracts: Social Capital and Network Governance In Procurement Contracts' (2015) 7 *J Legal Anal* 561 and Hugh Collins, *Regulating Contracts* (OUP 2005), 152.

13 Ian R Macneil, 'Contracts: Adjustment of Long-Term Economic Relations Under Classical, Neoclassical, and Relational Contract Law' (1978) 72 *NWULR* 854 at 887. He recognised the emergence of service contracts and that "services are inherently more relational than the transfer of goods". Ian R Macneil, 'Many Futures of Contracts, The' (1973) 47 *SCalLRev* 691 at 694.

14 See e.g. Jonathan Morgan, *Contract Law Minimalism* (CUP 2013), 62, Oliver E Williamson, *The Mechanisms of Governance* (OUP 1996), Robert E Scott, 'Contract Design and the Shading Problem' July 2015http://ssrncom/abstract=2628256 Columbia Public Law Research Paper 14.472, and Chapin Cimino, 'The Relational Economics of Commercial Contract' (2015) 91 *Texas A & M Law Rev* 91.

15 Douglas G Baird, 'Self-Interest and Cooperation in Long-Term Contracts' (1990) 19 *JLS* 583 at 586. DF Maltese and M Farina, 'Theory of the Firm and Organisational Contracts: The Remedial Aspects of Good Faith' (2016) 27 *EBOR* 51 recognises potential complexity but says at 56: "Contracts can be grossly divided into two broad categories – spot contracts and relational ones.". See Robert Cooter and Thomas Ulen, *Law and Economics: Pearson New International Edition* (6th edn, Pearson 2013), Jeffrey L Harrison, *Law and Economics* (WW Norton & Co. 2008) 163 et seq, and Thomas J. Miceli, *The Economic Approach to Law* (2nd edn, Stanford Economics and Finance 2009) 134 et seq. All examples are transactional.

16 Williamson, *Mechanisms of Governance*. Jonathan Michie and SF Deakin (eds), *Contracts, Cooperation, and Competition: Studies in Economics, Management, and Law* (OUP 1997), 9.

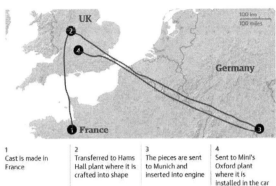

The modern supply chain can mean that components can cross the
Channel several times before the final product reaches the customer

1	2	3	4
Cast is made in France	Transferred to Hams Hall plant where it is crafted into shape	The pieces are sent to Munich and inserted into engine	Sent to Mini's Oxford plant where it is installed in the car

Figure 4.1 The Journey of the Mini's Crankshaft[17]

product or plant. Services do not rate a mention, far less[17] mixed service and product and system contracts. The commercial world becomes three types of contract,
three investment characteristics and two transacting frequencies.[18] This always was
over-reductionist and over-simplistic – "too tidy".[19]

He prophesied that as transactions become more "idiosyncratic", more
"occasional", such as plant construction, vertical integration will "ordinarily"
result.[20]

Purchasing professionals had already identified governance issues. In 1983,
Peter Kraljic developed a very famous "four-box" model which mapped contracts against two key dimensions – risk and profitability – together with guidance as to governance and relationship considerations associated with the
position on the matrix (Figure 4.3).[21]

Beale and Dugdale make a simple and obvious point that "a high degree of planning was
often explained by a high risk", 'Contracts between Businessmen' at 47 and see 56–57.

17 *The Guardian* www.theguardian.com/business/2017/mar/03/brexit-uk-car-industry-mini-
britain-eu.

18 Oliver E Williamson, *The Economic Institutions of Capitalism* (Free Press 1985) at 73–79. Jan
B Heide and George John, 'Alliances in Industrial Purchasing: The Determinants of Joint
Action in Buyer-Seller Relationships' (1990) 27 *J Mark Res* 4 –Williamson does not "does
not identify operational dimensions of governance structure" at 24.

19 See Mitchell, *Bridging the Gap*, 51–53.

20 Williamson, *Mechanisms of Governance*, 78–79.

21 Peter Kraljic, 'Purchasing Must Become Supply Management' (1983) 61 *Harvard Bus Rev*
109. At this time, I was working in the oil and gas industry, in a specialist department dealing
with important, complex subcontracts.

		Investment Characteristics Fig 3.1 and 3.2 combined Governance in bold, transaction type in italics		
		Nonspecific	Mixed	Idiosyncratic
Frequency	Occasional	**Market Governance** **Classical Contracting** *Purchasing standard equipment*	**Trilateral governance (neoclassical contracting)** *Purchasing customized equipment*	*Constructing a Plant*
	Recurrent	**Market Governance** **Classical Contracting** *Purchasing standard material*	**Bilateral Governance Relational Contracting** *Purchasing customized material*	**Unified Governance** **Relational Contracting** *Site specific transfer of intermediate product across successive stages*

Figure 4.2 Oliver Williamson's Governance Charts

	The Kraljic Four Box Supplier Segmentation Model	
High Profit Risk	**Leverage items** Exploit purchasing power Targeted pricing strategies Abundant Supply	**Strategic items** Develop long term relationship Collaborate/Innovate Analyse and manage risks Scarce resource Consider making in-house
Low Profit Risk	**Non-critical items** Standardise Automated procurement Abundant supply	**Bottleneck items** Low control over suppliers Innovation/Substitution Scarce product
	Low Supply Risk ⟶ High Supply Risk	

Figure 4.3 Kraljic's Four Box Model (Updated)

As Lyons and Mehta say, Williamson's analysis "belies the deep complexity of real world contractual governance".[22] Ian Duncan-Wallace describes the fundamental

22 In Michie and Deakin, *Contracts,* chapter 2, 'Private Sector Business Contracts: The Text between the Lines' at 63. Equally, the best example of a complex contract given in Victor P Goldberg (ed.) *Readings in the Economics of Contract Law* (CUP 1989), chapter 1.2, 'Relational Exchange: Economics and Complex Contracts is in Franchising', at 16.

move from professional led contracts to contractor led contracts, missed by William-son, in the construction contracting landscape in 1970.[23] Moreover, Williamson's analysis is undermined by the development of ever more complex outsourcing (Figure 4.4). Nowadays, contracts involve hospitals, offices or infrastructure; mixing service provision and equipment supply, even sharing of management techniques.[24] Rentokil, a facilities management contractor, provides this brief history:

> [FM] started as little more than janitorial and caretaker services during the 1970s … It now comprises "a mix of in-house departments, specialist con-tractors, large multi-service companies and consortia delivering the full range of design, build, finance and management".[25]

Zoe Ollerenshaw describes modern contracts as "a 'thick web' of interfaces … a complex web".[26]

In general, outsourcing/management and construction contracts are medium–long term, fixed term, fixed scope contracts with heavyweight, semi-boilerplate change management, dispute management, force majeure and commercial and technical variation provisions built in. They are not "call-off" or umbrella agree-ments. Nor are they always long-term; Jane Wiggins quotes a Mintel survey suggest-ing an average length of four years for UK facilities management contracts

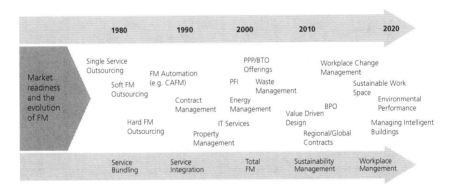

Figure 4.4 ISS Graphic Showing Development of Outsourcing, 1980s–2000+

23 Alfred A Hudson and IN Duncan Wallace, *Hudson's Building and Engineering Contracts* (Sweet & Maxwell 1970), esp. at 82–84.

24 Collins, *Regulating Contracts,* makes a similar comment at 138. See Rachel Burnett, 'The Changing Context of IT Contracts' (2004) 154 *NLJ* 343.

25 www.rentokil.com/facilities-management/history/. See Jane M Wiggins, *Facilities Manager's Desk Reference* (Wiley 2010), chapter 1.

26 In 'Managing Change in Uncertain Times' in Larry A DiMatteo and others (eds), *Commer-cial Contract Law: Transatlantic Perspectives* (CUP 2013), 203.

Such modern contracting represents a major change in commercial practice (see Figure 4.5 which relates to ISS, a £9bn (approximately) corporation with 43,000 employees; www.publications.issworld.com/ISS/External/iss world/White_papers/Perspectives_on_the_FM_market_development/Hodge). In 1953 Stoljar observed, using very old-fashioned language, that in employment contracts: "the usual and typical problem is whether the servant has been guilty of such misconduct as will entitle the master to dismiss him".[27] An implied term that employer and employee will maintain mutual trust and confidence, meaning that neither party will conduct itself in a manner likely to destroy or seriously damage that trust and confidence, emerged in the 1970s; explained by Lord Hoffmann: "a person's employment is usually one of the most important things in his or her life. It gives not only a livelihood but an occupation, an identity and a sense of self-esteem. The law has changed to recognise this *social reality*."[28] Lord Bridge implied the term,[29] in another case, "as a necessary incident of a definable category of contractual relationship".[30]

In the 1980s, about 90% of FM services were performed internally, with the rest by individual service providers. In the 1990s, it was evenly split between in-house and individual service providers, with a small percentage performed by IFM organisations. In the 2000s, Integrated Facility Services (IFS) started to capture market share from all three segments, with the largest reductions seen by individual service providers.

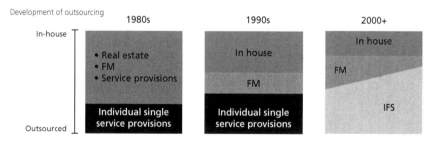

Figure 4.5 Evolution of Facilities Management Contracting

27 SJ Stoljar, 'Prevention and Cooperation in the Law of Contract' (1953) 31 *CanBar Rev* 231 at 249.
28 *Johnson v Unisys Ltd* [2000] UKHL 13, [2001] IRLR 279 at 35; my emphasis.
29 It originated in *Courtaulds Northern Textiles Ltd v Andrew* [1979] IRLR 84, EAT. A supervisor's comment – "Well, you can't do the bloody job anyway" – was held to destroy the continuing bond of confidence between the parties.
30 *Scally v Southern Health and Social Services Board* [1991] 4 All ER 563 (HL) at 571.

As such change is possible in Employment Law, significant change cannot be impossible in the commercial field, given changing commercial reality. Hugh Collins' transformation thesis suggests that as law moves from the classical era, becoming "more socialized", duties to cooperate must be imported.[31] My argument is based on the need to reflect expectations arising from the changing needs of commerce.

In one study (using 136 surveys and 67 interviews) corporate counsel explained how they chose governing laws. The survey authors concluded that "the most important factor is the perceived neutrality and impartiality of the legal system" (66%). Jonathan Morgan quotes Roy Goode saying that what gives English Law pre-eminence is "the quality of our judges, their sensitivity to legitimate commercial needs and their receptiveness to new legal instruments".[32]

Nowadays, a supplier of defective software may have a right to cure defects.[33] Toulmin J's implied term of active cooperation in IT contracts springs from a change in contracting/commercial reality.[34] Similarly, Leggatt J's implication of good faith in *Yam Seng*.[35] One derives from the realisation that IT contracts are new and different; the other from the idea that distributorship contracts require new forms of governance to make them work. Change is possible.

4.1.2 Meaning of commercial expectations

There are multiple definitions of reasonable or commercial expectations. Ian Macneil describes them as "inevitably present … tacit assumptions" and at their "extreme relational pole" their absence means that the relationship cannot survive.[36] My survey exposes various expected behaviours, reactions and activities, norms, which underpin successful performance, indeed, which are necessary for successful performance of symbiotic contracts. These include behavioural norms, some arguably fuzzy, such as good communication and relationship building (active cooperation). and bright-line norms such as rights to cure defects.

John Wightman describes "implicit understandings" as: "the knowledge, practices and or norms … of which the parties … are actually aware, (or can … reasonably be expected to be aware)".[37] This implies that such norms are

---

31 Thomas Wilhelmsson, *Perspectives of Critical Contract Law* (Dartmouth 1993) at 293.

32 Morgan, *Contract Law Minimalism*, 180.

33 *Eurodynamic Systems Plc v General Automation Ltd* unreported. *Saphena Computing Limited v Allied Collection Agencies Limited [1995] FSR 616.*

34 *Anglo Group plc v Winther Brown & Co. Ltd* [2000] EWHC Technology 127 (TCC); see subchapter 2.6.

35 *Yam Seng Pte Ltd v International Trade Corporation Ltd* [2013] EWHC 111 (QB); see subchapter 2.6.

36 Macneil, 'Contracts: Adjustment of Long-Term Relations', 903.

37 In Wightman, 'A Comparison of British and American Attitudes Towards the Exercise of Judicial Discretion in Contract Law' in David Campbell and others (eds), *Implicit Dimensions of Contract: Discrete, Relational, and Network Contracts* (Bloomsbury 2003) at 147.

party specific and objective. In this subchapter I concentrate on the work of the formidable neo-relationists, Hugh Collins and Catherine Mitchell, as well as the good faith focused Roger Brownsword, each of whom bring more meaning to relationalism than most scholars.

Catherine Mitchell describes commercial expectations as: "the collection of beliefs that surround the commercial contracting process … subjective beliefs … an external [non-legal] vantage point … on top of legal coherence".[38] Of commercial expectations she says that they "Should be understood as a more general appeal to the law to recognise the social values and behavioural norms that almost all commercial contractors … bring to bear on their relationship".[39] In her explicit appeal for a "substantial shift to a more relationally constituted contract law",[40] she suggests that "the point … is to achieve some sense of how *the parties* understood their agreement".[41] Steps which might facilitate this shift include:

- Opening up analysis of contracts to the "wider business relationship" and the "economic imperatives" underlying the deal[42] – I consider the context of negotiations and actual conduct below in subchapter 4.2.5.
- Giving legal recognition to previous dealing and trade customs: "such reasonable expectations may be compelling because, if shared, they are an important foundation upon which the parties build their relationship"[43] – see subchapters 4.2.1 and 4.2.4.
- Placing the Court in the "situation of the parties who make these decisions and trade-offs"[44] – see subchapters 4.2.4 and 4.2.6.
- Using as "contextual enquiries" – Williamson's factors of "asset-specificity" and "level of uncertainty".[45]
- Ensuring that judges "develop some sense of norms operating in particular industries and the contexts in which a more formalist approach might be expected".[46] I deal with how such norms might be unearthed in subchapter 4.2.1, and judicial self-knowledge in subchapter 4.2.5

In an examination of the "wider" relationship, I wonder how cultural factors, as one example, play out. In many cases dealt with in the commercial court parties

---

38 Mitchell, *Bridging the Gap*, 12–14.
39 Ibid.
40 Ibid. 236.
41 Ibid. 265. See also Catherine Mitchell, 'Obligations in Commercial Contracts: A Matter of Law or Interpretation?' (2012) 65 *CLP* 455.
42 Mitchell, *Bridging the Gap*, 237.
43 Catherine Mitchell, 'Leading a Life of its Own? The Roles of Reasonable Expectation in Contract Law' (2003) 23 *OJLS* 639 at 654.
44 Mitchell, *Bridging the Gap*, 246.
45 Ibid. 245–246.
46 Ibid. 247.

come from different jurisdictions and the idea of examining cultural factors in play appears to me to be hazardous at best and impossible at worst.[47] It is possible to illustrate the difficulties by observing that whereas it is common practice for relationships to be formed or continued on the golf course in the UK, that is extremely uncommon in Germany. A beer with German colleagues is just that: a beer. It is not part of the business relation. How one measures this aspect of the relationship in domestic cases is hard to determine; how one does it when multiple cultures are in play is impossible.

Mitchell is aware that identifying the location of a deal on the "relational continuum" may not be straightforward and suggests using Williamson's factors of "asset-specificity" and "level of uncertainty" as "contextual enquiries".[48] This is far from simple, not least because asset-specificity is not well-defined. Christian Ruzzier claims, citing empirical work, that "there are problems with the operationalization and measurement of asset specificity".[49] De Vita and colleagues suggest that "the impact of asset specificity on inter-firm relationship performance may not follow a constant, linear effect, but rather be governed by an inverted U-shaped function".[50] The way one might deal with "level of uncertainty" is not easy to envisage. It is, therefore, somewhat unclear what asset-specificity might mean to a Court. Bespoke assets may be built-to-design or built-to-purpose; there is no one size fits all in these transactions.

Hugh Collins' overall position is best described in his own words as committed contextualism: "Thorough-going contextualism ... context determines how much text matters".[51] Described by John Gava and Janey Greene as a "hybrid"[52] law of contract, Collins suggests that we should distinguish between, and use for legal analysis, three frameworks/dimensions/normative systems which govern action in contract[53] and are "always present in contractual relations".[54] Collins argues that regulation might proceed through: "evaluative discourse ... recognizing the force of [reasonable] expectations based upon the economic deal and the parties' history".[55]

---

47 See *Schuler (L) AG v Wickman Machine Tool Sales Ltd* [1974] AC 235, [1973] 2 All ER 39 (HL) and *RTS Flexible Systems Ltd v Molkerei Alois Muller Gmbh & Co. Kg (UK Productions)* [2010] 1 WLR 753: [2010] 3 All ER 1.

48 Mitchell, *Bridging the Gap*, 245–246.

49 Christian A Ruzzier, 'Asset Specificity and Vertical Integration: Williamson's Hypothesis Reconsidered' Harvard Business School Working Paper 2009.

50 Glauco De Vita, Catherine L Wang and Arafet Tekaya, 'The Many Faces of Asset Specificity: A Critical Review of Key Theoretical Perspectives' (2011) 13 *Int J Manage Rev* 329.

51 Collins, 'Objectivity and Committed Contextualism in Interpretation' in Worthington, *Commercial Law,* 193.

52 John Gava and Janey Greene, 'Do we Need a Hybrid Law of Contract? Why Hugh Collins is Wrong and Why it Matters' (2005) 63 *CLJ* 605.

53 Collins, *Regulating Contracts,* 129.

54 Ibid. 141.

55 Ibid. 180.

In other words, the use of the following three frameworks in legal analysis will support identification of reasonable expectations:

- Business relation – comprising numerous interactions, including deal-making and execution plus the social relationship (including business lunches, family links, club membership and ethnic identity), providing trust and "customary standards of trade".[56]
- Economic deal – which specifies the reciprocal obligations, whose normative framework is "economic rationality", which establishes economic incentives and non-legal sanctions.[57]
- Contract – the "standards of self-regulation", the "identification of rights and obligations established by any formal documents, explicit agreements, and accepted customary standards".[58]

The law, he says, must give due weight to each framework, being sensitive to the "history of prior dealings" and an "understanding of the informal conventions".[59] Collins recognises that "The courts possess unrivalled expertise in the details of private law. At the same time, they lack all the necessary dimensions of expertise and information for the task of setting standards for regulating markets."[60]

He argues that without diminishing its "reflexivity" private law can overcome these "weaknesses":

> by ... permitting *amicus curiae*, granting standing to collective groups, the admission of statistical evidence, and using the burden of proof ... require the evolution of reasoning to incorporate references to externalities, public goods, and the articulation of policy objectives ...[61]

The business relation is amorphous and confusing. One dimension is the "social relation" and that is similar to the "wider" relationship called into action by Catherine Mitchell. Collins drafts in business lunches and club memberships without explaining why and how the number of business lunches or who paid for the taxi home or the Cru Bourgeoise should affect the meaning of a contract. As with the cultural factors I discussed above these are intangible and friable (and irrelevant?).[62] I discuss the deal-making and execution phases in subchapters 4.2.4–4.2.6.

---

56 Ibid. 129.
57 Ibid. 129–131.
58 Ibid. 131–132.
59 Ibid. 181.
60 Ibid. 82.
61 Ibid. 93.
62 See *Sheikh Tahnoon Bin Saeed Bin Shakhboot Al Nehayan v Ioannis Kent (AKA John Kent)* [2018] EWHC 333 (Comm) where Leggatt J gives weight to the disputants' personal friendship.

The framework of the economic deal includes non-legal sanctions and it is hard to see why a Court might give these weight. Economic rationality can be conflated with determination of the purpose of the deal, business efficacy or common sense. The reciprocal obligations seem to be mundane contract matters.

It isn't clear into which framework the use of statistical evidence, the amicus curiae or the admission of class actions fits. Courts will already receive survey evidence (see subchapter 4.2.8). I am not sure how commercial actions will be affected by the other two possibilities.

Gava and Greene rather go to town on Collins' lack of detail on how this is to be achieved, claiming that it requires judges with "God-like capacity":

> a superhuman made up of Oliver Williamson, Max Weber, Ronald Dworkin's Hercules and Sir Humphrey Appleby might succeed at doing some of this but even this superhuman would baulk at getting into the heads of disputing contracting parties![63]

This is a little unfair. Much of what Collins proposes does not require too much in the way of revolutionary change (see subchapter 4.2) but the last extension, to externalities, public goods and policy objectives feels very ambitious; requiring judicial law-making in spades.

Roger Brownsword refers to expectations as "practice-based"[64] and suggests that we might define unacceptable commercial pressure by locating: "the standards recognized and accepted within the business community".[65] In developing this theme, he says that where in a particular contracting context the community has a shared understanding of where the line is to be drawn between fair and unfair dealing and "concomitantly, shared expectations about the conduct of fellow contractors", community requirements include regular dealing, no gross disparity of power and relational contracting to the extent that there is a body of experience capable of handling matters when they go wrong.[66] This is less helpful. Why does an imbalance of power matter? If parties, irrespective of size or power, are new to each other, why can "community standards" not apply to the relationship? If each party is an experienced participant should that not be sufficient to create a presumption that they are aware of the community's expectations?

Adams and Brownsword explore a procedural approach, the identification of community standards and a substantive approach, the identification of a community

---

63 John Gava and Janey Greene, 'The Limits of Modern Contract Theory: Hugh Collins on Regulating Contracts [Review Essay]' (2001) 22 *AdelLR* 299 at 306.

64 In DiMatteo and others, 'Contract in a Networked World' in *Commercial Contract Law*, 140.

65 Michie and Deakin, *Contracts*, at 273.

66 Roger Brownsword, *Contract Law: Themes for the 21st Century* (OUP 2006), 131.

of interest.[67] The advantage of this approach is that it elevates commercial expectations to the status of an evidence based, objective standard in which norms or practices can apply to parties who do not have long-term, iterative, relationships.

In considering how to "operationalize" a "co-operative ideal", involving regulation of or limiting of self-interest (still a little vague), Adams and Brownsword liken cooperation to a partnership model, accepting the need for a "non-speculative" strategy for filling out substantive requirements. Accepting that collection of empirical data might help identify community standards they observe that this might result in some variability, "happenstance". Variance may be explained objectively by variables such as industry, culture or context; so this should not be regarded as a problem. As my survey shows, standards can, in respect of cooperation in the management of complex contracts, be reduced to concrete principle and practice and explained in detail by reference to reactions to real-world vignettes. One might compare, for example, the ruthless concealment of information in the *Rabobank* case,[68] accepted as normal practice, with the observation of Mr Tyre in *Ritchie* that concealment of the information in that case was "not sensible commercial practice".[69]

A more intransigent problem would be that we might find "standards shared only at a high level of generality".[70] My survey avoids this possibility by exploring both high levels of generality and detailed vignettes to provide standards with content.

My sample is hard to describe as a community, except to the extent that respondents are engaged in similar transactions. The community relationship between an estates manager at the University of Leicester and a former Executive Vice-President in an oil super-major is hard to imagine unless we say that everyone so engaged is part of what must be an amorphous, incommunicado, community.

For a community of interest, Adams and Brownsword, "grappling with some complex moral theory", develop a logical model, based on Alan Gewirth's dialectical approach. This, they essay, creates a "generic requirement that the exchange be performed as agreed" and this would "shed light on co-operative requirements". Because party X must take a favourable view of the "generic conditions of exchange", non-fulfilment of generic conditions by another agent is impermissible and based on considerations of reciprocity all such agents must be

---

67 John Adams and Roger Brownsword, *Key Issues in Contract* (Butterworths 1995), 302–327. See John Wightman in 'Beyond Custom: Contract, Contexts, and the Recognition of Implicit Understandings' in Campbell and others, *Implicit Dimensions*, 155, discussing community models meaning "specialist shared trading practices".

68 *National Westminster Bank plc v Rabobank Nederland* [2007] EWHC 1056 (Comm). See Woo Pei Yee, 'Protecting Parties' Reasonable Expectations: A General Principle of Good Faith' (2001) 1 *OUCLJ* 195 at 223.

69 *J & H Ritchie Ltd v Lloyd Ltd* [2007] UKHL 9; [2007] 1 WLR 670.

70 Adams and Brownsword, *Key Issues*, 326.

under a duty to respect generic conditions. This doesn't disclose those generic conditions, so why they would be "cooperative" is not clear. Although this strategy shows reciprocal rights to "freedom and well-being" it is still not clear why this infers cooperation as opposed to freedom to exercise self-interest. Part of the matrix might be that parties can rat, or hide information.

They accept that the difficulty with the dialectical approach is that it might not be favoured by commercial contractors; the answer to which, they say, would be to allow contracting out. These expectations should, in other words, be the default position; defeasible only through very clear language.

Roger Brownsword and Lord Steyn[71] each link reasonable expectations to good faith. Professor Brownsword discusses three possible models of good faith, the first acting to protect "standards of fair dealing already recognised in a particular contracting context" (discussed above), the second concept attempting to "make the market" and impose certain external obligations and the third he describes as "judicial licence" or "visceral justice" (in a phrase he borrows from Michael Bridge).[72] However, good faith does not assist us in finding out what parties actually expect; asking parties does. The fair dealing standard is too vague, unless it means recognising that conduct, dealings and/or necessity create expectations and those expectations should be recognised. Otherwise there is a risk of circularity.

4.1.3 Why these expectations should be given legal force

Many of the expectations revealed by the survey are core to the contract, necessary incidents of successful performance. These shared, normative, commercial expectations of the morally reasonable and commercially experienced (in making symbiotic contracts work) emerge from the recognition that contracts are made to be performed, and provide content for the duty to cooperate; but why should they be enforced? My claim is rights centred, based on the argument that autonomous parties make contracts, creating new rights and obligations,[73] and that party intention, including unexpressed commercial expectation, should be at the core of adjudication.

Waitzer refers to reasonable expectations as: "legal Polyfilla – moulding themselves around other structures to plug the gaps".[74] A market or trade practice is not a gap. It is unexpressed agreement, perhaps unexpressed because it is an "ordinary reaction", perhaps because it is widely known, perhaps because that is how the parties have always operated, perhaps because it is so obvious that

---

71 Brownsword, *Contract Law*, 127–128. Steyn, 'Contract Law', 459.

72 Brownsword, *Contract Law*, 130.

73 Stephen A Smith, *Contract Theory* (OUP 2004) says, correctly, that this is what is distinctive about contract law – "it represents a method of creating new rights where none existed before".

74 Edward J Waitzer and Douglas Sarro, 'Protecting Reasonable Expectations: Mapping the Trajectory of the Law' (2016) 57 *CBLJ* 285 at 287.

writing it down would be seen as somewhat gratuitous distraction; as Mackinnon LJ colourfully remarked: "if, … an officious bystander were to suggest some express provision …, they would testily suppress him with a common 'Oh, of course!'"[75] The expectation in *Tradax* is not a gap; but an unspoken term of the contract.[76] Drawing the miscalculation to the charterer's attention is what the parties expected and had, therefore, agreed.

My starting point is that, in David McLauchlan's words, there is: "no conceivable reason … for foisting on the parties an agreement that is contrary to their actual intention".[77]

Adam Kramer asserts that "serious cases of incompleteness of meaning are likely to be rare" describing reasonable expectations as not being empty because all contracting behaviour occurs in a "social context",[78] which includes "mutually known norms of behaviour".[79] Professor Carter says that "expressed intention is a relatively narrow concept"[80] and that extending contract scope "far beyond" express intention is one of many functions of contract law. He describes such extensions under an objective theory of contract, entailing entry into contract as an express commitment to the institution of contract, including its rules for dealing with unexpressed intention.

Referring to "background assumptions", in an endeavour to account for how "agreements are determinate", Brian Langille and Arthur Ripstein say that customary practice and uses can have that effect. A default position of those assumptions being binding is "simply a special case of the need for contracting parties to make any unusual expectations clear".[81] Discussing frustration cases Andrew Robertson criticises this, saying that their "explanation seems to be firmly grounded in the imaginary world of the reasonable person … in which behaviour and expectations are so predictable and uniform that meaning is 'plain' and 'obvious'".[82] That risk can, where usage and

---

75 In *Shirlaw v Southern Foundries (1926), Limited.* [1939] 2 KB 206.

76 Bingham J did not treat the "ordinary reaction" as a trade practice – *Tradax Export SA v Dorada Compania Naviera SA (The "Lutetian")* [1982] 2 Lloyd's Rep 140.

77 David McLauchlan, "Some Fallacies Concerning the Law of Contract Interpretation" at 514. E. Allan Farnsworth, *Contracts* (3rd edn, Aspen Law & Business 1999) says "In the rare cases of a common meaning shared by both parties, the subjectivists have had the better of the argument" at 505.

78 Adam Kramer, 'Common Sense Principles of Contract Interpretation (and How we've Been Using Them All Along)' (2003) 23 *OJLS* 173 at 193.

79 Ibid. 182.

80 JW Carter and Wayne Courtney, 'Unexpressed Intention and Contract Construction' (2016) *OJLS* 326. Randy E Barnett, 'The Sound of Silence: Default Rules and Contractual Consent' (1992) 78 *Virginia Law Rev* 821 makes a similar claim but regards unexpressed agreements as gaps – see 860–867.

81 Brian Langille and Arthur Ripstein, 'Strictly Speaking – it Went Without Saying' (1996) 2 *Legal Theory* 63 at 79. At 154 in 'Beyond Custom' in Campbell and others, *Implicit Dimensions* John Wightman describes such expectations as customary.

82 Andrew Robertson, 'The Limits of Voluntariness in Contract' (2005) 29 *MULR* at 247.

practice is in dispute, be averted by using evidence of expectation; as we shall see in the next subchapter.

Stephen A Smith describes a normative claim for enforcing or recognising expectations as through the notion that it should "protect the expectations of morally reasonable contracting parties", especially "about how they (the contracting parties) ought to act in the future".[83] He says that this is the only universal claim but his key objection to it lies in his view that it is the subjective views of the parties which are in focus. It follows from that that a further objection is that it provides no method of dealing with parties with unreasonable expectations. In dismissing a normative variant, that practices in the community in which the parties trade may help, he asks us, fantastically, to "Consider the views of the Mafiosi community regarding what is appropriate contracting behaviour. It seems quite likely that at least some of these views are unreasonable on general moral grounds."[84] As an offer one cannot refuse[85] is not an offer in the conventional sense, this is not persuasive as a serious example of contracting behaviour. Notions of autonomy, or agreement, do not apply in Mafioso dealings.

Catherine Mitchell says of normative claims: "We may think it important that contracting processes and outcomes reflect some requirement of fair dealing ... [parties] have an entitlement to fair treatment."[86] In my survey, few referred to fairness as an expectation. In around half the mentions fairness meant a fair contract, followed closely by meaning it was fairly managed and then a few thought it meant a fair price (which might be the same as generally fair). It may be that we are discussing different aspects of fairness. The deal itself may be unfair but it should be executed in line with its terms, paper and expectation; procedurally fair. Another problem with fairness is reflected in her opinion that: "Maintaining that fairness requires that reasonable expectations should be protected and that we have a reasonable expectation of fair treatment simply traps us in a circle."[87]

That circularity can be avoided if one tries to find content for commercial expectation. Fairness may be part of the content; *Nash* and construction law cases are examples in point. It seems to me that if reasonable expectations are used in the way Lord Steyn uses them that one can put together a normative case. I can see the force in the assertion that these expectations are "implicit understandings" (ordinary reactions?) and diffuse (as contracts are diffuse) but they are far from informal.[88]

---

83 Smith, 'Reasonable Expectations', 369. His description of an empirical basis, at 375 is similar – "the parties' rational expectations about how [they] are likely to act in future".

84 Ibid. 375. He makes just this point at 370 that certain contracts are unenforceable, on the grounds of defective consent, including contracts "made at gunpoint".

85 The second most quoted film line – from *The Godfather* 1972.

86 Mitchell, 'Leading a Life of its Own?', 654–655.

87 Ibid. 660.

88 See also Zhong Xing Tan, 'Beyond the Real and the Paper Deal: The Quest for Contextual Coherence in Contractual Interpretation' (2016) 79 *MLR* 623 – "expectations must be infinitely variable and could be derived from a variety of sources".

In a wholesale rejection of relational theory Dori Kimel describes the core of its incorporation argument that the law should give: "legal force to parties' expectations that derive from such norms even inasmuch as the norms are merely implicit".[89] "Merely implicit" is an odd description. There is nothing "mere" about implicitness. Arguing that the fact that such norms are extra-contractual is what gives them viability and strength, the text being a "safety net", he says that absorbing such norms into the law may be "inhibitive"[90] – a similar position to that of Lon Fuller who argued that some acts only have value when performed voluntarily.[91] Text is clearly not unimportant and must be given prominence, but it must be read in context. Kimel's argument fails to recognise that expectations originate from multiple sources. Commercial expectations rarely arise from personal relationships. Some emanate from the desire, and the necessity, to make the contract work.

Catherine Mitchell refers to expectations as "slippery and elusive", before remarking that:

> Courts may prefer to speak of reasonable expectation rather than moral principles because it obscures the fact that an appeal to reasonable expectation is not so much a statement about the actual expectations ... as a judgment of the court ex post facto as to the standards the parties must observe.[92]

If the claim is, for example, that certain things are expected, for example that shipowners will quickly let an underpaying charterer know he has underpaid, then one can argue that the duty may be articulated by an appeal to the Court to recognise actual expectation. Where Courts use reasonable expectations as a vague touchstone without evidence of the existence of actual expectation, they may well impose their own standards of reasonableness.

That there are problems with the concept of reasonable expectations may be found in Smith's conclusion:

> The idea that the law ... should protect, the reasonable expectations of the contracting parties sounds eminently sensible ... It is nearly always unclear ... it invariably turns out that the meaning is better expressed using different terms. In practice, the idea that the law of contract protects ... reasonable expectations is a slogan.[93]

---

89 Dori Kimel, 'The Choice of Paradigm for Theory of Contract: Reflections on the Relational Model' (2007) 27 *OJLS* 233 at 244.

90 Ibid. 248.

91 Lon Fuller, 'Positivism and Fidelity to Law: A Reply to Professor Hart' (1958) 71 *HarvLRev* 630 at 672.

92 Mitchell, 'Leading a Life of its Own?'

93 Smith, 'Reasonable Expectations', 386.

There is force in this claim and my argument is limited to recognition of commercial expectation where content, common to actual or reasonable parties, is within the grasp of the commercial judge, if one limits the idea to those expectations or practices which can be or have been evidenced and which are used to determine what the parties have objectively agreed or understood as part of their bargain. In devising a strategy for finding and defining commercial expectations I ensure that such a notion can be connected, or, in the modern vernacular, hard-wired, to the parties. Giving legal recognition to these expectations, where that is a practical proposition, is in the interests of both commerce and law. The norms exposed by the survey arise from experience and a belief in performance of the bargain; not necessarily a non-legal vantage point and certainly not a slogan. They are driven by the desire to keep the contract alive and are consistent across multiple demographic groups. Some of them are clearly less susceptible to legal regulation than others. But some, described as "key", "absolutely critical" and "can't get the job done without it", should benefit from legal recognition.

From my survey of commercial expectation in the field I conclude that the content for commercial expectation emerges from an evidence-led examination of the matrix, the background. Expectations are part of the matrix, the mix; constituents of an alloy rather than a mould.[94] They emanate from trade or market practice (or assumption), from inter-party dealings, occasionally from custom or usage, perhaps from survey evidence. They explain the contract where something is unwritten, perhaps when something is unclear, or when something has an alternative meaning.

4.2 The source of the duty – commercial expectations – Polyfilla, penumbra or polysemia?

In this subchapter I explore how objectively determined commercial expectations can be exposed in proceedings (giving it some Ayr[95]).In reviewing sources, I include "x-phi" work, "philosophy with an empirical edge",[96] only for the purpose of elimination.

4.2.1 Evidence of market practice

Ferreting out Lord Steyn's paragons seems to me to be perhaps the most realistic, and pragmatic, method of finding commercial expectations. Sebastian Grammond is too pessimistic in his claim that: "They do not tell us much, however,

---

94 Lord Steyn's analogy in *First Energy (UK) Ltd v Hungarian International Bank Ltd* [1993] 2 Lloyd's Rep 194 at 196.
95 A trip to Ayr might help – "Auld Ayr, wham ne'er a toon surpasses; For honest men and bonnie lasses" – Robert Burns, *Tam O'Shanter*.
96 David Edmonds, *Would You Kill the Fat Man?* (Princeton UP 2013) at 87.

about where to look to supplement or replace a missing or incomplete or non-existent common intention."[97] Commercial courts have taken account of working methods in the industry or trade in question, textbooks and expert or factual evidence of trade or market practice or expectation, or "assumptions",[98] to assist them in understanding the context of commercial transactions for hundreds of years. Matrix material such as trade usage, custom or trade practice[99], and the opinions of "market men",[100] help explain the bargain.[101] As Lord Wilberforce explained, to understand the background to a commercial contract: "the court should know the commercial purpose of the contract and this in turn presupposes knowledge of the genesis of the transaction, the background, the context, the market in which the parties are operating".[102]

In 1648 the Master of Trinity House and other "esteemed" merchants were asked to advise the Court whether pirates were considered perils of the sea.[103] In 1761, in a case involving water damaged hogsheads of muscovado sugar, Lord Mansfield said:

> The special jury, (amongst whom there were many knowing and considerable merchants,) ... understood the question very well, and knew more of the subject of it than anybody else present; and formed their judgment from their own notions and experience.[104]

The practice did not end with Lord Mansfield's 1788 retirement. In *Syers v Jonas* in 1848 (citing several market practice cases) Parke B accepted: "evidence of the

---

97 Grammond, 'Reasonable Expectations', 365.
98 Neil Andrews, 'Interpretation of Contracts and "Commercial Common Sense": Do Not Overplay This Useful Criterion' (2017) 76 *CLJ* 36 at 43.
99 See *Gibson v Small* (1853) 4 HLC 353 Parke B – "the custom of trade, which is a matter of evidence, may be used to annex incidents ... upon the presumption that the parties have contracted with reference to such usage" at 397. Interestingly, Lisa Bernstein, 'Custom in the Courts' (2015) 63 *NWULR* 110 finds that independent expert evidence was used in less than one-third of the trade usage cases analysed.
100 See Steyn J in *Stratton v Dorintal Insurance* [1987] 1 Lloyds Rep 482.
101 Chitty, *Chitty on Contracts* (ed. Hugh Beale, 33rd edn, Sweet & Maxwell 2018), 14.033 citing *Gibson v Small*.
102 *Reardon Smith Line Ltd v Hansen-Tangen; The Diana Prosperity* [1976] 2 Lloyd's LRep 621 at 624, referred to in Andrews, 'Interpretation of Contracts', as one of six manifestations of commercial common-sense used by the judiciary; others including "trade practices and market assumptions".
103 *Pickering v Barkley* (1648) Sty 132. In *Buller v Crips* 87 ER 793 Holt CJ took advice from "two of the most famous merchants in London".
104 *Lewis v Rucker* (1761) 97 ER 769 (KB). For a history see C Oldham James, 'The Origins of the Special Jury' (1983) 50 UChiLRev 137. Prior to the 16th century juries of cooks and fishmongers are recorded – James B Thayer, 'The Jury and its Development' (1892) 15 *HarvLRev* 295 at 300. Mansfield's jury appears to have been advisory – Todd Lowry, 'Lord Mansfield and the Law Merchant: Law and Economics in the 18th Century' (1973) 7 *J Eco Issues* at 609.

universal usage, that on a sale of tobacco, it was understood to be by sample ... There is no doubt that in mercantile transactions ... evidence of established usage is admissible."[105] The special jury was abolished in 1949 by the post-war Labour Government and replaced by fact or opinion (usually expensive opinion) evidence.[106]

In 1914, the Court examined the discounting practices of brewers in the London area, concluding that tied houses and free houses were treated differently.[107] In 1933 Lord Warrington included methods of producing whale-oil, taking into account the introduction of factory ships in then recent years as facts assisting a correct construction of one contract.[108] In one very odd case Diplock J set aside the award of an arbitration Board because a well-known and accepted market practice, whereby an umpire might meet the Board in the absence of the parties, offended against the rules of natural justice.[109]

In a recent in-depth review of the law on penalties, the Supreme Court used evidence of market practice in determining whether an overstaying charge in a car park constituted a penalty. Lord Hodge noted, citing only evidence from those making profit in the business at hand (perhaps unaware that £85 represented more than one day's income for someone on the minimum wage):

> local authority practice, the BPA guidance, and also the evidence that it is common practice in the United Kingdom to allow motorists to stay for two hours in such private car parks and then to impose a charge of £85, support the view that such a charge was not manifestly excessive.[110]

Examining the question of a sub-broker's payment entitlement, where timing was not express, Sir Andrew Morritt remarked that Courts may: "have regard to market practices falling short of trade usage or custom. They are part of the factual context known to both parties."[111] This knowledge is "objective" as we can see from *Peter Darlington Partners Ltd v Gosho*, in which the buyer was not aware of a market practice whereby short delivery was acceptable subject to

---

105 *Syers v Jonas* 2 Ex 112 426. See Sir George Jessel in *Robert H. Dahl v Nelson, Donkin* (1881) 6 App Cas 38 (HL) and *Rey v Wyoherly* 8 C&P (1838) – a special jury skilled in landlord/tenant relations was impanelled.

106 HC Debate on abolition of Special Juries (1949). Quintin Hogg MP (later Lord Hailsham the Lord Chancellor) claimed that class was the reason for abolition.

107 *Charrington & Co. v Wooder* [1914] AC 71.

108 *Hvalfangerselskapet Polaris A/S v Unilever Ltd* (1933) 26 Lloyds LRep 29.

109 *London Export Corporation Ltd v Jubilee Coffee Roasting Co Ltd* [1958] 1 All ER 494.

110 *ParkingEye Ltd (Respondent) v Beavis (Appellant)* [2015] UKSC 67at 287. I parked my car in Abergavenny in early June 2017 and the local authority there provided an automated procedure allowing for a £5 overstaying charge if the overstay was under two hours. See *British Crane Hire Corpn Ltd v Ipswich Plant Hire Ltd* [1975] QB 303, [1974] 1 All ER 1059 where evidence of common understanding led the Court to conclude that the hirer's standard conditions applied to the contract.

111 *Crema v Cenkos Securities Plc* [2010] EWCA Civ 1444, [2010] EWHC 461 (Comm) at 70.

a pro rata rebate on the price, Glyn-Jones J saying that the buyer should have understood the phrase "pure basis" to mean just that.[112]

Jonathan Hirst QC, sitting as a Deputy High Court Judge, ruled in a City case:

> I also heard expert evidence from Glenn Cooper ... and Adam Hart ... both well qualified to give expert evidence and performed their obligations to the court impressively ... a broad measure of agreement ... on the basis of the expert evidence ... there is a general market practice or understanding in the City that a sub-broker is not paid until the broker receives payment from the client.
>
> So I would admit evidence of market practice which falls short of a usage as part of the matrix of fact ...[113]

In the Court of Appeal Aikens LJ strongly supported that holding, saying: "it has been common practice for the Commercial Court to hear evidence of 'market practice', which does not amount to evidence of an alleged 'trade usage or custom'".[114] The House of Lords considered market practice in North Sea operations in the twin dimensions of insurance practice and contracting terms in a major case arising from the 1998 Piper Alpha disaster, which cost 167 men their lives. It reviewed practitioners' works on both matters.[115] Lord Bingham described the market practices in insuring work as "customary".[116] And, in making a purposive construction of the complex (they all are) mutual indemnity clause at issue in the case, he quotes Daintith and Willoughby who describe the practice as:

> normal for the client and the contractor to assume full liability, and give each other mutual indemnities, for claims arising out of death of or injury to their own employees and for loss or damage to their own property ..., regardless of any negligence or default on the part of the other party or ...[117]

Catherine Mitchell is critical of the reluctance of the Courts to take account of "practices and understandings" in the industry[118] in *Total Gas Marketing v Arco*

---

112 *Peter Darlington Partners Ltd v Gosho* [1964] 1 LloydsLRep 149 at 152.
113 *Crema v Cenkos Securities Plc* (n. 112 above).
114 Ibid. at 42–50. See also Lord Hobhouse in *The Zephyr* [1984] 1 Lloyd's Rep 58.
115 David W Sharp, *Offshore Oil and Gas Insurance* (Witherby & Co. 1994) and Terence Daintith and Geoffrey Willoughby, *A Manual of United Kingdom Oil and Gas Law* (Oyez 1981).
116 *Caledonia North Sea Ltd v London Bridge Engineering Ltd* [2002] UKHL 4 at [7].
117 Ibid. at [8] citing Daintith and Willoughby, *Manual,* 171–172, also citing a US case, *Fontenot v Mesa Petroleum Co.* (1986) 791 F 2d 1207, describing the purpose of the scheme.
118 Mitchell, *Bridging the Gap,* 255–256.

British,[119] but this does not accord with my reading of that case. Perhaps not surprisingly, as Jonathan Parker J noted in the High Court, the spot price of gas had fallen – "Hence the termination of the Sale Agreement would be in Total's commercial interest". The case turned on the construction of a clause dealing with entry into an Allocation Agreement, without which users of the Bacton Gas terminal could not export gas for sale. The House of Lords and the Court of Appeal each noted that it is not unusual for allocation agreements to be agreed only shortly before gas delivery commences, which was mentioned in the High Court Judgment[120] but not as a market practice. There is nothing in any of the Judgments indicating that it was any more than an intermittent fact of life; not routine practice capable of giving rise to understanding or commitment.

On the role of the expert witness in banking litigation Peter Ellinger says that evidence is admissible as to whether: "a 'prudent banker' would have taken certain steps, ... an expert witness could indicate what would have been their own reaction, as a man working in the field, in the given circumstances".[121]

In examining an IT contract Steyn J took expert evidence, which allowed him to make what appears to be a significant change to the usual English Law default that there is no right to cure a defect, and concluded that it

> convincingly showed that it is regarded as acceptable practice to supply computer programmes (including system software) that contain errors and bugs. The basis of the practice is that, ... the supplier will correct errors and bugs that prevent the product from being properly used.[122]

The Privy Council accepted expert evidence on the application of price escalation clauses. Although the expert, Mr McKenzie, was a statistician, his long business experience allowed Goddard J to rule that his conclusion would have been "obvious to the parties".[123]

In one City case the expectations of traders were considered, Colman J accepting

---

119 *Total Gas Marketing Ltd v Arco British Ltd* [1998] All ER (D) 227 (n. 75). Lord Hope refers to the argument that the clause was drafted for the Seller's benefit, without remarking that such evidence should not be allowed.

120 CH 1997 T no. 318.

121 Peter Ellinger, 'Expert Evidence in Banking Law' (2008) *JIBLR* 557 and see *United Bank of Kuwait v Prudential Property Services Ltd* [1995] EG 190 .

122 *Eurodynamics* (n. 34 above).

123 *Contact Energy Ltd v The Attorney General* [2005] All ER (D) 428 (Mar). In *Zeus Tradition Marine Ltd v Bell* [1999] 1 Lloyd's Rep 703 – evidence as to market understanding of the meaning of a "subject to survey" clause was admitted.

the evidence of Mr Thompson, derived as it was from a wealth of experience in workout procedures, that amongst London banks it was in the 1990s considered good practice for co-workout banks to disclose to each other what those concerned with the workout personally considered to be material information.[124]

In another City case the evidence of two experts showed that there was no "universal" method (or market practice) of valuing stocks or bonds in a case where an Exxon Mobil subsidiary had divested itself of a portfolio of assets it held as security, on the event of Lehman Brothers entering into administration.[125]

In one case Moore-Bick LJ supported the use of evidence in relation to a finding that low-cost airlines depend upon being able to operate schedules requiring early morning and late-night aircraft movement;[126] and in another, in which the parties accepted that the customary deposit was 10%, Lord Browne-Wilkinson[127] decided that providing for a higher deposit militated against forfeiture unless justified by special circumstances. In a case on discrepant shipping documents Jonathan Hirst QC accepted evidence that an issuing bank electing to return documents should do so promptly, without delay.[128]

In the *Ritchie* case, used as the pattern for vignette 1 in Chapter 3, Lord Brown said, of Lloyd's refusal to provide any information: "Mr Colin Tyre, QC for the respondents acknowledged in argument that this was 'not sensible commercial practice'".[129] The role of the expert witness or that of the witness of fact is to provide the Court with the context, matrix or background; Moore-Bick J indicating that an expert should "inform the court of any aspects of the commercial background which have a bearing on the construction of the contract".[130] Andrew Robertson says that "Social or business practices may also play a role: by convention, some contracts [e.g. doctor and patient] contain no express terms, leaving the law to imply all rights and obligations on each side."[131] At least some of those obligations are likely to hinge on evidence of the practice of the reasonable doctor.

---

124 *NatWest v Rabobank* (n. 69 above) at 114.
125 *Lehman Brothers International (Europe) (In Administration) v Exxonmobil Financial Services BV* [2016] EWHC 2699 (Comm) Blair J at [21]. See also *Novus Aviation Ltd v Alubaf Arab International Bank BSC(c)* [2016] EWHC 1575 (Comm) – expert evidence was described as helpful in determining background.
126 *Jet2.com Ltd v Blackpool Airport Ltd* [2012] EWCA Civ 417 [2012] 1 CLC 605 at para 17.
127 *Workers Trust & Merchant Bank Ltd v Dojap Investments Ltd* [1993] AC 573 at 580. In the US *Nanakuli Paving & Rock Co. v Shell Oil Co.* 664 F2d 772 (9th Cir 1981) the Court referred to "overwhelming evidence" of market practice known to Shell.
128 *Fortis Bank Sa/Nv v Indian Overseas Bank* [2010] EWHC 84 (Comm) at [32].
129 *Ritchie* (n. 70 above) at [41].
130 *Kingscroft Insurance Co. v Nissan Fire & Marine Insurance Co. Ltd (No. 2)* [2000] 1 All ER (Comm) 272, [1999] Lloyd's Rep IR 603, 622. See also *Galaxy Energy International Ltd v Assuranceforeningen Skuld (Ejensidie) (The "Oakwell")* [1999] 1 Lloyd's Rep 249.
131 Robertson, 'Limits of Voluntariness', 207.

The notion that trade custom might be one source of commercial expectations[132] has, on its face, been dealt a serious blow by the empirical and historical work of Lisa Bernstein who reviews trade usages in US hay, grain and feed, textile, silk and lumber industries; concluding:

> "usages of trade" and "commercial standards … may not consistently exist, even in relatively close-knit merchant communities. While merchants … sometimes do and did act in ways amounting to loose behavioral regularities, most such regularities are either much more geographically local in nature or far more general in scope and conditional in form than is commonly assumed.
> … trade custom… is often amorphous and unsettled.[133]

The caveat "may not" tells one that they may exist. As Stewart Macaulay says, in a comment true of almost all trade practices and usages, Bernstein's findings "raise questions of evidence".[134] In almost every case, the custom or practice will have to be identified as applying to the particular contract and the particular parties. The fact that Virginia and New York traders have different ideas of the meaning of "bale" would not, Macaulay says, prevent a Court from finding meaning as between two New York traders.[135] Tantalisingly Bernstein cites a number of trade custom cases without providing verdicts or rationales.[136] She accepts, citing two cases, that trade body appointed arbitrators, "experienced industry members", who may "implicitly" take custom into account, also consider custom where "trade rules and the contract are silent" – an analogue of the rule that usage must not contradict express terms.[137] These arbitrators appear to be expert in the trade in question, filling the role ascribed to "merchant juries" by Jody Kraus.[138]

---

132 Mitchell, *Bridging the Gap*, 63.

133 Lisa Bernstein, 'The Questionable Empirical Basis of Article 2's Incorporation Strategy: A Preliminary Study' (1999) 66 *UChiLRev* 710.

134 Stewart Macaulay, 'Relational Contracts Floating on a Sea of Custom? Thoughts about the Ideas of Ian Macneil and Lisa Bernstein' (2000) 94 *NWULR* 775 at 788. See the same point by Rhidian D Thomas, 'Custom of the Port' (2016) *LMCLQat* 443. And Jody S Kraus, 'In Defense of the Incorporation Strategy', http//papersssrncom/papertaf?abstract_id=170011 at 39.

135 Macaulay, 'Relational Contracts Floating', 788, also asking "Why isn't it enough to say that one who wants to rely on a usage must prove it?"

136 Bernstein, 'Questionable Empirical Basis'. These include *Nanakuli Paving & Rock Co. v. Shell Oil Co.* (n. 28 above) and *Ore & Chemical Corp v Howard Butcher Trading Corp*, 455 F Supp 1150 in which one issue was whether conditions contained in a telex were standard for this type of transaction.

137 Lisa Bernstein, 'Merchant Law in a Merchant Court: Rethinking the Code's Search for Immanent Business Norms' (1996) *University of Pennsylvania Law Review* at 1780 and 1777.

138 Kraus, 'In Defense of the Incorporation Strategy', 39.

As we can see, John Gava goes somewhat too far in his claim that "obtaining information about the typical expectation of traders … runs into problems of their existence … as well as problems about who will do the work necessary to discover them".[139] Like Lord Mansfield, and contradicting Jonathan Morgan, the modern judge does have access to something analogous to a "group of tame merchant jurymen to give evidence of commercial norms and understandings".[140] Having listened to the "contextual officious bystander"[141] the Court can determine content for commercial expectations of the parties. The difficulty may come in the reluctance of parties to place trade practice or market practice or expectation evidence in front of the judge for tactical or cost reasons, their decisions on what to place before the Court being largely a matter for them, but Courts can use the *Tradax*[142] approach, asking witnesses of fact.

4.2.2 Custom

Christian Twigg-Flesner blames doctrinal certainty for the fact that custom is no longer a "revivifying source of commercial law"[143] but it seems more likely that the world simply moves too fast.[144] Facilities Management and outsourcing organizations have not had time to develop "reasonable, certain, and notorious"[145] customs, for example. It is possible, as shown in one empirical study, that even terms such as "fair wear and tear" or "vandalism" do not have agreed meanings in the relevant trade.[146] In the context of shipping port customs might

> serve to give meaning to key concepts, such as when a ship is to be regarded as an "arrived ship", the obligations of the receiver to assist the vessel …, and, once the ship has arrived at her berth, the preparations to be made for loading and/or discharging the ship …[147]

---

139 John Gava, 'False Lessons from the Real Deal' (2005) 21 *JCL* 182 at 185. Scott makes a similarly wide and similarly incorrect claim at 16.
140 Morgan, *Contract Law Minimalism*, 167.
141 Mark James, *Expert Evidence: Law and Practice* (3rd edn, Sweet & Maxwell 2010) at 295.
142 *The Lutetian* (n. 77 above).
143 Christian Twigg-Flesner and Gonzalo Villalta Puig (eds), *Boundaries of Commercial and Trade Law* (Sellier 2011) at 12.
144 Hugh Beale, 'Bridging the Gap: A Relational Approach to Contract Theory' (2014) 41 *JLS* 641. Mitchell, *Bridging the Gap*, 79, puts it more elegantly – the difficulty is "the inconsistency between the dynamic nature of commerce and the relatively static nature of law".
145 *Devonald v Rosser & Sons* [1906] 2 KB 728 (Court of Appeal Kings Bench Division).
146 Joseph HK Lai and others, 'Disputes Arising from Vaguely Defined Contractual Responsibilities in Building Services Maintenance Contracts' (2004) 22 *Facilities* 44.
147 Thomas, 'Custom of the Port', 445. See also Chitty at 14.004 and 14.033.

Although "likely to be rare" in construction contracts[148] custom "forms the basis of the contract"[149] (trade practice forms part of the matrix) and must be "so well known in the market ... that those who conduct business in that market contract with the usage as an implied term".[150] I am yet to find a custom which could be applied to sophisticated modern contracts. If one is buying or selling rabbits in Suffolk it may help to know that 1,000 means 1,200. In other contexts, it may be useful to know that a hundred could mean "six-score" in ling, cod, nails and herring.[151] It is less than helpful when one is looking at a contract involving the outsourced administration of a complex payroll or pension scheme.

Beale and Dugdale found that there "seemed to be positive resistance" to the written incorporation of trade customs in contracts, but this seems to derive from an interview with one lawyer.[152] Richard Austen-Baker's view that custom is largely a "dead letter" is fair; certainly, for modern, emergent forms of commerce.[153]

4.2.3 The parties' history – overview

One might expect party history to be fertile ground in matrix examination. It is where the parties are at closest quarters; in preceding business relations, armwrestling in negotiations and in the conduct of the business. English Law, however, places serious obstacles in the way of the commercial judge wishing to consider these elements. Lewison says "a large number of transactions" are required to establish a course of dealing.[154] Negotiations, arguably "a large part of the matrix",[155] are not generally admissible.[156] Performance, the actual modus operandi, is, equally and incomprehensibly inadmissible.[157] These are, therefore, currently a limited source of commercial expectation. Under the

---

148 Alfred A Hudson, *Hudson's Building and Engineering Contracts* (ed. Nicolas Dennys and Robert Clay, 13th edn, Sweet & Maxwell 2015) but adds that this may not be true in subcontracts, citing *Townsends (Builders) Ltd v Cinema News* [1959] 1 WLR 119 where it was demonstrated that, by custom, the architect was responsible for showing bye-law compliance.

149 Chitty at 14.033.

150 *Cunliffe-Owen v Teather* [1967] 3 All ER 561 at 573.

151 *Smith v Wilson* (1832) 3 B & Ad 728. See Chitty on Custom at 13.060. For the difficulty in software contracts see e.g. *Trumpet Software Pty Ltd v OzEmail* [1996] 560 FCA 1.

152 Beale and Dugdale, 'Contracts between Businessmen', 59.

153 Richard Austen-Baker, *Implied Terms in English Contract Law* (Edward Elgar 2011), 79.

154 Kim Lewison, *The Interpretation of Contracts* (6th edn, Sweet & Maxwell 2015) at 3.13 on *Hardwick Game Farm v Suffolk Agricultural etc Association* [1966] 1 All ER 309 (AC). See the summary of the law by Edwards-Stuart J in *Hamad M Aldrees & Partners v Rotex Europe Ltd* [2019] EWHC 574 (TCC) at [168].

155 Catherine Mitchell, *Interpretation of Contracts* (Routledge-Cavendish 2007) at 77.

156 *Investors Compensation Scheme v West Bromwich Building Society* [1998] 1 WLR 896. David McLauchlan, 'A Better Way of Making Sense of Contracts?' (2016) 132 *LQR* 577 at 584 – "a surprisingly large number of cases" contravene these rules.

157 *Prenn v Simmonds* [1971] 3 All ER 237, [1971] 1 WLR 1381 (HL). See Lord Steyn in Worthington, *Commercial Law*, at 128 – business people simply do not understand such a rule.

current law the hypothetical expectations of hypothetical parties not involved in the transaction are more important than the parties' own expectations.

In writing the following three subchapters it became clear to me that demarcation in these three categories, prior dealings, negotiations and subsequent conduct, is not easy. In a medium to long term relationship, especially one where repeat orders are being performed, but also in relationships where multiple orders for bespoke work are being performed (I am thinking of examples such as machining or event management), conversations about the course of business will range over current events, future business, past business and performance will/may form a part. These conversations will not be easy to disaggregate and may include comments making future orders or even current orders conditional on performance improvement. What sort of conversation is that? Is it a negotiation? (It may be if the parties are in the course of working on the next order.) Is it about preserving the current deal? Or is it a mere social discussion?

4.2.4 The parties' history – prior dealings

Roger Brownsword suggests that relational elements might include repeat dealings as "an unstated factor of some significance",[158] and Catherine Mitchell says that one contextual enquiry should be into the frequency of transacting.[159] Although Sir Kim Lewison (see above) and Richard Austen-Baker ("must be quite significant"[160]) suggest that a course of dealing requires numerous transactions, the law is unpredictable. Kerr LJ ruled, in *Nichimen Corporation v Gatoil Overseas Inc,* that the fact of opening credits late in nine previous dealings did not establish a course of dealing, "let alone a trade practice", because the reasons for the earlier latenesses were unknown.[161] Rix J, in a well-known passage, ruled that: "In principle ... it is always admissible to look at a prior contract as part of the matrix ... I do not see how the parol evidence rule can exclude prior contracts, as distinct from mere negotiations."[162]

It is tolerably clear that the course of dealing must be clear and consistent (even unequivocal), which may explain *Nichimen* as the "practice" could not be reduced to particularity.[163] Evans LJ considered three years of intermittent dealings in *First Energy (UK) Ltd v Hungarian International Bank Ltd* in

---

158 Brownsword, *Contract Law*, 44.

159 Mitchell, *Bridging the Gap,* 245–246.

160 Austen-Baker, *Implied Terms*, at 5.34–5.39.

161 *Nichimen Corporation v Gatoil Overseas Inc.* 1987 2 Lloyd's Rep 46 at 53.

162 *HIH Casualty and General Insurance Ltd v New Hampshire Insurance Co.* [2001] 2 Lloyds Rep 161 at [83].

163 In *Hamad M. Aldrees & Partners v Rotex Europe Ltd* at [168] "The course of dealing by the party contending that its terms and conditions are incorporated has to be consistent and unequivocal". See also *Cleveland Bridge UK Ltd v Sarens (UK) Limited* [2018] EWHC 751 (TCC).

explaining the "background of dealings",[164] and in another case 11 clear prior dealings were held to create a course of dealing sufficient to incorporate specific conditions.[165] In *Arcadis Consulting (UK) Ltd v AMEC (BCS) Ltd (Arcadis)* an earlier interim contract preceding the deal was examined to underline a conclusion that the parties had intended to provide for a limit of liability in the final contract.[166] In *Gunvor SA v Sky Oil and Gas Ltd* Butcher J said that "it was the usual practice of the Claimant to send out such formal terms and the Defendant would have known that that was their ordinary practice from their prior dealings", finding that, as the Defendant had not formerly objected to these terms, they formed part of the contract. It is not clear how far back these dealings stretched, although there is some indication that they were the negotiations involved in reaching the deal in issue.[167] In a charter party case the Court examined 28 voyages, 19 between the same parties, finding that in all but the first three the owners had bunkered at Constantza. Although course of dealing in terms, did not form part of the dispute, the practice was taken into account by the Court.[168] And in *CEL v Nedlloyd* Baroness Hale noted that – "Furthermore, the meaning of those provisions has to be construed in the context in which this agreement was negotiated".[169]

Where parties had had dealings for over 20 years the Court of Appeal applied a last-shot/battle of the forms analysis, despite saying that the context of a long-term relationship and the conduct of the parties might sometimes be strong enough to displace the result of a traditional offer and acceptance analysis.[170] Dyson LJ explained the result as "having the merit of a great degree of certainty",[171] but it seems more likely to increase upfront transaction costs or to diminish the capacity of parties to operate in mutually agreed ways.[172] It does not help that it is wholly unclear from any of the three Judgments what might suffice to displace the "traditional" analysis. In this case the dispute was, almost inevitably, over liability for delay and non-conformance. It seems likely that such issues must have arisen in past dealings and it does not appear to impose major costs or uncertainty in litigation to ask the parties to provide evidence of past practice and to analyse terms and conditions in that light. The evidence was that the battle of the forms was an administrative (automatic)

---

164 *First Energy (UK) Ltd v Hungarian International Bank Ltd* (n. 95 above) at 205.
165 *Circle Freight International Ltd v Medeast Gulf Exports Ltd* [1988] 2 Lloyd's Rep 427.
166 *Arcadis Consulting (UK) Ltd (formerly Hyder Consulting (UK) Ltd) v AMEC (BCS) Ltd (formerly CV Buchan Ltd)* [2018] EWCA Civ 2222.
167 *Gunvor SA v Sky Oil & Gas Ltd (Previously Known as Keystone Trade Oil & Gas Group (UK) Ltd)* [2018] EWHC 1189 (Comm) (16 April 2018) at [30] and at [4]–[5].
168 *Reardon Smith Line v Black Sea and Baltic General Insurance Co* [1939] AC 562 (HL).
169 *CEL Group Ltd and others v Nedlloyd Ltd* [2003] All ER (D) 323 (Feb) at [19].
170 *Tekdata Interconnections Ltd v Amphenol Ltd* [2009] EWCA Civ 1209.
171 Ibid. at [25].
172 Mitchell, *Bridging the Gap*, 124, says it may "give rise to the possibility of opportunism".

affair, so the result seems to place mechanical matters above the need to find out what parties have actually agreed.

One possible source of prior dealing might be umbrella agreements. These are usually framework agreements, allowing the simplification of repeated trans- actions including provisions which "record and mould expectations".[173] They may include general management interactions, problem solving and even dispute resolution provisions. They are usually not legally binding in themselves but may become an intrinsic component of individual transactions.[174] The way in which they have been operated by the parties over years might give rise to common core expectations, say as to dealing with defects. Such expectations would have to be concrete, arising through consistent practice of a type redu- cible to a bright-line.

In *Baird Textile Holdings v Marks and Spencer plc*[175] an "exceptionally close and inter-active commercial relationship", that had lasted 30 years, came to an abrupt end at the behest of Marks and Spencer. This involved close relation- ships between senior executives, regular consultations on strategy, sales, design, technology, quality and logistics, Baird's appointment of managers selected by M&S, Baird working to M&S's seasonal timetables and compliance with M&S's procurement policies and production standards. In her very good description of how new-form umbrella agreements work Lisa Bernstein finds similarly close relationships in her analysis of Master Service Agreements.[176] She presses the case that these are relationship based; but my reading of the Quality and Governance requirements is that they are highly formal managerial imperatives and deep planning requirements. As she observes, in a passage that many modern managers will recognise as correct and describing sensible com- mercial practice:

> Breaches due to one-off manufacturing glitches are largely ignored, unless they are frequent. Breaches due to systematic production problems (even large ones) that the buyer thinks can be remedied are initially met with offers of technical assistance, sometimes at the buyer's expense.[177]

This is the kind of area that I think might, and should, create the type of expectation that becomes contractual. If a practice developed, order by order, in which minor defects were accepted or remedied by the supplier and major defects are subject to discussion and root cause analysis over a period of years, it would seem very curious for the law to support a sudden change in behaviour

---

173 Ibid. 60–61.

174 Stefanos Mouzas, 'Negotiating Umbrella Agreements' (2006) 22 *Negotiation J* 279. See also Heide and John, 'Alliances'.

175 *Baird Textiles Holdings Ltd v Marks & Spencer plc* [2001] EWCA Civ 274, [2002] 1 All ER (Comm) 737.

176 Bernstein, 'Beyond Relational Contracts'.

177 Ibid. 584.

from that collaborative and pragmatic approach to a bright-line imposition of a contractual remedy. At this stage I would point out that this example shows how hard it is to separate prior dealing from subsequent conduct.

In the *Post Office Litigation* Fraser J described how default was dealt with as in practice – "if there were 'performance issues' these would be explored firstly with the SPM who would be given the opportunity to remedy them".[178] That is a good analysis of the contract and almost certainly how the parties understood it. Gava and Greene would disagree:

> a history of waivers ... might be understood by the breaching party as just part of the normal give and take of daily business, while the other side might see it as increasing evidence of the unreliability ... to be put up with only until an alternative source of supply is found. ... evidence for either point of view is likely to be non-existent or extremely fragmentary and ambiguous. How is a judge supposed to find the "true" nature of the business relation?[179]

In litigation each party will provide documentation under the usual disclosure rules which should give the judge a clue, perhaps even make matters "crystal clear" (as in *Chartbrook*). The ordinary reaction of any professional manager considering how to react would be to issue a relatively formal warning. It is certainly what any reasonable party would expect.

Baird's case suggested an implied contract[180] recognising "broad obligations" to continue the relationship. Under this Baird would be obliged to meet a reasonable or appropriate share of M&S's actual requirements, where it had the capability to do so and their price was reasonable. Baird submitted that the Court could, by examining the parties' past performance, work out the minimum purchase obligations that M&S should be taken to have committed to place and Baird to have committed to supply during a three-year notice period. The Vice-Chancellor ruled that this would involve the court writing a "reasonable" contract for the parties, after making a complete review of their situations, needs, abilities and expectations, but that the "informal business partnership" was insufficient to give any contractual protection, as there had been no agreement on essentials (distinguishing *Hillas v Arcos*[181]). M&S had made it clear that the only legal relationship it wanted was an order-by-order relationship.[182]

---

178 *The Post Office Group Litigation* [2019] EWHC 606 (QB) at [892].
179 Gava and Greene, 'Do we Need a Hybrid Law of Contract?', 617. At 618 they confirm my point, somewhat unexpectedly – "best evidence is likely to be found in past conduct, such as previous dealings or deviations ... in practice".
180 *Baird v M&S* (n. 176 above) at [67]–[68].
181 *Hillas & Co. Ltd v Arcos Ltd* (1932) 38 Com Cas 23, [1932] All ER Rep 494.
182 Robert Bradgate, 'Contracts, Contract Law and Reasonable Expectations' in Worthington, *Commercial Law*, at 675 – the "very flexibility of the arrangements made creating a contract

There is something missing in the analysis. Some form of umbrella agreement subsisted between the parties involving clear obligations to continue to discuss strategy, needs, prices and other requirements.[183] Contracts can be created by conduct as well as by words.[184] This would infer a duty to communicate, discuss and try to agree. My difficulty is that I suspect that the outcome would have been the same; no deal.

One of the many problems associated with reviewing the wider or even entire business relationship can be illustrated with a consideration of one of the cases considered by Catherine Mitchell in which she says that the Courts did have ways of making the two worlds of documents and understandings consistent.[185] In *Total Gas Marketing Ltd v Arco British Ltd* the Court was faced with giant oil and gas companies (there were three defendants) disputing the effect of a failure to enter into an "allocation agreement" into which entry was a condition of a gas supply contract, the gas being delivered to a terminal owned by yet another player in the industry: AMOCO.[186] That the oil and gas business is complex, even incestuous, can be gauged by remembering the fire at the Buncefield Oil Depot in Hertfordshire. Here is an extract from the HSE report.[187]

The Buncefield oil storage and transfer depot is a tank farm in Hemel Hempstead, Hertfordshire, England, close to Junction 8 of the M1 motorway. In December 2005 there were three operating sites at the depot:

- Hertfordshire Oil Storage Ltd (HOSL), a joint venture between Total UK Ltd and Chevron Ltd and under the day-to-day management of Total UK Ltd. HOSL (the site) was divided into East and West sites;
- British Pipeline Agency Ltd (BPA), a joint venture between BP Oil and Shell Oil UK, though assets were owned by UK Oil Pipelines Ltd (UKOP). This tank farm was also in two parts, the north section and the main section which was located between HOSL East and West; and
- BP Oil UK Ltd, at the southern end of the depot.

---

difficult". Hugh Collins, *The Law of Contract* (CUP 2008) – M&S "indicated clearly that it did not intend to enter into a long-term binding contractual relationship ... and its conduct was entirely consistent with that position".

183 See Bradgate, 'Contracts, Contract Law and Reasonable Expectations' in Worthington, *Commercial Law* at 678 – an argument based on M&S being estopped from claiming that there was no umbrella agreement could have been constructed.

184 *The Aramis* [1989] 1 Lloyds Rep 213 Bingham J – if the parties would have acted as they did without a contract that is fatal to any implication.

185 Mitchell, *Bridging the Gap*, at 255–256.

186 *Total Gas Marketing Ltd v Arco British Ltd* (n. 120) above.

187 www.hse.gov.uk/comah/buncefield/buncefield-report.pdf.

Total is the fourth largest oil company in the world, with revenues of circa $127Bn and Arco was purchased by BP for $27bn in 2000.[188] These are giant companies with networks of infrastructure investments, joint operations (almost all oil fields are developed by consortia), business to business sales of less or more preferred products and intertwined strategic interests. How a Court would examine their entire relationship is wholly unclear to me.

Frequency of transacting is not always a good guide. Large businesses transact with other large businesses on multiple levels and between different divisions; frequency does not imply homogeneity. Corporations are not always consistent in their approach and one manager's methods and tolerance levels will differ from another's.[189]

One problem with too relaxed a course of dealing principle is that implies that one interprets a contract by reference to a previous contract. And one wonders how far that process can go back in time. In *Baird v M&S* the relationship extended over 30 years. Any examination of such a background becomes increasingly complex and increasingly difficult for parties who may then be exposed to major problems with control and retention of records going back many years even beyond conventional limitation periods.

If parties experienced amicable, constructive relations in previous dealings or, for example, a defaulting party has usually been allowed to cure a defect, a Court might enquire into why a relationship had dissolved with that in mind as part of the background, confining it to consideration of the parties' method of dealing with similar problems in the past.

4.2.5 *The parties' history – negotiations*

Melvin Eisenberg describes negotiations as: "A relatively norm-free process centred on the transmutation of underlying bargaining strength into agreement by the exercise of power, horse-trading, threat and bluff."[190] As a rough and ready description it has serious explanatory power and one lesson which should be drawn from it is that it is likely to be difficult to locate a point in time, prior to full agreement, where a commitment intended by both parties to be binding has been made. English Law excludes evidence of prior negotiations, but the basis appears to be protean, Lord Hoffmann explaining that they are admissible in rectification actions but not otherwise for reasons of practical policy.[191] Lord Wilberforce preferring to base exclusion on grounds, which are not "technical",

---

189   Hugh Collins says something similar; that in larger firms "different departments may select rival normative contexts": *Regulating Contracts,* 135.
190   Melvin Aron Eisenberg, 'Private Ordering through Negotiation: Dispute-Settlement and Rulemaking' (1976) 89 *Harvard Law Rev* 637 at 638.
191   *Investors* (n. 157 above) at 913A.

that "simply that such evidence is unhelpful".[192] Beatson LJ has clarified this; extending admissibility to include rectification, estoppel and facts relevant to the background.[193] A further exception is that words deleted during negotiations may be treated as background.[194]

Ewan McKendrick comments that the rule is "suspect", and that negotiation evidence should be available unless it relates to the subjective intent of the parties.[195] Catherine Mitchell points out that negotiating evidence as background for determining content is admissible and hard to distinguish from interpretation.[196] Gerard McMeel says that the "boundaries of these exceptions are notoriously porous,[197] and circumventable", noting the power of the Courts to control evidence and Rules that ensure that evidence can be limited.[198] Illustrating the difficulty of using negotiation evidence, Lord Neuberger in *re Sigma* said that "documents often have different provisions drafted inserted or added to by different lawyers at different times ... last minute amendments agreed in a hurry, frequently in the small hours of the morning".[199] It is not always the lawyers who negotiate; indeed, lawyers are, in many cases, backroom advisers.[200] Lord Wilberforce said, correctly, that during negotiations the parties' positions are changing with "each passing letter" (or, today, email).[201]

In a case which surprised Denning MR, being the first time he had dealt with container traffic, a pre-contract conversation in which it was agreed that an expensive bespoke injection moulding machine would not be carried on deck was incorporated as the oral part of a part oral and part written contract, despite the use of written standard terms.[202] This appears to be a fictional way of circumventing the exclusionary rule.

---

192 *Prenn v Simmonds* (n. 158 above) at 1348E.

193 *Globe Motors Inc v TRW Lucas Varity Electric Steering Ltd* [2016] EWCA Civ 396 at [69].

194 *Bou-Simon v BGC Brokers LLP* [2018] EWCA Civ 1525.

195 In 'The Interpretation of Contracts: Lord Hoffmann's Re-Statement' in Worthington, *Commercial Law* at 160.

196 Mitchell, *Interpretation*, 76–77. Catherine Mitchell, 'Contract Interpretation: Pragmatism, Principle and the Prior Negotiations Rule' (2010) 26 *JCL* 134. Ewan McKendrick in Worthington, *Commercial Law* at 156 – it is hard to distinguish between evidence of the background and genesis and negotiating positions.

197 See *Vitol E&P Limited v New Age (African Global Energy) Ltd* [2018] EWHC 1580 (Comm) at [53]–[57] – Moulder J discusses the changed placement of a comma, saying at [55] that "one would have expected a significant change at this stage to have been highlighted in the covering email".

198 Gerard McMeel, 'Foucault's Pendulum: Text, Context and Good Faith in Contract Law' (2017) *CLP*.

199 *Re Sigma Finance Corp* [2008] EWCA Civ 1303 at [100].

200 My claim is experience based. See *Vitol E&P Ltd v New Age (African Global Energy) Ltd* at [60]–[74].

201 *Prenn v Simmonds* at 1384.

202 *J Evans & Son (Portsmouth) Ltd v Andrea Merzario Ltd* [1976] 2 All ER 930.

In another case the Court used evidence of prior negotiations to choose between two possible meanings of a term.[203] This principle was described (limited) by Lord Hoffmann in his last case in the House of Lords as allowing evidence that a party "habitually used words in an unconventional sense".[204] In this case, *Chartbrook*, one of the pre-contract documents disclosed by Chartbrook contained a holograph note which inferred that Persimmon's construction of the contract was what the parties had intended. Baroness Hale said of the note "On any *objective* view; that made the matter crystal clear".[205] Despite this she followed the majority in supporting the principle that the material was inadmissible.

In another recent case negotiation evidence formed part of the background to a complex Sale and Purchase Agreement, O'Farrell J saying that "There is strong evidence that the above interpretation was shared by the parties at the time of the SPA".[206] Such evidence was already in front of the judge, as disclosure is not limited to admissible documents.[207]

In *Arcadis* the Court looked extensively at the negotiations between the parties, disguising this as a review of the background, Dame Elizabeth Gloster ruling:

> The judge's conclusion is ... that ... Hyder assumed an unlimited liability for its contractual performance, when it never would have assumed such liability under any contract which it entered into. ... that is even more extraordinary in the current context, where the parties had specifically agreed that limit of liability in relation to the interim contract.[208]

Background may also include prior contracts; Carnwath LJ saying that Courts should take a "cautious and sceptical approach" when undertaking a review of a prior contract and consider that "prima facie" differences between the new

---

203 *The Karen Oltmann* [1976] 2 Lloyd's Rep 708. Lord Nicholls used narrow language, sometimes described as the "private dictionary" exception – "parties have in effect negotiated on an agreed basis that the words bore only one of the two possible meanings, then it is permissible for the Court to examine the extrinsic evidence". See *Proforce Recruit Ltd v The Rugby Group Ltd* [2006] EWCA Civ 69 where the Court of Appeal allowed a review of the negotiations but found that the parties had not agreed a special meaning for the term "preferred supplier status". Romilly MR in *Fechter v Montgomery* (1863) 23 Beav 22 used pre-contract "conversations" to unearth the purpose of the agreement; at 26.

204 *Chartbrook Ltd v Persimmon Homes Ltd* [2009] UKHL 38 at [45].

205 Ibid. at [99].

206 *Triumph Controls – UK Ltd, Triumph Group Acquisition Corporation v Primus International Holding Company, Primus International Inc., Primus International Cayman Co* [2019] EWHC 565 (TCC) at 312.

207 J Edward Bayley, 'Prior Negotiations and Subsequent Conduct in Contract Interpretation: Principles and Practical Concerns' (2012) 28 *JCL* 179.

208 *Arcadis Consulting (UK) Ltd (formerly Hyder Consulting (UK) Ltd) v AMEC (BCS) Ltd (formerly CV Buchan Ltd)* at [123].

contract and the old one are deliberate.[209] In the *Thorney Park* case McCombe LJ reviewed the history of the relationship, an earlier contract and the negotiations to conclude that an apparently open-ended termination provision (inserted during the negotiations for this contract) should be read together with another provision referring to an "initial term of three years".[210]

The exigencies of negotiation require that deals are done in multifarious ways, at different levels and in different "channels".[211] Ekaterina Pannebakker describes the corporate process as ending by appointing negotiators, and then finding agreement "through successive signals and through a more or less formal form, – letters of intent, protocols et cetera".[212] Deal-makers step in and out, make deals for different reasons, sometimes connecting apparently unrelated issues in order to cut through commercial impasses. Sometimes this is done simply to make progress, without much logic, to get negotiators onto new matters. In a typical sales environment, in my experience, in major corporate environments, a salesperson will discuss a contract with a customer. Amongst other things, the topics of termination and defects will probably crop up when the suppliers' expert reviews conditions. When the salesperson meets their opposite number, the procurement person, they usually encounter two obstacles:

- Neither is a contract expert.
- Each must follow complex compliance processes which make changing contract conditions difficult.

The customer way well agree that termination won't be triggered without allowing the supplier an opportunity to cure and that the supplier would be offered an opportunity to cure defects. Typically, the salesperson then writes to me, or one of my team (the paranoid contract/commercial expert), who advises that a verbal agreement like this is useless.[213] The best thing is to take a step which may well be regarded as aggressive and/or displaying a lack of trust: writing to the counterpart to record the discussion. Even then, my advice is that this is unlikely to work. It is clear that the supplier knew that there was a risk that the agreement was ineffective. Of itself, this suggests one of the evidential difficulties; my advice is likely to have been oral and hence unlikely to reach the Court. However, what would a reasonable commercial person make of this matrix? Despite the fact that recording this might provoke suspicion I would do so and

---

209 *KPMG LLP v Network Rail Infrastructure Ltd* [2007] All ER (D) 245 (Apr) at [83].

210 *Thorney Park Golf Ltd. v Myers Catering Ltd* [2015] EWCA Civ 19.

211 See the "phases" described in RE Fells, *Effective Negotiation: From Research to Results* (2nd edn, CUP 2012) at 67–70.

212 Ekaterina Pannebakker, 'Offer and Acceptance and the Dynamics of Negotiations: Arguments for Contract Theory from Negotiation Studies' (2013) 6 *Erasmus Law Rev* 131 at 136.

213 The salesman will, I know, regard this as incomprehensible; see Steyn, 'The Intractable Problem of the Interpretation of Legal Texts' in Worthington, *Commercial Law* at 128, saying that "business people just do not understand" this rule.

hope that a Court would recognise it as part of the matrix. If the agreement is recorded in an email or minutes there is no good reason why that should not be admissible as to what the condition actually means.[214] This is only a minor step from the *Karen Oltmann/Chartbrook* principle.

In a Canadian case one party wrote to the other providing its, allegedly "mutual", understanding of a clause in the contract. There being no reply the letter, being, according to Spigelman CJ, "drenched in subjectivity", was inadmissible; which seems right; although the opposite conclusion might be better were the letter from the party not seeking reliance on it. It's a lesson to dealmakers to follow up where that is important.[215]

In a survey he describes as "indicative" J Edward Bayley provides evidence that litigation practitioners consider the background, including negotiations and that documentation relating to subsequent conduct and precontract negotiation is usually (or often) disclosed.[216] 48% of litigators agreed that negotiation evidence is "frequently admitted", concluding that "cost awards are perhaps the most powerful device … [to deter production of] … futile evidence".[217] This together with case management powers, should answer cost and complexity issues. If judges do flout the rules almost routinely, they may also be disguising their reasoning, which cannot lead to coherent law.[218]

Applying this to *Lymington*, had Commodore MacNamara enquired of the marina's solicitors how the sublicensing provision worked and were the answer, in writing, that the owners would consider any request and be reasonable about granting permission, it would be perverse to deny that any force. Catherine Mitchell, quoting Lord Nicholls, suggests that documentary evidence should be admissible if it "sheds light on the language".[219] Hugh Collins suggests that prior negotiations should be "relevant if they would have influenced the reasonable promisee".[220] Neil Andrews describes the inadmissibility of the evidence of

---

214 Jody S Kraus and Robert E Scott, 'Contract Design and the Structure of Contractual Intent' (2009) 84 *NYU L Rev* 1023 at 1029 – tentative agreements may be abandoned during negotiations. See *Tekdata Interconnections Ltd v Amphenol Ltd* (n. 171 above) where Dyson LJ says, at [30], "an obvious example is where there is an issue as to whether a term was orally agreed and in post-contractual correspondence the party who denies the existence of the term admits that it was agreed".

215 *Phoenix Commercial Enterprises Pty Ltd v City of Canada Bay Council* [2010] NSWCA 64 at [30].

216 Bayley, 'Prior Negotiations' 183–184.

217 Ibid. 186–187.

218 Ibid. 183. Judges may allow "crafty counsel" to "sneak in evidence" of negotiations under the guise of demonstrating contractual purpose – Ryan Catterwell, 'The "Indirect" Use of Evidence of Prior Negotiations and the Parties' Intentions in Contract Construction: Part of the Surrounding Circumstances' (2012) 29 *JCL* 183.

219 Mitchell, *Interpretation*, 79.

220 Worthington, *Commercial Law*, chapter 8 'Objectivity and Committed Contextualism in Interpretation', 197.

negotiations as a "powerful restraint" on the over use of "commercial common sense" as Courts are "alive to the chance that a transaction's odd, curious or tough wording is the result of compromise or obfuscation".[221] I would suggest that that such a chance was worth exploring to determine how the parties got there and whether there was a discernible common intention. As Coulson J has said, judges should give effect to the intention of the parties "however inelegantly expressed".[222]

In considering how this might apply to modern complex contracts, we should consider that the constructive engagement which underpins their success is a continuous process and not an event. During negotiations parties will discuss, in outline, governance routines, Balanced Scorecard principles and the timescale for developing a full-blown, working Contract Management Plan. They expect that these management principles and documents will be fully developed during kick off meetings and reworked as the contract progresses. Minutes reflecting these agreements and discussions will probably exist and will probably not form part of the contract. In cases of doubt as to how the parties agreed that their contract should be governed and managed, these materials should be available to judges.

Catherine Mitchell argues that it is hard to maintain a claim that admitting evidence of prior negotiations would create uncertainty after *Chartbrook*, in which the judges fell 6–3 in favour of Persimmon.[223]

If the purpose of interpreting contracts is to find the objective intention of the actual parties and parties have identical subjective intentions, as shown by evidence, what logic might allow a Court to conclude that their objective intention was different? In summary the material is usually already disclosed, Judges frequently read it, and it may make matters "crystal clear". So long as one-sided or one-sided subjective material is not admitted, and material which is admitted either shows or probably shows common party intention, and there is a serious possibility of cost consequences for putting forward futile material, there is no good reason for the exclusionary rule.[224]

4.2.6 *The parties' history – subsequent conduct*

If judges can treat trade or market practice as part of the matrix or background it is difficult to understand why the parties' actual conduct is not so treated. Hudson suggests that the rules excluding such evidence are "not easy to apply ... particularly so when there is a series of contracts",[225] and Hugh Collins

---

221 Andrews, 'Interpretation of Contracts', 57.

222 *Fitzroy Robinson Ltd v Mentmore Towers Ltd* [2009] EWHC 1552 (TCC) at [65].

223 Mitchell, 'Contract Interpretation', 146.

224 See Andrew Milner, 'Contract Interpretation: Potential for Relaxing the Exclusionary Rule' (2011) 3 *IJLBE* 205.

225 Hudson at 1.031. For an example see *Gunvor SA v Sky Oil & Gas Ltd (Previously Known as Keystone Trade Oil & Gas Group (UK) Ltd)* (n. 168 above).

suggests that they "are widely ignored in practice".[226] Interestingly, Sir Kim Lewison opens his subchapter on subsequent conduct by saying that "At one time the Courts were prepared to admit evidence of subsequent conduct where the contract was ambiguous and the conduct was probative".[227] Lord Hoffmann has ruminated that: "when both parties are agreed about what they understood their mutual obligations ... to be, it is a strong thing to exclude their evidence".[228] In *New Zealand Diving Equipment Ltd v Canterbury Pipelines Ltd* an ambiguous provision said that rates for divers would be paid while divers were "on the job or in the water".[229] During performance, invoices included divers' time in transport to the offshore site and each invoice was paid on this basis, the client having checked them meticulously. McGregor J found that this provided unequivocal support for the contractor.[230] One wonders how the issue might have been resolved in the face of contradictory trade practice.

Judges can simply ignore the rule. For example in *Mamidoil-Jetoil Greek Petroleum Co. SA v Okta Crude Oil Refinery AD* Rix LJ decided that objective criteria for deriving a new oil-handling fee could be found on the basis that this had been possible over a 20-year relationship.[231] In *Medirest*, Lewison LJ used performance to support a narrow interpretation of the cooperation clause; Cranston J having found "that the dispute over SFPs and Deductions did not affect the day to day provision of services".[232] In *CEL v Nedlloyd* Hale LJ construed the contract referring to the substantial investment made in the haulage fleet; which must be subsequent conduct.[233]

David McLauchlan describes one "remarkable" case where a Court used negotiation evidence to establish that there was a contract, but excluded it when it interpreted the contract using: "the orthodox objective approach ... But why does a court have to look for a presumed intention when their actual intention that quota was to pass is established? Is our law of contract really so silly?"[234]

---

226 In 'Objectivity and Committed Contextualism in Interpretation', in Worthington, *Commercial Law*, at 197.

227 Lewison, *Interpretation*, at 3.19 citing *Watcham v Att Gen of East Africa Protectorate* [1919] AC 53. The East Africa Protectorate is, roughly speaking, Kenya.

228 *Carmichael v National Power plc* [1999] 1 WLR 2042 at 2050–2051.

229 *New Zealand Diving Equipment Ltd v Canterbury Pipelines Ltd* [1967] NZLR 961.

230 Ibid. at 977.

231 *Mamidoil-Jetoil Greek Petroleum Co. SA v Okta Crude Oil Refinery AD* [2001] EWCA Civ 406.

232 See *Mid Essex Hospital Services NHS Trust v Compass Group UK and Ireland Ltd (t/a Medirest)* [2013] EWCA Civ 200 at [145] citing *Compass Group UK and Ireland Ltd (t/a Medirest) v Mid Essex Hospital Services NHS Trust* [2012] EWHC 781 (QB) at [62]. See Lewison, *Interpretation*, 89 and 91.

233 *CEL Group Ltd and others v Nedlloyd Ltd* (n. 170 above) at [19]. She makes a similar comment about investment in *Rice (t/a Garden Guardian) v Great Yarmouth Borough Council* [2000] All ER (D) 902 (AC).

234 David McLauchlan, 'Contract Formation and Subjective Intention' (2017) 25 U Queensland LJ 77 at 85 citing *Edwards v O'Connor* [1991] 2 NZLR 542. From *Brambles Holdings Ltd v Bathurst City Council* (2001) 53 NSWLR 153 the answer appears to be yes, as the Court ruled that a common party interpretation of the contract was simply "wrong".

The rule has an obverse. For example, in Australia subsequent conduct may be weighed in the light of a No Oral Modification clause as a way of determining whether the parties intended to vary a contract.[235] This may operate by way of waiver in English Law cases.[236]

In developing, for example, Contract Management Plans and Balanced Scorecards those responsible will have an eye to the constructive engagement, give and take, problem solving, expected as part of the management of the contract, which may include some "aftercare" such as providing a full-time client presence to respond to queries, transfer knowledge to assist in settling in.[237]

In Chapter 3 I found that commercially experienced people can define what is required to make these modern complex contracts work. I also found that parties use give-and-take, adjust obligations and negotiate their way through problems. This conduct should be admissible to determine what the parties intended when they entered into the contract – the "Liberal approach" according to McLauchlan.[238] Lisa Bernstein accepts that "norms" will emerge over a relationship and may even contradict express terms but says that these are "extra-legal" and that conduct will not normally be taken into account by trade arbitrators where it departs from express language; a relatively narrow exclusion.[239]

As Johan Steyn observes, parties will simply not understand a rule that excludes such management work from the purview of the Court. They would be outraged if, having made such deals, the other party then insisted on black-letter performance, and a Court then found management work to have no legal status.

4.2.7 Surveys

My survey would be of value to support a commercial expert giving evidence. For example, it suggests that the "ordinary reaction" of a supplier asked for a report on a once defective, apparently now repaired harrow would be to provide a report sufficient to allay the farmer's concerns.[240] Market research surveys are admissible, as is[241] survey evidence if it is of "real

235 *Mathews Capital Partners v Coal of Queensland Holdings* [2012] NSWSC 462
236 *Reveille Independent LLC v Anotech International (UK) Ltd* [2016] EWCA Civ 443 in which negotiation evidence was also reviewed. Another possibility is that conduct varies the contract – see *Patel v Patel* [2019] EWHC 298 (Ch) – conduct in a partnership context at least must be "clear and unambiguous".
237 From Wiggins, *Facilities Manager's Desk Reference*, 194.
238 McLauchlan, 'Contract Formation and Subjective Intention', 94.
239 Bernstein, 'Questionable Empirical Basis', 767–768.
240 *Ritchie* (n. 70 above).
241 Sidney Lovell Phipson and Hodge M Malek, *Phipson on Evidence*, vol. 18 (Sweet & Maxwell 2013) at 33.02.

utility", and Courts may review responses without much guidance from stat-istical experts,[242] although the quality of the survey and data collection will go to weight.[243] A survey such as that undertaken by Lai, Yik and Jones,[244] reviewing market participants' opinions on the meaning of "fair wear and tear" and "vandalism", will be useful to a Court.

As I have argued in Chapter 3.1 the use of avatars in laboratory conditions is unlikely to provide useful data on commercial expectation because, not only are the experiments themselves wholly unrealistic, but one cannot trans-late avatar reaction to real-world conditions. X-phi experiments, despite their popularity, tell us nothing about the commercial world, which is more nuanced and complex than one can replicate in a laboratory filled with ingé-nues. Experiments should be transferable and test real-world hypotheses.[245] As Edmonds observes:

> In the real world we are not constrained by having just two options, X and Y: we have a multitude of options, and our choices are entangled in com-plex duties and obligations and motives. In the real world, crucially, there would be no certainty.[246]

The real-world/real-people, complex nature of my survey makes its findings much more credible than those emanating from students asked unrealistic ques-tions in laboratory conditions.

4.2.8 The commercial judge

When interpreting contracts judges take responsibility for determining whether an unexpressed term of the contract provides "business efficacy", or whether a particular interpretation accords with "common-sense"[247] or "business

---

242 *A Baily v Clark Son and Morland* [1938] AC 557 (HL), *Marks & Spencer Plc v Interflora Inc* [2012] EWCA Civ 1501 and see the robust decision in New Zealand in *Ritz Hotel Ltd v Charles of the Ritz Ltd* [1989] RPC 333.

243 James, *Expert Evidence* at 18.009. See also *Amey LG Limited v Cumbria County Council* [2016] EWCH 2856 (TCC) .

244 Lai and others 'Disputes'.

245 See also Russell Korobkin, 'Empirical Scholarship in Contract Law: Possibilities and Pitfalls' (2002) *U IllLRev* 1033 and Dennis Patterson, 'The Limits of Empiricism' (2000) 98 *MichLRev* 2738.

246 Edmonds, *Kill the Fat Man*, 100. Collins, *Regulating Contracts*, 131 – empirical work fails to "appreciate the presence" of several "normative frameworks".

247 *Rice (t/a Garden Guardian) v Great Yarmouth Borough Council* (n. 234 above) – Lady Justice Hale invoking "common sense", "in the context of a contract intended to last for four years, involving substantial investment … involving a myriad of obligations", inter-preted a power to terminate the contract for "any" breach as any breach which amounted to a repudiation – at [18].

common sense",[248] or other synonyms for multiple manifestations of the idea collected under the term "commercial common sense" by Neil Andrews.[249] There is an overlap between these concepts and the search for commercial expectation.[250] In this subchapter I explore the role of the commercial judge in identifying commercial expectation. Although some judges have "profound and secure" commercial expertise and may be able to deal "magisterially" with certain transactions as a result, Andrews' advice that judges "must not assume that they are master of all trades" is sensible.[251] Lord Reed counsels against "an excess of confidence that the judge's view as to what might be commercially sensible coincides with the views of those actually involved in commercial contracts".[252] While Lord Hodge also urges humility "about our ability to identify commercial purpose",[253] Sir Kim Lewison deprecates the tendency of judges to determine commercial purpose based on their own experience[254] and Lord Millett claims that invoking common sense "really gives the game away",[255] Lord Steyn takes a more gnostic view: "Modern judges usually have well in mind the reason for a rule and in a contract case that means approaching the case from the point of view of the reasonable expectations of the parties."[256] In *Equitable Life Assurance Society v Harman*[257] Lord Steyn based an implied term limiting the Society's discretion on the parties' "reasonable expectations" which were that contractual guarantees should not be deprived of any value. Lord Grabiner remarks, in unusually frank criticism, that Lord Steyn's approach is "speculative":

> It is very unclear ... where Lord Steyn found the "self-evident commercial object" ... or the "reasonable expectations of the parties". It was certainly not from anything any of the policyholders were told or promised ...

---

248 Lord Clarke in *Rainy Sky SA and others v Kookmin Bank* [2011] UKSC 50; [2011] 1 WLR 2900 at [21] and [23]. Lord Hodge in *Wood v Capita Insurance Services Limited* [2017] UKSC 24 at [10]. See also Cranston J in *Medirest High Court* (n. 233 above) at [25] saying (correctly) that Medirest's interpretation of the cooperation clause was more aligned to common sense.

249 Andrews, 'Interpretation of Contracts'.

250 *Rickman and another v Brudenell-Bruce* [2005] EWHC 3400 (Ch) George Bompas QC – a limit on discretion under a conveyance gave effect to the "reasonable expectations" of the parties and provided "business efficacy".

251 Andrews, 'Interpretation of Contracts', 52–53.

252 *Grove Investments Ltd v Cape Building Products Ltd* [2014] CSIH 43.

253 'Can Judges Use Business Common Sense in Interpreting Contracts?' in Larry DiMatteo and Martin Hogg (eds), *Comparative Contract Law: British and American Perspectives* (OUP 2016), 283. See Paul S Davies, 'Interpreting Commercial Contracts: A Case of Ambiguity?' (2012) *LMCLQ*.

254 Lewison, *Interpretation* at 2.06.

255 Lord Millett, 'The Common Lawyer and the Chancery Practitioner' in Daniel Clarry and Christopher Sargeant (eds), *The UK Supreme Court Yearbook*, vol. 6 (2015) at 92.

256 Steyn, 'Reasonable Expectations', 442.

257 *Equitable Life Assurance Society v Hyman* [2000] 3 All ER 961 at 971, [2002] 1 AC 408.

By contrast, Sir Richard Scott VC did consider the reasonable expectations of the parties ... by reference to the relevant policy documents.[258]

Evans LJ, dismissing a bank's claim that it was not bound by the conduct of a manager acting without actual authority, without reference to evidence, ruled: "It is not the practice, so far as I am aware, in normal commercial transactions for written proof eg of board decisions to be demanded ..."[259] There is some evidence that the Courts take the commercial expectations of "sophisticated" parties to be that Courts should not interfere readily with the language used; Jonathan Sumption observing in a recent lecture that the "more precise the words used and the more elaborate the drafting, the less likely it is that the surrounding circumstances will add anything useful".[260] Paul Finn says that "Judges commonly seem to regard the parties to commercial contracts as well-advised leviathans"; going on to say that for the most part neither is true.[261]

In *Rosserlane Consultants Ltd v Credit Suisse International*, despite finding the bank's conduct "reprehensible" Peter Smith J found that a "lengthy and carefully-drafted contract" drafted by experienced lawyers was "a commercial contract between sophisticated investors and the Bank".[262] Refusing to imply any limit on a bank's ability to force a borrower to extend a hedge, Mrs Justice Andrews described a party as "an astute and sophisticated businessman ... capable of making an educated and informed decision on hedging".[263]

This attitude might cut both ways; in *Thorney Park*, McCombe LJ took into account the fact that the contract had been prepared by "lay people"; a curiously condescending term.[264]

A Court may also conclude that that the natural meaning of the words is subject to forensic examination, Lord Reid saying of termination of an "elaborate" distribution agreement:

> if Schuler's contention is right, failure to make even one visit entitle them to terminate ... This is so unreasonable that it must make me search for some other possible meaning ... If none can be found then Wickman must suffer the consequences. But only if that is the only possible interpretation.[265]

---

258 Lord Grabiner, 'The Iterative Process of Contractual Interpretation' (2012) 128 *LQR* 41 at 57–59.

259 *First Energy (UK) Ltd v Hungarian International Bank Ltd* (n. 95 above) at 205.

260 Jonathan Sumption, *A Question of Taste: The Supreme Court and the Interpretation of Contracts* (Harris Society Annual Lecture 2017) at 9. Leggatt J deploys the reverse argument in *Yam Seng* (n. 132) at [161] using the "skeletal" nature of the agreement to justify implying a term.

261 "Fiduciary and Good Faith Obligations under Long Term Contracts" in Dharmananda, *Long Term Contracts*, 137.

262 *Rosserlane Consultants Ltd v Credit Suisse International* [2015] EWHC 384 (Ch).

263 *Greenclose Ltd v National Westminster Bank* [2014] EWHC 1156 (Ch) at [150].

264 *Thorney Park Golf Ltd v Myers Catering Ltd* (n. 211 above) at [24].

265 *Schuler (L) AG v Wickman Machine Tool Sales Ltd* (n. 48 above) at 251.

Ewan McKendrick refers *Schuler* in a discussion on how one draws the line between commercial construction and impermissible rewriting.[266] One can compare *Rice* to the *Schuler* case above and see that in two very similar cases senior judges reach similar conclusions with different logic; each seeming to search for a commercial common-sense meaning.

Judges appreciate the exigencies of complex matters. As case managers they read dispute resolution obligations widely and purposively. Mutuality and active cooperation lie at the heart of the Court's approach to parties' contractually arising obligations in arbitration; Lord Diplock saying: "The obligation is ... mutual; it obliges each party to cooperate with the other in taking appropriate steps to keep the procedure in the arbitration moving".[267] Coulson J observed that providing too much information in an adjudication might breach a duty to cooperate: "Unless parties and their solicitors co-operated properly and complied with the TCC guide, the court would refuse to hear cases with promiscuous and unnecessary bundling."[268] The dispute resolution Judgments have similarities with Judge Toulmin's implied term, which includes the acceptance of reasonable solutions and acting reasonably where relatively unimportant items cannot be delivered, and demonstrate that the Courts can construe contracts in ways that encourage to parties to work together.[269]

In complex modern symbiotic contracts experience and expertise on which to base an analysis of what the parties would expect is, in my opinion, likely to be no more accessible to the judiciary than expertise in banking or medical cases; notwithstanding that judges know how important cooperation is once complex machinery grinds into action. It is arguable that they should have some idea of relative priorities once problems arise, once disputes become apparent and in the general hurly-burly of business.

Bringing into play commercial expectations, commercial common sense, business efficacy or synonymous aspects as a deus-ex-machina, or, worse, acting as an undeclared amiable compositeur, using judicial intuition, carries the risk of diluting the concept; allowing the claim that the "notion explains too much".[270] Most judges have, however, served long

---

266 'The Interpretation of Contracts; Lord Hoffmann's Restatement', in Worthington, *Commercial Law,* 160–161.

267 *Bremer Vulkan Schiffbau und Maschinenfabrik v South India Shipping Corp Ltd* [1981] AC 909 HL at 25. In *The Hannah Blumenthal* [1983] 1 AC 854, [1983] 1 All ER 34 (HL) The Court ruled that "The mutual obligation. to keep the arbitration moving is not merely a matter of each party co-operating with any initiative taken by the other but a positive obligation imposed on each party to take the initiative himself, with or without the co-operation of the other party".

268 *Deluxe Art & Theme Ltd v Beck Interiors Ltd* [2016] EWHC 238 (TCC).

269 See *Laporte and another v Commissioner of Police of the Metropolis* [2015] EWHC 371 (QB).

270 Mitchell, 'Leading a Life of its Own?', 663.

apprenticeships at the Bar, giving them some idea of whether parties are holding back, attempting to make them "hostages of the arguments deployed by Counsel"[271] and the expertise of specialist Technology and Commercial Court judges in construction and engineering contexts should not be underestimated. The parties are best placed to identify the purpose of any transaction, which identification may be well supported by evidence of negotiations. The best context is that of the performance interest. Businesspeople contract on the footing that contracts will be performed, as Lewison suggests.[272] Nevertheless, Judges should restrain themselves and deliver opinion based on the documentation, witness evidence, Counsel's views or serious and declared experience in the type of transaction under review. Judges do not normally possess sharp-end commercial experience.; their experience is normally "warped".[273]

4.3 Conclusion

Commercial expectations, the unwritten part of the bargain, however encapsulated can be exposed by parties, documents, witnesses of fact, experts, those engaged in the trade or concessions by Counsel. Such expectations are, as I have shown, far from impervestigable (i.e. they can be thoroughly investigated). If practices or understandings are sufficiently general, well-enough known and understood, probative or otherwise clearly part of the bargain, Courts should and do use them in construing the paper contract and in putting the unsaid down on paper.

The tools for unearthing expectations already exist. Deeply contextual contract construction, balanced with one eye to commerciality,[274] is the most promising possibility. The doctrinal rules which prohibit the asperate commercial material inherent in negotiation and execution from exposure to judges are easy for judges to ignore and are without even the merit of reducing cost. Replying to criticism of the "background" principle Gerard McMeel notes that judges are "not averse to striking out inadmissible or irrelevant material"[275] and Arden LJ has indicated that case management powers are sufficient to control to allow judges a constructive rummage around the matrix without allowing in much unhelpful

---

271 Lord Steyn, lamenting a circuitous approach by Counsel to third-party rights, in *Darlington Borough Council v Wiltshier Northern Ltd* [1995] 1 WLR 68 at 78.

272 Lewison, *Interpretation* at 6.11.

273 Little has changed since Sir Mackenzie Chalmers, *The Sale of Goods Act; 1893* (Clowes 1902) used this term – at 129.

274 See Arden LJ in *Re Golden Key Ltd* [2009] EWCA Civ 636 at [28].

275 In 'Overview: The Principles and Policies of Contractual Construction' in AS Burrows and Edwin Peel (eds), *Contract Terms* (OUP 2007) at 33.

material.[276] The *Admiralty and Commercial Courts Guide*, for example, now explicitly provides for parties in their statements of case to "specifically set out in his pleading each feature of the matrix which is alleged to be of relevance".[277]

Relevant context and factual background can be revealed by evidence. Francois du Bois says that commercial practice, a key part of the background, whether it is trade or market practice, party conduct, the assumptions of the business relationship (to some extent), "provides a source of norms about how to exercise our practices, about how to be a good contractant".[278] The explanation of commercial practice which is displayed by survey participants may or may not show how to be a "good" contractant; but it shows how to be an effective and successful contractant. It exposes community standards and uncovers norms in commercial practice which can be used to articulate a concept of commercial expectation of cooperation, with an agreed description of what cooperation means and how to apply cooperation in practical settings. These expectations are "non-speculative" and do not suffer from Adams and Brownsword's concern that they might only be found at a "high level of generality".[279] They are neither open-textured nor a slogan as suggested by Stephen A Smith,[280] who observes elsewhere that it is not unreasonable for judges to consider existing practices to determine whether they provide a solution.[281]

I invite readers to consider this from their quotidian experience. Most of us have had a new kitchen or bathroom fitted. Many will have had an extension, or a garage built. It is unlikely that a perfect bathroom, kitchen, garage or extension was constructed. It is highly likely that there were defects. How did you deal with them? May I suggest that you called the builder, talked about the defects and expected the builder to fix them? Further, may I suggest that you did this without recourse to the contract; because it's the obvious, common-sense, way to proceed, your "ordinary reaction". Your role was to tell the trader of the defects.[282] Another possibility is that, during discussions, you had emailed the supplier to say "move the double socket in the kitchen to location x" and the supplier emailed back saying "sure; no problem. Will do". Would either of

---

276 In *Static Control Components v Egan* [2004] EWCA 392. See also *NLA Group Ltd v Bowers* [1999] 1 Lloyds Rep 109; involving a short point of construction Counsel tried to call five witnesses, subpoena two more and provide expert evidence, which Timothy Walker J described as "wholly unreasonable" at 111 awarding some costs on an indemnity basis.

277 HM Courts & Tribunals Service, *Admiralty and Commercial Courts Guide* (2014; updated March 2016), para C1.2(h).

278 Du Bois, *Good Faith, Good Law?*, 12.

279 See Adams and Brownsword, *Key Issues*, 326.

280 Smith, 'Reasonable Expectations', 386.

281 Ibid.

282 Collins, *Regulating Contracts*, 152, citing Beale and Dugdale, says of defects that recourse to law "does not seem to have occurred to the actors themselves".

you be other than incredulous to find that the Court would refuse to allow this exchange to be referred to in proceedings?

Once shown by trade or market practice, assumption or custom/usage a term could become a default. For example, the evidence in *Eurodynamics* having shown that an opportunity to repair defects was market practice in IT contracts, there seems no reason why later IT contracts should not be similarly so construed without the need for further evidence.

In Chapter 5 I will review these expectations, showing which might credibly be articulated as a deep, concrete, duty to cooperate.

5 The third way
How it is different

In the Introduction, I describe my search for a duty to cooperate as pragmatic or functional, seeking a better fit between the law and the expectations of those at the sharp end. The commercial expectations and changes in commercial reality identified in Chapters 3 and 4 underline the need for a coherent, higher-level concept of cooperation which meets the needs of modern commercial actors. In this Chapter I provide content for a deep, concrete duty to cooperate, and compare this to other definitions of cooperation.

5.1 The third way

There is a third way to bring concepts of cooperation in modern complex contracts into play in English Contract Law. It is neither necessary to rewrite the law and principles entirely, as relational theorists require, nor to undermine the commercial strengths of the Common Law, which minimalists and formalists assume would be the result. Using well-known constructs, it is possible to draft a concrete, overarching duty of cooperation for modern symbiotic contracts.

My survey reveals that commercial expectations in the background to many modern forms of contract arise from the pathway to success in performing these contracts lying in active cooperation, communication and problem solving. The goal is performance and is achieved by good management and leadership worked in formal and informal channels. Reciprocity and punishment are regarded as useful but ineffective. Those at the sharp end know that they must build relationships to discern what drives the other party, providing a foundation for cooperation, solid communication and practical problem solving. Dennett observes that: "I can still take my task to be looking out for Number One while including under Number One … my family, the Chicago Bulls, Oxfam, you name it …" [1]

Below is my idealised "transcendent" duty to cooperate (hereinafter TDTC), specifically for symbiotic contracts; but with application to others:

---

1 Daniel C Dennett, *Freedom Evolves* (Penguin 2004), 180.

In complex, highly interactive contracts, characterised by a high degree of inter-dependency, which require significant communication, active cooperation, and predictable performance for their success it is implicit, an inevitable inference from the spirit and the background, that parties must engage constructively and professionally, and do those things necessary to be done for the full realisation of the bargain. This duty to cooperate requires the parties to work together constantly, to plan, manage and organise the work, and accept where possible reasonable solutions to those problems which occur from time to time, transmitting information in good time to ensure that informed decisions can be made, providing each other with the opportunity to cure errors and defects (including an active duty to advise the other of defects, unsuitable materials, processes or instructions or defective performance as soon as practicable), undertaking consultation and making concessions where there is uncertainty or matters have been left to be resolved, and when taking decisions arrogated to them, which affect the other party, act impartially, honestly, fairly and reasonably, making a genuine examination of each's relevant commercial expectations.

This third way bears analogy to concepts of "contemplation", or "neighbour" at a high level of abstraction, leaving room for debate and allowing parties to adjust their relationships without abandoning their autonomy. Following Lord Atkins' logic from *Donoghue v Stevenson*,[2] I "content myself" with claiming that there is a "general conception" of a duty to cooperate, which "cannot in a practical world" extend to the protection of every injury or breach of contract.[3] The duty is an enabling/facilitating mechanism[4] which controls day-to-day conduct by requiring parties to ensure that each can take advantage of their bargain.

Dori Kimel observes, in a passage which begs the question of which norms should be regulated by contract law:

> One of the most important functions of contract law … is to support personal detachment by way of enabling parties to transact without relationships, at arm's length … What often enables parties to contracts to develop co-operative relationships … is the very existence of a "detached core": a certain stable baseline, comprising of clearly articulated … enforceable rights and obligations.[5]

In drafting the TDTC, I have separated "informal" elements of relationship building from the formal. In formal elements, I worked from doctrine and

---

2 *Donoghue v Stevenson* [1932] UKHL 100; [1932] AC 562.

3 Ibid, esp. at 580 and 599.

4 JF Wilson, *Principles of the Law of Contract* (Sweet and Maxwell 1957), 262. SJ Stoljar, 'Prevention and Cooperation in the Law of Contract' (1953) 31 *Can Bar Rev* 231 at 231.

5 Dori Kimel, 'The Choice of Paradigm for Theory of Contract: Reflections on the Relational Model' (2007) 27 *OJLS* 233 at 248.

analogy to build a "core" of rights and obligations which could be applied to symbiotic contracts. Activities such as "team-building", are categorised as useful but they and commercially "informal" values such as respect and transparency give way to a need for constructive engagement. In short, I separate out first, those elements not amenable to legal protection, then consider the background elements which are necessary to success, according to respondents, and which "would have affected the way in which the language of the document would have been understood by a reasonable man".[6]

The TDTC does not originate in, is not derived from nor depend on, cognate notions of good faith or mutual trust and confidence. Mutual trust and confidence in employment contracts means that neither party will conduct itself in a manner likely to destroy or seriously damage their relationship of confidence and trust.[7] This is asserted by judges to reflect a new "social reality"[8] entitling Courts to take account of "wider considerations" such as balancing an employer's interest in managing his business and the employee's interest in not being unfairly exploited.[9] In one key case, Lord Bridge accepted that it could only be justified on "wider considerations ... as a necessary incident of a definable category of contractual relationship".[10] Some commentators see a possible transformation of commercial contracts to align them with these values.[11] I am not convinced that this principle is necessary or workable for enabling or facilitating performance in commercial contracts. The TDTC's source lies in the objective expectations of experienced commercial parties. There is no immanent loyalty, fidelity, crypto-fiduciary, mutual trust and confidence, improper/unconscionable practice or quasi-agency, or fair dealing element. Such requirements are wholly unnecessary.

I articulate the duty at a similar level of abstraction to Lord Atkin in *Donoghue v Stevenson* or Baron Alderson in *Hadley v Baxendale*.[12] David Howarth might consider this as design:

---

6 Lord Hoffmann's description of background in *Investors Compensation Scheme v West Bromwich Building Society* [1998] 1 WLR 896 at 913.

7 The term originated in *Courtaulds Northern Textiles Ltd v Andrew* [1979] IRLR 84, EAT where a supervisor's comment to Mr Andrew "Well, you can't do the bloody job anyway" was held to destroy the bond of confidence between them amounting to constructive dismissal. Andrew's solicitors (Reynolds Porter Chamberlain) pleaded it as an implied term.

8 Lord Hoffmann in *Johnson v Unisys Ltd* [2000] UKHL 13, [2001] IRLR 279 at [35].

9 Lord Steyn in *Mahmud v Bank of Credit and Commerce International SA (In Liquidation)* [1998] AC 20; [1997] 3 WLR 95 (HL) at [46], Ewan McKendrick, *Contract Law: Text, Cases, and Materials* (OUP 2014), 361, observes that it is based on a lower standard than necessity.

10 *Scally v Southern Health and Social Services Board* [1991] 4 All ER 563 (HL) at 571. See also RV Upex, *Encyclopedia of Employment Law* (Sweet & Maxwell 1992) at 1A.2.5 and Chitty, *Chitty on Contracts* (ed. Hugh Beale, 33rd edn, Sweet & Maxwell 2018) at 40.151-152.

11 See Douglas Brodie, 'Fair Dealing and the World of Work' (2014) 43 *Ind Law J* 29 at 50–51 and Hugh Collins, *The Law of Contract* (CUP 2008), 337–338, on duties of disclosure.

12 *Hadley v Baxendale* (1854) 23 LJ Ex 179, 9 Exch 341 at 354.

Lawyers design social structures and devices in a way that parallels engineers' designs of physical structures ... Contracts, companies, trusts, constitutions, and statutes are the buildings, bridges, machinery, roads, and railways of social life.[13]

Although making and testing my social device is design in this sense,[14] the analogy to me (and I spent 35 years in engineering environments) of this as engineering has major mismatches. Engineers work from experimentally derived, verifiable, material. 1 + 1 = 2 in the engineering world. In law, it depends on the context of the 1. Or the other 1. Or the 2. Or the +. But his point that academics do not spend enough time drafting new concepts at a level of abstraction that might prove useful in a courtroom is a strong one.

5.2 Definitions of cooperation

In this subchapter, I describe how obligations academics define cooperation, considering similarities to and differences between these ideas and the TDTC. Interestingly, there is no listing for cooperate or cooperation in legal dictionaries.[15]

Survey respondents consider that cooperation goes further than "coordination and planning",[16] which one might call mechanical or techno-cooperation. To them cooperation is about making contracts work, supporting performance. It is similar to Bruce Schneier's definition: "cooperation doesn't imply anything moral; it just means going along with the group norm".[17] The TDTC differs from other definitions in combining physical and managerial elements and is based on legal authority plus the expectations of reasonable commercial actors. In the sense that it bears similarities to some judicial exposition it is not, at heart, radical.

5.2.1 Good faith in Civil Law

In Civil Law jurisdictions a duty of good faith applies to the performance of contractual obligations. The proposed Common European Sales Law provided, at Article 2, that "good faith and fair dealing" was "a standard of conduct characterised by honesty, openness and consideration for the interests of the other party to the transaction or relationship in question".[18] In France for example

---

13 David Howarth, 'Is Law a Humanity: (Or is it More Like Engineering)?' (2004) 3 *Arts Humanities Higher Educ* 9 at 12.
14 See also D Howarth, *Law as Engineering* (Edward Elgar 2013).
15 E.g. David M Walker, *The Oxford Companion to Law* (Clarendon Press 1980).
16 Harold Canfield Havighurst, *The Nature of Private Contract* (Northwestern UP 1961), 21–22.
17 Bruce Schneier, *Liars and Outliers* (Wiley 2012), 53.
18 Proposal for a Regulation of the European Parliament and of the Council on a Common European Sales Law Com/2011/0635final-2011/0284 (COD).

the French Civil Code provides that "agreements lawfully entered into … must be performed in good faith". Although vague this has, by judicial decisions, been given content which we can consider and compare to the TDTC.[19] According to Peter Rosher the duty as it applies to construction contracts governed by French law can be broken down into four elements:

- a duty of contractual loyalty;
- a duty of cooperation/collaboration;
- a duty of coherence;
- a duty of information.

The duty of loyalty includes a duty "not to act in a way that would render the performance impossible or more difficult".[20] The first part of this clearly has an analogue in the prevention principle. Rosher indicates that altering plans for the works in an "incoherent manner" is a breach of the loyalty part of the duty of good faith.[21] In England this would simply result in a justified claim for additional cost and, probably, an extension of time; under the TDTC it might result in a requirement to discuss the problems that followed such action. The loyalty requirement also infers a duty to "respect the interests of their contracting partners and to respect proportionality and equilibrium".[22] The TDTC does not require any respect for proportionality but it does require parties to engage constructively and to attempt to resolve problems; which might mean respect for the equilibrium. The next duty, that of cooperation and collaboration, has, as Rosher puts it, a "more dynamic and positive dimension", which includes an obligation to facilitate performance (similar to some of the duties in English law and the TDTC), but which appears to be, at its limit, more stringent, in that "a party must do *everything* in its power to *ease* the other party's performance" . It may be similar to the TDTC when there is a requirement to inform the other party of events that may impact performance or a duty to warn of unsuitable materials.[23] The duty of coherence means, it appears, that parties must act in a consistent manner; for example, a sudden change in the way that a particular provision is applied would offend.[24] This is not covered by the TDTC directly, but it may come into play when constructive engagement and problem solving come into play; a change

---

19 Peter Rosher, 'Good Faith in Construction Contracts under French Law' (2015) *ICLR* 302 at 304–305.
20 Ibid. at 305–306.
21 Ibid. at 306.
22 Ibid.
23 Ibid. at 306–307. This includes commercial and technical support throughout a franchise agreement – see Mark Abell and Victoria Hobbs, 'The Duty of Good Faith in Franchise Agreements – A Comparative Study of the Civil and Common Law Approaches in the EU' (2013) 11 *Int J Franchising Law* 1 at 3.
24 Rosher, 'Good Faith', 307.

of position should be explained and discussed. The duty of information goes further than that in the TDTC, requiring the employer to advise the contractor of adverse ground conditions or of pipes but its obverse, the duty of a contractor to warn of unsuitable materials, is similar. Under this duty many of the risks taken by the contractor appear to be placed on the employer such as a requirement to advise a client that they might be better off building a new ship as repairs would cost more than replacement.[25]

In France a change in external circumstances might lead to a requirement to renegotiate the deal; which goes much further than the TDTC and is close to a relational concept.[26] In German law a franchisor must "exercise its discretion reasonably" and taking the overall interest of the franchise network into account, which goes much further than either the TDTC or English law.[27]

In the case of Canada, "The court has been bounteous: Canadian contract law now has just about every kind of good faith there is" according to John Enman-Beech, who suggests that the width of the reception in Canada raises "rule-of-law concerns about the reckonability of court outcomes and a lack of fit with commercial expectations".[28] In contrast the TDTC yields determinate and bounded rules, based on party intention and the needs of the instant contract. E Allan Farnsworth says that the US duty extends to using discretion "fairly" and to give "fair warning", for example in calling in loans or refusing to provide further advances.[29] This goes further than English law or the TDTC.

Although Gerard McMeel, calling this a "functional equivalence" approach, suggests that there are English law doctrines which give the same result, it seems from the necessarily brief overview above that continental, US and Canadian doctrines of good faith do in fact go considerably further than the English doctrine does.[30]

---

25 Ibid. 308.
26 Abell and Hobbs, 'Duty of Good Faith', 5. See for the similar German position Werner Ebke and Bettina Steinhauer, 'The Doctrine of Good Faith in German Contract Law' in J Beatson and Daniel Friedmann (eds), *Good Faith and Fault in Contract Law* (Clarendon 1997), chapter 7 at 182–183. See also Severine Saintier, 'The Elusive Notion of Good Faith in the Performance of a Contract, Why Still a Bete Noire for the Civil and the Common Law?' (2017) *J Bus Law* 441 at 457. In Louisiana the duty "consists of honesty in a party's contractual behavior, or loyalty to, or collaboration with, the other party" – Jumoke Dara and Olivier Moreteau, 'The Interaction of Good Faith with Contract Performance, Dissolution, and Damages in the Louisiana Supreme Court' (2018) 10 *J Civ L Stud* 261 at 267.
27 Abell and Hobbs, 'Duty of Good Faith', 3. See for the similar German position Ebke and Steinhauer, 'Doctrine of Good Faith' in Beatson and Friedmann, *Good Faith and Fault*, 172.
28 John Enman-Beech, 'The Good Faith Challenge' (2019) 1 *J Commonwealth Law* 35 at 41–42 and 62.
29 'Good Faith in Contract' in Beatson and Friedmann, *Good Faith and Fault*, 159.
30 Gerard McMeel 'Foucault's Pendulum: Text, Context and Good Faith in Contract Law' (2017) *CLP*.

5.2.2 *Full-blooded relational scholarship*

In relational contract literature cooperation represents a basic real-world dynamic and is a major component of norms such as preservation of the relationship or solidarity.[31] Jonathan Morgan describes relational contract theory as requiring "the regulation of opportunism",[32] making the correct point that opportunism is not easy to differentiate from legitimate self-interest, and may require examination of "inner motivation".[33] This is certainly part of the relationist construct but relationists go further, placing duties on parties to renegotiate where one party is disadvantaged (likely in my opinion to open the door to even more opportunism), and a (necessarily) inchoate obligation to maintain the relationship, and tend not to address the need for cooperation in the daily working environment in reasonably well specified medium- and short-term contracts.[34] Ian Macneil described cooperation in a fairly vague way without detail as to how it might work in hard cases: "Relational responses to a breakdown of cooperation thus tends ... necessary or desirable to restore current and future cooperation ... negotiation, mediation, arbitration and orders to do things."[35]

Jay Feinman describes it: "The substantive core ... proceeds from two propositions; that contract is fundamentally about cooperative social behaviour".[36] Richard Speidel, for example, says that cooperation includes

> at a minimum, a duty to bargain in good faith and, at a maximum, the duty to accept an equitable adjustment proposed in good faith **by** the disadvantaged party. These duties promote the norms that the relationship should be preserved, and conflict harmonized ... the parties should share through compromise.[37]

---

31 E.g. Ian Austen-Baker, 'Comprehensive Contract Theory – A Four Norm Model of Contract Relations' (2009) 25 *JCL* 216, at 222 – "Relational contract theories assume that ... contracting parties are likely to want to perpetuate exchange relations"; Ian R Macneil, 'Contracting Worlds and Essential Contract Theory' (2000) 9 *Social Legal Stud* 431.

32 Jonathan Morgan, *Contract Law Minimalism* (CUP 2013), 137.

33 Ibid. 139.

34 Richard E Speidel, 'The Characteristics and Challenges of Relational Contracts' (2000) 94 *NWULR* 827 (n23) at 829.

35 Ian R Macneil, 'The Many Futures of Contract' (1973) 47 *Cal L Rev* at 741; which reminds me of King Lear "I will do such things. What they are yet I know not. But they shall be the terror of the earth". See also Alessandro Arrighetti, 'Contract Law, Social Norms and Inter-firm Cooperation' (1997) 21 *Cambridge J Econ* 171 at 175 suggesting that relational theory requires "flexibility" in contract enforcement partly because express terms are not sufficiently flexible.

36 Jay M Feinman, 'Relational Contract Theory in Context' (2000) 94 *Nw ULRev* 742 at 743.

37 Richard E Speidel, 'Court-Imposed Price Adjustments under Long-Term Supply Contracts' (1981) 76 *NWULR* 369 at 421.

And Hugh Collins makes a similar claim:

> It may be a reasonable expectation, for instance, that despite the presence of a fixed price contract, the parties will anticipate a price adjustment in the event of either mistaken assumptions about costs or unforeseen contingencies.[38]

Robert Gordon describes cooperation in relational contracts (memorably saying they are more like marriages than one-night stands) as: "In bad times, the parties are expected to lend one another mutual support, rather than standing on their rights."[39]

There are multiple elements of renegotiation implied in these definitions of cooperation. Hard relational cooperation means renegotiation, requiring that parties renegotiate contractual rights in the light of externalities, or continue trading, in the interests of maintaining a relationship. Constructive engagement, or internally driven cooperation, means the professional management of "infelicities and oddities" and defects, the resolution of legitimate discussion about the meaning of vague or wide terms, the review of over-eager manipulation of words and remedies, all in the pursuit of successful performance.

Hard relational cooperation is described as "highly questionable" and "quixotic" by Melvyn Eisenberg. Ewan McKendrick agrees, in the same volume, with a US Judgment that such a construct "cannot withstand scrutiny".[40] This objection is supported by a reading of Terry Daintith's analysis of a "very violent" shake-up in the iron ore supply industry which resulted in long-term contracts "surviving":

> at the expense of an almost total change in the character of the contracts … From fixed-term, fixed-quantity, fixed-price contracts, they have been converted into requirements contracts which may, through extension, have an indefinite term, with annually negotiated prices.[41]

---

38 Hugh Collins, *Regulating Contracts* (OUP 2005), 145–147.
39 RW Gordon, 'Macaulay, Macneil and the Discovery of Solidarity and Power in Contract Law' (1985) *Wis L Rev* Lyons and Mehta say in 'Private Sector Business Contracts: The Text between the Lines' in Jonathan Michie and SF Deakin (eds), *Contracts, Co-operation, and Competition: Studies in Economics, Management, and Law* (OUP 1997), 51, that relational contracting allows vulnerable partners to trust that counterparties will "respond in a co-operative manner" to unforeseen events. Kimel, 'Choice of Paradigm', quotes this at 245–246 to support his argument that not all relational norms can or should be legally regulated in "affective" and analogous agreements.
40 'Relational Contracts' and 'The Regulation of Long-Term Contracts in English Law' in Beatson and Friedmann, *Good Faith and Fault*, 300 and 314 respectively.
41 Terence Daintith and Gunther Teubner, *Contract and Organisation: Legal Analysis in the Light of Economic and Social Theory* (De Gruyter 1986), 186.

It is, in my opinion, impossible to construct legal principles, absent express terms, which could lead to such results, without replacing party autonomy with judge-made contracts. The contracts analysed by Terry Daintith were the subject of major renegotiations and it is likely that each result was different. Even if the contract is used as a "tool of cooperation",[42] cooperation is voluntary and involves a commercial negotiation as opposed to reliance on legal rights. My survey tends to bear this out. In the blackmail vignette most respondents were willing to renegotiate, but conditionally and contextually. It wasn't seen as a right or an expectation but as a commercial solution.

Commenting on *Baird Textiles Holdings plc v Marks and Spencer plc*[43] (discussed at 4.2.3) John Wightman notes relational elements which might have been relevant such as solidarity/fidelity.[44] Linda Mulcahy and Cathy Andrews, masquerading as "Lady Mulandrew", provide us with an alternative, feminist Judgment, saying that feminist and relational values each emphasise cooperation and concern for others, masculine behaviour being more arms-length, strategic. My survey does not bear this out; there is almost no difference between male and female respondents on reactions to difficult situations. Lady Mulandrew says that the various risks undertaken by Baird were "unlikely" to have been accepted without a broader set of obligations and that "it seems very implausible to suppose that Baird would have invested in such additional production capacity".[45] I agree with that, although Baird had the option of negotiating guarantees, or providing for an express break clause, providing for a decent notice period. They make one poor point – "in short M&S enjoyed the benefits of having subsidiaries without the full costs" – without remembering that M&S did not receive the profits from those quasi-subsidiaries either.[46]

It is very difficult to see how one can force a result onto free parties. One can ask them to behave professionally and to try to settle disputes, notwithstanding that they remain free to disagree. I am not sure that "share" or "mutual support" can be made to work. They go too far to be commercially practical. Parties expect that in bad times they will find ways to make the contract work. But if they can't, they then have to take their chances.

Michael Trebilcock's observation that relationalism "entails a highly amorphous sociological enquiry that seems well beyond the courts in case to case adjudication" is fair comment, when limited to hard relational cooperation.[47]

---

42 Thomas Wilhelmsson, *Perspectives of Critical Contract Law* (Dartmouth 1993), at 19–20, describing the findings of Daintith and Teubner, *Contract and Organisation*, 186.

43 *Baird Textiles Holdings Ltd v Marks & Spencer plc* [2001] EWCA Civ 274, [2002] 1 All ER (Comm) 737.

44 Rosemary C Hunter and others (eds), *Feminist Judgments: From Theory to Practice* (Hart 2010) 'Commentary on Baird Textile Holdings v Marks Spencer Plc' at 188.

45 Ibid. 193.

46 Ibid. 189.

47 Michael J Trebilcock, *The Limits of Freedom of Contract* (Harvard UP 1993), 141–142.

There is no question that the constructive engagement and active cooperation required by the TDTC can be categorised as renegotiation. That would be too crude. It implies professional management, and good governance in the pursuit of contract success, recognising the inevitability that in these complex contracts, problems will arise, whether because the contracts are incomplete or unclear or both. There is some congruence between the relational concept of cooperation and the TDTC, but only in management of execution. The negotiation aspect is necessary to restore the contract to normality, to allow proper performance, to create content in interstices and clarify obligations. The TDTC requires a certain amount of bargaining but for in-contract issues which might require some legitimate debate such as what, for example, "good quality" or "known brand" or "suitably qualified" might mean, as well as whether a deduction provision is being operated correctly. In that this seems to point to the need for the Court, as Catherine Mitchell describes it, to make a more "direct commitment" to supporting "commercial reasonableness", because the Court will have to consider whether serious effort to resolve issues has been made, this is a relational concept.[48]

Oliver Williamson (supported by Jonathan Morgan) provides a facile solution to relational contracting – a clause that parties "agree that they will co-operate over any problems encountered".[49] Medirest's General Counsel might be able to explain to them the pitfalls. Eisenberg claims that the relational literature has failed to show that there is a set of legal rules that should be applied to "relational" contracts, and this claim is fair, although, as I have argued above, if one limits the claim for new rules to constructive engagement on what one might call internalities, relationalism is not too vague nor wholly incapable of yielding determinate rules.[50]

5.2.3 Other academic constructs – mainstream obligations scholars and hybrid or para-relationists

In Samuel Stoljar's original review in 1953, describing duties to cooperate by category (Building, Commission, Employment and Notice), illuminating the principle with cases going back hundreds of years he says:

> Since the fundamental and pervasive theory of the common law of contract is that of a bargain between two parties the natural ... corollary is that the parties must mutually co-operate to enable and facilitate the fulfilment of their bargain ...[51]

---

48 Catherine Mitchell, *Contract Law and Contract Practice: Bridging the Gap between Legal Reasoning and Commercial Expectation* (Hart 2013) at 244.

49 Morgan, *Contract Law Minimalism* – "as Williamson points out, a simple clause could be inserted in every long term contract".

50 Eisenberg, 'Relational Contracts' in Beatson and Friedmann, *Good Faith and Fault*, 291.

51 Stoljar, 'Prevention and Cooperation'.

He explains the two parts to cooperation: "not to hinder [and] a distinctly positive duty ... to take all such necessary or additional steps ... that will either
materially assist or will generally contribute to the full realization of the
bargain".[52]

When one turns to other academic writings, things are apt to be a bit murky.
The nature of the cooperation, the meaning of cooperation and how it might
affect actual cases is oft-times not clear, reflecting Howarth's critique.[53]

For example, Adams and Brownsword, attempting to define cooperation, say:
"co-operation is not simply a matter of performing ... or making it possible for
the other party to perform ... On the other side co-operation is not a matter of
acceding to any demand made."[54] This is a bit vague. They suggest the classical
law is predicated on competition when cooperation would be "more rational".[55]
They place a modern notion of cooperation "somewhere between the classical
model ... and sheer altruism" (proponents of pure altruism are a rare breed),
saying that it implies "responsibility and restraint" and that the test is whether
conduct is compatible with the contractual community of interest.[56] My concept
is enabling and facilitating conduct which ensures that the contract is a success,
and requires some responsibility and restraint and is connected with a notion of
a contractual community.

They also argue that a cooperative model would require people to consider
how the scrupulous or honourable would react.[57] My model requires constructive engagement and professional attempts to resolve problems. This might
require people to consider how the experienced commercial professional would
react (the "ordinary reaction" per Bingham J in *Tradax*[58]). In other work,
Roger Brownsword says that a cooperative ethic of contract would be defined
by "equality of interest" in which contractors treat their interests as holding
equal weight.[59] The TDTC insists that where key decisions affecting one party
are taken by the other, fairness and impartiality play a central role.

Brownsword also says that Macaulay's work supports the view that business
operates on a cooperative level, maintaining that it is not important, as
a matter of practical ethic, whether cooperation is created through moral
principle or enlightened self-interest. Cooperation, in these terms, means

---

52 Ibid. 232 and he illustrates the prevention principle with the case of *Foreman S T and S Bank
    v* Tauber (1932) 348 Ill 280 – see subchapter 2.2 above.
53 Howarth, 'Is Law a Humanity?' and *Law as Engineering.*
54 John Adams and Roger Brownsword, *Key Issues in Contract* (Butterworths 1995), 301–302.
55 Ibid. 295.
56 Ibid. 302. At 297 they refer to the "relevant body of commercial opinion".
57 Ibid. (n.34) criticising Cockburn J's famous/cynical epigram in *Smit v Hughes* (1871) LR 6
    QB 597 (QB) – "The question is not what a man of scrupulous morality or nice honour
    would do ... "
58 *Tradax Export SA v. Dorada Compania Naviera SA (The "Lutetian")* [1982] 2 Lloyd's Rep
    140 at 157.
59 Roger Brownsword, *Contract Law: Themes for the 21st Century* (OUP 2006), 28–29.

roughly what Macaulay describes as disputes being "suppressed, ignored or compromised in the service of keeping the relationship alive";[60] described by Adams and Brownsword as "emphasising that for many business people co-operation is the name of the (relational) game".[61] If relationship means contract, then my model is aligned with this, but future business is a by product, a "nice-to-have".

Donald Harris and David Campbell say that "precise conduct cannot be specified in advance … [parties accept] … a general and productively vague norm of fairness". As a definition of cooperation this has some resonance and aligns tolerably well with the TDTC except that there is no notion of fairness in the TDTC. The other problem with it is that their conception of cooperation is cooperative utility maximisation, which might come to the same thing, but the managers I dealt with were trying to make the instant contract work.[62] There was an element of win-win and give-and-take but this was all under the shadow of a known contract framework. What there is is an acceptance of a degree of vagueness and a requirement to manage that out through professional engagements; the productively vague norm would be of performance and this would be achieved by following the contract as far as possible but then by sorting out in-contract problems as they arise.[63]

Hugh Collins deals with the topic in some detail saying that in the classical law there was "no general obligation to cooperate, to assist each other, to perform in good faith, or to make the contract a success".[64] He suggests that cooperation might require "obligations of loyalty and mutual assistance", requiring parties to

> go beyond performance according to the strict terms … displaying trust, in assisting each other as far as possible in … use … of discretion a general obligation to cooperate, to assist each other, to perform in good faith, or to make the contract a success.[65]

One of the original dimensions of my survey was that it asked practitioners what success means. The answer was performance, in broad terms. Good faith, in terms, is not a material issue for practitioners. Communication was consistently cited as an essential part of cooperation in managing contracts and when asked how they would use discretion, in general practitioners consult and consider the

---

60 Stewart Macaulay, 'An Empirical View of Contract"' (1985) 1985 *WisLRev* 465 at 468.

61 Adams and Brownsword, *Key Issues,* 299.

62 David Campbell and Donald Harris, 'Flexibility in Long-Term Contractual Relationships: The Role of Co-operation' (1993) 20 *JLS* 166 at 167.

63 Ibid.

64 Collins, *Law of Contract,* 330–363.

65 Ibid. 331–332. See Lyons and Mehta, 'Private Sector Business Contracts' in Michie and Deakin, *Contracts,* 107, that empirical work shows cooperation is associated with "flexibility to contractual performance".

interests of all parties; see subchapter 3.2.3. However, Professor Collins seems to confine the need for cooperation to longer-term transactions, arguing:

> If ... one regards the law of contract as offering an opportunity for entering into binding long term commitments ... calculations of self-interest ... should not be permitted to subvert the value of the institution in contracts. Instead the law must impose certain duties of co-operation.[66]

Elisabeth Peden says that it is appropriate to see cooperation as equivalent to good faith: "Cooperation basically must embrace a duty to act honestly and a duty to have regard to the legitimate interests of the other party."[67] That is quite close to my thinking on decision making but doesn't reach the level of detail required by Adams and Brownsword.

5.2.4 Law and economics definitions

Eric Posner claims: "Law and economics writing has become so paralyzed by complexity that a wise judge would simply ignore it."[68] As I have noted above (at 4.1.1) one problem with the law and economics literature is that it does not recognise the existence of symbiotic forms of contract which require cooperation as a practical day-to-day matter for performance; or perhaps it ignores these complex multi-layered instruments. Despite a good survey of the material available Richard Craswell discusses "a promise" or "the promise" throughout a discussion on economic theories of enforcing promises, it being very difficult to consider an outsourcing contract or a facilities management contract as "a" promise, as it is more the sum of thousands, perhaps tens of thousands of promises.[69]

The literature tends to the assumption that cooperation is about renegotiation and preservation, usually defining it in carrot and stick, Prisoner's Dilemma terms or as extended self-interest, enforced by the long-term relationship.[70] This almost bipolar literature provides support for both classical and relational

---

66 Collins, *Law of Contract,* 30.
67 Elisabeth Peden, *Good Faith in the Performance of Contracts* (LexisNexis Butterworths 2003), 170.
68 Morgan, *Contract Law Minimalism,* 60. He remarks that business wants the clear and simple rules of English Law instead – the rules in Chitty's 2000 or so pages and the multitude of cases cited? Mitchell, *Contract Law,* notes that the literature "appears to pull in different directions".
69 Richard Craswell, 'Two Economic Theories of Enforcing Promises', chapter 1 in Peter Benson, *The Theory of Contract Law: New Essays* (CUP 2001).
70 E.g. – Douglas G. Baird, 'Self-Interest and Cooperation in Long-Term Contracts' (1990) 19 *JLS* 583, Robert M. Axelrod, *The Evolution of Cooperation* (Basic Books 1984) Robert D. Cooter, 'Decentralized Law for a Complex Economy: The Structural Approach to Adjudicating the New Law Merchant' (1996) 144 *Univ Pennsylvania Law Rev* 1643, Robert E. Scott, 'Conflict and Cooperation in Long-Term Contracts' (1987) 75 *Cal LRev* 2005.

approaches to cooperation in the literature,[71] emphasising walk away, pay up later, theories of efficient breach (Richard Craswell points out that there are many methods of defining efficiency[72]) on one extreme and supporting relational models, finding ways to preserve the relationship, based on longer term contracting on the other.[73]

5.2.5 *Trust based definitions*

Lyons and Mehta distinguish between socially oriented trust (SOT) and self-interested trust (SIT), making the point that SOT is less powerful when difficulties arise.[74] They also claim that trust, not law, is the component that allows parties to "respond in a cooperative manner to unforeseen events".[75] In similar work, in an article discussing success factors in joint R&D projects, drawing from a survey of enterprises in three European Countries, Fink and Kessler[76] distinguish between instrumental trust which draws power from sanctions and maxim-based trust which draws power from "self-commitment", saying that where enterprises make use of maxim-based trust they seem to do better. Self-commitment includes some risk-management-like processes such as investigating the reputation of the other party and previous dealings. Others are attuned to making the project work such as communicating, modifying behaviour, taking a risk, accepting setbacks. They also note that the more "cooperative experience" the parties have, the more success can be expected.[77] It is worth remembering that these relationships have the support of legal systems in which good faith plays a larger role than it does in England and Wales. Their analysis is explicitly relational, rejecting governance or market mechanisms as controls, instead claiming trust as an increasingly significant coordination mechanism. The "structural" and "interpersonal" characteristics of maxim-based trust, however, include elements susceptible to governance and legal or market sanction such as

- resilience – inferring problem solving;
- communication – I can get right to the point;
- transparency – understanding other parties' processes.[78]

---

71 Baird n. 72 above, Trebilcock n. 48 above.
72 'Two Economic Theories' in Benson, *Theory*, 20.
73 Ibid. – for a survey of this material. See generally Anthony T Kronman and Richard A Posner, *The Economics of Contract Law* (Little, Brown 1979).
74 Lyons and Mehta, 'Private Sector Business Contracts' in Michie and Deakin, *Contracts*, 63–64.
75 Ibid. 51.
76 Matthias Fink and Alexander Kessler, 'Cooperation, Trust and Performance – Empirical Results from Three Countries' (2010) 21 *Br J Manage* 469. The survey received 458 responses from 10,000 requests.
77 Ibid. 479.
78 Ibid. 476 and 480.

These results align neatly with my survey results, showing that respondents' managerial ethos corresponds closely to conditions for success in R&D collaborations. In that certain expectations, such as good communication, and problem-solving endeavours are amenable to contractual regulation, I am unable to agree fully that the approach is either fully relational or is likely to be fully trust-based. The behaviours described by respondents do not appear to be truly extra-contractual, non-governance, market neutral. Survey results tend to demonstrate a correlation between good communication, solid management and success. Yadong Luo observes that in these types of contract completeness also drives performance, showing again that the deal needs formal and informal elements.[79]

In the same volume Deakin, Lane and Wilkinson describe cooperation in "supplier partnerships" or "networks" where there is a degree of information sharing, staff exchange and cross ownership of know-how and IPR as involving: "An intention or willingness to maintain a trading relationship over a period of time, to avoid adversarial behaviour and to adopt an attitude of flexibility with regard to contractual performance."[80] There are elements of this in the TDTC, save that there is no obligation to maintain a trading relationship, but the need for some give and take and management through constructive engagement is key.

Courts will not imply terms of mutual trust and confidence, which would allow parties to terminate should the conduct of the other result in a loss of trust and confidence in commercial contracts. Having reviewed the authorities, Flaux J., considering "tweets" made by a reality TV participant, declined to imply a term requiring the upholding of mutual trust and confidence, saying that if Mr Hendrick's behaviour evinced an intention not to be bound "that would amount to a renunciation of the contract entitling ITV2 to terminate for that breach".[81] Richard Spearman QC in a commercial property case said that "if the parties wish to produce [that] result ... then they should do expressly".[82]

In most commercial contracts, such trust and confidence are simply not necessary. They might come into play when Courts are considering mitigation, as in *Gul Bottlers* where "disgraceful" treatment had been meted out to the Pakistan distributor of double strength Vimto by the licensor. The refusal by the distributor to enter a new agreement offered during proceedings (a "legal stratagem") was found not unreasonable, and therefore not a failure to mitigate,

79 Yadong Luo, 'Contract, Cooperation, and Performance in International Joint Ventures' (2002) 23 *Strategic Manage J* 903.

80 In 'Contract Law, Trust Relations, and Incentives for Co-operation: A Comparative Study' in Michie and Deakin, *Contracts,* 107.

81 *MR H TV Ltd v ITV2 Ltd* [2015] EWHC 2840 (Comm). See also *Carewatch Care Services Ltd v Focus Caring Services Ltd* [2014] EWHC 2313 (Ch) and *Jani-King (GB) Ltd v Pula Enterprises Ltd* [2007] EWHC 2433 (QB) for similar Judgments.

82 *Chelsfield Advisers LLP v Qatari Diar Real Estate Investment Co* [2015] EWHC 1322 (Ch) and see *MR H TV Ltd v ITV2 Ltd.*

since Gul had wholly lost the trust and confidence in Nicholls necessary to underpin a long-term (five–ten year) agreement.[83] There will be circumstances in which trust and confidence has been lost but that, as in *Ritchie,* is the result of a breach and not the breach itself.

5.2.6 Managerial thoughts

Given that my respondents manage contracts it seems sensible to understand some of the academic literature on the topics of negotiation and cooperation in action. In particular it would help, if only to determine whether there is agreement between the literature and the practitioner on the value of constructive engagement. As we saw in Chapter 3 Jane Wiggins advises that facilities managers need good communications skills enabling them to build customer relationships.[84]

Cooperation in negotiation means to Fells "Integration, win-win, problem solving", which is very close to the views of my respondents.[85] Another echo of survey responses is found in Lewicki who, faced with "extreme" negotiations, advises "ask the supplier to explain why [the] problems" are occurring and to "Slow Down, Collaborate".[86] Again this emphasises the need to problem-solve and that is part of cooperation in contract management. Project managers recognise that when problems occur one needs to bring "key personnel together", that "escalation is the control mechanism" but that treating people unfairly may lead to the undermining of cooperation and cohesion.[87] On the Association for Project Management's website one finds "Spencer" describing a day in his life, and an unexpected problem: "For this, I'll get my team and our supply-chain delivery teams to work together collaboratively to develop solutions and eventually agree on one to resolve the issue."[88] In the complex area of providing human services, where service requirements and client demographics are dynamic, Bowen McBeath et al. observe that: "There appears to be a shared understanding among managers that partnership through regular dialogue is the most effective method of resolving service and contracting dilemmas."[89]

Charles Handy identifies cooperative employment contracts as those in which the individual identifies with the goals of the organisation and becomes creative

---

83   *Gul Bottlers (PVT) Ltd v Nichols Plc* [2014] EWHC 2173 (Comm).

84   Jane M Wiggins, *Facilities Manager's Desk Reference* (Wiley 2010) at 476.

85   RE Fells, *Effective Negotiation: From Research to Results* (2nd edn, CUP 2012), 68.

86   Roy Lewicki and others, *Negotiation: Readings, Exercises and Cases* (7th edn, McGraw-Hill 2015).

87   Erik W Larson and Clifford F Gray, *Project Management: The Managerial Process* (7th edn, McGraw Hill Education 2018).

88   www.apm.org.uk/jobs-and-careers/career-path/what-does-a-project-manager-do/a-day-in-the-life-spencer/.

89   Bowen McBeath and others, 'The Managerial and Relational Dimensions of Public-Nonprofit Human Service Contracting' (2017) 3 *J Strategic Contracting Negotiation* 51.

in the pursuit of those goals, with more voice on the goals and more discretion in how to achieve them: "in a cooperative environment expert or charismatic power works best and position power is less effective".[90] There is an echo of the views of my respondents here. The relationship is important and must be built through communication and engagement.

5.2.7 Tit-for-tat ≠ cooperation

> Farther on up the road, someone's gonna hurt you like you hurt me
> Farther on up the road, baby you just wait and see
> You got to reap just what you sow, that old saying is true
> Like you mistreat someone, someone's gonna mistreat you[91]

Prisoner's Dilemma (PD) games are so-called because the acme of the species is two prisoners, accomplices, who have been arrested (Figure 5.1). Their dilemma is that if each keeps quiet, they each get one year in gaol, if one rats, the rat goes free and the rattee goes to gaol for several years. If they each rat, each gets more than one but less than several years behind bars.

This popular pastime was invented in the 1950s by Merrill Flood and Melvin Dresser at the RAND Corporation and enormous efforts have been put into the design of PD experiments in endeavours to show why and how human beings work together.[92] The difficulty is explained by Hugh Mellor: "If this is philosophy then questionnaires asking people whether they think circles can be squares, is maths."[93]

The Payoff Matrix for a Typical Prisoner's Dilemma		
	Shahad	
Wayne	Confess	Keep Quiet
Confess	Each gets five years in gaol	No gaol for Wayne, ten years for Shahad
Keep quiet	No gaol for Shahad, ten years for Wayne	Each gets one year in gaol

Figure 5.1 Prisoner's Dilemma – Typical Payoff Matrix

90 Charles B Handy, *Understanding Organizations* (4th edn, Penguin 1993), 47 and 141.
91 Don Robey/Joe Medwick Veasey – 1957.
92 Schneier, *Liars and Outliers,* 262, refers to a database search yielding 73,000 academic papers with Prisoner's Dilemma in the title.
93 David Edmonds, *Would You Kill the Fat Man?* (Princeton UP 2013) at 93.

Anatol Rapaport, who designed the most successful algorithm for score maximisation in iterated PD games, tit-for-tat, understood the shortcomings of game theory. It must be supplemented by consideration of "the role of ethics, of the dynamics of social structure, and of social structure and of individual psychology".[94] It is not solely economists who refer to the most egregious outcome as resulting from cooperation but even authors who seek moral principles are not free from this error.[95] In the sense cooperation is used in this book and in the dictionary sense, not defecting, not ratting is not cooperation.[96] Prisoner's Dilemma games are often presented as offering a choice between cooperation and defecting. But there is no common goal. Each Prisoner has a separate goal: to avoid or minimise his own incarceration. There is no enabling or facilitation, and no joint work or activity.

Survey respondents were offered the option of reciprocation in vignette 4 and few found the idea attractive, just 6% rating it as their first choice and 12% as their second choice. It was said that it involved "stooping to their level", would dig "deeper trenches" or "relationships would sour". This is consistent with the relationship-building, communicate and make-it-work philosophy of those engaged in management of these contracts. There is some evidence, from a public good, pooled wealth game run by Fehr and Gachter, that free riders are so resented that cooperative players are willing to punish them even at a cost to themselves.[97] Deakin and Michie counsel, on PD games that: "The conditions under which contracts [are] renegotiation-proof are so extreme as to have only a tenuous connection with ... practice."[98] See also Gintis and Bowles and Engels in my subchapter 3.1.2 above who also describe the problem with game theory as failing to take the reality of human interaction into account (which might be thought to be fatal in a discipline supposedly examining human interaction).[99] Tit-for-tat, the bedrock of PD games, simply does not figure in the management of modern complex contracts. It is at once too simplistic, binary in nature, fails to consider social reality and does not provide the basis for a solution to the problem. Parties recognise that they must talk at some stage and that to reciprocate is mere adjournment.

---

94 Anatol Rapaport, *Fights, Games, and Debates* (University of Michigan Press 1974). See also Anatol Rapaport, 'The Use and Misuse of Game Theory' (1962) *Sci Am.*

95 Schneier, *Liars and Outliers*, 53, Joshua David Greene, *Moral Tribes: Emotion, Reason and the Gap between Us and Them* (Atlantic Books 2013), 30, Jesse J. Prinz, *Beyond Human Nature* (1st edn, Allen Lane 2012), 313.

96 Note Collins, *Regulating Contracts*, 130, describing PD experiments as non-cooperation games and "inherently unstable".

97 Ernst Fehr and Simon Gächter, 'Cooperation and Punishment in Public Goods Experiments' (2000) 90 *Am Econ Rev* 980.

98 'The Theory and Practice of Contracting' in Michie and Deakin, *Contracts,* 9–10.

99 PH Gulliver, 'Negotiations as a Mode of Dispute Settlement: Towards a General Model' (1973) 7 *Law Society Rev* 667 points out e.g. that the theories "universally ignore the distribution of power".

5.3 Conclusion

There is a certain amount of synthesis in the TDTC, which is a novel abstraction based on a unique combination of doctrinal, empirical and theoretical analysis. Burrows' unenthusiastic claim that cooperation "is a vague term and can be used to be used to cover a wide range of situations" is something of a counsel of despair.[100] The fact that cooperation will be required in a wide range of situations means that day-to-day requirements covered by a duty to cooperate will vary with the scope of the contract; which is roughly how Lord Atkin described the neighbour principle. In analysing academic opinion, I think that the level at which many academics approach cooperation is too abstract; it needs to get closer to the coal face (or the helpdesk).

My claim that the TDTC can be fairly described as a third way survives comparison to other conceptions of cooperation including Common Law articulations, relational constructs, academic opinion, good faith claims, and Prisoner's Dilemma experiments.

---

100 JF Burrows, 'Contractual Co-operation and the Implied Term' (1968) 31 *MLR* 390 (n. 81) at 390.

6 Remedies, antidotes, and enforcement mechanisms

From survey results, I argue that in these modern complex contracts, parties eschew termination and expect each other to engage constructively to manage, solve or prevent disputes and problems. A certain amount of give and take, communication and/or discussion is required. Accordingly, remedies should be available with this background in mind. In this Chapter I explore a few ideas, using standard, albeit seldom used, remedies, to demonstrate that the Common Law does have some flexibility in the way that it deals with parties unwilling to perform in a constructive and cooperative manner.

At the "extreme pole" of relational contracts, says Ian Macneil: "Trouble is anticipated and dealt with by 'cooperation and other restorational techniques'".[1] This may fit into the TDTC's constructive engagement requirements; but it needs detail. Courts should "mould the remedy to the circumstances",[2] a dualist approach to remedies.[3] I use the term "remedy" as a shorthand in the wide sense used by David Campbell, as a course of action open to someone who wishes to "take some step to cope with the consequences of [another's] failure to perform his contractual obligation".[4] In many cases, conventionally measured damages will be "inadequate",[5] and I endeavour to show that there are plausible alternatives. I concentrate on an analysis of remedies which might satisfy, in whole or in part, the need to deter termination and encourage constructive engagement. They are:

1 Ian R Macneil, 'Contracts: Adjustment of Long-Term Economic Relations under Classical, Neoclassical, and Relational Contract Law' (1978) 72 *NWULR* 854.
2 David J Ibbetson, *A Historical Introduction to the Law of Obligations* (OUP 1999) at 259 commenting on *Hong Kong Fir.*
3 Andrew Robertson (ed.), *The Law of Obligations: Connections and Boundaries* (UCL Press 2004). Michael Tilbury, 'Remedies and the Classification of Obligations', ibid., chapter 2, at 17. describes two theories of remedies; monist and dualist. Monist means that obligation and remedy are congruent rights; dualist that Courts make a determination of the obligation and then a context-specific evaluation of the remedy.
4 Donald Harris, *Remedies in Contract and Tort* (2nd edn, Butterworths 2002),t 3.
5 Lord Nicolls' description in *Attorney-General v Blake* [2000] UKHL 45 at [21].

- Remedies analogous to those for prevention. I will explore how remedies which "neutralise" prevention might be taken a step further. In these instances, Courts may substitute their own machinery and remedies may operate to create the fiction that a prevented obligation has been performed.
- "Wrotham Park"/negotiating damages. A remedy available where a hypothetical release fee, notionally the price a willing buyer and seller would have negotiated in circumstances where an asset or something in the nature of an asset is at the heart of the right infringed.
- Damages for failure or refusal to negotiate.
- Statutory adjudication. This provides a fast-track, rough and ready, temporarily final, dispute resolution framework.
- Limiting the right to terminate to encourage parties to engage with each other to keep the contract alive.
- Cost penalties, should the matter reach the Courts.

Although it might act as a deterrent, I excluded excommunication as a viable remedy, Sir Michael Latham recording:

> Mr Nisbet also kindly supplied a copy of his book "Fair and Reasonable – Building Contracts from 1550". … Conditions of contract in the Middle Ages were clearly onerous. A contract in York in 1335 required the carpenter to complete work within three months on pain of excommunication.[6]

Ralph Cunnington identifies four remedies which may be available to a Court where damages are not adequate.[7] These are specific relief, loss of amenity damages, gain-based damages and punitive damages. Loss of amenity damages are used where the object of the contract is the provision of amenity or pleasure, which is not usually the aim in symbiotic contracts (although there might be an argument that a contract to build a domestic garage or a kitchen fits this category) and punitive damages are not available in England.

Andrew Burrows classifies remedies functionally as: compensation, restitution, punishment, compelling performance of positive obligations, preventing wrongful acts, compelling the undoing of a wrong, declaring rights.[8] Prevention remedies tend to declare rights and/or compel performance. Negotiating damages and damages for failure to negotiate are compensatory. Limiting the right to terminate and allowing fast-track adjudication can compel the undoing of a wrong or declare rights. Cost penalties are deterrence-based, forcing parties to act in a commercially sensible manner.

---

6 Michael Latham, *Constructing the Team* (1994) at 4.4.
7 In 'The Inadequacy of Damages as a Remedy for Breach of Contract' in Charles Rickert (ed.), *Justifying Private Law Remedies* (Hart 2008), 114–127.
8 Andrew S Burrows, *Remedies for Torts and Breach of Contract* (3rd edn, OUP 2004), 8.

6.1 Remedies for prevention

Courts have various remedies at their disposal to deal with prevention of performance. One is proleptic, treating prevented obligations as performed, or forbidding reliance on them,[9] "a sort of estoppel" according to JF Burrows.[10] In *Mackay v Dick* Lord Watson ruled that where a party "impeded or prevented the event, it is held as accomplished".[11]

Another is to exonerate the innocent party from performance.[12] Most commonly experienced in construction or engineering contract cases, prevention bars an employer from claiming liquidated damages for employer caused delay. This dates back to the "first modern decision"[13] in 1838 in *Holmes v Guppy*,[14] described by Keating J as founded on the "most invincible reason".[15] The principle applies equally in shipping contracts.[16] Where an employer fails to provide proper drawings and instructions or access to site the obligation prevented will be "eliminated"[17] or the prevented party "exonerated", possibly even released from liability for forfeiture.[18] Attempts to create a contractual mechanism to manage preventative activity will be construed strictly against the employer.[19]

Where a party refuses to appoint a valuer, or interferes with certification, where a certifier declines to act,[20] where a certifier's conduct falls short of "a high standard of fairness" or is oppressive and "partisan",[21] the Court may substitute its own

---

9 John W Carter, *Carter's Breach of Contract* (Hart 2012), 11–47. *Colley v Overseas Exporters* [1921] 3 KB 302 – suing for the price was limited to cases in which delivery has taken place. In *Sir Richard Hotham v The East India Company* 99 ER 1295 at 1299 – Ashhurst J said: "it being rendered impossible ... by the neglect and default of the company's agents ... it is equal to performance".

10 JF Burrows, 'Contractual Co-operation and the Implied Term' (1968) 31 *MLR* 390 at 396.

11 *Mackay v Dick* (1881) 6 App Cas 251 (HL) (n. 70) at 270–271 "If the breach ... prevents the plaintiff from performing a condition ... he is to be taken as having fulfilled that condition". David M Walker, *Principles of Scottish Private Law* (2nd edn, OUP 1975) cites this case at 662–663, referring to the condition as "potestative": under the power or control of one of the parties.

12 *Roberts v The Bury Improvement Commissioners* (1870) LR 5 CP 310 (Exchequer) at 329.

13 Samuel J Stoljar, 'Prevention and Cooperation in the Law of Contract' (1953) 31 *CanBar Rev* 231.

14 *Holme v Guppy* (1838) 150 ER 1195. Stoljar, 'Prevention and Cooperation' at 237. See John E Stannard, *Delay in the Performance of Contractual Obligations* (OUP 2007) at 9.14 citing *Peak Construction (Liverpool) Ltd v McKinney Foundations Ltd* (1970) 69 LGR 1, 1 BLR 111 (CA) where Lord Salmon said at 121 "I cannot see how ... the employer can insist on compliance with a condition if it is partly his own fault that it cannot be fulfilled."

15 *Russell v Viscount Sa da Bandeira* (1862) 143 ER 59 (Common Pleas) at 205.

16 *The Mass Glory* [2002] EWHC 27 (Comm).

17 Stoljar, 'Prevention and Cooperation' at 233.

18 *Roberts v The Bury Improvement Commissioners, Joseph Hunt v Bishop* 155 ER 1523 (Exchequer).

19 *Peak Construction (Liverpool) Ltd v McKinney Foundations Ltd* (n. 14 above).

20 *Watts v McLeay* 19 WLR 916.

21 *Pawley v Turnbull* (1861) 3 Giff 70 cited by Alfred A Hudson and IN Duncan Wallace, *Hudson's Building and Engineering Contracts* (Sweet & Maxwell 1970) at 467. See also *Canterbury Pipelines v Christchurch Drainage Board* [1979] 2 NZLR 347.

machinery, taking matters into its own hands; Lord Fraser refusing to accept that one party could flout provisions "at his own sweet will":

> the machinery ... has broken down because the respondents have declined to appoint their valuer ... I prefer to rest my decision on the general principle that, where the machinery is not essential, if it breaks down for any reason the court will substitute its own machinery.[22]

The Court substituted the requirement for agreement on a valuer with an inquiry into a "fair and reasonable price"; perhaps because damages were not an adequate remedy.[23] In other prevention cases, such as one where a party refused to appoint a valuer, Courts have ordered specific performance.[24]

6.2 Wrotham Park/negotiating damages

In a line of cases, dating from *Wrotham Park Estate Co. v Parkside Homes Ltd* (*Wrotham Park*),[25] damages could be assessed as: "damages for loss of a bargaining opportunity or, which comes to the same, the price payable for the compulsory acquisition of a right".[26] At one stage it seemed that the law had advanced to allow Wrotham Park damages where it would be "just" to do so, not simply because no loss has been suffered but where the calculation of loss might present serious difficulty.[27] When I was completing my PhD I thought that the "loss of a bargaining opportunity" might be sufficiently flexible to provide a method of calculating damages where parties refused or failed to engage in a constructive manner, as in the "ketchup" vignette where I drafted as if only one party had refused to engage. In *Morris-Garner v One Step Ltd (Morris Garner)* the Supreme Court placed significant limits on such damages, asking us to "abjure" the term "Wrotham Park damages", replacing it with the prosaic term "negotiating damages",[28] in a case turning on the breach of a non-compete covenant. Negotiating damages are now strictly "compensatory", and appropriate only where, in Lord Reed's Judgment:

---

22 *Sudbrook Trading Estate Ltd v Eggleton* [1983] 1 AC 444 (HL) at 484.
23 Gareth Jones, 'Specific Performance: A Lessee's Covenant to Keep Open a Retail Store' (1997) 56 *CLJ* 488 at 490.
24 See *Richardson v. Smith* (1870) LR 5 ChApp 648 and *In re Malpass, Decd. Lloyds Bank Plc. v Malpass* [1985] Ch 42.
25 *Wrotham Park Estate Co. v Parkside Homes Ltd* [1974] 2 All ER 321, [1974] 1 WLR 798. Burrows, *Remedies*, 400, describes these as restitutionary.
26 *WWF-World Wide Fund for Nature v World Wrestling Federation Entertainment Inc* [2007] EWCA Civ 286 Chadwick J at [42].
27 See *Morris-Garner v One Step (Support) Ltd* [2016] EWCA Civ 180.
28 *Morris-Garner v One Step Ltd* [2018] UKSC 20, Lord Reed at [3]. The term was first used in senior Courts by Lord Neuberger in *Lunn Poly Ltd v Liverpool & Lancashire Properties Ltd* [2006] EWCA Civ 430 at [22].

the breach of contract results in the loss of a valuable asset ... the breach of a restrictive covenant over land, an intellectual property agreement or a confidentiality agreement. ... The claimant has in substance been deprived of a valuable asset, [or] the contractual right is of such a kind that its breach can result in an identifiable loss equivalent to the economic value of the right, considered as an asset, ... such as a right to control the use of land, intellectual property or confidential information. It is not easy to see how, in circumstances other than those of the kind described [above], a hypothetical release fee might be the measure of the claimant's loss. It would be going too far, however, to say that it is only in those circumstances that evidence of a hypothetical release fee can be relevant to the assessment of damages.[29]

Lord Sumption said of the use of a hypothetical release fee: "I consider that the notional price of a release may nonetheless be relevant, not as an alternative measure of damages but as an evidential technique for estimating what the claimant can reasonably be supposed to have lost."[30] In *Pell Frischmann Engineering Ltd v Bow Valley Iran Ltd*, approved in *Morris Garner*, parties negotiating a contractual joint venture fell out, and one party then continued negotiations with the National Iranian Oil Corporation using information covered by a confidentiality agreement; the Privy Council awarded Wrotham Park damages based on the "commercial value of PFE's veto",[31] saying that "The critical point was that the confidentiality agreements gave PFE a power of veto which stood between its erstwhile collaborators and what they saw as a valuable opportunity."[32]

This approval led Andrew Burrows (soon to be Burrows SCJ) to think that the "fuzzy edge" between the two cases will require "fine-tuning".[33] After all, there does not appear to be a great deal of difference between the breach of a confidentiality obligation and a breach of a non-compete covenant in that each appears to turn on the economic value of the right infringed and in each it appears that loss could be measured either conventionally or by reference to

29 *Morris Garner Sup Ct* at [91]–[95].
30 Ibid. at [106].
31 *Pell Frischmann Engineering Ltd v Bow Valley Iran Ltd* [2009] UKPC 45; [2011] 1 WLR 2370 at [57]. Lord Reed approved the Judgment in *Morris Garner Sup Ct* (n. 28 above) at [83] saying "The award of damages based on the commercial value of the right infringed treated that right as a commercially valuable asset, of which the claimant had been effectively deprived."
32 *Pell Frischmann* at [56].
33 AS Burrows, 'One Step Forward' (2018) 134 *LQR* 515 at 520. See also Caspar Bartscherer, 'Two Steps Forward, One Step Back: One Step (Support) LTD v Morris-Garner and Another' (2019) 82 *Mod Law Rev* 367 saying at 371: "It is unclear how Lord Reed foresees extending a quasi-proprietary right to extract economic value to some contractual rights while simultaneously withholding it from others without proffering any concrete criteria to draw the line between them."

hypothetical release fee. Without disagreeing too much with the majority, saying that he "broadly" took the same view on categories, Lord Sumption brought into play *Pell Frischmann* and *Experience Hendrix LLC v PPX Enterprises Inc.*,[34] in which Wrotham Park damages had been awarded against a party which owned various Jimi Hendrix copyrights but had agreed not to license them; and then did license them.[35] The Court of Appeal awarded damages based on the amount which would have been paid for the license (accepting that there may have been, in fact, no damage). Lord Sumption cites other cases where property rights are not in issue, one of misuse of the image of a racing driver,[36] and suggests that "the concept of treating a notional release fee as an evidential tool for assessing a party's true loss in appropriate cases has been found valuable and is certainly not impractical. It is frequently employed."[37]

It remains to be seen how much difference there is between Lord Sumption and Lord Reed and how valuable and widespread the use of a release fee, calculated hypothetically, will be. Burrows suggests that the Supreme Court had a choice between either allowing claimants always to elect for negotiating damages or drawing a defensible line around them.[38] The Supreme Court could, however, have taken an approach allowing negotiating damages only in cases where damage, albeit suffered, is either impossible or disproportionately costly to quantify, clarified the circumstances in which the hypothetical release fee might be available as an evidential tool and kept alive the idea of such damages as the loss of an opportunity to bargain where there had been an obligation to undertake some consultation or bargaining.

6.3 Damages for failure or refusal to negotiate

How, then, is a party subject to a failure to engage, to consult, to negotiate, to find recompense? Their damage is likely to comprise additional management time and loss of chance. They might consider hypothesising a release fee. I hope that the Supreme Court has not left parties with no remedy other than termination.

In *Pallant v Morgan* cases, where one party to a joint land deal rats, said to be based on agency concepts by Bowstead, Courts may hold that the land is held for both parties jointly and that if the parties fail to agree on the division of the property it will be resold, and the proceeds divided equally subject to reimbursement of some expenses.[39]

---

34 *Experience Hendrix LLC v PPX Enterprises Inc. and another* [2003] EWCA Civ 323.

35 *Morris Garner Sup Ct* (n. 28 above) at [122].

36 *Irvine v Talksport Ltd* [2003] 1 WLR 1576.

37 *Morris Garner Sup Ct* (n. 28 above) at [123].

38 Burrows, 'One Step Forward' (n. 33 above) at 521.

39 *Pallant v Morgan* [1953] Ch 43. Peter Watts and others (eds), *Bowstead and Reynolds on Agency* (20th edn, Sweet & Maxwell 2014) at 6.110.

In a case where a landlord failed to consult tenants affected by redevelopment works, Alan Steinfeld QC found that the landlord should have taken
the tenants' interests into account and agreed a pattern of quiet and noisy
times for the works. In addition, despite there being no evidence that the
tenant had lost profit, the Court awarded a 20% discount on the rent, indicating that this should have been considered by the landlord.[40] As I observe
in Chapter 3, the case shows that a duty to negotiate can bite. One could
explain the case as the Court awarding damages for a failure to engage or
negotiate.

6.4 Statutory adjudication

Always "intended to be rough justice", the UK's statutory adjudication
scheme, allowing an adjudicator to make a determination within 28 days of
a reference, has "spread around the world".[41] It "was, and is, a revolution that
has transformed the landscape of construction disputes".[42] The "rough and
ready" adjudication scheme for tenancy deposit disputes, equally, appears to
be transforming the handling of disputes around deposits.[43] The survey results
show that respondents (70–90%) would welcome fast-track adjudication.
Those with construction experience were more willing to describe it as effective or helpful.

As Chief Justice Wayne Martin suggests, expert determination is one possible
route for fast-track dispute resolution, but it carries the risk of finality even
when a determination is "idiosyncratic and extreme".[44] The advantage of adjudication lies in its temporarily binding nature. It allows for rough justice to be
reviewed in more refined tribunals.

If the numbers in Figure 6.1 are still valid, and Robert Fenwick Elliott's esti-
mate that adjudication costs are 10% of those of litigation is accurate, it seems
unarguable that the process is effective.[45] The number of adjudications appears
to have levelled off according to figures produced by the Adjudication Society
(Figure 6.2).[46]

In all three of the cases that I used as case studies in Chapter 3 I suspect that
access to adjudication, quick, cheap, rough and ready justice would have helped.
It focuses minds. It allows parties to get out of the hot atmosphere they have

---

40 *Timothy Taylor Ltd v Mayfair House Corporation* [2016] EWHC 1075 (Ch).
41 Keating Chambers Legal Update for Summer 2015.
42 James Pickavance, *A Practical Guide to Construction Adjudication* (John Wiley & Sons
   2015) at 1.10.
43 Julian Sidoli del Ceno, 'Adjudication in Tenancy Deposit Scheme Disputes: Agents' Perspectives' (2015) 7 *IJLBE* 162.
44 Kanaga Dharmananda (ed.), *Long Term Contracts* (Federation Press 2013), 352.
45 Robert Fenwick-Elliott, 'Building and Construction Industry Adjudication – The UK
   Experience'.
46 From Report 17 – www.adjudication.org/resources/research.

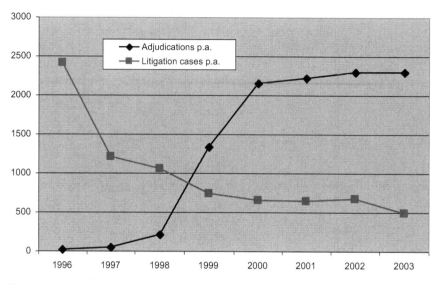

Figure 6.1 Approximate Numbers of Litigation Cases and Adjudications in the UK

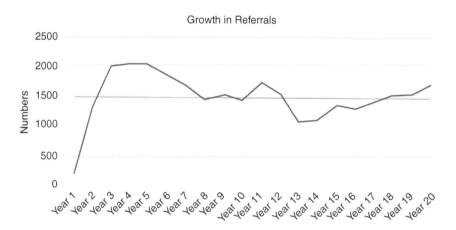

Figure 6.2 Adjudication Numbers 1998–2017 UK

created in a dispute and discuss it with a disinterested third-party expert. It also seems likely that most claims are not continued post-adjudication.[47]

47 Nicholas Gould, 'Adjudication and ADR: An Overview' – www.fenwickelliott.com/sites/default/files/nick_gould_-_adjudication_and_adr_-_an_overview_matrics_paper.indd_.pdf.

Remembering that, as soon as lawyers were engaged in *Medirest,* the Trust paid over withheld monies while not withdrawing their claims, it is not fanciful to suggest that placing the issues in front of an experienced adjudicator, who might well have taken the same approach as Cranston J, would have allowed the parties some breathing space before the two acts of termination were carried out.

6.5 Limiting the right to determine

In *Hong Kong Fir Shipping Company v Kawasaki Kisen Kaisha Ltd* (*Hong Kong Fir*),[48] in a falling market charterers cancelled a charter, alleging unseaworthiness. The Court found that there were no reasonable grounds for supposing that the vessel could not be made seaworthy in a reasonable time. Consequently, since the commercial purpose of the voyage had not been frustrated, the repudiation was wrongful. Following this case termination provisions will usually be classified as innominate, not as conditions, placing limits on parties' ability to terminate for minor breaches[49] and creating incentives to maintain the relationship. It is ancient law going back centuries.[50] Accepting that it may be possible to draft strict termination provisions, Hudson counsels against clauses apparently permitting "termination for any breach", referring to Courts' "reluctance" to "read such wording literally".[51] Hugh Collins says the case reinforces "the value of co-operation by forbidding reliance on the term as a pretext".[52] Roger Brownsword describes this as "covert manipulation of doctrine" which should be replaced by subjecting "withdraw[al] ... to a good faith proviso".[53] As I have argued in sub-chapter 2.5, it would be better to operate a simple principle, that where there is any rational doubt about the meaning of conduct the terminating party should be required to ask for an explanation before terminating. Neil Andrews alludes to this as the so-called "*Heisler*"[54] exception which applies where a party terminates wrongfully but has another existing justification for terminating. He goes on to indicate that, where an "opponent is clearly labouring under a misapprehension, which the innocent party could have readily dispelled ... [or] there was a clear chance to clarify whether the other party was taking a 'stand'", then termination will be wrongful. Much as I think that this takes the law in the right direction,

---

48 *Hong Kong Fir Shipping Co. Ltd v Kawasaki Kisen Kaisha Ltd* [1962] 2 QB 26, [1962] 1 All ER 474 (AC).

49 Note in *Fitzroy House Epsworth Street (No. 1) Ltd v Financial Times Ltd* [2006] EWCA Civ the conflation of material and substantial.

50 See e.g. *Sir Richard Hotham v The East India Company* (n. 75).

51 Alfred A Hudson, *Hudson's Building and Engineering Contracts* (ed. Nicolas Dennys and Robert Clay, 13th edn, Sweet & Maxwell 2015) at 8.046.

52 Hugh Collins, *The Law of Contract* (CUP 2008), 360.

53 Roger Brownsword, '"Good Faith in Contracts" Revisited' (1996) 49 *CLP* 111 at 127.

54 *Heisler v Anglo-Dal Ltd* [1954] 2 All ER 770, cited thus in Neil Andrews, 'Breach of Contract: A Plea for Clarity and Discipline' (2017) 134 *Law Q Rev* 117 at 119.

save that I think it behoves the terminating party to solidify the grounds for termination by making enquiries, the cases Andrews cites turned on misinterpretation (opportunistic in one case) of the other's conduct. In each case the terminating party accepted the other's conduct as repudiatory; in each case the Court found the conduct not to have been repudiatory. One case is based on *Mannai* – the terminating party who took advantage of an obviously incorrect notice being held not to be able to rely on it, which does provide an incentive to communicate and make enquiries, but which seems to be narrowly confined to contractual notices.[55] In the other a dealer in exotic cars, who innocently misinterpreted a contract for the sale of a Ferrari Testarossa (£179,500 worth), was held not to have repudiated the contract by asking for a significant increase in price, but the buyer was held to have repudiated, and lost their 25% deposit by reason of not making any effort to pay the sum he felt to be due (from the report it seems that the failure to complete the purchase may have been due to the fact that the buyer was no longer intending to return to Hong Kong and there may have been an element of opportunism) and it is not easy to drag out from the cases that attempts to clarify might have helped.[56]

John Wightman says that "cooperation is fostered by leaning against the use of technical breaches to escape".[57] Writing before corrective legislation (the 1979 Sale of Goods Act[58]), he laments the toleration of extreme uses of rejection rights (now limited by section 15A of the Act),[59] meaning Lord Atkin's lapse of judgement (which could be contrasted with Lord Reid's view in *Schuler* that such interpretation is only viable where there is no other explanation), in a case where goods were agreed to be fit for purpose but slightly non-conform to description:

> A ton does not mean about a ton, or a yard about a yard. Still less … does ½ inch mean about ½ inch. If the seller wants a margin he must and in my experience does stipulate for it. … recognized trade usage [particular figures] may be given a different meaning, as in a baker's dozen.[60]

The breach of a payment term, unless covered by an express provision, will, usually be insufficient to justify termination.[61] This may be different when non-

---

55 *Eminence Property Developments Ltd v Heaney* [2010] All ER (D) 193 (Oct).

56 *Vaswani v Italian Motors (Sales and Services) Ltd* [1996] 1 WLR 270.

57 John Wightman, *Contract: A Critical Commentary* (Pluto Press 1996).

58 Sale of Goods Act 1979 (1979 c 54).

59 Wightman, *Contract*, 91, says this of *Re Moore & Co. v Landauer* [1921] 2 KB 519 (KB). See also *Arcos v Ronaassen* [1933] AC 470 (AC).

60 *Arcos v Ronaassen* at 479. In Suffolk 1,000 rabbits, by custom, means 1,200 – *Smith v Wilson* (1832) 3 B & Ad 728.

61 *Dalkia Utilities Services plc v Celltech International Ltd* [2006] EWHC 63 (Comm), [2006] 1 Lloyd's Rep 599 and see *Spar Shipping AS v Grand China Logistics Holding (Group) Co Ltd* [2016] EWCA Civ 982.

payment is prolonged and "cynical" with "repeated complaints ... and broken promises".[62] In time clauses, as Lord Wilberforce once explained – there is only one breach possible: to be late.[63]

The Court may refuse to allow termination where it suspects opportunistic motive. In one IT case, it was clear to the Court that the defendant wanted to escape from the contract due to a change in his own circumstances, and consequently declined to accept that delays in performance or completing in a reasonable time were repudiatory.[64]

6.6 Cost penalties

In a series of cases in England Courts have punished parties in costs for unreasonable behaviour in ADR. They show a willingness by Courts to provide incentives to cooperate in dispute resolution; although they may not yet go far enough.[65] The *Halsey* rationale, cited in *Reid v Buckinghamshire Healthcare NHS Trust* is that:

> If the party unwilling to mediate is the losing party, the normal sanction is an order ... that they will have to pay their opponents costs even if those costs are not proportionate ... This penalty is imposed because a court wants to show its disapproval of their conduct.[66]

In one recent case, the Court of Appeal observed that:

> The message which the court sends out in this case is that in a case where bilateral negotiations fail but mediation is obviously appropriate, it behoves both parties to get on with it. If one party frustrates the process by delaying and dragging its feet for no good reason, that will merit a costs sanction.[67]

Noting that the ADR jurisprudence needs leadership and coherent jurisprudence from the Court of Appeal, Masood Ahmed says that *Thakkar v Patel* "oblige[s] litigating parties to actively engage with a call to mediation".[68] In essence,

---

62 *Alan Auld Associates Ltd v Rick Pollard Associates* [2008] EWCA Civ 655 at [20].

63 *Bunge Corpn v Tradax SA* [1981] 2 All ER 513, (HL) [1981] 2 Lloyds LRep at 5.

64 *Astea (UK) Ltd v Time Group Ltd* [2003] EWHC 725 (TCC).

65 *Halsey v Milton Keynes General NHS Trust* [2004] EWCA Civ 576. See also Masood Ahmed, 'Implied Compulsory Mediation' (2012) 31 *CJQ* 151 and Masood Ahmed, 'Bridging the Gap between Alternative Dispute Resolution and Robust Adverse Costs Orders' (2015) 66 *NILQ* 71.

66 *Reid v Buckinghamshire Healthcare NHS Trust* [2015] EWHC B21 citing *Halsey v Milton Keynes General NHS Trust* at [28].

67 *Thakkar v Patel* [2017] EWCA Civ 117 – Jackson LJ at [31].

68 Masood Ahmed, 'Mediation: The Need for a United, Clear and Consistent Judicial Voice' 13 *CJQ* 1.

paraphrasing Lord Diplock, parties are obliged to cooperate with each other to keep the proceedings "moving".[69] In that sense it must be possible for judges to craft remedies analogous to cost sanctions to deter parties from failing to engage constructively in-contract.

They may also punish parties who make extravagant claims and win only a small proportion of the claim.[70] By analogy Courts could punish parties who behave unreasonably, creating or exacerbating problems. At present they may do this indirectly; see the discussion below in subchapter 7.1.14 where a litigant's conduct was held to have contributed substantially to the problems encountered. In an employment law case surrounding a non-compete covenant the Supreme Court has just asked, not rhetorically, whether there might be a costs "sting in the tail" for winning parties who have left the Courts to clear up their "legal litter".[71]

---

69 *Bremer Vulkan Schiffbau und Maschinenfabrik v South India Shipping Corp Ltd* [1981] AC 909 HL.
70 *Business Environment Bow Lane Ltd v Deanwater Estates Ltd* [2009] EWHC 2014.
71 *Tillman v Egon Zehnder Ltd* [2019] UKSC 32 at [92].

7 A few hard cases

There is, in general, in the academic literature, limited linkage of cooperation to real cases showing how enforced, construed, or implied, cooperation might work,[1] what sort of rules might be used in enforcement and how case results and analysis might be affected.[2] In this chapter I demonstrate the TDTC at work, examining its implications when presented with the sort of problems encountered in the performance of modern complex contracts, with the aim of determining whether it can be applied in a coherent fashion and without undermining the certainty apparently required by commercial people.

I take some interesting cases, and hypotheticals, asking:

- What would happen if the TDTC were applied?
- What remedies might a Court use to encourage cooperation in such cases?

In some cases, I show that the TDTC is not engaged by the breach. I have examined these cases to show that the TDTC is an enabling duty with limited scope, there to facilitate performance. It is not an overarching duty, nor a tenebrous concept like good faith. It is distinctive and touches contracts only when parties must act jointly to enable or facilitate performance.

7.1 Medirest

7.1.1 The relevant facts

That imperfect behaviour is not confined to construction contracting may be seen by reading *Medirest*.[3] It provides a splendid example of the sort of activity

---

1 David Howarth, *Law as Engineering* (Edward Elgar 2013), commenting that academics do not do enough "design", says that this is typical.
2 None of my hard cases, other than *Baird Textiles*, is covered in Rosemary C Hunter and others (eds), *Feminist Judgments: From Theory to Practice* (Hart 2010) where there is a rare and welcome attempt to rewrite difficult cases from a different perspective.
3 *Compass Group UK and Ireland Ltd (t/a Medirest) v Mid Essex Hospital Services NHS Trust* [2012] EWHC 781 (QB).

that forced Parliament to legislate to ameliorate the behaviour of construction industry players by creating a statutory fast-track, adjudication process to provide temporary finality for disputes.[4] Cranston J describes some of this behaviour:

> In several cases, although a fault was remedied in the presence of senior Trust staff, the Trust asserted that it could not be reasonably satisfied that a fault had been remedied and continued to calculate service failure points because no email was received. That ... was not reasonable behaviour ...[5]

A few respondents reported experiencing similar behaviour in such contracts. When Medirest sent a conciliatory letter, the Trust issued internal instructions to "pull it to bits".[6] The final straw seems to have been the Trust's inquiry as to how much Medirest would be willing to pay to keep the contract. One respondent said: "In Contracting face-to-face meetings are much more beneficial than exchanging letters and notices. ... Parties are normally more considerate in meetings than in letters!"

7.1.2 *Applying the TDTC*

Cranston J described material breaches as including: "absurd calculations ... in many respects indefensible, a failure to respond positively when Medirest protested the calculations and sought to resolve the dispute".[7] It is not only the decision to make deductions that requires cooperation; it is the management of the aftermath, as Cranston J indicated and as the TDTC would infer. That requires good communication, and "constructive engagement". It is hard to imagine the officious bystander who would consider it to be sensible commercial practice to "pull" sensible proposals "to bits". I have been unable to find any contemporaneous commentary claiming that Cranston J's first instance Judgment would create uncertainty.

The ordinary reaction of a commercial manager receiving a request to discuss the deductions, I think, would be, without hesitation to agree to a meeting, to discuss in a constructive and professional manner how to resolve the issues, and I would expect them to consider that this is not only right but necessary for the success of such contracts. One respondent said:

---

4 For the background see Sir Michael Latham, *Constructing the Team* (1994), and James Pickavance, *A Practical Guide to Construction Adjudication* (John Wiley & Sons 2015) at 1.2 "Commercial intimidation was rife, ... thousands of firms were forced out of business."
5 *Medirest High Court* (n. 3 above) at [46].
6 Ibid. at [82].
7 Ibid. at [83].

I've not faced a customer quite this extreme but there are always customers who attempt to nickel and dime you when assessing backcharges ... Normally this ends up in long and arduous negotiations with us either charging back or having to escalate with management.

Additionally, the unfair and far from impartial decision-making would run afoul of the TDTC requirement to take decisions fairly and impartially.

7.1.3 What remedies should be considered?

Clearly disappointed by the *Medirest* decision, Mary Arden argues for a more balanced approach:

> Now what I say is this. We need to recognise more generally that there are some contracting situations where the parties expressly do not want to give each other the right to take decisions exclusively in their own interests ... They are not expecting to be told that their agreement to cooperate is meaningless ...[8]

A formal adjudication process might have forced the parties to reconsider their behaviour before the atmosphere had been wholly poisoned. An expert adjudicator might have helped the parties come to an opinion on whether they had fallen below some objective threshold in the management of the deductions or the aftermath.

One possible remedy is for the Court to take a view of the outcome of constructive engagement as it did in *Timothy Taylor Ltd v Mayfair House Corporation*, where a failure to consult led the Court to award affected tenants a 20% discount on their rent.[9]

Employing the general principle that where a certifier over-reaches or fails then the Court may substitute its own machinery could have two results.[10] The Court could make its own judgment on the appropriate deduction of service points or it could regard the provision as vitiated due to the constructive failure of the decision-making party to appoint a fair decision-maker, and make a decision based on normal principle; what damage has the contractor caused? Were the Trust forced to proceed along normal lines, proving damage, this would be a major deterrent since these liquidated damages clauses are designed, as liquidated quasi-disgorgement remedies, to substitute the requirement to prove damage (often onerous and time-

---

8 Mary Arden, 'Coming to Terms with Good Faith' (2013) 30 *JCL* 199 at 212–213. For some sense of the bewilderment that *Medirest* causes see Jan van Dunné, 'On a Clear Day, You Can See the Continent' (2015) 31 *ConstLJ* 3.

9 *Timothy Taylor Ltd v Mayfair House Corporation* [2016] EWHC 1075 (Ch).

10 *Sudbrook Trading Estate Ltd v Eggleton* [1983] 1 AC 444 (HL).

consuming) with agreed sums for defined events. After all; what damage is caused by wedging a spoon in a fire door (and how would you prove that this was the contractor's doing)? In an Australian case, discussed by Elisabeth Peden,[11] a franchisor's otherwise justified termination was held to be ineffective as a result of their breach of a good faith obligation, and, by analogy, one might consider a Court able to hold the deductions ineffective as a result of the breach of the cooperation obligations. This would have the same effect as a declaration that, by reason of the misuse of the deduction provision, and the subsequent failure to take steps to discuss or remedy the point, Medirest was held to have performed.

Cost penalties could be one method of deterring such behaviour. Although the Trust won, its behaviour, failing to pick up its "legal litter", should be reflected in the Court considering its cost recovery. This could be by analogy to a failure to mitigate; to act reasonably once it became clear that a dispute was in progress or for making extravagant claims and thereby prolonging the litigation. One could imagine, for example, a Court determining that the legal and managerial costs involved in investigating and analysing the service point deduction costs in *Medirest* might well be deducted from the winning party's costs or added to the losing party's costs.

7.2 Portsmouth City Council v Ensign Highways

7.2.1 *The relevant facts*

In this case Portsmouth City Council, advised by a consultant, embarked on a strategy of penalising Ensign, its Highways maintenance contractor, by deducting Service Points to force it to accede to commercial demands.[12] This included deducting the maximum amount of Service Points for every default, refusing to communicate in relation to breaches, finding breaches which Ensign might find hard to remedy and storing up deductions over several months so that Ensign could be "ambushed".

7.2.2 *Applying the TDTC*

The judge, Edwards-Stuart J, remarked "unsurprisingly, Esign was very disturbed at these developments".[13] Applying the TDTC means that parties should avoid such disturbances. Instead they should communicate, engage and problem-solve. Behaving in this hole-and-corner manner is plainly non-compliant with the TDTC. In the US it appears that "overreaching" interpretation of

---

11 Elisabeth Peden, *Good Faith in the Performance of Contracts* (LexisNexis Butterworths 2003), 205, discussing *Bamco Villa Pty Ltd v Montedeen Pty Ltd* [2001] VSC 192.
12 *Portsmouth City Council v Ensign Highways Ltd* [2015] EWHC 1969 (TCC).
13 Ibid. at [8].

contract language may breach the UCC's good faith requirements.[14] In Australia obligations to cooperate in good faith preclude parties "from cynical resort to the black letter".[15] A simple duty to engage and communicate professionally and constructively would be breached by PCC's behaviour.

7.2.3 What remedies should be considered?

The issues are similar to those in *Medirest*: the difference lies in the tactical ambushes planned by the Council. Effluxion of time would plainly make adjudication less useful; at least on the first occasion. One possibility is the one I ponder in *Medirest* above; that the Court substitutes its own machinery by way of an inquiry into actual damages, which would be complex and expensive. If Ensign fails to fill in a pothole what damage does the City suffer? The answer may be "none" but there may be an abatement type remedy available to allow the City to recover the cost saving made by the contractor.[16]

Ewan McKendrick's opinion that acting with the predominant purpose of injuring the other party may be bad faith[17] appears not to be borne out by *Ensign*, but it could be given life by the application of *Bamco* principles.

7.3 The Post Office litigation

7.3.1 The relevant facts

In a highly complex litigation between the Post Office (PO)[18] and around 550 Sub Post-Masters (SPMs), who ran branch offices under contract, Fraser J considered the quasi-franchise relationships. Identifying nine "characteristics" of a relational contract, all in the PO/SPM relationship,[19] he characterised the contracts as "relational" and ruled that the contracts "included an implied obligation of good faith" (implied-in-law logic[20]). The characteristics are similar to Leggatt J's broad definition in *Sheikh Tahnoon* to refer to contracts in which "the parties are committed to collaborating with each other, typically on a long term basis, in ways which respect the spirit and objectives of their venture ..., and which it may be impossible to specify, exhaustively in a written contract".[21]

---

14 Robert S Summers, '"Good Faith" in General Contract Law and the Sales Provisions of the Uniform Commercial Code' (1968) 54 *VaLRev* 195 at 203.

15 *Overlook v Foxtel* [2002] NSWSC 17.

16 *Amey LG Ltd v Cumbria County Council* [2016] EWCH 2856 (TCC).

17 Guido Alpa and Mads Andenas (eds), *Private Law beyond the National Systems* (British Institute of International and Comparative Law 2007), 697.

18 *The Post Office Group Litigation* [2019] EWHC 606 (QB) at [3] and [725]–[726].

19 Ibid. at [727].

20 Ibid. at [738].

21 *Sheikh Tahnoon Bin Saeed Bin Shakhboot Al Nehayan v Ioannis Kent (AKA John Kent)* [2018] EWHC 333 (Comm) at [167].

Much of the litigation arose from errors in the Post Office's accounting system "Horizon" which "threw up apparent shortfalls and discrepancies", for which the PO generally blamed SPMs. SPMs brought multiple claims against the Post Office.[22] In a 315-page Judgment, Fraser J was fairly critical of the PO, saying that "there is a lot to be desired from the Post Office's behaviour" and that it would "brook no dissent". He set out the following undesirable aspects of its behaviour:

- Legal representation is not permitted by the PO at interviews which deal with whether a suspended SPM is to have their engagement terminated.
- A Temporary SPM was told to destroy all documentation in the branch that related to an SPM's appointment. "There can never ... be any sensible rationale for such destruction".
- Liability for losses requires negligence or fault, routinely and comprehensively ignored by the PO.
- Specific grounds and proper particulars of potential termination were not clearly identified in advance.[23]

7.3.2 *Applying the TDTC*

Fraser J implied 13 detailed terms into the contracts,[24] as "incidents, examples or consequences ... of the duties of good faith",[25] including:

> *(c) Properly and accurately to effect, record, maintain and keep records of all transactions effected using Horizon*
> *(d) Properly and accurately to produce all relevant records and/or to explain all relevant transactions and/or any alleged or apparent shortfalls attributed to Claimants*

(c) and (d) are essentially the basic obligation to provide an adequate system capable of dealing with SPM's data and records efficiently and accurately, in order to effect production of accounts. This is similar to the *Kleinert* case discussed in Chapter 2 in which a client supplied a crusher inadequate to the duty required of it.[26] Horizon, which was "central to the operation of Post Office branches",[27] was a mandatory system, out of which SPMs could not opt. A failure by the Post Office to provide a fit-for-purpose accounting system

---

22 *Post Office Group Litigation* (n. 18 above) at [10].
23 Ibid. at [723].
24 Ibid. at [746]–[748] and [1122].
25 Ibid. at [690]–[701].
26 *Kleinert v Abosso Gold Mining Co. Ltd* (1913) 58 Sol Jo 45 (Privy Council).
27 *Post Office Group Litigation* (n. 18 above) at [344].

meant that the joint activity of production of accurate and proper accounts by the PO and the SPM(s) was undermined. Just as Abosso's inadequate crusher was inadequate to its duty so was Horizon. Good faith adds nothing.

(e) To co-operate in seeking to identify the possible or likely causes of any apparent or alleged shortfalls and/or whether or not there was indeed any shortfall at all
(f) To seek to identify such causes itself, in any event
(g) To disclose possible causes of apparent or alleged shortfalls (and the cause thereof) to Claimants candidly, fully and frankly
(h) To make reasonable enquiry, undertake reasonable analysis and even-handed investigation, and give fair consideration to the facts and information available as to the possible causes of the appearance of alleged or apparent shortfalls
(i) To communicate, alternatively, not to conceal known problems, bugs or errors in or generated by Horizon that might have financial (and other resulting) implications for Claimants
(l) Properly, fully and fairly to investigate any alleged or apparent shortfalls

(e) to (i) and (l) are very similar to *Anglo Group* terms. The PO litigation is in some way the obverse of *Anglo Group* in that the PO provided a new computer system for its SPMs to use. One might expect the terms to be similar to those identified by Toulmin J but *Anglo Group* is not referred to in the Judgment. One could rephrase Toulmin J:

> It is well understood that the design and installation of a computer system requires the active co-operation of both parties ... There would be aspects of the system which did not immediately fulfil the needs of the PO or of the SPMs and there would have to be a period of discussion between them to see how the problems could be resolved. The duty of co-operation in my view extends to both parties accepting where possible reasonable solutions to problems that have arisen.

Cranston J's formulation of the duty to cooperate in *Medirest* (reflected in the TDTC), requiring parties to "work together constantly, at all levels of the relationship [and] work together to resolve the problems which would almost certainly occur",[28] could also apply to these issues.

(j) To communicate, alternatively, not to conceal the extent to which other Subpostmasters were experiencing relating to Horizon ...
(k) Not to conceal from Claimants the Defendant's ability to alter remotely data or transactions upon which the calculation of the branch accounts ... depended

---

28 *Medirest High Court* (n. 3 above) at [27].

(m) Not to seek recovery from Claimants unless and until: ... (iii) the Defendant had carried out a reasonable and fair investigation as to the cause and reason for the alleged shortfall and whether it was properly attributed to the [SPM]

Turning to the management of shortages, in my opinion the PO, as the paymaster for SPMs, calculating their remuneration, especially as that remuneration was partly determined by the Horizon system, wholly under the control of the PO, should have been obliged to act as if in the position of a certifier acting "in a fair and unbiased manner ... holding the balance" . That is a slightly stronger term than the one implied by Fraser J but it has the merit of being consistent with existing law and being easy to understand. It implies a proper assessment of the SPMs' and PO's entitlements, examining all the relevant evidence.

(n) Not to suspend Claimants: (i) arbitrarily, irrationally or capriciously; (ii) without reasonable and proper cause; and/or (iii) in circumstances where the Defendant was itself in material breach of duty
(o) Not to terminate Claimants' contracts: (i) arbitrarily, irrationally or capriciously; (ii) without reasonable and proper cause; and/or (iii) in circumstances where the Defendant was itself in material breach of duty

(m), and (n) are typical TDTC duties and conflict directly with *Medirest*. They each seek to limit the ability of the PO to operate an "absolute contractual right".

On suspension and termination Fraser J said that the Post Office's submission: "amounts to one that it *is* contractually entitled to suspend and/or terminate SPMs arbitrarily, capriciously, irrationally and without reasonable or proper cause, and to exercise contractual powers other than honestly".[29] The PO's power to suspend is broad:

[the PO] may suspend the Operator ... [where the PO] considers this to be necessary in [its] interests ... 15.1.3 – there being grounds to suspect that the Operator is insolvent, to suspect that the Operator has committed any material or persistent breach of the Agreement, or to suspect any irregularities or misconduct in the operation of the Branch.[30]

Fraser J describes this as a "powerful weapon" so "It must therefore be used properly."[31] This, it seems to me, is right. Fraser J's description of PO practice

---

29 *Post Office Group Litigation* (n. 18 above) at [761]. As I discuss at subchapter 2.7 above, these powers are normally controlled under implied-in-law terms.
30 Ibid. at [886]–[887].
31 Ibid. at [884].

in cases of suspension, which usually leads to a loss of livelihood, underlines the need for a fair investigation:

> Suspended SPMs are not only entirely excluded from the Post Office part of their premises ... also are completely denied access to any information or records. ... Mr Abdulla ... was, at his interview with Mrs Ridge, not given access to documents that showed his account concerning the TC and the lottery in the sum of £1,092 was substantiated by internal Post Office records. ... I do not see how a decision about a SPM's future can sensibly be taken on proper grounds in the absence of such a document being made available either to the SPM, or to the Post Office personnel tasked with taking such a decision.[32]

The termination conditions are of two types, as Fraser J explains before he says: "I consider that in both instances – termination without notice, and termination summarily – the Post Office must take the decision in accordance with the obligation of good faith."[33] As I discuss at subchapter 2.7.2 the English Courts have declined, sometimes in strong terms, to imply limits on decisions to terminate. Fraser J simply ignores these authorities, treating the matter as one of controllable discretion.

7.3.3 What remedies should be considered?

I suspect that adjudication would not have been useful, probably being too rough and ready for a complex case like this. Fraser J has not made any ruling on remedies so far. There are three types of breach in this litigation.

- One is the failure to provide an adequate accounting system.
- Next is the failure to manage the problems which arose as a result of Horizon's inadequacies.
- The third is the failure to act fairly and impartially in making decisions.

They are interlinked and it is hard to determine what might have deterred the PO from operating these contracts as it did. One possibility would be to treat the SPMs as having performed their obligations to provide accounting data, and to vitiate the ability of the PO to recover shortages. Another is to change the burden of proof – to force the PO to prove that the SPMs were at fault for the shortfalls. That would allow relatively simple calculations of damages since much of the action taken by the PO, including recovery of shortfalls, suspension and termination, would be in breach of contract.

---

32 Ibid. at [886].
33 Ibid. at [899].

Another would be to limit the PO's ability to suspend or terminate to repudiatory conduct, using Lord Reid's *Schuler* logic. In many cases this would mean that the termination or suspension had been wrongful, providing an easier pathway to calculation of damage.

7.4 Yam Seng Pte Ltd v International Trade Corporation Ltd (Yam Seng)

7.4.1 The relevant facts

In *Yam Seng*,[34] the contract, under which Yam Seng obtained an exclusive licence to distribute "Manchester United" cosmetics, was short ("skeletal" according to Leggatt J), comprising eight clauses drafted by the parties. David Campbell described the problems:

> A warm business relationship cooled largely because ITC repeatedly failed to supply merchandise as agreed, so that YSL itself repeatedly made commitments … that it could not meet … ITC's explanations of its failures and assurances of improved performance justifiably came to be regarded as implausible or outright false.[35]

ITC's conduct was found to be repudiatory and Yam Seng entitled to damages.

7.4.2 Applying the TDTC

Leggatt J defined the contract as a relational contract, requiring: "a high degree of communication, cooperation and predictable performance based on mutual trust and confidence and involve expectations of loyalty".[36] The communication and cooperation requirements align perfectly with the TDTC but there seems little reason to imply good faith obligations, particularly given the depressingly quotidian nature of the breaches alleged; which consisted of late shipment of orders, failing to supply all the specified products (neither of which merit novel treatment), undercutting agreed prices and providing false information. The evidence suggested, this being described as the "decisive contextual feature", a commercial expectation par excellence: "common ground between Mr Tuli and Mr Presswell that there is an industry assumption that retail prices in domestic markets will be higher than the corresponding duty-free retail prices at airports or on-board aeroplanes".[37] That "industry assumption" is a routine

---

34 *Yam Seng Pte Ltd v International Trade Corporation Ltd* [2013] EWHC 111 (QB).
35 David Campbell, 'Good Faith and the Ubiquity of the "Relational" Contract' (2014) 77 *MLR*.
36 Leggatt J in *Yam Seng* (n. 34 above) at 142.
37 Ibid.

commercial expectation, core to the contract, a fundamental obligation. The third complaint, that of providing false information, offends the TDTC in that there is no constructive engagement or proper communication; indeed, there is the opposite.

David Campbell observes that: "good faith obligations essential even to a commercial contract of this sort must be implied in order to give efficacy to the fundamentally co-operative contractual relationship".[38] Leggatt J defined the communication requirements, showing that the contract could be construed with precision, with no need for supernumerary good faith duties:

> ITC needed to plan production and take account of the expected future demand from Yam Seng for Manchester United products. ... Yam Seng ... was arguably entitled to expect that it would be kept informed of ITC's best estimates of when products would be available to sell and would be told of any material change in this information without having to ask.[39]

7.4.3 What remedies should be considered?

If the parties felt that the relationship should continue fast-track dispute resolution through statutory adjudication might well help. In cases like *Yam Seng* I think that normal conditions apply; terminate for repudiatory breach and claim damages; which was exactly the outcome.

7.5 Bristol Groundschool Ltd v Intelligent Data Capture Ltd

7.5.1 The relevant facts

The parties had collaborated, in a contract described as relational by Spearman J, on the production of training manuals for commercial airline pilots.[40] Applying good faith "standards of commercial dealing" Spearman J held that unauthorised downloading of material was commercially unacceptable and in breach of an implied duty of good faith.

7.5.2 Applying the TDTC

The materials were created between the parties for the express purpose of producing training manuals. Any other use must breach the contract. That seems to me to be obvious – there is no need to create an implied term of good faith. Such a breach does not engage the TDTC.

---

38 Campbell, 'Good Faith and Ubiquity'.
39 *Yam Seng* (n. 34 above) at [143].
40 *Bristol Groundschool Ltd v Intelligent Data Capture* [2014] EWHC 2145 (Ch).

7.5.3 *What remedies should be considered?*

Normal damages for breach; perhaps on the basis of a hypothetical release fee.

7.6 Communication cases – Mona Oil, AE Lindsay and Peter Dumenil

7.6.1 *The relevant facts*

The facts of each case[41] are given in subchapter 2.5 above. The thread that unites the cases is that a telephone call, or a cable or a telex enquiry, might have elicited information which would have allowed the contract to be performed.

7.6.2 *Applying the TDTC*

The TDTC requires that, where there is uncertainty, there should be an onus on a party deciding to put an end to the contract to double-check that the breach is not deliberate. Jenkins LJ's Judgment in *Dumenil* that it "behoved" the buyer to follow up is commercially sensible, because, as he said, the mistake was puzzling.

I would express the general proposition using a mixture of the words of Jenkins LJ and Bingham J:

> It behoves any reasonable commercial actor, before terminating a contract, to consider whether it is reasonably possible that there is an alternative explanation for the situation which has arisen, in which case to contact the other party and make proper enquiries in an attempt to clarify matters.

There are similarities between this principle and a right to cure defects in that the underlying idea is that parties should keep the contract alive by providing an opportunity to rectify errors and defects. One wonders whether such a term is reasonable, necessary and obvious and could be implied under the normal rules. If the objective is to support performance, then the term is reasonable and necessary. Jenkins LJ and Bingham clearly considered it obvious.

The explanation of *Mona Oil* and *Dumenil* offered by JF Burrows – that the Court assigned liability to the party which made the error and which could have corrected it by following up – is deficient in that the mistaken party may not have realised that a mistake had been made.[42]

---

41 *Mona Oil Equipment & Supply Co. Ltd v Rhodesia Railways Ltd* [1949] 2 All ER 1014; *AE Lindsay & Co Ltd v Cook* [1953] 1 Lloyd's Rep 328 (QBD); *Peter Dumenil & Co. Ltd v James Ruddin Ltd* [1953] 1 WLR 815 (AC).

42 JF Burrows, 'Contractual Co-operation and the Implied Term' (1968) 31 *MLR* 390 and see also *Dumenil* where the terminating party failed to follow up and double-check a clearly erroneous message.

The provision of information should be handled carefully. Describing, in IT contracts, a trend to draft provisions which create obstacles to relief from delaying events Clive Davies points out the tension between a legal requirement to provide notices and the result of following the contract:

> the last thing the supplier executive tasked with delivery wants to do is unnecessarily upset the supplier's customer. Yet that is precisely what he or she is required to do under the contract. It is also what his or her professional adviser will be telling him or her to do.[43]

A general duty to communicate clearly might make such communication more of a matter of course and less likely to cause relations between the parties to strain. It is also consistent with modern forms of contract in which defaulting parties are offered a right to cure, where possible, before termination rights crystallise.[44]

The principles I suggest provide incentives for parties to follow up and ensure that they have not got hold of the wrong end of the stick, or the rabbitskin. Had the TDTC duty to consult and clarify been incorporated and, of course, followed, then Rhodesian Railways would probably have obtained its oil tanks, Mr Dumenil his skinned rabbits and Lindsay's their frozen chickens.

7.6.3 What remedies should be considered?

Assuming that one party makes no real attempt to manage the issue, refusing to enter sensible discussions or communicate, what are the legal alternatives that might force a change of heart? One is, in my opinion, adjudication. A rough and ready decision-making process, threatened by the other, might bring a recalcitrant to the table. In several of these cases the result of failing to consult or seek further information was that the contract was terminated, and the natural remedy is conventional damages. Another possibility is loss of chance damages as discussed by Sir George Leggatt.[45]

---

43 Clive Davies, 'The Successful Management of Delay in IT Outsourcing Contracts' www.sclorg/siteaspx?i=ed39430.

44 See e.g. Clause 36 of the Institution of Mechanical Engineers, *MF/1 (rev 6): Model Form of General Conditions of Contract* (rev. 6th edn, Institution of Engineering and Technology 2014). There are similar provisions in Institution of Civil Engineers, *The New Engineering Contract* (Thomas Telford 1991).

45 Sir George Leggatt, 'Negotiation in Good Faith: Adapting to Changing Circumstances in Contracts and English Contract Law' (Jill Poole Memorial Lecture) at [62]–[66].

7.7 J & H Ritchie Ltd v Lloyd Ltd

7.7.1 *The relevant facts*

A used but newly supplied harrow developed a vibration in its drive chain.[46] The supplier provided a replacement and took the harrow back to their workshop, for investigation, where it was discovered that it had a serious defect, in that two bearings were missing. They fixed the problem and returned the harrow, and then refused to tell the farmer what the problem had been. The farmer rejected the harrow.

7.7.2 *Applying the TDTC*

Lord Hope ruled that the farmer had been "deprived of the information that they needed to make a properly informed choice"[47] and Lord Mance said that: "a natural implication of the arrangement made that the seller would, at least upon request, inform the buyer of the nature of the problem".[48] It wasn't so natural as to have persuaded Lloyd. My sample seems to agree that it was both necessary and reasonable for the information to be given to the farmer. These opinions are fully in line with the TDTC. Indeed, the underlying idea of facilitating informed choice is core to the TDTC.

Accepting that the result in *Ritchie v Lloyd* was "desirable" Kelvin Low doubts whether the term implied passed either an officious bystander or business efficacy test,[49] but my survey shows solid commercial support for forcing the supplier to disgorge the information, easily passing both tests.

7.7.3 *What remedies should be considered?*

Fast-track adjudication would be helpful – one imagines a hard-bitten adjudicator asking Lloyd whether they really believed that their Trappist attitude was "commercially sensible". Hypothesising a win for Lloyd the Court could take the view that there had been a technical win but the "egregious" refusal to discuss the issue, where a discussion might have resulted in a formal or informal resolution, should mean that a very limited costs order would be made. On a win for Mr Ritchie one possibility would that the management time he had spent seeking the information should be recompensed by Lloyd.[50]

---

46 *J & H Ritchie Ltd v Lloyd Ltd* [2007] UKHL 9; [2007] 1 WLR 670.
47 Ibid. at 19.
48 Ibid. at 52.
49 Kelvin FK Low, 'Repair, Rejection and Rescission: an Uneasy Resolution' (2007) 123 *LQR* 536.
50 See e.g. *Tate & Lyle Food and Distribution Ltd v Greater London Council* [1981] 3 All ER 716.

7.8 D&G Cars Ltd v Essex Police Authority

7.8.1 *The relevant facts*

In this case,[51] "a relational contract *par excellence*" in Dove J's words,[52] in fact a fairly standard service contract, the authority terminated a long-term vehicle recovery and crushing contract on discovering that a recovered vehicle had been repaired and absorbed into the contractor's fleet.

7.8.2 *Applying the TDTC*

Dove J implied a term that the parties would act with honesty and integrity, explaining that such a contract required fair dealing and transparency. Even a superficial overview reveals that the basic obligation on the part of D&G was to crush cars on the instructions of the authority. D&G did not crush one such car. That appears to me to be a very clear breach of its basic obligation, exacerbated by the fact that permission had been granted on previous occasions for deviations.

The references to trust, integrity, fair dealing and confidence are wholly unnecessary. The TDTC is not engaged.

7.8.3 *What remedies should be considered?*

The reluctance of the Courts to imply terms of mutual trust and confidence into commercial contracts is explained by Richard Spearman QC in a case involving complex property development agreements: "if the parties wish to produce the result that each of them has the right to terminate the contract in the event that it loses trust and confidence in the other ... then they should do expressly".[53] This appears to me to be right. The rules relating to repudiation are clear and will often cover situations where one party has wholly lost confidence in the other.

If the Authority had wished to continue the relationship, negotiating damages might be appropriate allowing the Court to award damages based on the outcome of a hypothetical negotiated transfer of the diverted car. Another possibility is an abatement based on the contractor's cost savings.[54] Either might deter such breaches, forcing the contractor to be open and negotiate should he find a desirable car to add to his fleet. One potential difficulty is that the property in to-be-crushed vehicles may not pass to the Police Authority. For the purposes of this discussion I make the assumption that the vehicles have some value to

---

51 *D&G Cars Ltd v Essex Police Authority* [2015] EWHC 226 (QB).
52 Ibid. at [176].
53 *Chelsfield Advisers LLP v Qatari Diar Real Estate Investment Co.* [2015] EWHC 1322 (Ch) and see *MR H TV Ltd v ITV2 Ltd* [2015] EWHC 2840 (Comm).
54 See *Amey LG Limited v Cumbria County Council* (n.16 above).

the Authority; even if the Authority does not own the vehicle (and there are powers in some circumstances, notably proceeds of crime legislation, to take ownership of a vehicle) its possessory rights allow it to retain the vehicle until fines and fees are paid.[55]

7.9 Decision-making powers – Nash and Lymington

7.9.1 *The relevant facts*

The facts are set out above in subchapter 2.7.[56] In *Nash* the lender, Paragon, in financial trouble and consequently unable to borrow at normal market rates, raised interest rates by 2%. Mrs Nash and others challenged this use of decision-making power. In *Lymington* a licensee wished to sub-license the use of berths in a marina to his two brothers on a rolling basis. The marina owners demurred and were challenged on the use of this "absolute discretion".

7.9.2 *Applying the TDTC*

If one applies the TDTC to these decision-making cases, altering the general negative duty not to act capriciously, arbitrarily or irrationally (rules described by Jack Beatson as a limited concept of 'abuse of rights'[57]) to a positive duty to act fairly and impartially, perhaps allowing the *Esso* measure of genuine appraisal of one's own commercial requirements as a guide, it is hard to see that this would alter the result. This is unlikely to reduce certainty; since such standards have been in place in the construction industry for over a century. In both *Nash* and *Lymington,* the Court heard evidence that the decision-maker had considered its own requirements genuinely so there would appear to be no additional burden imposed.

Where an employer wishes to vary a contract two elements of the TDTC are engaged. These decisions are the sort of things which, says Zoe Ollerenshaw, are "heavily planned for",[58] with variations and extensions of time, in particular, providing fertile grounds for disputes.[59] Judges, when disputes arise on valuations and extensions of time, are fairly strict on the duties of certifiers and decision-makers. They will observe that asking for perfect information is not

---

55 See www.gov.uk/stopped-by-police-while-driving-your-rights/when-the-police-can-seize-your-vehicle.

56 *Nash v Paragon Finance Plc* [2001] EWCA Civ 1466; *Lymington Marina Ltd v Macnamara* [2007] All ER (D) 38 (Mar).

57 Jack Beatson and Daniel Friedmann (eds), *Good Faith and Fault in Contract Law* (Clarendon 1997), chapter 10 at 228.

58 'Managing Change in Uncertain Times' in Larry A. DiMatteo and others (eds), *Commercial Contract Law: Transatlantic Perspectives* (CUP 2013), 204.

59 Eric Eggink, 'Correct Scoping of Employer's Requirements: The Prevention of Change Orders' (2017) *ICLR* 4 at 4.

reasonable, noting that architects, for example "are not strangers to the project",[60] or that architects should not adopt a "passive" attitude to problems.[61] In addition they must act lawfully, fairly and even somewhat scientifically; making assessments of time in a "logical and calculated" manner which should not be "impressionistic".[62] The contractor will usually be obliged to provide information for review.[63] An offer to inspect records should be treated seriously, and the contractor should offer "such details ... as are reasonably necessary".[64]As Akenhead J said:

> it is necessary to construe the words in a sensible and commercial way that would resonate with commercial parties in the real world. The Architect ... must be put in the position in which they can be satisfied that all or some of the loss and expense claimed is likely to be or has been incurred.[65]

In New Zealand it has been held that an extension of time must be advised to the contractor as soon as reasonably practicable.[66] Tying these elements together, contractors are obligated to communicate reasonably sufficient detail to a certifier who is then obliged to deal with it professionally and expeditiously, ensuring that the contractor can then get on with the work with some underlying commercial certainty.

7.9.3 What remedies should be considered?

There are two possibilities. Where a decision-maker fails to reach decisions fairly and impartially the Court may either substitute its own decision, as I discuss in Chapter 5 above, or it may act as a reviewer, requiring the decision-maker to reconsider. Neither is particularly radical. In some cases, as I have discussed in Chapter 2, Courts have ordered specific performance where decision-making has been capricious.

7.10 Day-to-day management – the mundane and the more mundane

7.10.1 The relevant facts

This is an extract from a "day in the life of example" for a facilities manager:

---

60 Aikenhead J in *Walter Lilly & Co. Ltd v Giles Patrick Cyril Mackay and DMW Developments Ltd* [2012] EWHC 1773 (TCC) (n. 63) at 467.
61 *Holland Hannen and Cubitt v Welsh Health Technical Services Organisation* (1981) 18 BLR 1.
62 Brian Eggleston, *Liquidated Damages and Extensions of Time* (3rd edn, Wiley-Blackwell 2009), 329, citing *John Barker Construction Ltd v London Portman Hotel Ltd* 83 Build LR 35.
63 See generally Eggleston.
64 *Walter Lilly & Co. v Mackay and DMW* (n. 60 above).
65 Ibid. at 468.
66 *Fernbrook Trading v Taggart* [1979] 1 NZLR 556.

9am

I pop up to the canteen to get some breakfast. The catering is out-sourced, and I am responsible for management of that contract. I speak with the Catering Manager and he explains that some deliveries did not arrive, so one of the planned meals will be off the menu. It is the main vegetarian option, so I am slightly concerned, and go and speak to the chef to arrange an alternative. Again, I take a note to check in with the supplier in the week.[67]

Extending this example, let's say that our FM decides to make a service point deduction, despite the cure. In that case we have worked out how the parties should proceed. Let's assume, however, that, in running his eye over the offerings, our FM espies some "Harrison's" tomato ketchup sachets. He hasn't heard of Harrison's and asks the caterer why they are not using Heinz. The contract, he is told, requires the ketchup to be a "known brand". The FM argues that Harrison's is not a known brand and instructs the caterer, on pain of deductions, to offer Heinz in future. Heinz, I discovered from a quick internet search, costs around 6p per sachet whereas Harrison's costs around 2.5p. How to resolve this? One of my respondents says: "when people have the right approach and gel well, a contract can go well even if protocols aren't water-tight". In my opinion this is a legitimate debate. If the supplier was using a cheaper brand to save money that would be too bad for the employer, but it appears to be a fair debating point. Another day-to-day issue might arise if, say, a repeated fault arose in kitchen equipment; in which case one would expect a root cause analysis to be shared by the contractor. One empirical survey shows significant agreement on categorisation of a light bulb burning out but less on such things as a leaking fire hose.[68] These seem to me to give rise to legitimate debate but also to obligations to make reasonable efforts to resolve the disagreements.

7.10.2 Applying the TDTC

These seem to me to be issues that should be dealt with quickly. The parties should get together and work out solutions. If they can't they should escalate, in the hope that senior management might have heard of Harrison's. Although the survey I refer to above may demonstrate some variance it will provide material to a Court or adjudicator to consider which of the parties is more likely to be proposing a business-like approach to the matter.

---

67 www.maxwellstephens.com/blog/a-day-in-life-of-facilities-manager/.
68 Joseph HK Lai and others, 'Disputes Arising from Vaguely Defined Contractual Responsibil-ities in Building Services Maintenance Contracts' (2004) 22 *Facil* 44.

7.10.3 *What remedies should be considered?*

Adjudication would or should work. This could be statutory or informal. If the FM decides to refuse to discuss the matter, and to insist on Heinz or deduction, then an adjudicator could take that behaviour into account in wasted expenditure or cost awards. Cost penalties, should this "legal litter" reach the Courts, might deter.

7.11 Walter Lilly & Co. Ltd v Giles Patrick Cyril Mackay and DMW Developments Limited

7.11.1 *The relevant facts*

The outrageous behaviour of one Mackay towards his own team (!), is described in the Judgment:[69]

> his behaviour towards the Architects, some WLC employees and other consultants was not simply coarse … it was combative, bullying and aggressive and contributed very substantially to the problems on this project.
>
> Mr Mackay … accused Mr Davis of BLDA of being "the most unprofessional person" he had met, that he was a charlatan and liar and that his head was "so far on the chopping block that it is holding on by a thread"
>
> At a walk around meeting Mr Mackay referred to Mr Davis as a "f***ing Pussy" and said that he "wakes up in the morning wanting to kill him". At a similar meeting a week later he called Mr Davis to his face a "f*****g little twat"

7.11.2 *Applying the TDTC*

Applying the TDTC one would be forced to conclude that Mr Mackay's behaviour deviated somewhat from its standard of constructive engagement; and that he made few efforts to resolve matters reasonably. The TDTC requires that parties interact constructively, make efforts to cure (not cause) problems. Mr Mackay's behaviour would not meet that standard.

Tying this into vignette 4, the "ketchup" vignette, over 80% of respondents chose one of the top three options in question 11.2, when asked whether they would keep demanding the removal of the uncooperative manager, and over 67% thought that provisions allowing parties to demand the removal of uncooperative or aggressive managers would be helpful or more than helpful.

---

69 *Walter Lilly & Co. v Mackay and DMW* (n. 60 above).

Sweet & Maxwell's *Employment Law Encyclopaedia* says that the duty applies to employment contracts as a class.[70] For example, after a few incidents with his notoriously aggressive and foul-mouthed manager, a very highly paid City trader resigned. Newman J held that the term was not affected by the level of pay and that the frequent use of foul language does not sanitise it.[71] A manager's remark that his personal secretary was an "intolerable bitch on a Monday morning" irretrievably damaged the confidence which they should have in one another.[72] A night club owner called an employee a "big bastard", "pig-headed"[73] and, with further imprecation, said "I can talk to you any way I like", which destroyed that relationship.[74] A breach of the duty entitles the innocent party to treat the contract as repudiated.[75] This may be because a wronged employee may have no remedy, walking away excepted.[76] However, consider the position in a major employer with hundreds or thousands of employees on one site. In that case, an employee could, in most cases, be redeployed with ease, suffering little damage. In a small firm where such redeployment is not a possibility, I can understand the reasoning that says that repudiation is the only possible remedy but in a major enterprise this does not accord with common sense. In a large organisation, very few relationships are key and when a line manager and an employee fall out badly, redeployment of one or the other is usually possible. In that sense, the remedy could be moulded to fit *Hong Kong Fir* principles. In my own experience, I have created conditions in which the rights of either employee or employer have been preserved pending attempts to mediate or reorganise. In Scotland, the position is different, and an employer will be able to cure even a repudiatory breach.[77]

---

70 RV Upex, *Encyclopedia of Employment Law* (Sweet & Maxwell 1992) at 1A.2.5. See also Chitty, *Chitty on Contracts* (ed. Hugh Beale, 33rd edn, Sweet & Maxwell 2018) at 40.151-152.

71 *Horkulak v Cantor Fitzgerald International* [2004] EWCA Civ 1287. See also *Ogilvie v Neyrfor-Weir Ltd* EATS/0054/02 (EAT (Scotland)) and *Cantor Fitzgerald International v Bird* [2002] IRLR 267. See *Doman v Royal Mail Group Ltd* ET/2803550/10 where one instance of telling a manager to "fuck off" was, marginally, held to justify dismissal.

72 *Isle of Wight Tourist Board v Coombes* [1976] IRLR 413, EAT.

73 For a review of bad language cases see Julian Yew, 'Foul Mouths in the City' (2003) 153 *NLJ* 1298.

74 *Palmanor Ltd v Cedron* [1978] ICR 1008.

75 See *Courtaulds Northern Textiles Ltd v Andrew* [1979] IRLR 84, EAT Browne-Wilkinson LJ at 72 and *Buckland v Bournemouth University Higher Education Corporation* [2010] All ER (D) 299.

76 Frederic Reynold, 'Bad Behaviour and the Implied Term of Mutual Trust and Confidence: Is there a Problem?' (2015) *ILJ* 262 at 265. Daniel Friedman, in Beatson and Friedmann, *Good Faith and Fault*, 423–424, notes that employment contracts are unique in that a unilateral breach, wrongful dismissal, brings the contract to an end. The employee does not have the opportunity to affirm. Doctrinally this is inexplicable.

77 *Millars of Falkirk Ltd v Turpie* 1976 SLT (Notes) 66.

Some might question whether it is necessary or reasonable to imply a term requiring constructive engagement and some attempt at resolving issues in a reasonable way. In this case such a term appears to me to meet both requirements. A breach of it would provide a contractor with a possibility of relief and some flexibility in managing the project.

7.11.3 *What remedies should be considered?*

It is not clear that statutory adjudication would help. The link between behaviour and problem might be hard to pin down for particular issues.

I would have insisted to Mr Mackay that the personal abuse desist, as part of my obligations towards my people, and I would have replaced them with more robust personnel, sending the bill for doing so to Mr Mackay, plus a claim for wasted management time possibly as a wasted expenditure claim.[78] One respondent to the ketchup vignette said: "often the only way to gain their attention is to pull people off site when it comes to a critical event or juncture, combined with a demand for outstanding monies". Commercial contractors should be able to weather the sort of storms caused by even language as extreme as that used in this case and I would question whether facing the architect and the builder with the choice of repudiation or affirmation in these circumstances makes commercial sense. However, the possibility of having to deal with a changing team, with claims for additional expense, disruption and delay arising from the changes, might deter this sort of behaviour.

7.12 General thoughts on the cases

The review of various hard cases shows that the TDTC can be applied consistently across cases where contracts require an enabling or facilitating mechanism or are complex and constructive engagement is of the essence. The TDTC is more certain, and easier to apply, than the subjective, complex and nebulous requirements of good faith. Not every breach of a complex modern contract is a breach of the duty to cooperate. The duty is there as an enabling/facilitating mechanism, allowing contracts to be performed effectively.

The key good faith/relational contract cases are unpersuasive. In at least two such cases good faith was implied where there was a breach of the basic obligation in plain sight. In the more complex PO litigation, I show that the basic obligations were clear enough. Extant duties of active cooperation and basic cooperation were more than sufficient. The incorporation of a duty of good faith overcomplicates an already complex process by requiring first evidence of the "characteristics" of the contract (leading to a decision as to whether it is

---

78 See e.g. *Anglia TV v Reed* [1972] 1 QB 60, and *C&P Haulage v Middleton* [1983] 1 WLR 1461.

a relational contract), then argument that a duty of good faith be implied, subsequent to which then that duty is fleshed out into "incidents".

Elisabeth Peden argues that Courts should use good faith as a principle or tool of construction.[79] This, it seems to me, adds little but cost and complexity. She accepts that it is difficult to argue that a duty to perform in good faith is "necessary for the business efficacy" of the contract, or "so obvious it goes without saying", since the contract can "work" if the parties perform their obligations in their own interests.[80] This is not true of duties to cooperate, which exist to make the contract workable

---

79 Peden, *Good Faith*, 139 and 230.
80 Ibid. 228.

8 Concluding thoughts and suggestion for reform

The claim that contracts are made to be performed (the "only pure contractual interest"[1]) is reflected in responses to my survey.[2] Lewison notes that "both parties to a contract are taken to contract on the footing that they wish the contract to be performed".[3] Even where behaviour is deplorable parties seek to continue performance and to find a way through the issues by discovering root cause and seeking practical solutions. Respondents' expectations are based on respect for the deal, on a perceived need of successful performance, hedged by realism and a pragmatic approach. Hence, neither Courts nor parties should act as "destroyers of bargains",[4] but strive to make contracts work; and avoid putting "spanners in the works".[5] If commercial practitioners are correct to think that successful performance requires cooperation, even give and take, and are able to articulate what that cooperation means, Courts should endeavour to read contracts in such a way that those requirements are given effect. Based on respect for the paper deal, with a hard-edged, pragmatic realisation/expectation that in executing the deal a penumbra, an outer layer, of cooperation, involving

1 Roskill J in *Cehave v Bremer Handelsgesellschaft mbH* [1975] 3 All ER 739. See Daniel Friedmann, 'The Performance Interest in Contract Damages' (1995) 111 *LQR* 628 at 629.
2 And in other surveys – see e.g. Russell J. Weintraub, 'A Survey of Contract Practice and Policy' (1992) *WisLRev* 1 at 53 where he records corporate Counsel strongly supporting expectation measure damages. Andrew Robertson, 'The Limits of Voluntariness in Contract' (2005) 29 *MULR*, says, at 209, that Macaulay's finding that buyers expected to be able to cancel paying reliance damages is at odds with the law's use of expectation damages but this is inconsistent with Hugh Beale and Tony Dugdale, 'Contracts between Businessmen: Planning and the Use of Contractual Remedies' (1975) 2 *Br J Law Soc* 45, who report that, absent express termination for convenience provisions, "practice appeared to be quite close to the legal position" at 53 and I suspect that Macaulay's buyers relied on such provisions (which would be typical in manufacturing industry terms).
3 Kim Lewison, *The Interpretation of Contracts* (6th edn, Sweet & Maxwell 2015) at 6.11. See also Sir John Mummery, 'Commercial Notions and Equitable Potions' in Sarah Worthington (ed.), *Commercial Law and Commercial Practice* (Hart 2003), chapter 3, at 37: "Promises are usually made ... in the expectation that they will be kept rather than broken".
4 Lord Tomlin – *Hillas & Co. Ltd v Arcos Ltd* (1932) 38 Com Cas 23, [1932] All ER Rep 494.
5 Sir Robert Goff, 'Commercial Contracts and the Commercial Court' (1984) *LMCLQ* 382, adding "or even grit in the oil".

relationship building, communication and problem solving is required for successful performance, commercial actors eschew punishment or reciprocity in their dealings. These expectations are key to the contract, and they emerge through reading the contract and enquiring into the commercial matrix to discover what it was that the parties have agreed.

The "Intractable Problem of Interpretation" accounts for the "preponderant part of the legal work of English Judges", perhaps 90%, according to Lord Steyn and this is interesting in that it may point to judges spending considerably more time on content than formation.[6]

The real deal, the deal the parties think they have done, has two basic components: the paper contract and juxtaposed commercial expectations. It looks like Figure 8.1.

Underlying the survey answers is a theme that contract involves formal and informal, hard and soft elements.[7] The paper deal provides clarity and direction, but delivery requires communication, clarification, mutual understanding and cooperation. Terms and conditions and liabilities are ominous, undesirable,

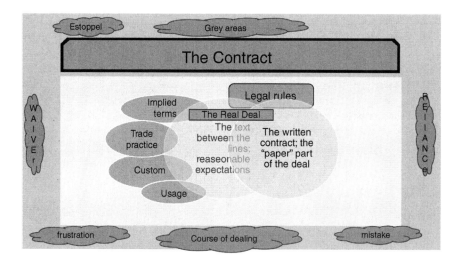

Figure 8.1 The Real Deal

6 Steyn, 'The Intractable Problem of the Interpretation of Legal Texts' at 123 in Worthington, *Commercial Law.* chapter 6.
7 Alessandro Arrighetti, 'Contract Law, Social Norms and Inter-firm Cooperation' (1997) 21 *Cambridge J Econ* 171 at 191 says that the contract is important but there is also an atmosphere of "flexible pragmatism".

necessary, background.[8] Scope, governance, pricing and specification provide direction and clarity. Management, constructive engagement and communication make it happen. Although it is not always easy to distinguish between hard and soft elements and which can, and which should, be legally enforced in proposing the TDTC I concentrated on those enforceable elements which achieve cooperation.

Contracts work, or, at least, complex contracts work at multiple levels; as shown in Figure 8.2. Deal makers create a framework between corporate entities but to make that work management teams must communicate, understand each other, work out what the problems are and how to resolve them. Active cooperation is implicit.

One respondent said this (other comments were similar):

> clear rules for governance and contract management as well as KPIs should be established ... implementation clearly communicated ... – and measured for effectiveness, corrections and adjustments – including refining and amending the contract to make it a success.

Contract structure, formal and informal, can be understood using the representation in Figure 8.3. The informal, formal and cloudy elements illustrate the "messy reality" that is contract. As we have seen, for example, it is often hard to determine when behavioural provisions will be given effect and when not and what the determinants are that separate agreement to agree from provisions which can be given content. There are elements of relationship building, such as governance and communication, which can be reduced to legal requirements and there are others, such as social functions, or visits to the opera, which might challenge even a Mackenzie Chalmers.

In some ways, the survey reflects Macaulay's view that contract is a mere device for the conduct of exchanges, but the paper contract is regarded as one part of a framework. Parties and contract managers make relationships in order to understand the other party, which, in turn, enables them to trim, give and take, in the shadow of the paper deal, the framework. As David Campbell trenchantly argues, although "exchange" is a rather narrow description of modern contracts, the limits of law and economics may well lie in the fact that "at the basis of exchange lie fundamentally co-operative social relations which are necessary for and cannot be explained by ... exchange relationships".[9]

---

8 This roughly aligns with the claim that law is a "reinforcer" or, to use a currently fashionable term, a "backstop" – Carol M Rose, 'Trust in the Mirror of Betrayal' (1995) 75 *Boston Univ Law Rev* 531 at 554–556. Collins says that the contract is a "point of reference": Hugh Collins, *Regulating Contracts* (OUP 2005), 137.

9 In 'The Relational Constitution of Contract and the Limits of "Economics"' in Jonathan Michie and SF Deakin (eds), *Contracts, Co operation, and Competition: Studies in Economics, Management, and Law* (OUP 1997), 320. His solution is a "rigorous" relational challenge to the classical model.

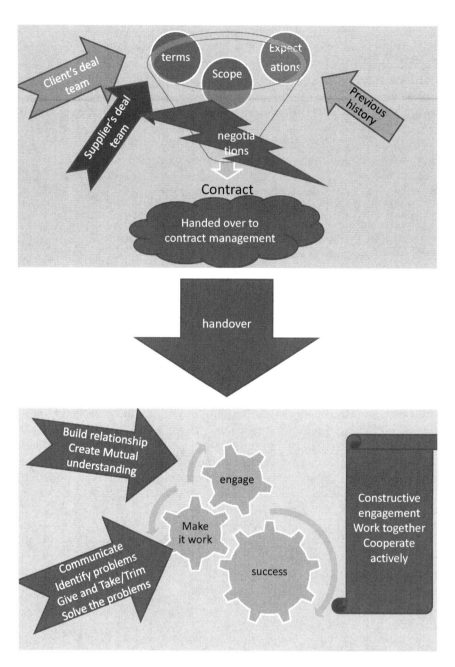

Figure 8.2 Making Contracts and Making Them Work

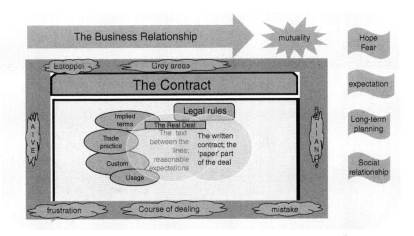

Figure 8.3 Contract Structure – Formal and Informal

As Stewart Macaulay advised: "We might at least focus the issues if … we accept that there is a text between the lines … and if we do not attempt to implement this implicit text we are denying reasonable expectations."[10] There is no separation of the paper deal from the real deal; they are two parts of the same whole. As I have shown in Chapter 3, the contract drives the relationship and not vice versa; the relationship is formed for the purpose of getting the work done. Participants referred to the paper contract as scene-setting, a fall-back, providing the "rules of the game" and governance, a roadmap and a management tool; not solely containing terms, conditions and liabilities.

Considering my argument that the duty to cooperate is a core part of the contract, expected as such by the parties (Chapter 3) and exposed by construction (Chapter 2), I argue, per Lord Donaldson, that defeating it should be difficult:

> I have on occasion found it a useful test notionally to write … a declaratory clause …. We then get a contract reading: "It is further agreed that Manchester United Football Club will pay a further sum of £27,770 … when Edward MacDougall has scored 20 goals … provided always that Manchester United Shall be under no obligation to afford MacDougall any reasonable opportunity of scoring 20 goals". It at once becomes clear that the inclusion of the proviso renders this part of the contract "inefficacious, futile and absurd".[11]

---

10 Stewart Macaulay, 'The Real and the Paper Deal: Empirical Pictures of Relationships, Complexity and the Urge for Transparent Simple Rules' (2003) 66 *MLR* 44 at 79.

11 *Bournemouth & Boscombe Football Club Ltd V Manchester United Football Club Ltd* 1974 B No 1531 (AC) (n. 95). Lady Hale used the formulation in *CEL Group Ltd and others v Nedlloyd Ltd* [2003] All ER (D) 323 (Feb) [2003] EWCA Civ 1716 at [18] "'provided also that NLL are at

Accordingly, to defeat the TDTC through express terms I argue for something like a "red hand" obstacle which "would need to be printed in red ink on the face of the document with a red hand pointing to it before the notice could be held to be sufficient".[12] Although Arthur Leff's warning that some people would sign a contract headed in pink "this is a swindle!" is valid,[13] we can, nevertheless, consider such a default as a way of replacing Lord Reid's "search for some other possible meaning".[14] Contracting out should be possible but the contract would have to say something along the lines of Figure 8.4.

Red Hand Clauses

Red Hand

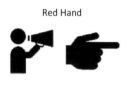

It is agreed that Party XXX may terminate this contract, without further notice, or any notice, for minor or inconsequential or technical breaches or minor defects irrespective of their effect on the work or service ...

Red Hand

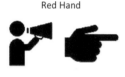

It is agreed that the Purchaser may make deductions from the price without notice or in an absurd manner and refuse to discuss the underlying rationale behind the deductions or provide information sufficient to allow the Contractor to make an informed judgement...

Red Hand

It is agreed that the Purchaser may use the discretion granted at clauses [x,z,y and b] to make decisions on a whim or in a manner which is unfair, or irrational, or capricious, or arbitrary or unreasonable, or wholly selfishly without any regard to the interests of the Contractor.

Red Hand

It is agreed that exact payment is a condition of this contract. Should the Buyer pay too little or fail to provide a precisely conforming letter of credit the Purchaser may terminate the contract forthwith, without further notice.

Figure 8.4 Red Hand Clauses

liberty to dispose of their business as a going concern to whomsoever they please whenever they please during the period of this contract.' Such a declaration would have rendered the exclusive right to provide for their transport requirements similarly inefficacious, futile and absurd."

12 Lord Denning in *Spurling (J) Ltd v Bradshaw* [1956] 2 All ER 121, [1956] 1 WLR 461 at 125.

13 Arthur A Leff, 'Contract as Thing' (1970) 19 *Am ULRev* 131.

14 *Schuler (L) AG v Wickman Machine Tool Sales Ltd* [1974] AC 235, [1973] 2 All ER 39 (HL) at 521.

I limit my other suggestions for reform to five.

- Statutory adjudication, largely based on that imposed on the construction industry, should be made available for all non-consumer contracts. As I have argued above, in subchapter 5.3.3, a fast-track, temporarily final, rough and ready scheme for dispute resolution, could reduce costs and provide a speedy solution to disputes. My survey respondents appeared to support such a scheme, and there were comments from them that problems should not be allowed to "fester" or that one should take the difficult problems early, and that problems should be pre-empted. As James Pickavance asks: "Why should it be confined to the construction industries?"[15]
- Courts should try harder to unearth commercial expectation. As I have shown in subchapter 4.2 such expectations come from multiple sources, including surveys, previous cases, judicial experience and witness evidence. Judges can and should try to get at meaning through deeper enquiries into background. If the source is the parties, then the judge is not making law but finding it.[16] If that also infers more judicial activism this should be made clear by judges as they question witnesses. Lord Reid is right that among the responsibilities of the Common Law Judge is development of the law to meet "changing economic conditions and habits of thought".[17]
- Courts should take a more relaxed approach to interpretation; allowing some leeway in adducing evidence of negotiations, taking more seriously the prior conduct of the parties and allowing actual performance as pointers to meaning. This is unlikely to reduce certainty and, as Lady Arden says, the case management powers now available to judges enable them to get rid of extraneous material.[18]
- In considering remedies Courts should be more innovative, making use of their review and replace powers where "machinery" is not essential, taking advantage of the flexibility offered together with damages based on a hypothetical release fee (the Sumption variant+), damages for a failure to consult or something analogous to the *Pallant v Morgan* equity. A party which abuses agreed damages clauses to the extent that the relationship

---

15 James Pickavance, *A Practical Guide to Construction Adjudication* (John Wiley & Sons 2015) at 1.10.

16 Robert D. Cooter, 'Decentralized Law for a Complex Economy: The Structural Approach to Adjudicating the New Law Merchant' (1996) 144 *Univ Pennsylvania Law Rev* 1643 at 1646. When Courts "apply community standards they find law not make it"; but, as I have shown, this is far from being New Law.

17 *Myers v DPP* [1965] AC 1001 (HL) at 1021. See also Lord Hoffmann's reference to changes in social reality discussed in subchapter 4.1.1.

18 See subchapter 4.3 and *Static Control Components v Egan* [2004] EWCA 392.

becomes rocky should not be able to rely on advantageous provisions once it has abused them.

•   A more robust attitude to costs might go some way to supporting, for example, ADR, adjudication and constructive engagement.

Lord Devlin said in 1957 that: "The danger in any branch of the law is that it ossifies. If all lawyers were made doctors overnight they would flock to the dissecting rooms for I am sure that they prefer corpses to live patients."[19]

I have shown that there is no need for the law to become an ossuary when confronted with modern forms of commerce. The Common Law would be strengthened by a deeper recognition of the role of cooperation; founded on the expectations of reasonable parties. Although I see room for pessimism there is plenty of scope for optimism and the appearance of a great commercial judge who might take on Lord Blackburn's mantle and those of Lord's Steyn and Reid. Perhaps between prospective SCJs Burrows and Leggatt and Lady Arden, already a member, the Supreme Court can, for example, rationalise the good faith cases using more typical common law methodology, circumscribe *Medirest,* take aboard the powerful arguments for a wider application of hypothetical release fees[20] and find a way to meet the expectations of commercial actors in a new contract reality. My vision is of a contract law that helps modern complex contracts work, which infers the incorporation of objectively gleaned commercial expectations.

19 Patrick Devlin, 'The Relation between Commercial Law and Commercial Practice' (1951) 14 *MLR* 249.
20 See Sir George Leggatt, 'Negotiation in Good Faith: Adapting to Changing Circumstances in Contracts and English Contract Law' (Jill Poole Memorial Lecture) on negotiating damages at [62]–[65] where he takes a wider view than the current Supreme Court.

Bibliography

Abell, M and Hobbs, V, 'The Duty of Good Faith in Franchise Agreements – A Comparative Study of the Civil and Common Law Approaches in the Eu' (2013) 11 *International Journal of Franchising Law* 1.

www.academyofexperts.org/guidance/users-experts/what-an-expert-witness.

Adams, J and Brownsword, R, *Key Issues in Contract* (Butterworths 1995).

'A Day in the Life of a Facilities Manager' – www.maxwellstephens.com/blog/a-day-in-life-of-facilities-manager/

'A Day in the Life of a Project Manager' – www.apm.org.uk/jobs-and-careers/career-path/what-does-a-project-manager-do/a-day-in-the-life-spencer/

'Adjudication Society Report No 17' – www.adjudication.org/resources/research.

Ahmed, M, 'Mediation: The Need for a United, Clear and Consistent Judicial Voice' (2018) 13 *CJQ* 1.

Ahmed, M, 'Implied Compulsory Mediation' (2012) 31 *CJQ* 151.

Ahmed, M, 'Bridging the Gap between Alternative Dispute Resolution and Robust Adverse Costs Orders' (2015) 66 *NILQ* 71.

Aivazian, VA, Trebilcock, MJ and Penny, M, 'The Law of Contract Modifications: The Uncertain Quest for a Bench Mark of Enforceability' (1984) 22 *OHLJ* 173.

Alpa, G and Andenas, M (eds), *Private Law beyond the National Systems* (British Institute of International and Comparative Law 2007).

Alvesson, M and Deetz, S, *Doing Critical Management Research* (Sage 2000).

Ambadipudi, A, Brotschi, A, Forsgren, M, Kervazo, F, Lavandier, H and Xing, J, 'Industrial Aftermarket Services: Growing the Core'. 2017 McKinsey electronic article at www.mckinsey.com/industries/advanced-electronics/our-insights/industrial-aftermarket-services-growing-the-core

Andrews, N, *Contract Rules* (1st edn, Intersentia 2016).

Andrews, N, 'Interpretation of Contracts and "Commercial Common Sense": Do Not Overplay This Useful Criterion' (2017) 76 *CLJ* 36.

Andrews, N, 'Breach of Contract: A Plea for Clarity and Discipline' (2018) 134 *LQR* 117.

Arbitration LSoI, *2010 International Arbitration Survey* (2010).

Arden, M, 'Coming to Terms with Good Faith' (2013) 30 *JCL* 199.

Arrighetti, A, 'Contract Law, Social Norms and Inter-firm Cooperation' (1997) 21 *Cambridge J Econ* 171.

Atiyah, PS, 'Judicial Techniques in the Law of Contract' (1968) 2 *Ottawa LR* 244.

Atiyah, PS, *The Rise and Fall of Freedom of Contract* (Clarendon Press 1979).

Atzmüller, C and Steiner, PM, 'Experimental Vignette Studies in Survey Research' (2010) 6 *Methodology* 128.

Austen-Baker, I, 'Comprehensive Contract Theory – A Four Norm Model of Contract Relations' (2009) 25 *JCL* 216.

Austen-Baker, R, *Implied Terms in English Contract Law* (Edward Elgar 2011).

Axelrod, RM, *The Evolution of Cooperation* (Basic Books 1984).

Babbie, ER, *Survey Research Methods*, vol. 2 (Wadsworth Publishing 1990).

Bagchi, A, 'The Perspective of Law on Contract' (2013) 88 *Washington LR* 1227.

Baird, DG, 'Self-Interest and Cooperation in Long-Term Contracts' (1990) 19 *JLS* 583.

Bartscherer, C, 'Two Steps Forward, One Step Back: One Step (Support) LTD V Morris-Garner and Another' (2019) 82 *Mod Law Rev* 367.

Bateson, A, 'The Duty to Cooperate' (1960) *JBL* 187.

Bayley, JE, 'Prior Negotiations and Subsequent Conduct in Contract Interpretation: Principles and Practical Concerns' (2012) 28 *JCL* 179.

BBC, 'Waste Collection Costs Double After Firm's Collapse' www.bbc.co.uk/news/uk-scotland-48169029 6 May 2019.

Beale, H and Dugdale, T, 'Contracts between Businessmen: Planning and the Use of Contractual Remedies' (1975) 2 *Br J Law Soc* 45.

Beatson, J and Friedmann, D (eds), *Good Faith and Fault in Contract Law* (Clarendon Press 1997).

Beheshti, R, 'Anticipatory Breach of Contract and the Necessity of Adequate Assurance under English Law and the Uniform Commercial Code' (2018) *LMCLQ* 276.

Benson, P, *The Theory of Contract Law: New Essays* (CUP 2001).

Berg, BL, *Qualitative Research Methods for the Social Sciences* (7th edn, Ally & Bacon 2009).

Bernstein, L, 'The Questionable Empirical Basis of Article 2's Incorporation Strategy: A Preliminary Study' (1999) 66 *UChiLRev* 710.

Bernstein, L, 'Beyond Relational Contracts: Social Capital and Network Governance in Procurement Contracts' (2015a) 7 *J Legal Anal* 561.

Bernstein, L .E, 'The Myth of Trade Usage: A Talk for KCON'(12 Dec. 2017) *Barry Law Review* (forthcoming) https://ssrn.com/abstract=3086727 or http://dx.doi.org/10.2139/ssrn.3086727.

Bernstein, L, 'Custom in the Courts' (2015) 63 *NWULR* 110.

Bernstein, L, 'Merchant Law in a Merchant Court: Rethinking the Code's Search for Immanent Business Norms' (1996)144 *U Penn LR* 1764.

Booysen, S, '"Pay Now – Argue Later": Conclusive Evidence Clauses in Commercial Loan Contracts' (2014) *JBL* 31.

Bowles, S and Gintis, H, *A Cooperative Species: Human Reciprocity and its Evolution* (Princeton UP 2011).

Braucher, J, Kidwell, J and Whitford, WC (eds), *Revisiting the Contracts Scholarship of Stewart Macaulay: On the Empirical and the Lyrical (International Studies in the Theory of Private Law* 10*)* (1st edn, Hart 2013).

Bridge, M, 'The Exercise of Contractual Discretion' (2019) 135 *LQR* 227.

Bridge, MG and Benjamin, JP, *Benjamin's Sale of Goods* (Sweet & Maxwell 2014).

Brinkmann, S, *Understanding Qualitative Research: Qualitative Interviewing* (OUP 2013).

Brodie, D, 'Fair Dealing and the World of Work' (2014) 43 *Ind Law J* 29.

Brownsword, R, '"Good Faith in Contracts" Revisited' (1996) 49 *CLP* 111.

Brownsword, R, *Contract Law: Themes for the Twenty-First Century* (OUP 2006).

Bryman, A, *Social Research Methods* (4th edn, OUP 2012).

Burnett, R, 'The Changing Context of IT Contracts' (2004) 154 *NLJ* 343.

Burrows, AS, *Remedies for Torts and Breach of Contract* (3rd edn, OUP 2004).

Burrows, AS, *A Restatement of the English Law of Contract* (OUP 2016).

Burrows, AS, 'One Step Forward' (2018) 134 *LQR* 515.

Burrows, AS and Peel, E (eds), *Contract Terms* (OUP 2007).

Burrows, JF, 'Contractual Co-operation and the Implied Term' (1968) 31 *MLR* 390.

Cameron, E, 'Major Cases' (2000) 14 *IRLCT* 259.

Campbell, D, 'Good Faith and the Ubiquity of the "Relational" Contract' (2014) 77 *MLR* 475.

Campbell, D, Collins, H and Wightman, J (eds), *Implicit Dimensions of Contract: Discrete, Relational, and Network Contracts* (Bloomsbury 2003).

Campbell, D and Harris, D, 'Flexibility in Long-Term Contractual Relationships: The Role of Co-operation' (1993) 20 *JLS* 166.

Campbell, D and Vincent-Jones, P (eds), *Contract and Economic Organisation* (Dartmouth 1996).

Carter, JW, *Carter's Breach of Contract* (Hart 2012).

Carter, JW and Courtney, W, 'Unexpressed Intention and Contract Construction' (2016) vol. 37 issue 2 *OJLS* 326.

Carter, SM and Little, M, 'Justifying Knowledge, Justifying Method, Taking Action: Epistemologies, Methodologies, and Methods in Qualitative Research' (2007) 17 *Qual Health Res* 1316.

Catterwell, R, 'The "Indirect" Use of Evidence of Prior Negotiations and the Parties' Intentions in Contract Construction: Part of the Surrounding Circumstances' (2012) 29 *JCL* 183.

Chalmers, M, *The Sale of Goods Act; 1893* (Clowes 1902).

Chartered Institute of Building, *CIoB's Facilities Management Contract* (John Wiley 2015).

Chitty, *Chitty on Contracts* (ed. H Beale, 33rd edn, Sweet & Maxwell 2018).

Cimino, C, 'The Relational Economics of Commercial Contract' (2015) 91 *Texas AM Law Rev* 91.

Clarry, D and Sargeant, C (eds), *The UK Supreme Court Yearbook*, vol. 6 (2015).

CIPS Balanced Scorecards – www.cips.org/Documents/Knowledge/Third%20Party% 20Materials/Example-Balanced-Scorecard.pdf

Cleavely, J and Collins, T, 'Risk in Facilities Management Contracts' (2014) 15 *Ed LJ* 284.

Cockram, R, *Manual of Construction Agreements* (Jordan Publishing 2016).

Coleman, A, 'Spot the Signs of a Failing Project' (2015) *Sunday Times* (2 August).

Collins, H, 'Implied Duty to Give Information during Performance of Contracts' (1992) 55 *MLR* 556.

Collins, H, *Regulating Contracts* (OUP 2005).

Collins, H, *The Law of Contract* (CUP 2008).

Collins, H, 'Implied Terms: The Foundation in Good Faith and Fair Dealing' (2014) 67 *CLP* 297.

Cooter, R and Ulen, T, *Law and Economics: Pearson New International Edition* (6th edn, Pearson new international edn, Pearson Education MUA 2013).

Cooter, RD, 'Decentralized Law for a Complex Economy: The Structural Approach to Adjudicating the New Law Merchant' (1996) 144 *U Penn LR* 1643.

Courtney, W, 'Reasonableness in Contractual Decision-Making' (2015) 131 *LQR* 552.

Courtney, W and Carter, J, 'Implied Terms: What Is the Role of Construction?' (2014) 31 *JCL* 151.

Cox, A, *Strategic Procurement in Construction* (Thomas Telford 1998).

Daintith, T and Teubner, G, *Contract and Organisation: Legal Analysis in the Light of Economic and Social Theory* (De Gruyter 1986).

Daintith, T and Teubner, G (eds), *Contract and Organisation Legal Analysis in the Light of Economic and Social Theory* (De Gruyter 2011).

Daintith, T and Willoughby, G, *A Manual of United Kingdom Oil and Gas Law* (Oyez 1981).

Dara, J and Moreteau, O, 'The Interaction of Good Faith with Contract Performance, Dissolution, and Damages in the Louisiana Supreme Court' (2018) 10 *J Civ L Stud* 261.

Davies, C, 'The Successful Management of Delay in IT Outsourcing Contracts' www.sclorg/siteaspx?i=ed39430

Davies, M, *Doing a Successful Research Project: Using Qualitative or Quantitative Methods* (Palgrave Macmillan 2007).

Davies, PS, 'Interpreting Commercial Contracts: A Case of Ambiguity?' (2012) *LMCLQ* 26.

De Vita, G, Wang, CL and Tekaya, A, 'The Many Faces of Asset Specificity: A Critical Review of Key Theoretical Perspectives' (2011) 13 *Inter J Manage Rev* 329.

Dennett, DC, *Freedom Evolves* (Penguin 2004).

Denzin, NK and Lincoln, YS, *Collecting and Interpreting Qualitative Materials* (Sage 1998).

Depoorter, B, Hoeppner, S and Freund, L, 'The Moral-Hazard Effect of Liquidated Damages: An Experiment on Contract Remedies' (2018) 173 *JITE* 1.

Devlin, P, 'The Relation between Commercial Law and Commercial Practice' (1951) 14 *MLR* 249.

Dharmananda, K (ed), *Long Term Contracts* (Federation Press 2013).

DiMatteo, L and Hogg, M (eds), *Comparative Contract Law: British and American Perspectives* (OUP 2016).

DiMatteo, LA, Zhou, Q, Saintier, S and Rowley, K (eds), *Commercial Contract Law: Transatlantic Perspectives* (CUP 2013).

Dingwall, R, 'Quantophrenia is Back in Town' (2014) www.socialsciencespacecom/2014/05/quantophrenia-is-back-in-town/

Du Bois, F, 'Good Faith, Good Law?' www.archivelegalscholarsacuk/edinburgh/restricted/downloadcfm?id=312

Dunné, J, 'On a Clear Day, You Can See the Continent' (2015) 31 *Const LJ* 3.

Eder, HB and Scrutton, STE, *Scrutton on Charterparties and Bills of Lading* (Sweet & Maxwell 2011).

Edmonds, D, *Would You Kill the Fat Man?* (Princeton UP 2013).

Edwards, R and Holland, J, *What Is Qualitative Interviewing?* (Bloomsbury Academic 2013).

Eggink, E, 'Correct Scoping of Employer's Requirements: The Prevention of Change Orders' (2017) *ICLR* 4.

Eggleston, B, *The ICE Design and Construct Contract: A Commentary* (Blackwell Scientific Publications 1994).

Eggleston, B, *Liquidated Damages and Extensions of Time* (3rd edn, Wiley-Blackwell 2009).

Eisenberg, T and Miller, GP, 'The Flight to New York' (2009) 30 *Cardozo LRev* 1475.

Eisenberg, MA, 'The Duty to Rescue in Contract Law' (2002) 71 *Fordham LRev* 647.

Eisenberg, MA, 'Private Ordering through Negotiation: Dispute-Settlement and Rulemaking' (1976) 89 *HarvLRev* 637.

Ellinger, P, 'Expert Evidence in Banking Law' (2008) 23 *JIBLR* 557.

Engel, C, 'The Proper Scope of Behavioral Law and Economics' (2018) Discussion Papers of the Max Planck Institute for Research on Collective Goods.

Engineers IoC, *The New Engineering Contract* (Thomas Telford 1991).

Engineers IoM, *MF/1 (rev 6): Model Form of General Conditions of Contract* (rev 6th edn, Institution of Engineering and Technology 2014).

Enman-Beech, J, 'The Good Faith Challenge' (2019) 1 *J Commonwealth Law* 35.

Enonchong, N, *Duress, Undue Influence and Unconscionable Dealing* (2nd edn, Sweet & Maxwell 2012).

Ernst & Young, *The Journey Continues: PPPs in Social Infrastructure* (2008) http://infrastructureaustralia.gov.au/policy-publications/publications/Ernst-Young-The-journey-continues-PPPs-in-social-infrastructure-2008.aspx

Farnsworth, EA, *Contracts* (3rd edn, Aspen Law & Business 1999).

Fehr, E and Gächter, S, 'Cooperation and Punishment in Public Goods Experiments' (2000) 90 *Am Econ Rev* 980.

Feinman, JM, 'Relational Contract Theory in Context' (2000) 94 *Nw ULRev* 742.

Fells, RE, *Effective Negotiation: From Research to Results* (2nd edn, CUP 2012).

Fenwick-Elliott, R, 'Building and Construction Industry Adjudication – The UK Experience' (2006) http://feg.com.au/papers-articles/building-and-construction-industry-adjudication-%E2%80%93-the-uk-experience/

Fink, M and Kessler, A, 'Cooperation, Trust and Performance – Empirical Results from Three Countries' (2010) 21 *Br J Manage* 469.

Frank, RH, *The Darwin Economy: Liberty, Competition, and the Common Good* (Princeton UP 2012).

Fried, C, *Contract as Promise* (Harvard UP 1981).

Foxton, D, 'A Good Faith Goodbye? Good Faith Obligations and Contractual Termination Rights' (2017) 2017 *LMCLQ* 361.

Friedmann, D, 'The Performance Interest in Contract Damages' (1995) 111 *LQR* 628.

Fuller, L, 'Positivism and Fidelity to Law: A Reply to Professor Hart' (1958) 71 *HarvLRev* 630.

Furst, S, Keating, D, Ramsey, V, Uff, J and Williamson, A (eds), *Keating on Construction Contracts* (Sweet & Maxwell, 2006).

Gava, J, 'False Lessons from the Real Deal' (2005) 21 *JCL* 182.

Gava, J, 'Taking Stewart Macaulay and Hugh Collins Seriously' (2016) 33 *JCL* 108.

Gava, J, 'What We Know about Contract Law and Transacting in the Marketplace – A Review Essay (2014)' (2014) 35 *U Adelaide Law Rev* 409.

Gava, J and Greene, J, 'The Limits of Modern Contract Theory: Hugh Collins on Regulating Contracts [review Essay]' (2001) 22 *AdelLR* 299.

Gava, J and Greene, J, 'Do We Need a Hybrid Law of Contract? Why Hugh Collins Is Wrong and Why It Matters' (2005) 63 *CLJ* 605.

Gherardi, S and Turner, B, 'Real Men Don't Collect Soft Data' (1987) 13 *Quaderno.* 4.

Gilbert, GN, *Researching Social Life* (Sage 2008).

Gillham, B, *The Research Interview* (Continuum 2000).

Goetz, CJ and Scott, RE, 'Principles of Relational Contracts' (1981) 67 *VaLRev* 1089.

Goff, SR, 'Commercial Contracts and the Commercial Court' (1984) *LMCLQ* 382.

Gold, N, Colman, AM and Pulford, BD, 'Cultural Differences in Responses to Real-Life and Hypothetical Trolley Problems' (2014) 9 *Judgment Decis Making* 65.

Goldberg, VP (ed.), *Readings in the Economics of Contract Law* (CUP, 1989).

Goode, RM and McKendrick, E, *Commercial Law* (4th edn, LexisNexis 2009).

Gordon, R, 'Macaulay, Macneil and the Discovery of Solidarity and Power in Contract Law' (1985) *WisLRev* 565.

Gould, N, Adjudication and ADR: An Overview – www.fenwickelliott.com/sites/default/files/nick_gould_-_adjudication_and_adr_-_an_overview_matrics_paper.indd_.pdf.

Grabiner, L, 'The Iterative Process of Contractual Interpretation' (2012) 128 *LQR* 41.

Grammond, S, 'Reasonable Expectations and the Interpretation of Contracts across Legal Traditions' (2009) 48 *Can Bus LJ* 345.

Gray, A, 'Termination for Convenience Clauses and Good Faith' (2012) 7 *J Int Commer Law Technol* 260.

Greene, JD, *Moral Tribes: Emotion, Reason and the Gap between Us and Them* (Atlantic Books 2013).

Griffith, JAG, *The Politics of the Judiciary* (Fontana 1997).

Gullifer, L and Vogenauer, S (eds), *English and European Perspectives on Contract and Commercial Law,: Essays in Honour of Hugh Beale* (Hart 2014).

Gulliver, PH, 'Negotiations as a Mode of Dispute Settlement: Towards a General Model' (1973) 7 *Law Soc Rev* 667.

Hadfield, GK, 'Problematic Relations: Franchising and the Law of Incomplete Contracts' (1990) 42 *StanLRev* 927.

Hale, B, 'Maccabean Lecture in Jurisprudence – A Minority Opinion' (2008) 154 *Proceedings of the British Academy* 319–336.

Halson, R, 'Opportunism, Economic Duress and Contractual Modifications' (1991) 107 *LQR* 649.

Handy, CB, *Understanding Organizations* (4th edn, Penguin 1993).

Harris, D, *Remedies in Contract and Tort* (2nd edn, Butterworths 2002).

Harrison, D, 'Is a Long-Term Business Relationship an Implied Contract? Two Views of Relationship Disengagement' (2004) 41 *J Manage Stud* 107.

Harrison, JL, *Law and Economics* (WW Norton & Co. 2008).

Havighurst, HC, *The Nature of Private Contract* (Northwestern UP 1961).

Heide, JB and John, G, 'Alliances in Industrial Purchasing: The Determinants of Joint Action in Buyer-Seller Relationships' (1990) 27 *J Marketing Res* 4.

HM Courts and Tribunals Service, *Admiralty and Commercial Courts Guide* (2014; updated March 2016).

Hobhouse, JS, 'International Conventions and Commercial Law' (1990) 106 *LQR* 530.

Hooley, R, 'Controlling Contractual Discretion' (2013) 72 *CLJ* 65.

Howarth, D, 'Is Law a Humanity: (Or Is It More like Engineering)?' (2004) 3 *Arts Humanities Higher Educ* 9.

Howarth, D, *Law as Engineering* (Edward Elgar 2013).

Hudson, AA, *Hudson's Building and Engineering Contracts* (ed. N Dennys and R Clay, 13th edn, Sweet & Maxwell 2015).

Hudson, AA and Wallace, IND, *Hudson's Building and Engineering Contracts* (Sweet & Maxwell 1970).

Hudson, AA and Wallace, IND, *Hudson's Building and Engineering Contracts* (11th edn, Sweet & Maxwell 1995).

Hunter, RC, McGlynn, C and Rackley, E (eds), *Feminist Judgments: From Theory to Practice* (Hart 2010).

IACCM, '2013/2014 Top Terms' (2014) www.iaccm.cm/resources/?id=7619

Ibbetson, DJ, *A Historical Introduction to the Law of Obligations* (OUP 1999).

Inabuaye-Omim, S, 'Industrial Gas Turbine Condition Monitoring System: An Overview' (39th Engine Systems Symposium, Cranfield University).

James, CO, 'The Origins of the Special Jury' (1983) 50 *UChiLRev* 137.

James, M, *Expert Evidence: Law and Practice* (3rd edn, Sweet & Maxwell 2010).

Johnson, S, MacMillan, J and Woodruff, C, 'Courts and Relational Contracts' (2002) 18 *J Law Econ Org* 221.

Jolls, C, 'Contracts as Bilateral Commitments: A New Perspective on Contract Modification' (1997) 26 *JLS* 203.

Joly, E, 'Baseball and Jet Lag: Correlation Does Not Imply Causation' (2017) 114 *Pro Nat Acad Sci US Am* E3168.

Jones, G, 'Specific Performance: A Lessee's Covenant to Keep Open a Retail Store' (1997) 56 *CLJ* 488.

Jones, MT, 'Strategic Complexity and Cooperation: An Experimental Study' (2014) 106 *J Econ Behav Org* 352.

Kimel, D, 'The Choice of Paradigm for Theory of Contract: Reflections on the Relational Model' (2007) 27 *OJLS* 233.

Klatch, RE, 'The Methodological Problems of Studying a Politically Resistant Community' (1988) 1 *Stud Q Sociol* 73.

Korobkin, R, 'Empirical Scholarship in Contract Law: Possibilities and Pitfalls' (2002) *U IllLRev* 1033.

Kostritsky, JP, 'Context Matters – What Lawyers Say about Choice of Law Decisions in Merger Agreements' (2014) 13 *DePaul Bus Commer Law J* 211.

Kraljic, P, 'Purchasing Must Become Supply Management' (1983) 61 *Harvard Bus Rev* 109.

Kramer, A, 'Common Sense Principles of Contract Interpretation (and How We've Been Using Them All Along)' (2003) 23 *OJLS* 173.

Kraus, JS, 'In Defense of the Incorporation Strategy' *University of Virginia Law School, Legal Studies Working Paper* 99–4. https://papers.ssrn.com/sol3/papers.cfm?abstract_id=170011

Kraus, JS, 'Contract Design and the Structure of Contractual Intent' (2009) 84 *NYU LRev* 1023.

Kronman, AT and Posner, RA, *The Economics of Contract Law* (Little, Brown 1979).

Kuklin, BH, 'Justification for Protecting Reasonable Expectations' (2000) 29 *Hofstra LRev* 863.

Kurczewski, J and Frieske, K, 'Some Problems in the Legal Regulation of the Activities of Economic Institutions' (1977) 11 *Law Soc Rev* 489.

Landers, RN and Behrend, TS, 'An Inconvenient Truth: Arbitrary Distinctions between Organizational, Mechanical Turk, and Other Convenience Samples' (2015) 8 *Ind Org Psychol* 142.

Langille, B and Ripstein, A, 'Strictly Speaking – It Went without Saying' (1996) 2 *Legal Theory* 63.

Lai, JHK, Yik, FWH and Jones, P, 'Disputes Arising from Vaguely Defined Contractual Responsibilities in Building Services Maintenance Contracts' (2004) 22 *Facilities* 44.

Larson, EW and Gray, CF, *Project Management: The Managerial Process* (7th edn, McGraw Hill Education 2018).

Latham, MS and Britain, G, *Department of the E, Constructing the Team: Joint Review of Procurement and Contractual Arrangements in the United Kingdom Construction Industry; Final Report, July 1994* (HMSO 1994).

Leff, AA, 'Contract as Thing' (1970) 19 *Am ULRev* 131.

Leggatt, SG, 'Contractual Duties of Good Faith' (Lecture to the Commercial Bar Association on 18 October 2016).

Leggatt, SG, 'Negotiation in Good Faith: Adapting to Changing Circumstances in Contracts and English Contract Law' (Jill Poole Memorial Lecture 2018).

Lewicki, R, Barry, B and Saunders, DM, *Negotiation: Readings, Exercises and Cases* (7th edn, McGraw-Hill 2015).

Lewis, R, 'Contracts between Businessmen: Reform of the Law of Firm Offers and an Empirical Study of Tendering Practices in the Building Industry' (1982) 9 *JLS* 153.

Lewison, K, *The Interpretation of Contracts* (6th edn, Sweet & Maxwell 2015).

Lim, E and Chan, C, 'Problems with Wednesbury Unreasonableness in Contract Law: Lessons from Public Law' (2019) 135 *LQR* 88.

Lindgren, K, 'Book Review: Catherine Mitchell - Bridging the Gap' (2015) 33 *JCL* 160.

Llewellyn, KN, *The Common Law Tradition: Deciding Appeals* (Little, Brown 1966).

Lorenz, E, 'Trust, Contract and Economic Cooperation' (1999) 23 *Cambridge J Econ* 301.

Low, KFK, 'Repair, Rejection and Rescission: An Uneasy Resolution' (2007) 123 *LQR* 536.

Lowry, T, 'Lord Mansfield and the Law Merchant: Law and Economics in the Eighteenth Century' (1973) 7 *J Econ Issues* 605.

Luo, Y, 'Contract, Cooperation, and Performance in International Joint Ventures' (2002) 23 *Strategic Manage J* 903.

Lyotard, J-F, Bennington, G and Massumi, B, *The Postmodern Condition: A Report on Knowledge* (Manchester University Press 1984).

Macaulay, S, 'Non-Contractual Relations in Business: A Preliminary Study' (1963) 28 *A Sociol Rev* 55.

Macaulay, S, 'Elegant Models, Empirical Pictures, and the Complexities of Contract' (1977) 11 *Law Soc Rev* 507.

Macaulay, S, 'An Empirical View of Contract' (1985) 1985 *WisLRev* 465.

Macaulay, S, 'The Real and the Paper Deal: Empirical Pictures of Relationships, Complexity and the Urge for Transparent Simple Rules' (2003) 66 *MLR* 44.

Macaulay, S, 'Freedom from Contract: Solutions in Search of a Problem?' (2004) 2004 *WisLRev* 777.

Macaulay, S, 'Relational Contracts Floating on a Sea of Custom? Thoughts about the Ideas of Ian Macneil and Lisa Bernstein' (2000) 94 *NWULR* 775.

Macneil, IR, *Contracts, Instruments for Social Cooperation* (FB Rothman 1968).

Macneil, IR, 'The Many Futures of Contract' (1973) 47 *Cal L Rev* 691.

Macneil, IR, 'Contracts: Adjustment of Long-Term Economic Relations under Classical, Neoclassical, and Relational Contract Law' (1978) 72 *NWULR* 854.

Macneil, IR, 'Relational Contract: What We Do and Do Not Know' (1985) *WisLRev* 483.

Macneil, IR, 'Contracting Worlds and Essential Contract Theory' (2000) 9 *Social Legal Stud* 431.

Macneil, IR, 'Uncertainty in Commercial Law' (2009) 13(1) *EdinLR* 68.

Mak, V, 'The Seller's Right to Cure Defective Performance – A Reappraisal' (2007) *LMCLQ* 409

Mak, V, 'According to Custom? The Role of 'Trade Usage' in the Proposed Common European Sales Law (CESL)' (2014) 10 *ERCL* 64.

Malek, A and, Quest, D, *Jack: Documentary Credits: The Law and Practice Including Standby Credits and Demand Guarantees* (4th edn, Tottel 2009).

Malhotra, D and Murnighan, JK, 'The Effects of Contracts on Interpersonal Trust' (2002) 47 *Administrative Sci Q* 534.

Maltese, DF and Farina, M, 'Theory of the Firm and Organisational Contracts: The Remedial Aspects of Good Faith' (2016) 27 *EBOR* 51.

Mason, AF, 'Contract, Good Faith and Equitable Standards in Fair Dealing' (2000) 116 *LQR* 66.

McBeath, B and others, 'The Managerial and Relational Dimensions of Public-Nonprofit Human Service Contracting' (2017) 3 *J Strategic Contracting Negotiation* 51.

McCann, S, 'Managing Partnership Relations and Contractual Performance in the Operating Phase of Public Private Partnership' (2014) 15 *Int Public Manage Rev* 111.

McCloskey, DN, *Enterprise and Trade in Victorian Britain: Essays in Historical Economics* (Routledge 2003).

McCunn, J, 'Belize It or Not: Implied Contract Terms in Marks and Spencer V BNP Paribas' (2016) 79 *MLR* 1090.

McGregor, H, *McGregor on Damages* (Sweet & Maxwell 2012).

McKendrick, E, *Contract Law: Text, Cases, and Materials* (OUP 2014).

McLauchlan, D, 'A Better Way of Making Sense of Contracts?' (2016) 132 *LQR* 577.

McLauchlan, D, 'Contract Formation and Subjective Intention' (2017) 25 *U Queensland LJ* 77.

McLauchlan, D, 'Some Fallacies Concerning the Law of Contract Interpretation' https://ssrn.com/abstract=3123371

McMeel, G, *The Construction of Contracts Interpretation, Implication, and Rectification* (OUP 2011).

McMeel, G, 'Foucault's Pendulum: Text, Context and Good Faith in Contract Law' (2017) 70(1) *CLP* 365.

Miceli, TJ, *The Economic Approach to Law* (2nd edn, Stanford Economics and Finance 2009).

Michie, J and Deakin, SF (eds), *Contracts, Co-operation, and Competition: Studies in Economics, Management, and Law* (OUP 1997).

Miles, MB and Huberman, AM, *Qualitative Data Analysis: An Expanded Sourcebook*, vol. 2 (Sage 1994).

Milner, A, 'Contract Interpretation: Potential for Relaxing the Exclusionary Rule' (2011) 3 *IJLBE* 205.

Mintz, A, Redd, SB and Vedlitz, A, 'Can We Generalize from Student Experiments to the Real World in Political Science, Military Affairs, and International Relations?' (2006) 50 *J Conflict Resolut* 757.

Mitchell, C, 'Leading a Life of Its Own? The Roles of Reasonable Expectation in Contract Law' (2003) 23 *OJLS* 639.

Mitchell, C, *Interpretation of Contracts* (Routledge-Cavendish 2007).

Mitchell, C, 'Contracts and Contract Law: Challenging the Distinction between the "Real" and "Paper" Deal' (2009) 29 *OJLS* 675.

Mitchell, C, 'Obligations in Commercial Contracts: A Matter of Law or Interpretation?' (2012) 65 *CLP* 455.

Mitchell, C, 'Contract Interpretation: Pragmatism, Principle and the Prior Negotiations Rule' (2010) 26 *JCL* 134.

Mitchell, C, *Contract Law and Contract Practice: Bridging the Gap between Legal Reasoning and Commercial Expectation* (Hart 2013).

Mitchell, C, 'Publication Review – Contract Law Minimalism: A Formalist Restatement of Contract Law' (2014) 25 *ICCLR* 324.

Morgan, J, 'Against Judicial Review of Discretionary Contractual Powers' (2008) *LMCLQ* 230.

Morgan, J, *Contract Law Minimalism* (CUP 2013).

Morgan, J, 'Resisting Judicial Review of Discretionary Contractual Powers' (2015) *LMCLQ* 484.

Morrison, N, 'Once Bitten, Twice Shy' (2009) *J Law Soc Scotland* www.journalonline.co.uk/magazine/54-9/1006975.aspx

Mouzas, S, 'Negotiating Umbrella Agreements' (2006) 22 *Negotiation J* 279.

Nettle, D, 'The Watching Eyes Effect in the Dictator Game' (2013) 34 *Evol Hum Behav* 35.

Network Rail, *Standard Suite of Contracts* (2016) www.networkrail.co.uk/browse%20documents/standardsuiteofcontracts/documents/nr11%20mf1%20(rev%205)%20v3%204(tp).pdf

Neuberger, L, '"Judge Not, that Ye Be Not Judged": Judging Judicial Decision-Making', FA Mann Lecture: www.supremecourt.uk/docs/speech-150129.pdf.

Okasha, S, *The Origins of Human Cooperation: Samuel Bowles and Herbert Gintis: A Cooperative Species* (Princeton UP 2011).

Pannebakker, E, 'Offer and Acceptance and the Dynamics of Negotiations: Arguments for Contract Theory from Negotiation Studies' (2013) 6 *Erasmus Law Rev* 131.

Parker, D and Hartley, K, 'Transaction Costs, Relational Contracting and Public Private Partnerships: A Case Study of UK Defence' (2003) 9 *Journal of Purchasing and Supply Management* 97.

Patterson, D, 'The Limits of Empiricism' (2000) 98 *MichLRev* 2738.

Peden, E, *Good Faith in the Performance of Contracts* (LexisNexis Butterworths 2003).

Peel, E, 'Terms Implied in Fact' (2016) 132 *LQR* 531.

Peel, E and Treitel, SGH, *Treitel on the Law of Contract*, vol. 13 (Sweet & Maxwell 2011).

Phang, A, 'The Challenge of Principled Gap-Filling' (2014) *JBL* 261.

Phipson, SL and Malek, HM, *Phipson on Evidence*, vol. 18 (Sweet & Maxwell 2013).

Pickavance, J, *A Practical Guide to Construction Adjudication* (John Wiley & Sons 2015).

Pollock, F, *Principles of Contract: A Treatise on the General Principles Concerning the Validity of Agreements in the Law of England* (5th edn with a new chapter, Stevens 1889).

Prinz, JJ, *Beyond Human Nature* (1st edn, Allen Lane 2012).

Rapaport, A, 'The Use and Misuse of Game Theory' (1962) 207 *Scientific American* 108.

Rapaport, A, *Fights, Games, and Debates* (University of Michigan Press 1974).

Rentokil's website – www.rentokil.com/facilities-management/history/

Rickert, C (ed.), *Justifying Private Law Remedies* (Hart 2008).

RICS, *Professional Standards and Guidance, UK – UK Residential Real Estate Agency* (RICS 2017).

Rimington, S, *Open Secret* (Hutchinson 2001).

Robertson, A, *The Law of Obligations: Connections and Boundaries* (UCL Press 2004).

Robertson, A, 'The Limits of Voluntariness in Contract' (2005) 29 *MULR* 179.

Robertson, A, 'The Limits of Interpretation in the Law of Contract' (2016) 47 *Victoria Univ Wellington Law Rev* 191.

Robson, C, *Real World Research* (3rd edn, Wiley 2011). 179.

Rose, CM, 'Trust in the Mirror of Betrayal' (1995) 75 *Boston Univ Law Rev* 531.

Rosher, P, 'Good Faith in Construction Contracts under French Law' (2015) *ICLR* 302.

Rosher, P, 'Partnering/Alliancing – A New Way of Thinking about Construction: Part 1' (2015b) *IBLJ* 237.

Ruzzier, CA, 'Asset Specificity and Vertical Integration: Williamson's Hypothesis Reconsidered' Harvard Business School Working Paper 2009.

Sanga, S, 'Choice of Law: An Empirical Analysis' (2014) 11 *JELS* 894.

Scheurich, JJ, *Research Method in the Postmodern* (Falmer 1997).

Schilke, O and Lumineau, F, 'The Double-Edged Effect of Contracts on Alliance Performance' (2018) 44 *J Manage* 2827.

Schmitthoff, CM and others, *Schmitthoff's Export Trade* (12th edn, Sweet & Maxwell 2011).

Schneier, B, *Liars and Outliers* (Wiley 2012).

Sharp, DW, *Offshore Oil and Gas Insurance* (Witherby & Co. 1994).

Scott, RE, 'Conflict and Cooperation in Long-Term Contracts' (1987) 75 *Cal LRev* 2005.

Scott, RE, 'Contract Design and the Shading Problem' http://ssrncom/abstract=2628256 (Columbia Public Law Research Paper 14-472 accessed July 2015).

Scott, T, 'Failed Joint Ventures: The Search for the "Pallant V Morgan Equity"' www.wilberforce.co.uk/wp-content/uploads/2014/10/PUBLICATION-Development-Disputes-2012-Chapter-4-Failed-joint-ventures-TS.pdf

Schwartz, A and Scott, RE, 'Contract Interpretation Redux' (2010) 119 *Yale LJ* 926.

Sergeant, M, 'No EOT Provision for Variations: Why the Right to LADs Should Not Be Lost' (2016) 32 *Const LJ* 352.

Sergeant, M and Wieliczko, M, *Construction Contract Variations* (Informa Law 2014).

Saintier, S, 'The Elusive Notion of Good Faith in the Performance of a Contract, Why Still a Bete Noire for the Civil and the Common Law?' (2017) *JBL* 441.

Shapiro, FR, 'The Most-Cited Law Review Articles Revisited' (1996) 71 *Chi-Kent LRev* 751.

Sheppard, E, 'Good Faith in the Aftermath of Yam Seng' (2015) 7 *JIBFL* 407.

Sidoli Del Ceno, J, 'Adjudication in Tenancy Deposit Scheme Disputes: Agents' Perspectives' (2015) 7 *IJLBE* 162.

Smith, SA, *Contract Theory* (OUP 1993).

Smith, SA, *Contract Theory* (OUP 2004).

Smith, SA, 'Reasonable Expectations of the Parties: An Unhelpful Concept' (2009) 48 *CBLJ* 366.

Soper, CH, *Contract, Conflict and Cooperation: A Critical Analysis of the Common Law Approach to the Breakdown of Modern, Complex, Symbiotic Contracts* (Leicester 2018).

Speidel, RE, 'Court-Imposed Price Adjustments under Long-Term Supply Contracts' (1981) 76 *NWULR* 369.

Speidel, RE, 'The Characteristics and Challenges of Relational Contracts' (2000) 94 *NWULR* 827.

Stannard, JE, *Delay in the Performance of Contractual Obligations* (OUP 2007).

Steyn, J, 'Contract Law: Fulfilling the Reasonable Expectations of Honest Men' (1997) 113 *LQR* 433.

Stoljar, S, 'Prevention and Cooperation in the Law of Contract' (1953) 31 *CanBar Rev* 231.

Stolte, J, 'The Context of Satisficing in Vignette Research' (1994) 134 *J Social Psychol* 727.

Sue, VM and Ritter, LA, *Conducting Online Surveys* (Sage 2007).

Summers, RS, '"Good Faith" in General Contract Law and the Sales Provisions of the Uniform Commercial Code' (1968) 54 *Va L Rev* 195.

Sumption, J, *A Question of Taste: The Supreme Court and the Interpretation of Contracts* (Harris Society Annual Lecture 2017).

Tan, ZX, 'Beyond the Real and the Paper Deal: The Quest for Contextual Coherence in Contractual Interpretation' (2016) 79 *MLR* 623.

Thayer, JB, 'The Jury and Its Development' (1892) 15 *HarvLRev* 295.

Thomas, RD, 'Custom of the Port' (2016) *LMCLQ* 436.

Tillotson, J, *Contract Law in Perspective* (Butterworths 1985).

Todd, P, *Bills of Lading and Bankers' Documentary Credits* (Lloyds of London Press 1998).

Tosato, A, 'Commercial Agency and the Duty to Act in Good Faith' (2016) 36 *OJLS* 661.

Trebilcock, MJ, *The Limits of Freedom of Contract* (Harvard UP 1993).

Twigg-Flesner, C and Villalta Puig, G (eds), *Boundaries of Commercial and Trade Law* (Sellier 2011).

Twining, W, *Karl Llewellyn and the Realist Movement* (CUP 2012).

UK Government, 'The Commercial Agents (Council Directive) Regulations 1993 Proposal for a Regulation of the European Parliament and of the Council on a Common European Sales Law' (2011) Com/2011/0635final-2011/0284 (COD) www.gov.uk/stopped-by-police-while-driving-your-rights/when-the-police-can-seize-your-vehicle

UK Government, *The Outsourcing Playbook – Central Government Guidance on Outsourcing Decisions and Contracting* (https://assets.publishing.service.gov.uk/government/uploads/system/uploads/attachment_data/file/780361/20190220_OutsourcingPlaybook_6.5212.pdf 2019).

UK Parliament, Work and Pensions and BEIS Committees Publish Report on Carillion (The Stationery Office 2018). www.parliament.uk/business/committees/committees-a-z/commons-select/work-and-pensions-committee/news-parliament-2017/carillion-report-published-17-19/

Upex, RV, *Encyclopedia of Employment Law* (Sweet & Maxwell 1992).

Vigen, T, 'Spurious Correlations', www.tylervigen.com/spurious-correlations

Vogenauer, S and Weatherill, S (eds) *The Harmonisation of European Contract Law: Implications for European Private Laws, Business and Legal Practice*, vol. 1 (Hart 2006).

Waddams, SM, *Principle and Policy in Contract Law* (CUP 2011).

Waitzer, EJ and Sarro, D, 'Protecting Reasonable Expectations: Mapping the Trajectory of the Law' (2016) 57 *CBLJ* 285.

Walker, DM, *Principles of Scottish Private Law* (2nd edn, OUP 1975).

Walker, DM, *The Oxford Companion to Law* (Clarendon Press 1980).

Watkins, D and Burton, M (eds), *Research Methods in Law* (Taylor & Francis 2013).

Watts, P, Reynolds, FMB and Bowstead, W (eds), *Bowstead and Reynolds on Agency* (20th edn, Sweet & Maxwell 2014).

Webster, *New International Dictionary of the English Language* (G Bell & Sons 1928).

Weintraub, RJ, 'A Survey of Contract Practice and Policy' (1992) *WisLRev* 1.

Whitford, WC, 'Jean Braucher's Contracts World View' (2016) 13 *ACJ* 58.

Wiggins, JM, *Facilities Manager's Desk Reference* (Wiley 2010).

Wightman, J, *Contract: A Critical Commentary* (Pluto Press 1996).

Wilhelmsson, T, *Perspectives of Critical Contract Law* (Dartmouth 1993).

Wilken, S, *The Law of Waiver, Variation and Estoppel* (OUP 2012).

Wilkinson-Ryan, T, 'Incentives to Breach' (2015) 17(1)*ALER* 290.

Williamson, OE, *The Economic Institutions of Capitalism* (Free Press 1985).

Williamson, OE, *The Mechanisms of Governance* (OUP 1996).

Wilson, JF, *Principles of the Law of Contract* (Sweet & Maxwell 1957).

Wiseman, ZB, 'The Limits of Vision: Karl Llewellyn and the Merchant Rules' (1987) 100 *HarvLRev* 465.

Worthington, S (ed), *Commercial Law and Commercial Practice* (Hart 2003).

Wright, RT and Decker, SH, *Burglars on the Job: Streetlife and Residential Break-ins* (Northeastern UP 1996).

www.scotlawcom.gov.uk/files/1115/2222/5222/Report_on_Review_of_Contract_ Law_-_Formation_Interpretation_Remedies_for_Breach_and_Penalty_Clauses_ Report_No_252.pdf

Wynn-Evans, C, 'Contractual Powers: How to Reach a Reasonable Opinion' (2015) 21 *EmplJ* 18.

Zakrzewski, R, *Remedies Reclassified* (OUP 2005).

Index